The Food of Italy

ALSO BY CLAUDIA RODEN

Coffee
Picnic
A New Book of Middle Eastern Food
Mediterranean Cookery
The Book of Jewish Food
Claudia Roden's Invitation to Mediterranean Cooking

THE FOOD OF ITALY
REGION BY REGION

Claudia Roden

Chatto & Windus
LONDON

For Simon, Nadia and Anna
and for the Italian *appassionati di cucina*
who helped me with this book

Published by Chatto and Windus 2002

2 4 6 8 10 9 7 5 3 1

Text copyright © Claudia Roden 1989
Maps by Mark Lewis. Photography by Carol Sharp

Claudia Roden has asserted her right under the Copyright, Designs
and Patents Act, 1988 to be identified as the author of this work

First published in Great Britain in 1989 by
Chatto & Windus
Random House, 20 Vauxhall Bridge Road,
London SW1V 2SA

Random House Australia (Pty) Limited
20 Alfred Street, Milsons Point, Sydney,
New South Wales 2061, Australia

Random House New Zealand Limited
18 Poland Road, Glenfield,
Auckland 10, New Zealand

Random House South Africa (Pty) Limited
Endulini, 5A Jubilee Road, Parktown 2193, South Africa

Random House Group Limited Reg. No. 954009
www.randomhouse.co.uk

A CIP catalogue record for this book is available from the British Library

ISBN 0 7011 7361 0

Papers used by Random House are natural,
recyclable products made from wood grown in sustainable forests;
the manufacturing processes conform to the environmental regulations
of the country of origin

Designed by Caz Hildebrand

Typeset in Franklin Gothic ITC
Printed and bound in Hong Kong by C & C Offset Printing Co., Ltd

Contents

Acknowledgements

My greatest debt is to Brenda Jones and Philip Clarke, who sent me to Italy to write 'A Taste of Italy' for the *Sunday Times Magazine* (London). They made it possible for me to visit most cities in every region, to try every dish and discover the local produce and to meet hundreds of people connected with food. Without their support this book could never have been written. Brenda advised and encouraged me, and I owe her more than I can ever repay her.

I owe a great deal to Massimo Alberini, culinary historian and journalist, who made information available and introduced me to cooks and gastronomes all over Italy. I cannot thank him enough. He has just turned eighty and still rushes around the country attending and putting on events, choosing menus and encouraging cooks as vice-president of the Accademia Italiana della Cucina. The Accademia was founded in 1953 by Orio Vergani, a sportswriter who, while covering the Tour de France, realised how France was making the most of her regional cooking traditions while Italy was neglecting hers. The aim of the Accademia is to save Italy's culinary heritage and maintain the standard and authenticity of regional cooking.

Because I travelled alone, without plans and pre-arrangements, I depended greatly on the help of people I met for guidance. I cannot name all those whose food I ate, who gave me recipes and information, who let me see them at work and took me to see cheese- and salami- and pastry-makers, who extended the hospitality of their homes and taught me about Italy, but I am grateful to them all, and something of what they told me is in this book. I cherish every contribution, and all the warmth that came with it.

I have very special thanks for the following people who gave generously of their time and their knowledge and expertise: Gianna Modotti, who teaches cooking in Udine; Renzia Sebelin, who teaches in Treviso; Gianni Gosetti of Tolmezzo in Friuli; in the Veneto, Sergio Luciano Preo, Giuseppe Carlotto, Dino Boscarato, Francesco and Jenny Rizzo; Cipriani's Natale Rusconi; in Bolzano, Giorgio Grai; in Merano, Horst Auerbach; Piero Bolfo in Pavia; Fulvio de Santa at the restaurant Peck in Milan; Franco Colombani at the Albergo del Sole at Maleo; Antonio and Nadia Santini at Dal Pescatore in Canneto sull'Oglio, near Mantua; Giorgio Gioco of the 12 Apostoli in Verona; Vito Quaranta and Attalo Paparello of Verona; Vittorio Bisso of Da 'O Vittorio in Recco, near Genoa; Giovanni Goria in Asti; Anna Maria Alvano; Signor Giardino of the Enomotel Il Convento and Danilo of La Crota in Roddi d'Alba; Pierro Bertinotti of Pinocchio in Borgomanero; Paola Buldini and Bruno Simoni in Bologna; Giorgio Fini and Giuseppe Giusti in Modena; Rino Azzali of Al Tartufo in Salsomaggiore; Giancarlo Ceci of the Ristorante Maria Luigia in Collecchio, near Parma; Gianfranco Neri in Parma; Carla Schuani of Sandri in Perugia; Vittorio Battilocchi in Norcia; in Tuscany, Mariapaola Dettore and Lorenza Stucchi de' Medici; Professore Corrado Barberis in Rome; Dottore Nello Oliviero in Naples; Dottore Aielli of the Ristorante Cappuccini Convento on the Amalfi coast; Nico Blasi in Martina Franca, in Apulia; Franco Frassinato of Otranto; Paola Pettini, who has a cooking school in Bari; Antonio Stanziani and the teachers at the Cooking Institute at Villa Santa Maria in the Abruzzi; Paolo Cascino in Palermo; Salvatore Schifno in Agrigento; Giuseppe Catalano of the Hotel Moderno in Erice; Fiorella Badalucco in Trapani; Maria Guccione on Favignana Island, near Trapani; the Mother Superior of the Monastero Santo Spirito in Agrigento; Franco Azzolini of the Palm Beach Hotel in Villa Grazia di Carini; Angelo Lauria of the Pasticceria Italia in Licata, near Agrigento; the Canuscio family in Palermo and Corleone; Antonio Tantilo at the Charleston in Palermo; in Sardinia, Natalina Laconi of Su Meriagu Sant'Andrea at Quartu Sant'Elena, Cagliari; Cesare Murgia of Sa Cardiga e Su Schironi at Maddalena, near Cagliari; Giancarlo Deidda of Dal Corsaro in Cagliari; Signora Sacchi of Monte Ortobene; Antonio Licheri of the Scuola Alberghiera near Nuoro.

I thank Nico Passante, of the Gritti Palace in Venice, for an invitation to a banquet with the regional chefs who demonstrate at the hotel's cooking school, and to Avvocato Giorgio Bernardini of Parma Alimentare for the splendid Renaissance banquet in Parma for the presentation of the Maria Luigia prize for journalism.

I am grateful to Dottore Francesco Varola Ancillotti, who wrote from Rio de Janeiro and Rome correcting spelling and points of geography and history in my *Sunday Times* pieces, and to Mr Gianfranco Spaggiari and Dottore Massimo d'Amico of the Italian Trade Centre in London for their advice. I have special thanks for Maxine Clark, Marion Maitliss, Jenny Cowgill and Alec Chanda – Alec particularly – who cooked and ate the dishes with me.

I wish to acknowledge my debt to a wide collection of regional cookery books that I have used for reference, among them Jeanne Carola Francesconi's *La cucina napoletana* (Edizione del Delfino), the equally monumental *Le ricette regionali italiane* (Casa Editrice Solares) by Anna Gossetti della Salda, which has been my bible, and *Le migliori ricette della scuola del Gritti* (Edizioni Acanthus), from which several of the chefs' recipes have come.

Introduction

Travelling up and down the country through every corner of Italy over the course of a year to research the 'Taste of Italy' series for the *Sunday Times Magazine* was an undreamt-of opportunity to get to know the food and the country in an intimate kind of way. This book is based on the series and on additional material collected during the many trips.

Every recipe brings a rush of memories – a dinner in a piazza in the warm night air; a discussion about a dish on a train, with the whole carriage joining in; the back streets of Naples full of bustle and drama, glittering with carnival lights and shrines to the Virgin Mary; a wedding party in Sicily; fishing boats bringing their catch into a tiny Ligurian port; nuns making almond pastries in a convent. The taste of basil, parmesan and olive oil, the smell of garlic frying with sage and rosemary, bring back the brilliant light and pure primary colours, with images of Italy and feelings of joy and enchantment.

It is easy to fall under the spell of Italy. The French writer Stendhal wrote in the early part of the nineteenth century that in the art and the joy of living, Milan was two hundred years in advance of Paris. This can hardly be said of Milan today, but everyone can still be irresistibly charmed by a country so full of natural beauty, art, music and tradition; by a quality of life that warms the heart and by food that is simple and unaffected but full of rich flavours and delightful touches.

Part of the fascination of Italy is its incredible diversity. The landscape, the vegetation and the climate constantly change. There are hills, mountains, plains and coastline, and every town and village is quite different from the next. The architecture, the ambience, the way people behave are different, and you can hear different dialects and even different languages. The cooking too is different. There is no such thing as Italian cooking, only Sicilian, Piedmontese, Neapolitan, Venetian, Florentine, Genoese and so on. That is what makes a culinary tour of the regions such an enormous pleasure. The extraordinary diversity is a legacy of Italy's fragmented past and its division, until the unification of the country over a hundred years ago, into many independent sovereign states. There were kingdoms, duchies, lordships and republics, papal and city states, and each had its own history, culture and traditions.

After the decline of the Roman Empire, Italy became a many-centred universe. In the Middle Ages each big town, in central and northern Italy especially, conquered and managed the surrounding land, and the great sea towns had their own colonies around the Mediterranean. These towns and communes were ruled by different laws and institutions and they were constantly divided by economic and political rivalries, bitter conflicts and wars. A kaleidoscope of foreign influences – the French in Piedmont; Austrians in Lombardy, Trentino-Alto Adige and Veneto; Yugoslavs in Venezia Giulia; Spaniards in the south; Arabs in Sicily – reinforced the differences. The south has a tradition of unity in diversity because the regions shared the same rulers and destinies, but in the north and in central Italy there are hardly two cities that shared the same succession of rulers or had the same cultural heritage. When King Victor Emmanuel II of Sardinia-Piedmont was proclaimed king of a united Italy in 1861, the component parts of the new nation were disconnected and extremely diverse. The great cleavage, partly historical, partly climatic and economical, was the one which divided the north from the south, the former Kingdom of Naples, whose inhabitants belonged to another civilisation.

The twenty administrative regions which were formed after the war correspond more or less to the states that existed before unification, and their particularism has not been cancelled out. Each region is a world in itself with its own identity. Local patriotism – *campanilismo* – is such that each feels strongly about its food and lays claim to having the best cooking in Italy.

Italy has changed dramatically since the Second World War and it is still changing. The political writer Giorgio Bocca writes in *Italia che cambia* (Changing Italy) that it has changed more in these last few years than in the three thousand preceding ones. Although there were some industries in the north at the end of the nineteenth century, until the 'economic miracle' after the war Italy was still an agricultural country, where *mezzadria*, a system of sharecropping by which peasant farmers lived on estates as tenants and cultivated the land, giving half the produce to the landlord as rent, prevailed. Estates were large and divided into fields, or *poderi*, each housing a family community headed by a *mezzadro* or *capoccia*. Farming methods were archaic. Peasants were busy all year round growing wheat, corn or rice, vegetables and fruit. Wine was made on each estate, and in many olive oil was made as well. Every farm kept pigs, rabbits and poultry. In the north and centre peasants also bred a few calves for the market, made cheese and cured pork. But the harvest often failed and life was hard. Cooking remained little changed from what it had been hundreds of years before.

When Italy was rapidly transformed in the 1950s and 1960s into a highly industrialised modern consumer society where women went to work, the old life was swept away. The *mezzadria* system was abolished. The government gave credit to tenants to buy their land at an interest rate of only three per cent, but peasants still abandoned the land for the cities and factories. People from the poorer south invaded the richer north in search of work and a better life or went abroad. With this industrial, economic and social revolution came a change of eating and cooking habits and a homogenising of cultures.

Now the culinary borders have been confused and there is no longer a precise geography of food. The great differences were between north and south. Before the war you could divide Italy according to cooking fats. There was butter in the north, pork fat in the centre and olive oil in the south. The Italy of polenta and rice and boiled meats was in the north, and the Italy of pizza and dry pasta was in the south. Black pepper was used in the north, hot red pepper in the south. In the north they cooked with wine, in the south with tomatoes.

The past twenty-five years have seen the *invasione pizzaiola* and the adoption of pasta, both hardly ever eaten in the north before, in every corner of Italy. Mass production of foods has brought standardisation. The same factories make all the different regional salamis and cheeses. Even buffalo that provide rich milk for making mozzarella, which were once found only in the south, are now raised also in the north. The use of olive oil has become widespread (in the past a bottle might have lasted a whole year for a family in the north) and few people now will eat pork fat, even in the south. Cooks in all the main cities are mostly from the south – from the Abruzzi, Apulia and Sicily – and this has had a major influence on national tastes.

Italy has succumbed to fast foods and has gone through many fashions in eating, from steak and salad after the war (a reaction against meat only once a week, which had been the case for most country people) and French cuisine in restaurants, to a proliferation of hamburger, sandwich and salad bars and *nouvelle cuisine*, and even the phase of the 'threes and fours', when everything – spaghetti, omelettes, pizza – had three or four cheeses and three or four herbs. Now there is

concern with health and dieting and the cult of the new (they call it *cucina creativa*). I was offered a *risotto tricolore* in the national colours with chopped tomatoes and kiwi, and another with wild strawberries, and I found menus full of things such as prawns with whisky, and ravioli filled with crab and vodka or with smoked salmon. Almost every restaurant offers smoked salmon in various forms – chopped into tagliatelle, sliced with mushrooms or mixed with salad. One could say that smoked salmon from Scotland and Canada is the most important unifying factor in restaurants throughout the country. Italians have also developed a great passion for green things, wild things and raw things, especially for radicchio, *rucola* (arugula, or rocket) and porcini mushrooms, which are available all year round.

But despite all this, regional cooking has survived, and perhaps because of this, it is reflowering. Nostalgia and fascination with the past and the quest for identity have brought a revival of interest in traditional cooking and a respect for genuine produce. As their world changed and the old traditions seemed to be vanishing, and when they seemed to lose touch with their roots, people began to hanker for the good things of the past. Afraid to lose forever their culture and their link with the land, Italians have started to 'rediscover' their individual heritage in the old everyday foods of the countryside. They call this rediscovery *il ricupero* or *la riscoperta*. The dishes that evoke the 'happy days' when peasant farmers had ten children and families were close and patriarchal, when the kitchen was the living room and meals were convivial, are very much in fashion. Poor peasant dishes such as polenta and bean soup and those based on bread or dried chestnuts or made with offal or wild plants are particularly popular.

In Italy the past is not far away. The generation that cooks in the old way, that of the *nonnine* (little grandmothers), is still there, and inspired chefs go to them for recipes. Many showed me handwritten recipe books as well as old cookery books, including facsimiles of books written during the Renaissance, that they used. These chefs follow the seasons, use local ingredients, track down home-grown produce and band together to get farmers to raise quail, ducks, geese and game (which had almost disappeared). They explained to me that they wanted to update and revitalise tradition, not embalm it.

There is a certain mystification going on, and what someone called 'nostalgic kitsch'. Some of the dishes that are 'revived' never really existed, for instance tortelloni filled with nettles. At a restaurant in Parma, the chef-owner offered me tortelli stuffed with apple, saying it was an old local dish. When Massimo Alberini, a culinary historian who was of the party, told him not to make up stories, he said that the recipe might not have been codified but that his grandmother made them.

Authentic local food is not easy to find in restaurants, because Italians do not want to spend very much to eat what their grandmothers make – they want to try something new. For years French food guide books commended only those restaurants with 'creative' cooking, so there was no incentive to stick to tradition. State catering schools teach classic French and international cooking with the more well-known Italian dishes, so that students are able to find work anywhere. It is in the trattorias and family-run restaurants, where the owners themselves cook, that you get the real thing. Since tourists have become more adventurous and started to ask for local specialities, more and more *piatti tipici* have begun to appear on menus during the tourist season. Some restaurants offer the kinds of things that no one wants to do at home anymore because they take too long or make the house smell of frying.

Because the cooking of Italy is so varied and because it was never formalised as it was in France, there is no *haute cuisine* or *cuisine bourgeoise* or classic national cuisine. It is basically country cooking for large families, a combination of peasant food and the grand dishes that belonged to the nobility and were eaten by the peasantry on special occasions – some only once a year, at carnival time. The different styles may have a city stamp but they have their roots in the land because town and country in Italy have always been closely bound. Since the Middle Ages big towns in north and central Italy owned the land around them and the rich and noble spent a good part of the year in their country houses. In the south, feudal landlords had castles in the countryside while the agricultural population lived in walled hilltop towns for protection and worked in faraway fields every day.

The aim of this book is to feature real traditional recipes from all the regions of Italy. The selection reflects what is popular in Italy today, what I liked best and what I feel you will most enjoy cooking and eating. I did not try to be comprehensive. Many things are missing. I adore snails and frogs, newborn (jelly-like) fish and cardoons, but have found it difficult to buy fresh ones, and I expect you to be squeamish about frogs, sheep's heads and certain offal. I like salt cod and stockfish, but I hate cooking them; I love a *pasticcio di tortellini* – a pie filled with a sweet béchamel and tiny pasta stuffed with meat – but it is too fattening and takes too long to make; and although I tried the famous dessert *zuppa inglese* in different versions in many places, I never thought much of it. Because many dishes have several regional versions, I tried as many as I could and chose the best one.

I have not included many of the old traditional pastries, such as the yeast cake panettone, the fruity *panforte* of Siena and the macaroon-type amaretti, which people buy rather than make at home, nor the dozens of pastries traditionally made for religious feasts. Every town has its own version of petits fours, sweet bread-rings, fritters in the shape of ribbons, hard dry biscuits to dunk in wine, and variously filled pastries. These sweets are all part of ancient rituals to celebrate Christmas, Easter, Carnival, the Day of the Dead and saints' days. They are delightful and fascinating, but I preferred to include here the luscious modern desserts you can find in Italy and reproduce at home.

Every generation pulls from tradition what suits it best. We are keener now on fish and vegetables and prefer quick and easy, fresh, light foods with rich flavours, less fat and less stodge. My intention was to keep to the original, authentic way of preparing the dishes and to make the kind of improvements that young Italian chefs are making, in a way that both respects tradition and takes into account modern tastes. Generally, I have reduced the amount of fat, and I have used oil in preference to butter and pork fat when it did not spoil the flavour. If you wish, you can make your own adjustments and use oil – olive or sunflower (the latter is also used in Italy) – exclusively throughout. The cooking times are shorter than they once would have been, so that vegetables are still crisp and fish and meat are not overcooked. These refinements and the importance of exquisite presentation are what Italians have learned from *nouvelle cuisine*. There is an Italian saying, '*L'occhio vuole la sua parte*', which means that the eye needs to be satisfied. If it is true that Italians have an innate sense of taste, they use it to make their food look exquisite in a natural, simple way, and that is what you should do too.

The owner of a restaurant in Umbria was angry that I wanted only traditional local foods. 'Why must we remain stuck in the past?' he complained. Food is always changing and that is natural, but now that changes come through the media and all the world is getting to be the same, what appeals and fascinates and touches the heart is that which distinguishes Italy, which recalls her past and is part of her precious heritage and traditions.

Planning a meal

I have grouped the recipes in this book by region, but you are meant to pick from all over when you plan a meal. To make it easier for you to choose, the dishes are listed on pages 11–14 by category in the order in which they would appear in a meal, but bear in mind that they are flexible. Many antipasti, for instance, can also make a perfect second course or side dish or can be part of a buffet, and many dishes can be served on their own as a meal in itself.

A formal meal in Italy is a succession of courses, with no main course, starting with an antipasto, followed by a first course (*primo*) of either pasta, risotto or soup, and a second course (*secondo*) of meat, poultry or fish, accompanied by one or two vegetable side dishes (*contorni*). Then there is salad (*insalata*), sometimes cheese, and the meal ends with fruit or dessert (*dolce*) or both.

Antipasto never played an important part in Italian eating. Not long ago it consisted of only a few slices of cured meat or salami, and these are still the favourites. Antipasto is meant only to whet the appetite, so do not make too much. For most people in Italy the first course is the most important, and pasta is the favourite food. Although most people prefer the simplest treatment – olive oil and garlic with fresh raw tomato and basil or a dressing of butter melted with sage leaves, sprinkled with freshly grated black pepper and parmesan – the versatility of pasta is extraordinary. Risotto and other rice dishes, gnocchi and *canederli* (bread dumplings) are also versatile. Soups can be a meal in themselves or light and delicate.

With so much coast (only four out of the twenty regions do not have contact with the sea), Italy has a wide range of fish and seafood. Until recently fish was considered to be a Friday dish only, and not grand enough to serve to guests, but now it is one of the most popular foods.

Meat and poultry dishes are mostly grills, roasts and stews; there are lovely game dishes, and offal is particularly good. Egg dishes and vegetable dishes can also be served as a second course. Vegetable dishes are an important part of every meal, so make good use of the repertoire. Salad can be a green salad or cooked vegetables dressed with olive oil and lemon juice.

Cheese is served at the end of the meal in northern Italy, especially in Piedmont, but not usually in the south. At home, dessert is generally fruit, sweets being reserved for special and festive occasions. After fruit or dessert, strong black coffee from a 'high' or 'after dinner' roast may be served in small cups, and perhaps followed with brandy or grappa, an amaro (bitter), anise-flavoured sambuca or a sweet wine such as vin santo, accompanied by almond pastries or hard biscuits for dunking.

Recipe list by type of food

I CONTORNI, INSALATE E VERDURE
Side Dishes, Salads and Vegetables

I DOLCI
Desserts

Ingredients

With few exceptions, all the ingredients you need for cooking Italian dishes are available in the UK. Just make sure that they are of the best quality and that they taste good. There are plenty of olives that taste bad, pine nuts and walnuts that are stale, capers that are too vinegary, ricotta and mozzarella that are slightly 'off'. They will spoil your dish.

Bread

Mass production is known to bring uniformity where once there was diversity, and this is true for bread. Throughout Italy now you find soft, elongated rolls (*panini*), called *banane* because of their shape, to make into sandwiches, and little hard, crusty rolls, light and airy or half empty inside, called, according to their shape, *michetta*, *rosetta*, *ciriola*, *parigina*, *fisarmonica*, *treccia* or *torcigliato*. These are the original breads of northern Italy – Lombardy, the Veneto and Piedmont. Because polenta once reigned there and took the place of bread, the latter was a luxury food, small, elegant, insubstantial. In the south, starting in Tuscany, bread was large and the farther south you went, the larger it became. The rough country loaf called *pagnotta* is heavy and compact and made to last at least a week. This coarse solid bread was one of the most important ingredients in cooking. It was used as a bed for food, in salads, soups and stews, in dumplings, fillings, puddings and cakes. Bakers have now started to make it again, as they have many other popular regional breads that had disappeared, but it is never like the old homemade kind, which had the strong taste and rich texture needed for recipes such as *bruschetta*, *panzanella* and *pappa al pomodoro*.

To name a few of the many regional breads still to be found, there is the ring-shaped *ciambella*, which is made in various regions; the Sardinian paper-thin *carta di musica*; Sicilian sesame bread; a rye bread of Alto Adige with cumin seeds; the famous twisted *manine* of Ferrara; the flat *focacce* of Tuscany and Liguria; the thin unleavened *piadina* of Romagna, baked on a grid; the Friulian *pan de frizze*, with bits of bacon; the Tuscan *panini al rosmarino* with rosemary and raisins; and the Apulian large and hard *frisedda*.

Ritual breads are still made for weddings, baptisms, Carnival, Easter and every type of feast and festival, while a whole new range of modern breads, such as those with walnuts, olives and onions, are offered in restaurants.

Pasta

Pasta is the most important food of Italy. There are hundreds of different types, shapes and sizes and at least two thousand Italian and dialect names, from fresh noodles such as tagliatelle, tagliolini, fettuccine and the wider pappardelle, stuffed pasta like ravioli, cappelletti, tortelloni and the large lasagne and cannelloni, all made with egg and soft wheat, to dry hard-wheat pasta. In this category you find spaghetti, spaghettoni and spaghettini (depending on their diameter), vermicelli and all the versions of pasta with a hole: ziti, maccheroncelli, bucatini with tiny holes, penne which are short and smooth quills, ridged rigatoni, and a whole world of shells, ears, snails, hats, tubes, twists, corkscrews, bird's tongues, little stars, ribbons, bow ties, butterflies, coins and wheels.

There is no unity of nomenclature. Every region uses its own names, and industrial production has not always made it easier. The same industrial pasta is called cravattine, farfalle or gasse, trenette or linguine. Pasta illustrates more than anything the anarchic, independent spirit of Italy, which unification did not change. The importance of shapes and textures has to do with the amount of sauce they can collect and hold. Every region has its favourites. In the Veneto and Alto Adige they sometimes mix wholewheat, rye or buckwheat flour with white flour. Many types are available in the UK now, and it is worth experimenting and finding your own favourite combinations of pasta and sauce.

There are differences in quality in commercial pasta. For hard-wheat dry pasta, it is far better to get Italian brands, but they too vary in quality. The test is if they cook perfectly al dente.

Olive oil

It is always worth buying extra-virgin olive oil. The blander, cheaper kind of extra-virgin now available in supermarkets is not much more expensive than that labelled simply 'olive oil' and is very good for cooking and deep-frying fish and vegetables. For salads, and when the oil is to be used raw, you should experiment and taste some of the very best quality extra-virgin oils. Some are light and delicate, but most are so strong that you are meant to use only a little drop. Many Italians prefer to use a light vegetable or seed oil such as sunflower oil for cooking meat and for dishes in which olive oil would overpower the delicate flavours. I do too. See also page 195.

Parmesan

It is far better to buy a nice chunk and to grate it yourself (or to have it grated at the shop) than to buy it already grated. Freshly grated parmesan is about double the volume of dry grated parmesan in jars. See also page 103.

Mozzarella

Mozzarella made in Campania or Apulia with buffalo or cow's milk and eaten on the day it is made is something sensational. But in this country, when you have the choice between the vacuum-packed Italian variety, the kind imported loose in its whey and the American version, all of which are quite acceptable, what really matters is freshness and the expiration date. The smoked mozzarella affumicata, with a dark chestnut exterior and cream-coloured interior, keeps its delicate flavour better.

Ricotta

Ricotta made in the UK may not be as good as that made around Rome and in Sicily (ricotta is made everywhere in Italy, but in these areas they make it best). Always use the freshest available, as ricotta goes off quickly and has an unpleasant flavour when slightly stale. Unless it is vacuum-packed, it is best eaten within twenty-four hours.

Mushrooms

Mushrooms, especially wild ones, are extremely popular in Italy, where there are said to be more than forty varieties. Most popular of all are the large, pale brown, meaty porcini, or *Boletus edulis* (*cèpes* in French), which seem to be available everywhere at all times of the year. When not in season they are brought in from other parts of Italy or from abroad. My substitute for them is the cultivated shiitake mushrooms.

Among other highly prized wild mushrooms are the orange-capped, yellow-gilled ovoli (so called because they look like eggs when they are small), or Caesar's mushrooms, which are found in northern Italy; the *gallinacci* (also called *cantarelli*, *finferli* and various other dialect names), which are the yellow, funnel-shaped, peppery, fruity *chanterelles* or *girolles*; the spongy-capped *spugnole*, which are morels; the slightly bitter *funghi ostrichi*, which are oyster mushrooms; the *chiodini*, called 'little nails' in Italy because of their shape, and here called honey fungus because of their honey colour and also bootlace fungus because of the black

rhizomes by which they spread; the aromatic trumpet-shaped *trombetta dei morti*, or black trumpet; and the delicately flavoured *steccherino dorato*, or hedgehog fungus.

Dried mushrooms, or *funghi secchi* (generally porcini), have a slightly musty and stronger, more intense flavour than fresh ones. They are used as a flavouring for sauces, soups and stews, and sometimes a few are added to fresh mushrooms to deepen the flavour of the dish. They are very expensive, but only very few are needed. Look for cream-coloured slices in preference to dark brown, crumbly ones, and keep them in a dry, tightly closed jar. They can last forever. They must be soaked for at least half an hour before using, and the soaking water, which is also prized (it is good in soups), should be strained to get rid of any grit.

Tomatoes

Italians use canned peeled tomatoes a great deal. My recipes call for fresh, ripe, peeled tomatoes because that is what I like to use. Although fresh tomatoes in some places might not be as good as those grown and ripened in Italy, a teaspoon of sugar in a sauce made with 500g (1lb) tomatoes can improve their flavour. But good-quality canned tomatoes are far better than fresh tomatoes with a bad taste or with no taste at all. In all the recipes that call for fresh tomatoes for cooking, you can use canned ones instead.

Olives

Italy produces many different kinds of olives. The most famous are Gaeta, Taggiasca, Frantoio, Leccino, Moraiolo and Coratina. Most of the canned olives available in this country in supermarkets have hardly any flavour at all, so look for olives that come from Italy, Greece, Spain or France, which have a strong, intense flavour, and taste them, if you can, before buying.

Stock cubes

In all the kitchens I visited I saw the cooks use stock cubes for dishes such as soup and risotto, so there is no reason why you should not use them too, except when an especially good broth is required. I noticed that their stocks are very light and that they use more water than is usually recommended in the directions on the packet.

Pepper

Where I say pepper in recipes it always means freshly ground black pepper. For hot red pepper you can use any little chillies, fresh or dried. Be careful with the amounts you use. You can use little chillies whole and leave them in the ingredients while they are cooking for just a short time if you do not want the dish to be too hot. Many of the recipes call for hot chilli powder. You can use cayenne or substitute red pepper flakes, which are also used in southern Italy.

Herbs
Use fresh herbs if you possibly can – you can find them in most places all year long. Parsley in Italy is the flat-leaf kind, but you can use the curly-leaf kind as well.

Capers
It is best to use capers preserved in brine or in salt (which you remove by soaking in water for a short time). Those more commonly available in the UK are preserved in vinegar. Squeeze them to remove some of the vinegar or soak them first in water if you like.

Anchovies
In Italy, the anchovies used for flavouring in cooking are those preserved in salt. They are whole and much larger than the fillets in oil available here, and they have a better flavour. The quantities I give in the recipes are for fillets in oil, which are sometimes a quarter of the size of the salted ones in Italy. If you have salt-pressed anchovies, wash the salt off under running water, then scrape off some of the skin and lift the fillets from the bone with a pointed knife.

Prosciutto
When Italians say prosciutto, which means ham, they always mean prosciutto crudo – raw ham. They use the less prestigious parts of this, cut thick, for cooking. It is much more expensive than prosciutto cotto (boiled or baked ham), but its distinctive flavour makes a difference to any dish.

Pancetta
Pancetta is unsmoked bacon cured in a way that makes it sweeter than bacon, but you can use plain unsmoked bacon instead.

Basics

To clean and prepare live mussels

You can keep mussels (uncleaned) for a day in the refrigerator or longer in a bucket of cold salted water. Sandy ones will disgorge some of their sand in the water.

To clean mussels, scrub them, pull off their beards (the stringy bits that hang out of the shell) with a knife, and wash in several changes of cold water. Test them to see if they are alive. Discard any that are broken and any that are too heavy or too light or that do not close when they are tapped or dipped in cold water.

To steam the mussels open, put them in a saucepan with about 2cm ($\frac{3}{4}$in) of water at the bottom – enough to produce steam. Put the lid on and bring to the boil. The shells will open in 1–5 minutes. Take off the heat and discard any that remain closed.

You can also open (and cook) mussels by putting them on a hot grill or griddle or in a hot oven for a minute or two. Clams are prepared in the same way.

To clean and prepare squid

Pull the head away from the body pouch and discard the soft innards which come out with it. Cut out the eyes (be careful that the ink does not squirt out at you) and the small round cartilage at the base of the tentacles. Discard the insides of the pouch: the ink bag if any (carefully, without breaking), the icicle-shaped transparent cuttlebone and the soft gelatinous innards. You do not need to peel off the reddish membrane which covers the pouch or cut off the fins from the body (though some people do for aesthetic reasons). Rinse very thoroughly in running water.

To clean and prepare octopus

Octopus is now almost always sold already cleaned and tenderised and all you need to do is cut out the eyes and gristle with the help of a sharp knife.

If it has not already been cleaned and tenderised, cut partway through the muscle which unites the tentacles to the inside of the head and discard all the contents of the head cavity; pull out the ink bag carefully without breaking it, the hard oval beak and the gelatinous innards. Cut out the eyes, then beat the tentacles with a mallet until they feel soft and have lost their spring. Remove any scales that may be left on the suckers. Wash well in cold running water.

Only a very large octopus needs to be skinned; otherwise the skin acquires a lovely pinkish colour when it is cooked.

To cook pasta al dente

The main thing about cooking pasta is not to overcook it. It must be al dente – firm to the bite, not soft and mushy. Southern Italians like it even a little hard and complain that northern Italians overcook theirs and turn it into *colla da manifesti* (poster glue).

For 4 people and 500g (1lb) of pasta, bring about 4 litres (7 pints) of water to the boil. Add salt, let it come to a rapid boil and put in the pasta all at once. Bend long hard pasta in the middle with a wooden spoon or by pressing it down, so that all the pasta is quickly under water and cooks evenly.

Stir and put the lid on so that the water comes more quickly back to the boil. Take the lid off and cook at a lively boil. Stir the pasta to keep it from sticking together and very quickly start trying it for doneness. The cooking time depends on the type of pasta and varies from 2–3 minutes for fresh egg tagliatelle to about 10–12 minutes for spaghetti and macaroni. Drain quickly in a colander as soon as the pasta is tender enough to bite through – it is best drained slightly underdone as it continues to soften out of the boiling water. Southern Italians do not drain their pasta too well and leave a tablespoon or so of cooking water to keep it moist. Mix in the sauce and serve at once.

To make tomato sauce

(salsa al pomodoro)

2 cloves garlic, finely chopped
2 tablespoons olive oil
1kg (2lb) tomatoes, peeled and chopped

1 teaspoon sugar
Salt and pepper
3 tablespoons chopped basil leaves or parsley

Fry the garlic in oil until golden, add the tomatoes, sugar, salt and pepper and simmer for about 25 minutes. Add the herbs.

To make broth

(brodo)

Broth in Italy is much less concentrated, lighter and more delicate in flavour than stock. It is made with meat – beef, veal or chicken is used – and with a few bones, but you may use a chicken carcass and less meat.

FOR 2 LITRES (3½ PINTS) BROTH

1 chicken carcass
1 stalk celery, cut into large pieces
1 carrot, cut into large pieces
1 onion, cut in half

1 tomato
A few parsley stalks
Salt

Put the chicken carcass in 3 litres (6¼ pints) cold water and bring to the boil. Remove the scum, then add the rest of the ingredients and simmer for 3 hours. Strain. If there is too much fat, use a large spoon to remove it from the surface or cool in the refrigerator and remove the fat when it solidifies.

Variations

You may add 2 bay leaves, and sprigs of thyme, sage and rosemary.

I have seen a cook add a glass of white wine, and the result was good.

Choosing the wine

In Italy no meal is complete without wine. It is good to combine the food and wine of the same region, if only because they have been paired traditionally. Some, such as Piedmontese, are natural partners. But just as I have encouraged you in this book to mix dishes from all over Italy in the eclectic way that Italians do now, there is no reason why you should not cross regional borders with wine. The important thing is to please yourself and to choose the right one for the food and the occasion. In the past, most Italian wine was cheap mass-market wine. But Italy's wine-making industry has changed itself so dramatically in the last twenty-five years that you now have an unparalleled variety of fine world-class premium wines to choose from.

Italy has always produced huge quantities of wine – more than any other country in the world and about twenty per cent of the world output. There are seas of grapes everywhere and every region is wine country. Most of the wine is merely drinkable *vino da tavola* to be consumed on the spot, or to be used for blending at home or abroad, or for distilling. Only about twenty per cent represents quality wines that are classified under denominations of controlled origin, which govern grape variety, yields per acre, methods of vinification, alcoholic strength and ageing requirements. These are *denominazione di origine* (DOC) and the higher 'guaranteed' (DOCG), as well as a new, more flexible category of *indicazione geografica tipica* (IGT) of wines from specific areas. A few acclaimed and prestigious wines do not fit into these categories because of their unorthodox blendings and methods and are labelled *vino da tavola*. It is in the area of premium quality wines that Italy's vineyards and wineries have undergone the most radical transformation that has ever been seen in any country. For a country that has been making wines since Greek and Roman times, it is both a revolution and a renaissance.

Until the 1960s, when the profits of wine-making were shared between peasant farmers and landowners under the old *mezzadria* system, there had been little incentive for either to produce good wines. Anyway, the world wanted only cheap wines from Italy. But now quality wines are in demand – people are prepared to pay high prices for them and the market for bulk wines has shrunk. There are new men with an enlightened approach in the field, a new attitude and spirit in wine-making and viticulture and much excitement and enterprise.

In a first wave of transformation, famous French (now international) grape varieties such as Cabernet Sauvignon, Chardonnay, Merlot, Sauvignon Blanc and the Pinots, with universally recognised names and flavours, were introduced in many regions and French methods, such as ageing and fermenting in small oak barrels from Bordeaux, have been emulated to produce first rate wines. New techniques from California, where many wine-makers are of Neapolitan origin, and from Australia, have also been adopted, and the industry has been transformed from rustic to high tech and has come up with stylish new wines appealing to modern tastes.

Traditionalists who have persisted in the old heroic mould with local grapes, have refined old classics. With better methods of planting and growing and more rigorous standards of production, and sometimes with a little blending with foreign grapes, they have enhanced and maintained the true regional character of their wines. Most excitingly, and following recent trends, some have revived abandoned traditions and reintroduced long-neglected native grapes. There is an incredibly vast resource of indigenous grape varieties – about four hundred – that are unique to Italy. Some are famous such as: Piedmont's Nebbiolo and Dolcetto, Liguria's Vermentino, Veneto's Prosecco, Friuli's Tocai, Tuscany's Sangiovese, Umbria's Sagrantino, the Abruzzi's Montepulcciano, the Marches' Verdicchio, Lazio's Malvasia, the South's Aglianico, Fiano, Greco, Primitivo and Negroamaro, Sicily's Nero d'Avola, and Sardinia's Vernaccia. Viticulture has acquired a new importance. Many producers now grow their own grapes and control cultivation. They clone and select the best grapes for the best sites and reduce yields by cutting off excess grapes to concentrate the wine.

The leading regions that produce great wines are Piedmont and Tuscany, which are rivals for the best reds (Italy is traditionally red wine country), and Trentino-Alto Adige, the Veneto, and Friuli-Venezia, which are famous for fine whites. But in every part of Italy, and most impressively in the much maligned southern regions and islands, the former home of bulk wine for blending and distillation, where the heat produces powerful alcoholic wines, there are some very pleasant, satisfying wines and also some really great ones. The world of Italian wines is perplexing and many-splendoured. The extraordinary diversity reflects differences in terrain and microclimates, in grape varieties and local traditions as well as the independent, individualistic, sometimes anarchic spirit of producers who want to follow their own way and forge their own style. It is especially appealing in an international market awash with ever more standardised global tastes.

In every chapter I have indicated the best wines I discovered when I travelled around Italy in the late eighties, but more have come on the scene to international critical acclaim. Burton Anderson is the world's leading expert on Italian wines and there is no better guide than his *Best Italian Wines* (Webster's/Little, Brown) published in 2001.

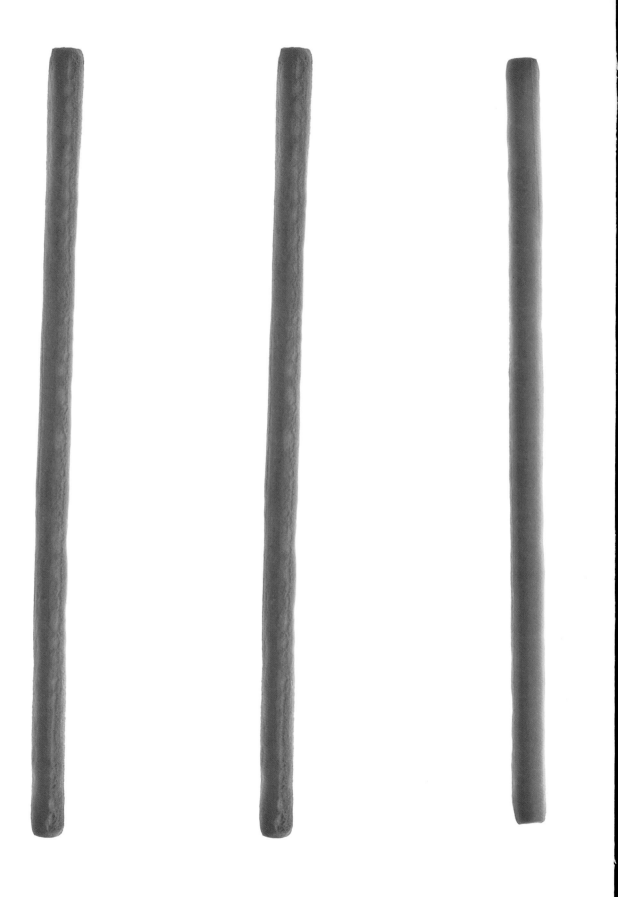

Piedmont & Valle d'Aosta

Piedmont and Valle D'Aosta

The region of Italy that played the most important part in the country's struggle for unification during the nineteenth century, whose king, Victor Emmanuel II, became the first king of Italy, has recently gained a reputation as the great gastronomic region with centres such as Alba, Asti and Monferrato. A region whose cooking is based on the most perfumed truffles and the best wine in Italy, and on wild mushrooms and game, is bound to be gastronomic, yet until not very long ago the cooking of Piedmont was generally thought to be only a derivation of the French because the dialect is French and cooking terms are French. One of the first cookery books published in Turin, in 1767, was *Il cuoco piemontese – perfezionato a Parigi* (The Piedmontese Cook – Perfected in Paris).

In those days the cooking from across the mountains (the border with France runs as far north as Mont Blanc) was followed in all well-to-do families, not only in Piedmont but in the whole of Italy and Europe. But Piedmont was part of the once French province of Savoy that became the Kingdom of Savoy (of which Turin was the capital from 1559). French was the language of the court until the middle of the nineteenth century and the French influence continued to dominate in the kitchens of the court into the twentieth.

There was also a rich tradition of country cooking, and today that cooking, especially of the gastronomic enclave of the wine country in the area of the Langhe, attracts thousands of people from all over the world. They come mainly in the truffle season, when the famous white truffles are hunted (they do it with the help of dogs; in France, pigs are used) around oak, hazel and poplar trees in the hills around Alba, Asti and Monferrato.

White truffles are a rarity (the only other place you find them is Morocco, where they are quite different), and although less prized abroad than the black ones of France, they are highly scented. In their season, autumn, they appear in restaurants in almost every dish, shaved on at the last minute with a special slicer, and you can smell them from one part of the restaurant to the other.

The medieval city of Alba, capital of the Langhe, is the most important market for them, and its October truffle fair is a great attraction for gourmets.

The people of Piedmont – of Asti and Alba especially – are great ones for festivals and pageantry. They have them all the time, and everyone has a medieval costume and a flag ready to bring out. The most important are the wine and gastronomic festivals. For the festival *delle sagre* (festival of festivals) people come from all around the countryside, in ox carts, dressed in pre-war clothes, bringing mountains of their own local specialities for the great feast in the main square.

The truffle season, which comes at the same time as the grape harvest, at the end of October, is also the wild mushroom season (there is another one in the spring), the game season (for partridge, pheasant, wild duck, quail and hare), and the season for frogs and snails. So autumn is the time when Piedmontese cooking blossoms and comes into its own. Truffles have become so expensive that few can afford to buy them and the alternative perfume which you can detect everywhere is that of garlic, married often with anchovies.

When Piedmontese cooking was thought to be derivative, it was the middle-class cooking of Turin alone that people were thinking of. The extraordinarily rich variety of country dishes was ignored until they arrived at the capital with the influx of peasants who were to form the new working class (it is now massive, with immigrants from the south), and restaurants opened offering the dishes of the hinterland.

Turin – the great industrial and business city, the most hard-working city in Italy, the elegant baroque city of gracious squares, tree-lined streets and lovely gardens with graceful bridges over the river Po – has no cooking of her own and few things which can be called entirely hers. The most representative is *giandujotti* – hazelnut chocolates, which take their name from the carnival mask *gianduja*. Turin is said to be the place where chocolate was first introduced in Europe. At the end of the sixteenth century, Duke Emanuele Filiberto brought cocoa back from Spain, and at the end of the eighteenth, Turin became the centre of a great chocolate industry (Suchard, the founder of the Swiss chocolate firm, went there as a young man to learn chocolate-making).

Another product of Turin known all over the world is grissini, the hard sticks made with bread dough. In Turin people only want the hand-pulled, uneven, long, thin and crisp ones, sometimes with a dusting of flour clinging to them. There are two varieties: *stira* is thin, usually half to one metre (two to three feet) long and dusted with rice flour; *rubata* is fatter and less even, with finger marks, as it is made by rolling rather than pulling. Napoleon is said to have sent regularly for supplies of '*les petits bâtons de Turin*' from the city which the French affectionately named 'Grissinopoli' and 'the *commune* of San Grissino'.

The Turinese are famous for their passion for pastries and desserts, and pastry-making is more developed here than anywhere else in Italy. Many of the wonderful sweets served in the old cafés, where you go to drink coffee and hot chocolate, were developed by cooks at the court of Savoy. These cafés also make their own ice cream and are among the most enjoyable features of city life. Otherwise Turin has absorbed the culinary traditions of the countryside.

Turin is the only real city in Piedmont. Everything else is the antithesis of the city: entirely rural with small provincial towns filled with the smell of the country, love of the good life and people whose energies are directed towards wine and gastronomic festivals and singing sessions. The contrast is amazing.

Piedmont lies within an arc of high mountains which embraces its northern and western borders and fans into the gentle hills of the Langhe and Monferrato and down into the plain around Vercelli and Novara. The Valle d'Aosta, the smallest region of Italy, to the north-west of Piedmont, has deep river valleys alternating with high mountains, which make it one of the loveliest tourist spots in the Alps. Because the geographical variety is so great, this part of Italy has the greatest possible agricultural differences. Maize, barley and wheat and also rye and oats are grown on the plain. Novara and Vercelli produce sixty per cent of Italy's rice. The celebrated vineyards are in the hills, where vegetables and fruit also grow: apples and pears in the Aosta valley, peaches around Canale, walnuts at Feisuglio, hazelnuts at Alba. Each valley and hillside specialises, and that is also the case with cherries and strawberries. There are plenty of trout and freshwater fish in the mountain streams and in the rivers Po and Tanaro, and frogs flourish in the rice fields. Cattle-rearing in the mountain pastures makes Piedmont the greatest producer of meat in Italy and one of the most important of butter and cheese. In the old days the cooking fats used were butter, pork fat, hazelnut and walnut oils. Now olive oil (from neighbouring Liguria) is important.

The numerous alpine valleys produce a vast range of cheeses. Fresh cheeses are served as antipasti, sometimes dressed with olive oil and also herbs; a Piedmontese meal must always finish with sharp, piquant cheeses, served with red wine, followed by fruit and sweets served with Asti Spumante. Bread and cheese is a favourite accompaniment for wine-tasting.

The most famous cheese, fontina, is made in the Valle d'Aosta with cow's milk. The cheese made in summer, when the cows feed on mountain pastures, is aromatic and more highly prized than that made in winter, when the cows eat dry forage in their sheds. Fontina is made into great rounds that weigh up to 18kg (40lb) and is matured for up to 100 days. It is used a great deal in cooking and goes into the famous *fonduta*, a speciality of the Valle d'Aosta, and in a sauce for gnocchi and a layered polenta.

Other famous cheeses are paglierino, made industrially with cow's milk (the name comes from the straw, *paglia*, in which it was originally ripened), which can be fresh, matured or aged, and robiola (also called tuma), a sharp creamy goat's cheese usually eaten within a week of its making but also found aged. There are a number of varieties of robiola: robiola del bec is made from October to November, during the mating season (the ram is *becco*), when the milk has a particular flavour; robiola di cocconato is round and flat (like a large mushroom, *coccone* in dialect), has no crust and is eaten very fresh; robiola delle Langhe is dry but soft, and usually served with a dribble of olive oil; similar robiola d'Alba is ready after two weeks; robiola bossolasco is strongly scented and can be aged for a month; robiola di roccaverano, made around Asti and Alessandria from a mixture of goat's and cow's milk, is large, white, grainy, delicately flavoured and very slightly acid. Even when they look the same, cheeses taste different in every valley.

Piedmont is strong on goat's cheeses. There is the long, cylindrical caprino piemontese of the Valle d'Aosta; the tiny round and very fresh caprino di rimella from around Vercelli and Valsesia; the flat cevrin di caozze produced in the Sangone Valley, which can be very sharp and piquant when seasoned. Sora from the Cuneo hills is light, fresh and aromatic.

Of the cheeses made with cow's milk, toma, aged for at least three months, is the most common – it is semi-hard and can be more or less sharp and contain more or less fat; tometta is fresh with a little fermentation, tomino is very fresh, and usually eaten as an antipasto with a strong sauce; sweet and aromatic tumet from Vercelli is made from skimmed summer milk; testun is hard and dry; press, from the valleys of d'Ossola, Formoza and Vigezzo, is semi-hard, piquant and almost bitter and is aged for up to a year for grating; motta from Vercelli is flavoured with fennel seeds; reblochon is soft and creamy with a crust. Other cheeses are grasso d'Alpe, Montebore, Moncenisio, nostrano del monregalese. Blue-green gorgonzola and the hard grana padana of Lombardy are also made in Piedmont, and there are mixtures: *brus*, from around Cuneo and Asti, is a mixture of different cheeses, mashed together, flavoured, left to ferment, then enriched with grappa or other alcohol to make a powerfully piquant cream that can be savoured only in tiny quantities. *Sargnon*, a speciality of Vercelli, is made from remaindered pieces of gorgonzola and other fermented cheeses mixed with alcohol and left for a month to become a rich, strongly flavoured cream.

There is quite a large range of homemade pork sausages and salamis. One of the most characteristic is *salamin d'la duja*, which is kept in pork fat (the air is too humid for drying out), traditionally in a clay pot called a *duja* – hence the name. The region is also famous for its goose and donkey salamis (tender young donkeys less than one year old are used), its cured goose (*prosciutto d'oca*), smoked goose breasts (*petti stagionati*) and goose liver pâté, and *violini*, salted and cured venison.

A Piedmontese meal can be an overwhelming experience, with from five to thirty antipasti, called *assaggi* (tastings), followed by several often substantial courses. People have reduced the amount they eat in these diet- and health-conscious days, but the habit of the important meal, especially on Sunday, remains an institution.

The countryside, to which all those with roots in the land and memories of parents and grandparents pruning the vine and feeding the chickens are deeply attached, has remained much the same, although everyone has become rich as the wine industry has prospered. The peasants here always put money aside, and when the landlords were forced to sell them their homes cheaply, they bought them and a bit of land. Their children went to work in local factories and the wages helped to invest in machinery. Half the agriculture is still in the hands of the old farmers, and their farmhouses (*cascine*), where once they had a bit of everything including ducks, geese, a few cows in the barn and a pig which made them self-sufficient, are still there, next to modern villas in a sea of vines, vegetable gardens and fruit trees.

Giovanni Goria, a lawyer from Asti and a great Piedmontese gastronome who organises festivals, advises and encourages restaurants and even teaches cooking (all for love), remembers the long list of typical dishes that figured year after year in the ritual cycle of feast days. To celebrate the *svinatura*, when newly made wine was put in the barrels, people ate *bagna cauda*, a strongly flavoured sauce, kept simmering on a little stove on the table, and a plate of raw vegetables for dipping. It was a convivial affair, with everyone dipping into the same bowl, eating masses of bread, drinking rivers of wine and singing. The Piedmontese are not spontaneous and exuberant like the Italians of the south – quite the opposite. They are quiet, reserved, hard-working, a little taciturn and closed in, so these moments of conviviality are extra precious.

For the Festa dei Santi e dei Morti (Feast of the Saints and the Dead) they prepared a huge minestrone with beans, chickpeas and bacon, flavoured with onion and garlic, sage and rosemary. On the feast of killing the pig, farmers invited their friends to come and enjoy the perishable parts. The basis of the Piedmontese *fritto misto* is the brains, sweetbreads, liver (all the parts that had to be eaten at once), dipped in egg and breadcrumbs and fried in a mixture of oil and butter. The dish has developed into a magnificent combination of savoury and sweet which includes slices of veal, chicken croquettes, mushrooms, macaroons, balls of thick semolina cream flavoured with vanilla and sugar, or with chocolate, and also apple slices. *Batsoa*, boiled pig's trotters (the word comes from the French *bas de soie* – silk stocking), also got into the *fritto misto*, boned and cut into slices, or were boiled in an aromatic broth with vinegar, bay leaf, cloves and cinnamon. Black pudding was made with fried onion and spices and cooked on a bed of chopped leeks. *Grive*, liver mixed with juniper, was grilled in a net of lacy caul.

Christmas Eve (a day of abstinence from meat) always began with *lasagne della Vigilia*, pasta simply dressed with butter, garlic and Spanish anchovies (since the Middle Ages every farmhouse had a barrel of salted anchovies brought from Spain by Provençal 'anchovy men'), great spoonfuls of parmesan and lots of black pepper, and continued with fried tench, stewed eels and salt cod. Christmas lunch started with a variety of pâtés made with liver, pheasant, goose and rabbit, followed by agnolotti, crescent-shaped dumplings stuffed with roast veal, pork and rabbit mixed with sausage, egg, parmesan and nutmeg. Next came a very concentrated meat broth with *pasta reale* (omelette cut into little squares) and tiny peas which were kept in jars, followed by a great big pike and the festive turkey stuffed with sausage meat, minced veal and parmesan. Dessert was *dolce Monte Bianco* with chestnuts and cream, perfumed with rum. The Piedmontese adore rum.

The great New Year's dish was the *gran bollito misto* (*buji* in dialect), in which beef, pork, veal and chicken were boiled in a herby broth with veal head (cotechino, pork sausage, was cooked separately) and served accompanied by an array of strongly flavoured sauces: green *bagnet verd*, with anchovies, garlic, parsley and breadcrumbs; red *bagnet d'tomatiche*, with tomatoes; *mostarda d'uva*, a fruit preserve made with grape must and mustard essence; and *saussa d'avie*, a mixture of honey, ground walnuts or almonds and a little broth, with a few drops of mustard essence. The *bollito* was preceded by rice with *fonduta* poured over, and followed by sliced fruit cooked in butter with sugar, then, finally, a Milanese panettone. The list continues with dishes for Carnival, Lent, Easter, Ascension and spring.

Recently hundreds of trattorias and restaurants have sprung up where these and other traditional dishes can be found. They feature antipasti such as pâtés, *carne cruda* (raw meat), and the famous *vitel tonne* (*vitello tonnato*), thinly sliced cold veal covered with a creamy sauce of tuna, anchovy and capers; *insalata di riso*, rice salad cooked with white wine, served with parsley and truffle shavings; *cipolle ripiene* (stuffed onions) and frittatas. There is always rice, combined with chickpeas or vegetables, with frogs or bits of cheese and ham or with meat gravy and truffles. Gnocchi are made with potatoes and served *alla bava*, with melted fontina and butter. This is also polenta country. Traditionally it is served poured out on the table for everyone to help themselves. The only pastas are agnolotti, dumplings stuffed with meat, as mentioned previously, or with spinach, ricotta and herbs; *tajarin*, or tagliolini, very finely cut noodles, a speciality of Alba, where they are served with chicken livers, meat gravy and truffles; and the wider lasagnette, which are served with a mushroom or asparagus sauce. There are great roasts and long-simmered stews and game cooked with wine, or *in civet* or *in salmi*. There is a wonderful range of desserts in Piedmont: stuffed peaches and baked pears; *zuppa inglese*, a kind of trifle; *zabaione*, which was born in Piedmont; and the most popular, *bonèt* a kind of crème caramel enriched with crumbled macaroons and flavoured with cocoa and rum. Every village makes its own special biscuits. Among these are *crumiri* of Casale, amaretti of Mombaruzzo, *baci di dama* of Tortona.

Every little part of Piedmont has its specialities and different influences, although there has been a symbiosis among them. Alessandria, for instance, has Ligurian dishes such as *panizza*, a soup made with chickpea flour; *pansoti*, stuffed pasta served with a walnut sauce; a black-olive paste – their 'mountain caviar' – and lettuce rolls; Lombard dishes such as agnolotti stuffed with pumpkin; a mysterious *polenta dei Sicuri*; and also Emilian dishes such as lasagne.

Until the fifteenth century, the region was divided among a small aristocracy into numerous little autonomous dukedoms and marquisates, continually fighting one another and continually fighting off French and Austrian invaders. The House of Savoy, which had been mainly in the mountains, gradually affirmed itself, and by the eighteenth century all the domains were united under the Savoy dynasty. Piedmont, which had always been on the sidelines, went into the heart of Italian history and, during the period of the Risorgimento (1849–1861), it became the protagonist of Italian unity, providing the ideology and the basis for government and driving the Austrians out of Italy. Count Camillo Benso di Cavour, the leading architect of Italian unity and the new nation's first prime minister, and Giuseppe Garibaldi (he was born in Nice, which was part of the Kingdom of Savoy), who led the bitter wars to unite the reluctant south, are the great heroes of Italian unity, with streets named after them in every city.

Cavour promoted the agricultural and industrial prosperity (mainly silk production) of the region, but while Turin grew into a powerful political and industrial capital, rural Piedmont continued with the old traditions, some of which date back to and reflect the diversity of the time of the old dukedoms and marquisates.

The Wines of Piedmont

Some of Italy's most prestigious wines are produced in Piedmont, which is the most traditional of Italy's wine-making regions. Piedmont is famous for strong reds from the days when wine was a nourishment – '*il vino che e pane*' (wine that is bread) – for the men who worked long hours in the fields. These wines are perfect partners for the *piatti forti*, the strong heavy dishes of Piedmont.

The most famous, Barolo, produced around the town of Alba, is not fashionable outside Piedmont these days, but it is regarded with awe as one of the greatest wines of Italy and it is always referred to as 'regal' – perhaps because of its association with the old royal courts of Piedmont. Made with the native Nebbiolo grape, it is a strong wine for strong men; dry, austere, vigorous, full-bodied and long-ageing, it can be rough and tannic, but at its best it loses its hard taste and develops unique and harmonious sensations of flavour and aroma. It can be balanced and velvety; it has a great deal of depth and intensity of flavour combined with the mingled scents of violets and old roses, truffles, tobacco, pepper, and even tar. It is a tradition in Piedmont to open a bottle, drink some, and leave the rest for a day or so for guests as a special treat, because a slight oxidation gives the wine a pleasant aftertaste.

Barbaresco, too, is an old legendary, almost mythical, big wine with a very particular personality. It is tannic and long-ageing; it is not as full-bodied as Barolo, but is more delicate and refined. Velvety, with a fruity, slightly bitter taste and an intense perfume of violets, it is said to be an elegant 'feminine' wine among the great range of full-bodied virile reds made in Piedmont with Nebbiolo grapes. These include Boca, Carema, Fara, Gattinara, Ghemme, Lessona and Sizzano, all very attractive wines with some of the qualities of Barolo, but lighter-bodied and much cheaper and easier to drink. Like Barolo and Barbaresco, they are meant to be served at a warmish temperature with game, red meat, rich sauces and strong sharp cheeses, and they should be left to breathe for a few hours before drinking.

Another fine red, Nebbiolo d'Alba, can be drunk young and is particularly refined and elegant. Connected with the House of Savoy and the old nobility, it features in seventeenth-century accounts of banquets, and is currently reliving moments of glory. It can be dry to pleasantly sweet and also sparkling, with a perfume of raspberries and violets, and is popularly served with *fonduta*. Roero is another thoroughly modern fragrant and fruity wine. Dolcetto d'Alba, also at its best when young, is a hearty wine for simple, friendly occasions. It is medium-bodied, soft, dry and fruity, with a pleasantly bitter taste. Barbera, an ordinary Piedmontese red table wine, made with Barbera grapes from one of Italy's most prolific and wide-spread vines, has a low image but it is a good, warm, gutsy wine with plenty of charm, flowery fragrance and fruity, acid, resinous bite. It is what you often find in trattorias outside Italy.

Bubbly reds like the dry or semi-sweet Freiza with the perfume of raspberries and violets, the vivacious Malvasia and the flowery Brachetto are popular too, especially to take on picnics and for alfresco eating.

Piedmont is red wine country, but it also produces large quantities of white wines – dry, sweet and sparkling. One of Italy's most fashionable white wines is the young, crisp, tart, fresh and fragrant Gavi, made from Gavi grapes. Another is the young, nutty and aromatic Arneis. Both are excellent with fish, antipasti, primi and white meats.

And Piedmont is the home of the world-famous Asti Spumante, the white, sparkling, fruity, delicately sweet and sometimes dry, aromatic dessert wine which is made in the town of Asti. Asti Spumante is a wine of celebration. It accompanies cakes and desserts and it is always served with panettone at Christmas. Moscato d'Asti is another very perfumed and delicate, fruity dessert wine, while the sparkling Moscato d'Asti Spumante is brought out on festive and joyful occasions.

LIVER PATE
Pâté di fegato

The recipe for this pâté comes from Danilo, the young owner-chef of La Crota at Roddi d'Alba. Most of his customers ask for *assaggi* – small tastings of everything, a way of eating that has come into fashion in the last ten years.

250g (8oz) pound calf liver	3 tablespoons marsala
250g (8oz) pound chicken livers	Salt and pepper
125g (4oz) butter	3 tablespoons cognac
A sprig of rosemary	Small truffle, diced (optional)

Clean the livers and remove the veins. Cut the calf liver into small pieces.

In a frying pan, melt 15g (½oz) butter with the rosemary and sauté the chicken livers for moments only until browned but still pink and juicy inside. Remove, and sauté the calf liver, also for moments only and over high heat until lightly browned but still pink inside. Pour in the marsala and let it bubble for a second. Add salt and pepper. Put the livers and pan juices through the blender.

Let the mixture cool a little, then blend in the remaining butter and the cognac and finally stir in the truffle, if using. Scrape into a bowl and let cool in the refrigerator for a few hours to a firm consistency. Serve with toast.

HOT GARLIC AND ANCHOVY DIP
Bagna cauda

This hot garlicky sauce with vegetables to dip in it is the most representative of Piedmontese foods. It is eaten all year round, but it is associated by the Piedmontese with grape picking and pressing, the smell of fermenting grape juice, and the electric atmosphere that accompanies the rituals and celebrations of wine-making.

A drinking party invited me to join their long, narrow table. They explained that a group around a *bagna cauda* must be large, uninhibited and jolly. Actually, it was euphoric, and they sang Piedmontese ballads.

Once upon a time local hazelnut and walnut oils were used as a base for the sauce, but now a light and delicate olive oil from Liguria is used, and often it is mixed with melted butter.

SERVES 4

200ml (7fl oz) olive oil
4–5 cloves garlic, crushed

12 anchovies, drained and chopped
125g (4oz) butter

Put the oil in a small sauté pan, add the garlic and heat until the garlic is soft but not brown. Add the anchovies and cook, stirring, over low heat until the anchovies dissolve, being careful not to burn the garlic. Add the butter, and as soon as it has melted, serve, standing the pan on a table burner so the sauce does not get cold.

To serve

Have a variety of raw vegetables cut into pieces. In Piedmont they use peppers, celery, carrots, cauliflower, mushrooms, fennel, artichoke hearts, cardoons, turnips, spring onions, beetroot, boiled potatoes and Jerusalem artichokes. Serve lots of bread to mop up the drippings.

CHEESE FONDUE
Fonduta

Fonduta, a speciality of the Valle d'Aosta, the smallest Italian region, which has a very strong French character, can be found also in Piedmont. Fontina, the cheese with which it is made, takes its name from Mount Fontin at Quart in the Valle. *Fonduta* is often served over polenta or rice.

SERVES 6

500g (1lb) fontina, diced
300ml (½ pint) milk
50g (2oz) butter, melted

5 egg yolks
White pepper
White truffle (optional)

Put the cheese in a bowl, cover with the milk and leave for at least an hour to soften. Heat the cheese and milk in a double boiler, stirring continuously, until the cheese melts and starts to make threads. Add the butter and take off the heat. Beat in the egg yolks, return to the double boiler and stir vigorously until the mixture becomes smooth and creamy and thickens slightly. Do not let the mixture boil or the eggs will curdle. (I find this way is quicker and works better than the usual one of starting with egg yolks then adding the cheese and milk.) Add pepper, and if you have the truffle, sprinkle over some shavings. Serve in soup plates with plenty of bread or toast for dipping.

Note

Swiss gruyère is a good alternative to fontina.

PEPPERS WITH ANCHOVIES AND CAPERS
Peperoni alla piemontese

SERVES 6

4 peppers

6–8 anchovy fillets, finely chopped

1–2 cloves garlic, crushed

1 heaped tablespoon capers, finely chopped

A few sprigs of oregano, finely chopped

4–5 tablespoons olive oil

Roast the peppers in the oven at 200°C (400°F, gas mark 6) for 20 minutes, or until they are soft, then put them into a plastic bag, close it tight and leave for 10 minutes for the skins to loosen. Peel the peppers, remove the seeds and cut each into 4 pieces or into strips. Toss well with the rest of the ingredients.

POACHED EGGS WITH TOMATOES AND BASIL
Uova in camicia

SERVES 4

1 small or ½ medium onion, chopped

2 cloves garlic, crushed

2 tablespoons olive oil

500g (1lb) tomatoes, peeled and chopped

3 tablespoons chopped basil

2 tablespoons chopped parsley

Salt and pepper

2 teaspoons vinegar

4 eggs

To make the sauce, fry the onion and garlic in the oil until soft. Add the tomatoes and simmer for a few minutes until slightly reduced, then add the herbs and seasoning. Fill a high-sided sauté pan with salted water, add the vinegar and place on the heat. When it comes to the boil, break the eggs in one by one and reduce the heat to simmering point. When the white is set, put a little tomato sauce on each of four dishes, remove the eggs with a slotted spoon and place on the sauce.

ONIONS STUFFED WITH MEAT
Cipolle ripiene

SERVES 4

4 large (Spanish) onions, peeled

250g (8oz) minced veal

4 tablespoons grated parmesan

2 cloves garlic, crushed

A sprig or two of oregano or marjoram, finely chopped

2 tablespoons finely chopped parsley

2 tablespoons tomato paste

Salt and pepper

1 egg

Oil

Boil the onions whole for about 35 minutes, until tender. When they have cooled a little, cut in half horizontally and remove the centres, leaving a shell of about 3 layers and patching any little hole left at the bottom with a piece of onion.

Mix the meat (if it is not already minced you can chop it finely in a food processor) with the cheese, garlic, herbs, tomato paste, a little salt and pepper and the egg; work well until smooth. Fill the onions with this mixture, arrange them in an oiled baking dish, brush the tops with oil and bake in the oven at 200°C (400°F, gas mark 6) for 40–50 minutes.

Serve hot.

ONIONS STUFFED WITH PUMPKIN

Cipolle ripiene di magro

SERVES 4–8

6 large (Spanish) onions, peeled

500g (1lb) pumpkin

175g (6oz) amaretti, reduced to crumbs

125g (4oz) mostarda (fruit in syrup with mustard essence)

A good pinch of nutmeg

Salt and pepper

1 egg

Butter

Boil the onions whole in salted water for about 30–35 minutes, until tender, Peel the pumpkin, remove the seeds and stringy bits and boil until tender (you can put it in with the onion and lift it out when it is done). Drain the onions, let them cool, then cut them in half horizontally and remove the centres, leaving a shell about 3 layers thick. Patch up any holes left at the bottom with a piece of onion.

For the filling, mash the pumpkin, add the amaretti and mostarda, finely chopped, with a little of the syrup, season with nutmeg, salt and pepper, and add the egg to bind it. You can do this in a blender or food processor.

Fill the onion halves and place in a buttered baking dish. Top with butter shavings and bake in the oven at 200°C (400°F, gas mark 6) for about 40 minutes, or until nicely coloured.

Note

You can do the same with small onions and serve them with an array of little stuffed vegetables.

MIXED FRIED DELICACIES

Fritto misto piemontese

The tradition of deep-frying spreads across the country. *Friggitori* or *frittolini*, some of them street vendors, specialise in frying. But the combination of little delicacies that are put together in a *gran fritto misto* can be something so special that it makes you gasp with surprise and pleasure.

Fritto misto belongs to the great tradition of Italian cooking for grand occasions. It is part of the rituals celebrating births, weddings, saints' days, anniversaries and special events such as a return from abroad. Piedmont, Emilia-Romagna, Lombardy, Rome, Tuscany and Naples are all famous for the variety they offer. The Piedmontese *fritto* is the richest. Until only a few years ago many restaurants there, especially in the region of the Langhe and in Turin, owed their reputation to their sumptuous selection of *fritti*, which could go up to as many as twenty-five. But now, because it is so rich and so finicky to make, a *fritto misto* is never on a menu more than once or twice a week, and usually it has to be ordered and the ingredients discussed in advance.

Traditionally, the Piedmontese fry in a mixture of oil and butter, but now many fry meat in sunflower oil, and that is what I prefer. Most things are first dipped in flour, then in beaten egg and finally in fine dry breadcrumbs, but some vegetables and fruit are dipped in a batter.

Some ingredients need to be cooked beforehand. All have different frying times. When they are a nice golden brown, they must be drained, salted, and brought to the table piping hot. Although it is possible to do all the frying in advance and to heat everything up in the oven when you are ready to serve, the result will not be quite the same as when the dark golden crust is still crisp and light from the hot oil.

The components vary according to the season and to individual tastes. There can be chicken cutlets, potato and cheese croquettes, pieces of meat, all kinds of offal, vegetables and fruit. I once got a skewer with alternating pieces of bananas and strawberries. You could also be offered frogs, the cooked and flattened meat of pig's trotters, cockscombs and snails. Fried sweet semolina is always present; it is a must.

Method

Have ready a bowl of beaten egg, a plate of flour and another of fine dry breadcrumbs. Dredge the ingredients first in flour, then in beaten egg and lastly in breadcrumbs. Deep fry until golden.

For the batter (for vegetables and fruit), mix 100g (3½oz) flour with 1 egg and 1 tablespoon oil and beat in about 120ml (4fl oz) water or milk, or enough to make a light creamy batter.

Meats

Lamb or veal kidneys, trimmed, the first cut in half the second sliced (for preparation see page 37)

Lamb or calf's brains: remove as much of the thin membrane as you can, blanch in salted water with 1 tablespoon vinegar for a few minutes until firm, lift out and cool, then cut into large pieces

Lamb or calf's sweetbreads: peel off the thin membrane and blanch in salted water with 1 tablespoon vinegar for about 10 minutes, then lift out, pull off the remaining membrane and cut into pieces

Lamb or calf's liver, cut into small thin slices

Tiny lamb chops

Frying sausages, cut into bite-sized pieces

Vegetables

Fresh porcini mushrooms, sliced, or small mushrooms left whole

Aubergine, sliced

Asparagus: use only the tender part

Courgettes, sliced diagonally

Courgette or pumpkin blossoms, pistil removed and stem trimmed: wash and dry and dip in batter

Tomatoes, thickly sliced and seeds removed

Peppers

Artichoke hearts, sliced

Cauliflower florets, boiled in salted water until tender

Fruit, sweet things and other foods

Sweet firm apples, sliced and dipped in batter

Amaretti biscuits, slightly moistened in milk

Polenta sliced 1cm ($\frac{1}{2}$in) thick

Fried sweet semolina

To make this, bring to the boil in a saucepan 500ml (18fl oz) milk with 2 tablespoons sugar. Add 125g (4oz) semolina all at once and cook for about 15 minutes, stirring occasionally, over very low heat. Remove from the heat and mix in 1 egg yolk. Pour the mixture in a layer about 1cm ($\frac{1}{2}$in) thick on a wet tray or dish. When it has cooled, cut into diamond shapes. Turn them out and dredge first in flour, then in beaten egg and finally in breadcrumbs and deep-fry until golden.

Note

In Lombardy butter is used for frying; elsewhere, oil is used.

RAW MEAT SALAD

Insalata di carne cruda

I had this raw meat salad at the Castello Grinzane Cavour near Alba, which once belonged to Cavour's family and now belongs to the *comune*. The castle houses a wine museum, an *enoteca* where you can taste local wines, and a trattoria that specialises in the cooking of the Langhe.

SERVES 4–8

500g (1lb) fillet of beef or very tender veal

Juice of 2 lemons

6–8 tablespoons olive oil

Salt and plenty of pepper

2–3 cloves garlic, crushed

A good bunch of parsley, finely chopped

1 lemon, cut in wedges

4 pickled cucumbers, thinly sliced

2–3 tablespoons capers

Chop the meat very finely. Beat the lemon juice with the olive oil, add salt and pepper and garlic, and mix very well with the meat. Let the meat absorb the dressing for 2 hours, covered, in the refrigerator. Serve spread on a flat dish, sprinkled with parsley and garnished with lemon wedges, slices of pickled cucumber and capers spread around the edges.

Variations

There are those who add 1–2 finely chopped anchovies to the dressing and those who present the salad with a crown of truffle or parmesan shavings or very thin slices of raw porcini mushrooms.

A modern version, the Venetian carpaccio invented at the grand hotel Cipriani, is a very thin slice of raw beef dressed with the oil and lemon dressing, sometimes embellished with shavings of truffle or parmesan. According to legend, the dish was first offered at the time of an exhibition of the painter Carpaccio's work. When a lady asked the name of the slice of raw meat she was served, the waiter caught sight of an exhibition poster and simply said 'Carpaccio', and the name stuck.

TONGUE WITH RED SAUCE
Lingua in salsa rossa

Boiled tongue with red sauce is a speciality of Asti, where the dish is served warm as an antipasto, but elsewhere it often comes as a main dish. Tender tongue and a strongly flavoured and fragrant sauce make a delicious combination.

If you can't find fresh tongue, use cured tongue and soak overnight in a bowl of cold water.

SERVES 10–12

1 beef tongue, about 2kg (4lb)
1 onion
5 cloves
1 carrot, cut into large pieces
1 stalk celery, cut into large pieces
2 bay leaves

Wash the tongue, put it in a large saucepan with plenty of water to cover, bring to the boil and remove the scum, then add the onion stuck with the cloves, and the rest of the ingredients. Simmer gently, adding water to keep the meat covered, for about 4 hours, until the tongue feels very tender when you pierce it with a pointed knife.

Take out the tongue, peel the skin off while still hot and return to the broth. Cut into slices just before serving, hot or cold, and accompany with the hot or cold red sauce (recipe follows) or *salsa verde*, a herby green sauce (page 115).

RED SAUCE
Salsa rossa

1 onion, chopped
1 stalk celery, diced
1 carrot, diced
2–3 cloves garlic, chopped
1 red pepper, diced
2 tablespoons olive oil
2 anchovy fillets, finely chopped
1kg (2lb) tomatoes, peeled, seeded and cut
2 sprigs of rosemary
Salt
1–2 tablespoons red wine vinegar
1–2 tablespoons sugar
Up to $\frac{1}{2}$ teaspoon hot chilli powder
About 3 tablespoons chopped basil
About 3 tablespoons chopped parsley

Fry the onion, celery, carrot, garlic and pepper in olive oil until soft, stirring often. Add the anchovies and let them melt, then add the tomatoes, the rosemary and salt to taste, and simmer for 30–45 minutes, until much reduced. Take out the rosemary sprigs (they will have lost their leaves). Blend the sauce until smooth and return it to the pan. Add the vinegar and sugar and ground red chilli and more salt if necessary. Simmer for about 10 minutes, tasting to make sure that the flavour is rich and strong; then add the basil and parsley.

TAGLIATELLE WITH WHITE TRUFFLES
Tagliatelle con tartufi

If you want to try the old-style Piedmontese tagliatelle called *tajarin*, make the dough with 400g (14oz) flour, 2 eggs, 1 tablespoon grated parmesan and about 5 tablespoons water. Otherwise use the recipe on pages 110–111. Work the dough and roll out as described in that recipe and cut the noodles thin.

SERVES 4

1 small white truffle
125g (4oz) butter
40g (1½oz) freshly grated parmesan

Salt and pepper
Pinch of nutmeg
500g (1lb) tagliatelle or fettuccine

Scrub the truffle with a brush and wash it well. Melt the butter and add the grated parmesan and a little salt, pepper and nutmeg.

Boil the tagliatelle until al dente, drain quickly and serve immediately, tossed with the melted butter mixture. Shave a little truffle over each serving.

RISOTTO WITH HAM AND CHEESE
Antico risotto sabaudo

SERVES 4–6

50g (2oz) butter
1 medium onion, finely chopped
50–75g (2–3oz) cooked ham, diced
A sprig of rosemary
400g (14oz) Arborio rice

150ml (5fl oz) white wine
1.25 litres (2 pints) chicken or veal stock
125g (4oz) fontina or gruyère, cubed
Freshly grated parmesan
Sliced white truffle (optional)

Melt the butter in a saucepan, add the onion and cook for 5 minutes, until soft but not coloured. Add the ham and cook for 1 minute, then add the rosemary and rice, stirring until the rice is transparent.

Add the wine, stir and cook until it is absorbed. Add the stock, ladleful by ladleful, stirring until each is absorbed. After about 20 minutes the rice should be creamy but al dente. Stir in the fontina or gruyère and cook for 5 minutes more. To finish, add 3–4 tablespoons of parmesan. This risotto is sometimes crowned with a few shavings of white truffle.

RISOTTO WITH BAROLO
Risotto al Barolo

Wine is one of the most important ingredients in Piedmontese cooking – there are wine soups; game is marinated in wine; stews are simmered in wine; agnolotti (meat ravioli) are served with wine poured over them; and fruits are cut up and dropped in wine for dessert.

This risotto from the Langhe has been adopted by restaurants in Turin. In truffle season truffle shavings are added. Barolo is one of the great wines of the region. You can use another rich full-bodied wine instead.

SERVES 4

1 litre (1¾ pints) light chicken stock (you may
    use 1½ stock cubes dissolved in 1 litre/
    1¾ pints water)
350g (12oz) Arborio rice
Salt and pepper

1 onion, chopped
50g (2oz) butter
About 300ml (½ pint) Barolo or other good red wine
Grated parmesan

Bring the stock to the boil, add the rice, season with salt and pepper and simmer gently for 15 minutes, stirring occasionally, then drain. In the meantime, in another large saucepan, fry the onion in 15g (½oz) butter until soft and transparent, add the rice, pour in the wine a little at a time, and cook, stirring often, for 5–10 minutes, until the rice is tender. The risotto should be moist and creamy. Stir in the rest of the butter and let it melt in. I prefer to leave the parmesan for people to help themselves at the table.

MIXED BOILED MEATS
Bollito misto

The tradition of boiling meat belongs to the north of Italy, especially to the cattle- and pig-rearing valley of the river Po, where boiling different types of meat together has become an art. Emilia-Romagna (and Modena in particular) has a reputation for *bollito misto* as Lombardy once had.

But in Piedmont, where it is considered more a meal for big eaters than a dish for gourmets, and where it is offered on market days in the provinces, the *bollito* is an institution with a place of honour in restaurants – it features on Saturdays and Sundays on provincial menus and arrives on a splendid silver trolley, *il carrello dei bolliti*, and is always present on great occasions.

Usually it is a matter of only two meats, beef and chicken (*bollito di seconda*), or three meats (*di terza*), with tongue added. *Di quarta*, with four, is the richest. You find the dish in full regalia as the *gran bollito misto*, with seven (it's the magic figure) traditional components and at least three sauces, only in a few grand restaurants or at great family or civic events.

The typical Piedmontese protagonists of a *gran bollito misto* are beef, chicken, tongue, leg of veal and, less commonly, calf's head, a joint of pork and cotechino (a coarse boiling sausage). In Lombardy you may find calf's or pig's feet. In Emilia-Romagna sausages and pork products such as *cappello da prete*, *salame da sugo ferrarese* and zampone (stuffed pig's foot) are prominent, while in the Veneto, apart from Verona, which is the regional capital of *bollito*, the usual offering is likely to be sausage or chicken, often stuffed with bread and herbs.

In the days before the stock cube, when stock-making for soups and risotto was all-important, the rich and noble Piedmontese families made a habit of regularly boiling meats and chicken for stock. The practice was to put the meats in cold water and then to bring them to the boil; this method extracted the best from the meat for the broth. The impoverished meat formed the servants' meal.

Now the meats go into boiling water which is supposed to seal in their juices and allow the meats to cook to melting tenderness (you should be able to eat them with only a fork) while preserving their succulence. *Bollito misto* is now more often eaten out than at home because families are no longer large enough for the amount of meat it requires.

Some people are a little prejudiced against boiled meats, but everyone who eats them is usually won over, especially when there are wonderful sauces to enliven them.

Make your *bollito misto* as simple or as complicated as you like, with two, three, four or more meats – the choice is up to you. There is no merit in making it difficult for yourself. A good selection is chicken, beef or veal and tongue. The amounts in this recipe will serve sixteen to twenty people.

2 carrots, cut into chunks
2 stalks celery, cut into chunks
2 onions, cut into chunks
2kg (4lb) ox tongue (if you use a pickled tongue, cook it separately (see page 33) or its flavour will dominate the broth)
1 pig's trotter or calf's foot, scrubbed and blanched (optional)

1.1kg (2¼lb) brisket, topside or silverside of beef
Salt and pepper
1.75kg (3½lb) chicken
1kg (2lb) boneless veal (boned rump or rolled shoulder)
1 cotechino sausage, available precooked in Italian shops

Place the vegetables, tongue and pig's trotter or calf's foot, if using, in a very large saucepan with enough boiling water to cover them. Bring to the boil again and skim the scum from the surface. Add the beef and season to taste. Reduce the heat and simmer, covered, very gently for 1 hour. Add the chicken and veal and simmer slowly for 2 more hours. Add the precooked cotechino towards the end of the cooking time and heat through thoroughly.

Leave the meat in the broth while you remove the tongue. Skin and trim it and return it to the broth. Bring the meat, still in the broth, to the table and carve in thick slices. Or carve in the kitchen, cover the slices in broth and keep hot until you are ready to serve.

To serve
Accompany with potatoes, carrots, baby turnips and onions, boiled separately; and serve with a selection of sauces. You must have the green sauce (recipe follows) and a red sauce (page 33 or page 116) and, if you like, pickles, olives, *mostarda di Cremona* (fruit in syrup with mustard essence, which is typically served in Lombardy), *peperonata* (page 79), and other sauces such as *salsa di cren* (see page 72) of Friuli and Alto Adige and the old-fashioned *saussa d'avie*, made of ground walnuts or almonds, mustard and honey mixed to taste. (Instead of mustard, a few drops of mustard essence and broth can be used.)

Variations
For a Modenese (Modena is in Emilia-Romagna) version of *bollito misto*, add a zampone, a pig's trotter stuffed with sausage meat. They are sold already cooked and vacuum-packed. Follow the packet instructions and drop the zampone in at the end.

GREEN HERB SAUCE
Bagnet verd

This green sauce to be served with boiled meats is far better made with flat-leaf parsley than the curly kind. It is best made an hour before serving.

SERVES 8

1 large bunch (about 175g/6oz) flat-leaf parsley, finely chopped
3 tablespoons finely chopped mint
3 anchovies, finely chopped
1 tablespoon finely chopped capers
4 small pickled cucumbers, finely chopped
4 tablespoons fine dry breadcrumbs (optional)

2 hard-boiled egg yolks, mashed (optional)
2 cloves garlic, crushed
2–3 tablespoons vinegar
1 tablespoon sugar
Salt and pepper
150ml (4fl oz) olive oil

Everything can be done in the food processor but not all at once. First chop the parsley and mint and put them in a bowl. Then blend the anchovies, capers and pickled cucumbers, and the breadcrumbs and hard-boiled egg yolks, if using. Add to the chopped herbs and mix in the garlic, vinegar, sugar, salt and pepper. Finally, beat in the olive oil. The sauce should be slightly fluid.

FRUIT PRESERVE IN GRAPE JUICE
Mostarda d'uva

This delicate sweet preserve is made at grape-picking time. Grapes are pressed and the juice is kept in jars for serving with boiled meats.

About 600ml (1 pint) red grape juice (you can use the bottled juice available)
2 large hard pears, peeled and cored
2 apples, peeled and cored
1 teaspoon cinnamon

5 cloves
3 tablespoons walnut pieces or toasted and coarsely chopped hazelnuts or almonds (optional)

Boil the grape juice in a large saucepan until reduced by about half. Add the pears and apples, the cinnamon and cloves, and simmer gently, covered for most of the time, for at least 1 hour (break the fruit into little pieces when it is soft), until the fruit falls apart and the liquid has the consistency of syrup. If you like, add walnuts (but make sure they are not stale) or other nuts.

Variations

In Asti they make *mostarda* with pears and quince.

BEEF BRAISED IN BAROLO
Brasato al Barolo

Every region of Italy makes stews (*stufati*). In the Veneto they call them *pastizzade*, in Venezia Giulia *gulasch*, in Emilia-Romagna and Tuscany they are *stracotti* and in the south *ragù*. The *brasati* of Piedmont are different in that the piece of meat stays whole; it is first browned in fat, and the cooking medium is wine.

This recipe is from Signor Rocca of the Giardino da Felicin in Monforte d'Alba.

SERVES 8

3 tablespoons olive oil
2 stalks celery, finely chopped
3 carrots, peeled and finely chopped
2 cloves garlic, crushed
1 onion, chopped
Sprig of rosemary

1.5kg (3lb) beef topside in a piece, or rolled silverside
600ml (1 pint) Barolo
Salt and pepper
Freshly grated nutmeg

Heat the oil in a flameproof pot or casserole, add the celery, carrots, garlic and onion, and cook for about 5 minutes until soft. Add the rosemary and beef. Brown lightly, then pour in the wine, cover and simmer for 2½ hours, or until tender.

Remove the meat and keep warm. Pour the liquid and vegetables into a blender or food processor and process until smooth. Season to taste with salt and pepper and nutmeg and reheat. Slice the meat and serve with the sauce poured over.

At the restaurant this is usually accompanied by potato purée and carrots.

SAUTEED KIDNEYS
Rognoni trifolati

SERVES 4

4 veal or 12 lamb kidneys, cleaned
1 onion, chopped
1 tablespoon sunflower oil
25g (1oz) butter

Salt and pepper
4 tablespoons cognac, or 3 tablespoons dry marsala
2 tablespoons finely chopped parsley

Split the kidneys in half, remove the cores and white membrane, then wash and cut into slices (they do not need soaking in water with vinegar to remove strong flavours as large beef kidneys do). Small lamb kidneys can be simply cut in half. Fry the onion in a mixture of oil and butter until soft, add the kidneys, season with salt and pepper and fry very briefly, stirring, on high heat, until they change colour. Sprinkle with cognac or marsala and parsley and cook for a moment or two longer. They toughen if they are overcooked. Serve hot.

CHICKEN LIVERS WITH MARSALA
Fegatini di pollo al Marsala

I was first offered this as an hors d'oeuvre but I like to serve it as a main course or as a sauce with noodles.

SERVES 2

250g (8oz) chicken livers

1 small onion, chopped

15g (½oz) butter

2 slices pancetta or unsmoked bacon, chopped

Salt and pepper

6 tablespoons dry marsala

Clean the livers and leave them whole. Fry the onion in the butter until soft. Add the pancetta or bacon and fry for 2 minutes, stirring, then add the chicken livers and sauté quickly, turning over the pieces, until browned all over but still pink inside. Add salt and pepper and marsala and cook for 1–2 minutes longer.

DUCK STEWED IN WINE
Anatra di Palmina

SERVES 4

1 duck, jointed

1 onion, chopped

1 carrot, peeled and chopped

1 stalk celery with some leaves, chopped

300ml (½ pint) dry white or red wine

Salt and pepper

4 tablespoons cognac or brandy

Remove the fat from the duck by skinning it: pull the skin off with the help of a sharp knife.

Heat a piece of the skin, fat side down, in a large sauté pan until you have released about 2 tablespoons of melted fat. Throw away the skin.

Fry the onion, carrot and celery in the fat until soft, then put in the duck pieces. Pour in the wine, season with salt and pepper and simmer gently, covered, for 1 hour, or until tender. Add the cognac or brandy, cook a few minutes longer and serve very hot.

Note

The sauce can be served with pasta as a first course.

PHEASANT IN RED WINE
Fagiano in salmì

This is a nineteenth-century court dish, made a little differently now from the way it was prepared in the royal kitchens.

SERVES 6

3 pheasants, about 1kg (2lb) each

50g (2oz) butter

2 tablespoons oil

2 slices unsmoked bacon, chopped

1 large onion, chopped

1 large carrot, peeled and chopped

2 cloves garlic, finely chopped

2 anchovies, finely chopped

1 stalk celery with leaves, chopped

150ml (5fl oz) marsala

1 bottle (750 ml) red wine

Sprig of sage

2 sprigs of rosemary

3 bay leaves

5 cloves

1 teaspoon cinnamon

12 juniper berries

Salt and pepper

Sauté the pheasants in a mixture of butter and oil in a large flameproof casserole, turning them to brown them all over, then take them out. Drain off a bit of the fat, leaving some to fry the bacon and onion. When the onion is soft, add the carrot and garlic, and when the aroma rises, add the anchovies and celery. Pour in the marsala and the wine and add sage, rosemary, bay leaves, cloves, cinnamon, juniper berries and salt and pepper. Put the pheasants back in the casserole, add a little water and simmer, covered, for 30–45 minutes, or until tender, turning them over at least once.

Ladle most of the sauce into another pan and boil down to a rich consistency, then pour back over the birds and heat through.

Serve on toast or on grilled polenta (pages 86–87) with the sauce poured on top.

Note

You can also bake the pheasants, covered, in the oven at 200°C (400°F, gas mark 6) for 45–60 minutes.

PHEASANT WITH WINE SAUCE
Fagiano caldo in carpione

SERVES 4

4 pheasants, about 1kg (2lb) each
Sprigs of sage, rosemary and thyme
3 tablespoons olive oil
1 stalk celery, finely chopped
1 medium carrot, peeled and finely chopped
1 onion, finely chopped

1 bottle (750 ml) medium dry white wine
Salt and pepper
25g (1oz) butter
3 shallots, finely chopped
2 tablespoons vinegar
2 egg yolks

Stuff the pheasants with herbs and brown in the oil in a large flameproof casserole. Add the celery, carrot and onion, pour in the wine, add water to cover, and bring to the boil. Season and simmer, covered, for 30–45 minutes, or until the birds are tender. Remove the birds and keep warm.

Melt the butter in a saucepan, add the shallots and cook until soft and golden.

Strain the liquid from the pheasants into the shallots, add the vinegar and boil to reduce to 500ml (16fl oz). Stir 2 tablespoons into the egg yolks and return to the saucepan. Stir over gentle heat, a moment only to prevent curdling, until slightly thickened. Carve the pheasants and serve with the sauce. (For a smoother sauce, purée it in a blender.)

QUAIL ON GRILLED POLENTA
Quaglie su crostone di polenta

There is a long tradition of cooking game birds, and *polenta e osei* (polenta with birds) is a famous northern dish that arouses romantic nostalgia. Now that there is little to be caught, farmed quail is the usual alternative.

SERVES 4

8 quail
300ml (1/2 pint) white wine
A few sage leaves
2 sprigs of rosemary
Pepper

100g (3 1/2 oz) unsmoked bacon slices, cut into
     small pieces
3 tablespoons vegetable oil
Salt
8 slices polenta (pages 86–87)

Marinate the quail overnight in wine with sage, rosemary and pepper.

In a sauté pan large enough to hold all the quail, fry the bacon in oil for a few minutes, then add the birds, lifted out of the marinade. Turn to brown them all over, then pour in the marinade. Add salt, and simmer for 20–30 minutes, until the quail are cooked and the sauce is reduced, adding more wine or a little water if it becomes too dry, and turning over the quail.

Toast the slices of polenta under the grill, turning them over once. Serve the birds on top with the sauce poured over.

Variations

For grilled quail, cut the birds open at the breast, then pull them out and flatten them as much as you can so that they cook more evenly. Marinate as above. Brush with oil and cook over glowing coals or under the grill, turning them over once and leaving them longer with the open, bone side towards the heat. Be careful not to overcook.

HARE IN WINE SAUCE
Lepre in salmì

SERVES 4

$1/2$ onion, chopped

$1/2$ carrot, chopped

1 small stalk celery with leaves, chopped

1 clove garlic, chopped

2 tablespoons sunflower or other light oil

1 hare, about 1.25kg (2$1/2$lb), cut into 4 pieces

440ml (14fl oz) red wine

1 bay leaf

4 cloves

1 teaspoon cinnamon

Salt and pepper

3 tablespoons marsala

In a large sauté pan, fry the onion, carrot, celery and garlic in oil until soft. Add the hare and turn to brown the meat all over, then pour in the wine. Add the bay leaf, cloves, cinnamon, salt and pepper and simmer for 30 minutes. If you have the liver, put it into the pan and cook for 1 minute. Blend the liquid with the liver (to make a thicker sauce), return to the pan and cook a few minutes longer, until the meat is tender (with the young tender hare available now it takes less than 45 minutes altogether). Add marsala towards the end.

Note

It is quite usual to use the sauce with pasta, which is served as a first course.

Variations

Rabbit could be used instead of hare.

ALMOND PUDDING
Tartarà dolce

Tartarà is one of the old farmhouse foods that have been 'reborn'. A savoury *tartarà* with milk, eggs and cheese is also popular.

SERVES 4

4 egg yolks

6 tablespoons sugar

500ml (18fl oz) milk

Grated rind of 1 lemon

100g (3$1/2$oz) almonds, very finely chopped

A few drops almond essence

In a bowl sitting in boiling water, beat the egg yolks with the sugar until pale and fluffy. Boil the milk with the grated lemon rind, cool slightly and add to the egg mixture. Cook, stirring (to avoid lumps forming), until it thickens (it does so only a little). Add the almonds and almond essence, and continue to cook, stirring occasionally, to a thick cream. Serve hot or cold.

ZABAGLIONE
Zabaione

In the countryside, zabaglione is eaten hot for breakfast.

SERVES 6

8 egg yolks

75–125g (3–4oz) sugar

250ml (8fl oz) dry marsala or wine

Beat the egg yolks with the sugar until they are pale, then beat in the marsala or wine. (Some like to use a sweet wine, such as a delicately sweet white Moscato; some prefer a dry one.) Pour into a large saucepan and heat gently by standing the pan in a larger pan of barely simmering water. Beat constantly (a hand-held electric beater is a help) until the mixture swells to a thick foam. Serve in warm glasses with plain biscuits.

RUM AND CHOCOLATE CUSTARD
Bonèt

SERVES 4

5 eggs

7 tablespoons sugar

500ml (18fl oz) warm milk

100g (3½oz) plain amaretti biscuits, finely crushed

2 tablespoons unsweetened or dark cocoa powder

250ml (8fl oz) good strong coffee

3 tablespoons rum

Beat the eggs with 4 tablespoons of sugar. Mix in the milk, amaretti, cocoa, coffee and rum. Heat the remaining sugar with 2 tablespoons of water and let it become golden brown. Pour it into a warmed ovenproof dish and coat the inside. Let it cool, then pour in the milk mixture. Bake in the oven at 150°C (300°F, gas mark 2) for 1 hour, or until the cream sets. Chill before serving.

HAZELNUT CAKE
Torta di nocciole

1 tablespoon baking powder

3 eggs, separated

200g (7oz) sugar

125g (4oz) butter, melted and cooled

200g (7oz) flour

200g (7oz) hazelnuts, toasted, skinned and coarsely chopped

Grated rind of 1 lemon

4 tablespoons milk

Beat the baking powder with the egg yolks, add the sugar, butter, flour, hazelnuts, lemon rind and milk, and mix thoroughly. Beat the egg whites until stiff, then gently fold into the mixture. Pour into a buttered, floured 20cm (8in) cake tin and bake in the oven at 180°C (350°F, gas mark 4) for 35 minutes, or until browned and a skewer comes out almost dry.

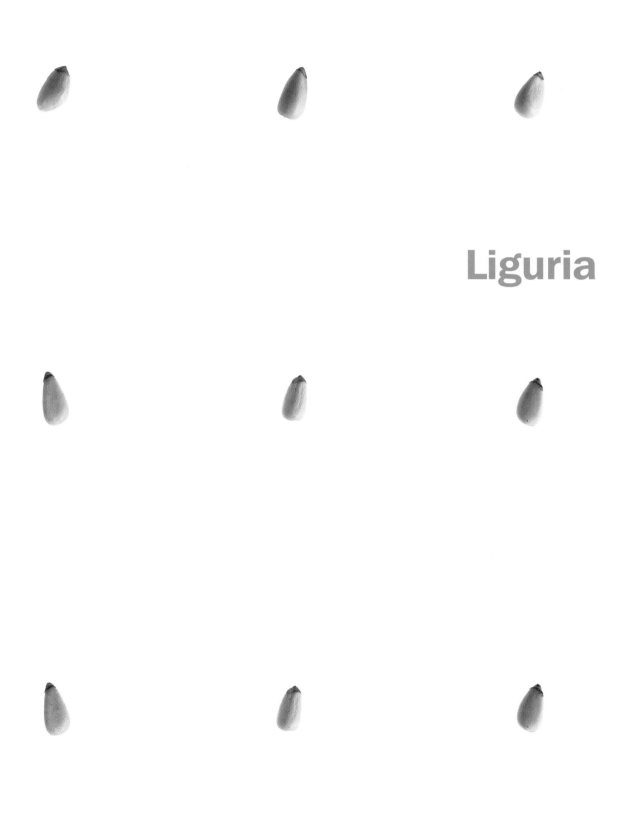

Liguria

Liguria

A tiny narrow arc on the sea below Piedmont framing the bay of Genoa, Liguria is all hills that rise up spectacularly from the sea into the high mountains of the Alps and the Apennines. The towns are perched on the coast, and almost a quarter of all Italian tourism is here, attracted by the lovely beaches, the sun and the deep blue sea. Every kind of vegetable is squeezed into the thin strip between the sea and the hills, which are terraced and planted with olives, vines and fruit trees, particularly peaches, apricots, oranges and lemons. The brilliant sun makes everything grow profusely. Colour bursts out from every corner. Bright flowers grow out of crevices and cascade down the walls that support the banks above the roads, and even in the winter mimosa and bougainvillaea bloom. There is intensive commercial cultivation of carnations and other flowers, and the western Ligurian coast is called the Riviera dei Fiori (the Riviera of flowers).

The hills are covered with wild herbs entangled in the scrub – thyme, sage, rosemary, oregano, marjoram and basil. They perfume the air and characterise the cooking. While Piedmontese food is winter fare, with all its *bolliti*, *fritti misti* and *brasati* (stews), the cooking of Liguria is at its best in the summer months. Both are highly aromatic – the Piedmontese with truffles, wild mushrooms and garlic, the Ligurian with garlic and herbs. Ligurians adore herbs and greenery, and they cook everything with their delicate olive oil, one of the best in Italy.

Ligurian cooking is surprising in many ways. It has none of the characteristics common to the other northern regions, nor is it a cuisine based on the sea, as you would expect from a region with so much coastline. Instead it makes great use of vegetables (as much as Apulia), and its most striking feature is the abundant use of aromatic herbs. The difference from its northern neighbours can be explained by the natural barrier of high mountains which left it isolated in the days when transport was difficult. All Liguria's traffic and exchanges were made across the sea: it received pine nuts from Pisa, pecorino cheese from Sardinia and salted anchovies in barrels from Spain. The list of special local dishes is extraordinary for such a small region; the cuisine owes more to the country than to the sea because it grew out of the hankerings of her sailors.

For centuries all the men of Liguria were sailors. Christopher Columbus was born in Genoa, which is still Italy's most active port, and La Spezia is one of Italy's two naval bases. In the days of sailing when voyages took months, sailors lived on foods that kept forever, such as beans, chickpeas, dry salami and hard biscuits, and, of course, they ate fish. They yearned for fresh vegetables and greenery and fragrance, and during their time ashore this is what their women made to please them.

Ligurians love herbs and make a cult in particular of basil. Everyone grows their own in every available space, in little plots, in window boxes, around the house. Their most famous food – they call it their flag – is the sauce called pesto, which is served with the local pasta: trenette (thin noodles), trofie (made with hard flour and water), lasagne and corzetti (coin-shaped and stamped with a motif), and also with gnocchi and minestrone. To make pesto, bunches of basil leaves are pounded in a mortar with garlic and salt. The basil, like all the herbs that grow in Liguria, is highly perfumed, and when it is crushed it releases such a wonderful scent that it is worth having the patience to pound rather than use the blender, which some do today. Every town along the coast has its own version of pesto. Some make it with pine nuts; some with walnuts; Nervi adds cream at the end; Recco adds a slightly acid ricotta. Provence in the south of France makes a similar sauce: *pistou*. Liguria, which became part of the French Empire in 1806, naturally has much in common with this part of France. They share another speciality: collections of tiny vegetables – courgettes, onions, tomatoes, aubergines and peppers – stuffed with a mixture of breadcrumbs, eggs, garlic, cheese and herbs, including marjoram, and then baked. Ligurian *minestrone con pesto*, a rich soup with a long list of green vegetables and pesto added in at the end, is very much like a Provençal equivalent. Ligurians, along with the people of Nice and Palermo, use chickpea flour to make a kind of thick pancake which is baked in a huge round tray in a baker's oven. They call it *panissa* or *farinata di ceci*.

Liguria is a truly Mediterranean region: here more than anywhere else you find similarities with southern France, Spain, Greece and the Arab world; as for instance the garlic and bread sauce beaten with oil in a mortar until it is like mayonnaise, and a kind of ratatouille, and fruits preserved in syrup. You even find Arab words. Square lasagne are *mandilli di sea* (*mandil* is the Arab word for 'handkerchief' and *sea* means 'silk' in dialect). Trenette or linguine are also called by an old Arab name, *tria*. There were Saracen coves on the Ligurian coast until the tenth century, but the culinary legacy may have come from the trading colonies Genoese merchants established on the coast of North Africa. Ligurian cooking is the cooking of Genoa, and as with all the great Mediterranean ports, many of the influences come from far away.

Another reason the cooking of the sea is not greatly developed here is that this part of the coast is not rich in fish. There are plenty of shellfish – a type of clam called *tartufo di mare*, sea dates (*datteri di mare*) and mussels (a hairy type, known as *cozze pelose*). Ligurians eat shellfish raw, sprinkled with lemon and pepper, or take them out of the shells, dip them in batter and deep-fry them. Shellfish are used with garlic and tomatoes in a sauce for pasta, are cooked in a soup, are stuffed with breadcrumbs, garlic and parsley and put under the grill or are simply cooked with oil, garlic, parsley, pepper and wine.

The fish found in Liguria are mostly anchovies, sardines and other 'poor fish', which are used in mixed fries or in *ciuppin*, a fish soup flavoured with onion, garlic and parsley, in which the fish turn into a sort of cream. Another typical fish dish is *burrida*: different fish are cooked in a sauce of fried onion, chopped anchovy, carrot, celery, tomato, parsley and pine nuts; people say it is of Saracen origin. Squid and cuttlefish are cooked *a zimino* – with white wine and tomatoes, and spinach or beet greens. There are several good stockfish dishes, all very simple: one includes potatoes cut into large pieces and a dressing of olive oil and lemon; in another the stockfish is cooked in white wine and accompanied by barely cooked tomatoes. The usual Mediterranean fish,

like bream, bass and red mullet, can be found, but they are not plentiful.

There is one sumptuous dish that no one makes outside Liguria – a most extraordinary and elaborate fish salad, *cappon magro*. It takes so long to prepare and requires such a variety of fish and vegetables that it is made only for special events. Some restaurants have it on the menu one day a week. Fish and vegetables, six or seven of each (the usual vegetables are cauliflower, green beans, broad beans, celery, carrots, artichokes, potatoes and beetroot), are each poached or boiled separately. The cooked fish is then skinned and boned, and the vegetables are cut into pieces. Everything is dressed with oil, vinegar, salt and pepper and arranged – first the vegetables, then the fish – on a huge oval plate on a base of hard biscuits (*galette*) softened in vinegar and water. The pyramid is decorated with slices of hard-boiled eggs, prawns, oysters, mussels, anchovies, olives and mushrooms in oil; there may even be lobster. The whole is then covered by a rich green sauce, a mixture of olive oil, vinegar, parsley and other herbs, pine nuts, anchovies and white breadcrumbs. As you can imagine, it can be quite a spectacular affair.

Until 1815, when it was incorporated into the Kingdom of Savoy, Genoa was the capital of the Ligurian republic, which in its heyday had been one of the great financial and commercial powers of the Mediterranean, a rival to Venice and Pisa. But Liguria always suffered from the division of the land into myriads of small, constantly warring estates of the local nobility. Some of the history is visible in the medieval city centre of Genoa, where the walls of the tall houses seem too close overhead, leaving only a slit of piercing sunlight to illumine the labyrinth of streets; and in the Romanesque, Gothic and Baroque churches and splendid Renaissance villas and palaces and the fortresses that dot the mountains. The history is present also in the dishes.

The Wines of Liguria

Almost all the wine in Liguria is consumed locally and privately. Only two wines are widely known and available: Cinque Terre and Rossese di Dolceacqua. Both are light and fresh but highly alcoholic. The white Cinque Terre also has a fortified dessert wine called Sciacchetra. The red Rossese di Dolceacqua is dry but with a touch of sweetness. Pigato, a fresh fruity white made with Pigato grapes, has won national acclaim.

FLAT BREAD
Focaccia

In Tuscany they call this *schiacciata* and sometimes flavour it with sage or rosemary.

SERVES 8 OR MORE

1kg (2lb) flour
Salt
50g (2oz) fresh or 25g (1oz) dried yeast or dry
    yeast
500ml (18fl oz) or more warm water

A pinch of sugar
150ml (5fl oz) olive oil
Coarse salt
2 sprigs of rosemary or sage

Put all but 50g (2oz) of the flour and a pinch of salt in a bowl and make a well in the centre. Dissolve the yeast in about 120ml (4fl oz) of the measured warm water, adding the sugar to activate it. Leave it to froth, then pour into the flour, stirring it in with a wooden spoon. (Or follow the packet instructions for dried yeast.) Stir in 4 tablespoons oil and enough of the remaining warm water, working it in with your hands, to make a soft dough. Add some of the remaining flour if necessary. Knead for 10–15 minutes until soft and elastic, adding a little flour if it is too sticky. Roll the dough in 1 tablespoon of oil so that a dry crust does not form, cover it with a damp cloth and leave to rise in a warm place for 1 hour, or until it doubles in bulk. Punch it down and knead it again briefly, then divide it into 2 balls and roll each out on a lightly floured surface with a lightly floured rolling pin to a thickness of about 1cm ($\frac{1}{2}$in). Lift each on to an oiled baking sheet, brush the tops generously with oil and sprinkle with salt and rosemary or sage leaves. Press your finger in the dough to make indentations all over and let the dough rise again for about 30 minutes on the sheet. Bake on the top shelf of the oven at 240°C (475°F, gas mark 9) for about 20 minutes, or until golden brown. Brush with olive oil and serve warm.

FLAT BREAD WITH OLIVES
Focaccia con le olive

Every seaside resort has its own special focaccia, eaten as a snack and often served to tourists as an antipasto. This one has plenty of olive oil, and also a little white wine.

SERVES 8

1kg (2lb) flour
Salt
50g (2oz) fresh or 25g (1oz) dried yeast
350ml (12fl oz) warm water
A pinch of sugar
150ml (5fl oz) olive oil plus 6 tablespoons to
    brush on at the end

150ml (5fl oz) dry white wine
400g (14oz) black olives, pitted and coarsely
    chopped
1 tablespoon dried thyme
2 tablespoons dried oregano

Put all but 25g (1oz) of the flour and a pinch of salt in a bowl and make a well in the centre. Dissolve the fresh yeast in about 120ml (4fl oz) of the warm water, adding a pinch of sugar to activate it. Leave it to froth, then stir into the flour. (Or follow the packet instructions for dried yeast.) Stir in 150ml (5fl oz) olive oil and the wine, then add the rest of the warm water, working it in with your hands, just enough so the dough sticks together in a ball. Knead well for 10–15 minutes until soft and elastic, adding the remaining flour if the dough is too sticky, then work in two-thirds of the olives and the thyme. Leave the dough to rise in a bowl covered with a damp cloth for 1–2 hours, or until doubled in bulk, then punch down and work for 1–2 minutes. Divide in two. Roll out each on a floured surface with a floured rolling pin to a thickness of about 1cm ($\frac{1}{2}$in) and place each on an oiled baking sheet, spreading it out with your hands. Sprinkle with salt and oregano and spread the rest of the olives over the top. Make many depressions all over the dough with your finger. Bake on the top shelf of the oven at 240°C (475°F, gas mark 9) for about 25 minutes, or until lightly browned. Brush with the remaining oil and serve warm.

STUFFED MUSHROOMS
Funghi ripieni

Liguria, like the French Riviera, is known for its great variety of stuffed vegetables. Ligurians do all kinds, including tiny courgettes, little onions and mushrooms. The usual stuffing is the cheesy one given as a variation here, but for mushrooms I prefer the following one.

SERVES 6

500g (1lb) large flat mushrooms

Olive oil

Salt and pepper

Large bunch of parsley

2 slices dry white bread, crusts removed

Milk

2 or more cloves garlic, crushed

2–3 tablespoons brandy or rum (optional)

Wash the mushrooms and cut off the stalks, then briefly fry in 2–3 tablespoons oil for 5 minutes, or until just tender, sprinkling with salt and pepper and turning them over once. Arrange them, stem side up, side by side in an ovenproof dish.

For the stuffing, chop the mushroom stalks and parsley finely in a food processor. Add the bread, soaked in milk and squeezed dry, and process a little longer. Turn into a bowl and add as much garlic as you like and a little salt and pepper. Moisten with brandy or rum to taste, if using, and with 2–3 tablespoons olive oil, and mix well. Press a little stuffing into each mushroom cap and put under the grill for about 5 minutes. Serve hot.

Variations

You can bake the mushrooms instead of frying and grilling them. Place the stuffing in the caps, brush with oil and bake at 200°C (400°F, gas mark 6) for about 20 minutes.

The more common Ligurian stuffing has 125g (4oz) grated parmesan and 50g (2oz) breadcrumbs moistened with milk and mixed with 2 eggs, some chopped fresh oregano and marjoram and salt and pepper. I found restaurants baking huge trays of many different vegetables, all tiny and all with this filling, which makes a charming display but also makes all the vegetables taste the same.

MUSHROOM-STUFFED LETTUCE IN BROTH
Zuppa di lattughe ripiene

SERVES 4

500g (1lb) shiitake or other mushrooms

2–3 tablespoons olive oil

4 cloves garlic, crushed

3 tablespoons chopped marjoram

200g (7oz) ricotta

2 eggs, lightly beaten

2–3 tablespoons grated parmesan

Salt and pepper

1 large head iceberg or cos lettuce

1 litre (1¾ pints) light meat broth

4 slices coarse-textured bread, toasted in the oven and brushed with olive oil

Finely chop the mushrooms in a food processor. Lightly fry in the oil with the garlic and marjoram for about 10 minutes until tender, stirring occasionally. Mash the ricotta with the eggs, add the mushrooms, parmesan, salt and pepper, and mix well.

Discard the outer leaves of the lettuce and separate the rest. Blanch them in boiling water for a few seconds until they soften, then drain. Open each carefully, put a heaped tablespoon of filling at one end and roll up towards the end where the rib is thickest, tucking in the sides so the filling does not fall out.

Pack the rolls into a wide saucepan. Bring the broth to the boil and pour over the rolls; simmer for a few minutes.

Serve the rolls in soup bowls on the toasted bread with a little of the broth poured over.

BASIL AND PINE NUT SAUCE
Pesto

Pesto is the prince of Ligurian dishes. Its making is a joyful ritual and the perfume which fills the air is a powerful appetite whetter. There is no place in the world which makes as much use of basil as Genoa, and no place where the plant has as much perfume. Every town has its own version. This is the way they make it at Da 'O Vittorio in Recco. It is served with trenette, tagliatelle or corzetti (coin-shaped pasta, stamped with a motif) and with gnocchi.

SERVES 4

2 cloves garlic, crushed, or more to taste
50g (2oz) pine nuts
Salt
50g (2oz) or more basil (weighed with the stems)

4 tablespoons grated pecorino sardo or parmesan
150ml (5fl oz) light olive oil
2–3 tablespoons prescinsoa (a creamy acid ricotta) or fromage frais (optional)

Pound the garlic and pine nuts in a large mortar with a little salt. Add the chopped basil leaves (the amount takes into account that basil found elsewhere is less perfumed than in Liguria), a few at a time, pounding and grinding the leaves against the sides of the bowl. You can also put everything in the blender. Stir in the grated cheese and mix very well, then gradually beat in the olive oil (the olive oil of Liguria is very light, delicate and perfumed) and the prescinsoa or fromage frais, if using.

VEGETABLE SOUP WITH PESTO
Minestrone con pesto

This is the kind of soup which is best made the day before to give the flavours time to mingle.

SERVES 6–8

4 medium potatoes, peeled and diced
250g (8oz) pumpkin, diced, or courgettes, sliced
1 small cauliflower, broken into small florets
75g (3oz) mushrooms, roughly chopped
125g (4oz) fresh or frozen peas
150g (5oz) broad beans, or green beans cut in pieces
400g (14oz) can cannellini beans
1 onion, finely chopped

2–3 tablespoons olive oil
6 ripe tomatoes, peeled and chopped, or 400g (14oz) can chopped tomatoes
3 tablespoons finely chopped parsley
Salt and pepper
125g (4oz) rice or pasta (ribbons or broken tagliatelle)
Pesto (see above)
Grated parmesan or pecorino

Fill a large saucepan with plenty of salted water and bring to the boil. Add the potatoes, pumpkin or courgettes, cauliflower, mushrooms, peas and broad or green beans and simmer for about 40 minutes, or until the vegetables are very tender. Add the cannellini beans and heat through. In the meantime, fry the onion in oil until soft, add the tomatoes and parsley, and cook for 5 minutes more. Pour the mixture into the soup and check the seasoning.

Twenty minutes before serving, bring to the boil and add the rice, or bring to the boil and add pasta 10 minutes before serving. When the rice or pasta is cooked, stir in some pesto, or pass it around along with the grated cheese and let everyone help themselves.

Variation
Diced aubergine is sometimes added to the soup, but I prefer it without it.

NOODLES WITH PESTO
Trenette al pesto alla genovese

SERVES 4

2 medium waxy new potatoes, peeled and sliced

4–6 green beans, strings removed

Salt

400g (14oz) trenette or fettuccine

Pesto (page 48)

Grated pecorino or parmesan

Put the potatoes and green beans in a large saucepan with plenty of boiling salted water and cook until both are nearly done, then throw in the trenette or fettuccine and cook until these are al dente. Drain, reserving a ladle of the cooking water. Serve with pesto, diluted if you like with a little of the cooking water, and grated cheese.

PASTA SQUARES WITH PESTO
Mandilli di sea

For *mandilli di sea* (which means 'silk handkerchiefs' in dialect) make egg pasta as described on pages 110 –111 there are those who mix a little white wine with the water – roll it out as thin as you can, let it dry for 30 minutes on a cloth, and cut into 15cm (6in) squares. Cook, 4 at a time, in boiling salted water with a tablespoon of oil to prevent them from sticking, until al dente. Serve as they are with plenty of pesto (page 48). You may also use store-bought lasagne.

This is not a dish you can make for a party, because you can make only a few *mandilli* at a time and you must serve them right away. It is the kind of food you eat in the kitchen while the next batch is being cooked.

TRIANGULAR HERB RAVIOLI WITH WALNUT SAUCE
Pansoti con salsa di noci

Pansoti means 'pot-bellied ones'. Different kinds of wild Ligurian herbs and leaves (*preboggion* is the general term) may go into the filling. I have made *pansoti* with spinach and watercress, but you may try adding herbs of your choice.

SERVES 10

For the filling

1kg (2lb) beet greens, Swiss chard or spinach
   and borage, or 500g (1lb) frozen spinach

2 bunches watercress (175–200g/6–7oz
   weighed with stems)

Salt

200g (7oz) ricotta

50g (2oz) freshly grated parmesan

25g (1oz) butter, melted

2 eggs

Pepper

$1/4$ teaspoon nutmeg

For the dough

400g (14oz) flour

Salt

1 egg

2 egg yolks

120ml (4fl oz) water

For the filling, wash all the fresh green leaves, remove the stems and cook in very little salted water, turning them over with a wooden spoon until they crumple to a soft mass. Drain and squeeze every drop of water out, then chop finely (in a food processor if you like) and mix well with the rest of the filling ingredients. Frozen spinach need only be defrosted and squeezed dry before mixing with the other ingredients.

For the dough, mix the flour and a pinch of salt with the whole egg and 1 yolk; add only enough water so that the dough holds together in a ball, working it in with your hands. Knead for 10–15 minutes, or until the dough is smooth and elastic, adding a little more flour if it is too sticky. Wrap in clingfilm and leave to rest for 30 minutes, then roll out as thin as you can on a lightly floured surface with a floured rolling pin. Cut the sheet into 5cm (4in) squares and brush the edges with the remaining egg yolk. Put a heaped teaspoon of filling in the centre of each square and fold it over into a triangle, pressing the edges firmly to stick them together. (You can bring the ends together to make the traditional headscarf shape but it is not worth doing if you risk tearing the dough.)

Cook the pansoti in plenty of salted boiling water for 3–5 minutes until al dente, then drain and serve covered with the following walnut sauce.

WALNUT SAUCE
Salsa di noci

300g (10oz) shelled walnuts
1 clove garlic, crushed
2 slices country bread, crusts removed
300ml (½ pint) milk

50g (2oz) freshly grated parmesan
5–6 tablespoons light olive oil
Salt and pepper

Blend the walnuts and garlic, the bread soaked in the milk, the cheese and olive oil (the Ligurian oil is light and delicately flavoured) to a cream, adding salt and pepper.

RICE AND SPINACH CAKE
Torta di riso e spinaci

SERVES 8

500g (1lb) fresh or 300g (10oz) frozen whole-leaf
    spinach
250g (8oz) Arborio rice
Salt
1 onion, chopped
1 tablespoon oil

25g (1oz) butter
3 eggs
4 tablespoons grated parmesan
Pepper
A good pinch of nutmeg

Wash the spinach and remove the stems. Cook until it softens (frozen spinach needs only to be defrosted), then drain and chop finely. Boil the rice in salted water for about 10 minutes until nearly done, throw the spinach in with the rice, stir well and drain at once.

Fry the onion in oil until golden and put it in a bowl with the rice and spinach. Add the butter, eggs and cheese, pepper and nutmeg. Mix well and press into a buttered non-stick mould or cake tin. Bake in the oven at 200°C (400°F, gas mark 6) for about 25 minutes, or until golden.

Turn out and serve hot. It is also good cold.

Variation

For *preboggion con riso*, add a bunch of chopped herbs, such as mint, basil, marjoram, oregano, thyme, sage, rosemary or parsley, and 1–2 crushed cloves of garlic with the spinach.

RED MULLET WITH OLIVES
Triglie alla ligure

This is how Gianni Bisso cooks red mullet at Da 'O Vittorio in Recco.

SERVES 2

2 × 250g (8oz) red mullets, cleaned and scaled

4 tablespoons olive oil

150ml (5fl oz) white wine

Pinch of salt

50g (2oz) black olives, pitted

2 cloves garlic, chopped

1 lemon, cut in half

2 tablespoons chopped parsley

Put the fish in a baking dish with the oil, wine, salt, olives, garlic and lemon halves. Cover with foil and bake in the oven at 180°F (350°F, gas mark 4) for 20 minutes, or until the fish flake easily when tested with the point of a knife. Serve sprinkled with parsley.

SPINACH WITH RAISINS AND PINE NUTS
Spinaci all'uvetta passolina e ai pinoli

The more common way of doing this Genoese dish of Spanish origin (you also find it in Spain) is with olive oil and anchovies and without tomatoes. I prefer this recipe, and I like using butter, which softens the taste of spinach.

SERVES 4

1kg (2lb) spinach

4 ripe tomatoes, peeled and chopped

3 tablespoons light olive oil or olive oil mixed
    with butter

2 tablespoons raisins, soaked in water, then drained

Salt and pepper

Pinch of nutmeg

2 tablespoons pine nuts, toasted

Wash the spinach well and remove the stems. Drain and squeeze the water out. In a large saucepan, heat the tomatoes in oil or a mixture of butter and oil until soft. Put in the spinach and the drained raisins and cook, stirring and turning the leaves over until they crumple. Season with salt, pepper and nutmeg, stir in the toasted pine nuts and serve hot.

QUINCES IN SYRUP
Cotogne in composta

This old-fashioned preserve makes a ready dessert which keeps well in a jar.

SERVES 6

1kg (2lb) quinces

250g (8oz) sugar

Thinly pared peel of $\frac{1}{2}$ lemon

Juice of $\frac{1}{2}$ lemon

$1\frac{1}{2}$ teaspoons cinnamon

6 cloves

150ml (5fl oz) dry white wine

Wash, peel and core the quinces and cut into thick slices. Put them with the peels and cores, which lend a jellied quality, into a saucepan with the rest of the ingredients and about 300ml ($\frac{1}{2}$ pint) water to cover.

Simmer for about 1 hour, until the fruit is tender, then lift out the quince slices and arrange in a serving bowl. Reduce the syrup a little and strain it over them. Serve cold.

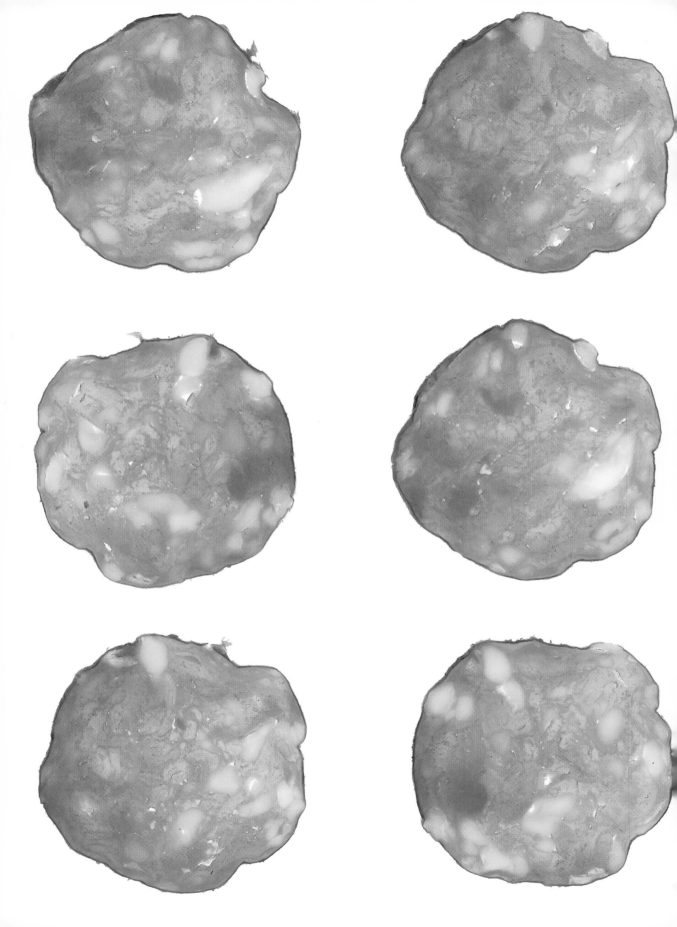

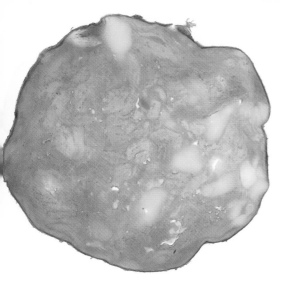

Lombardy

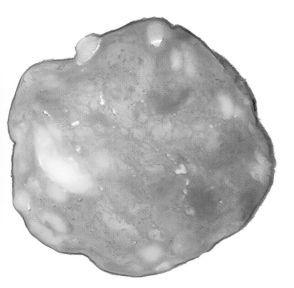
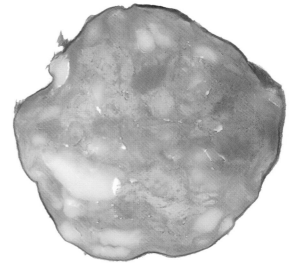

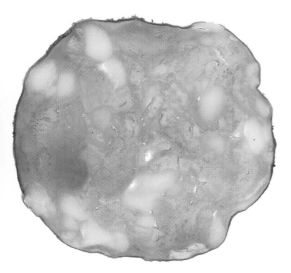
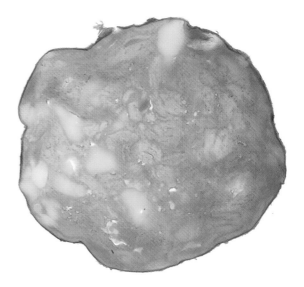

Lombardy

Lombardy is the richest of all the regions of Italy. It accounts for a third of all Italian exports, but it is not all a smoky industrial monster. Industries are studded around the most luxuriant and fertile of countrysides. The basin of the river Po is an immense flat plain with pale green fields alternating with wheat, maize and rice fields, divided by rivers and canals; fringed to the north by a succession of the most beautiful lakes in Italy (Maggiore, Lugano, Como and Garda) and by the foothills of the Alps, which rise to high snow-crested peaks. Woods scramble over hills, bell towers spring out from behind trees, a hazy mist gives an air of nostalgic melancholy. Towns with historic names, and palaces, castles and medieval streets carry you into the heart of the Renaissance.

Lombardy was already well advanced in agriculture by the fifteenth century. It was ruled by noble families who owned the land; first by the Viscontis and later the Sforzas, who were the richest and most powerful *signorie* in the peninsula (there were also the Gonzagas in Mantua and the Estes). By draining the marshes and irrigating the fields, they made Lombardy the most productive region in the world at the time. They grew wheat and maize and introduced the cultivation of rice; they bred cattle and made cheese. At that time Italy was the centre of Europe. Italian could be heard in the kitchens of the European courts, and the banquets of noble families were complex spectacles of gastronomic architecture and choreography.

The eighteenth century saw a growing movement of capital towards the countryside. Merchants and the nobility built villas and gardens and began to invest in large-scale agriculture. Large farm settlements and capitalist methods of production appeared, and the old feudal order fused into semi-feudal systems such as the *mezzadria*, in which tenant agricultural families gave half their produce to landowners.

This was when the cuisine of Lombardy took shape, combining the rustic cooking of the hungry *mezzadro*, who remained personally and economically dependent and locked in a cycle of subsistence, with a kind of cosmopolitan *haute cuisine* that retained elements of the old tradition of the court and was practised by a middle class passionate about the pleasures of the table.

The court cuisine had been in the great Italian Renaissance tradition codified by Bartolomeo Sacchi of Piadena (known as Platina) in his *De honesta voluptate e valetudine* (1457), the first cookery book to be published in Italy, in which most of the recipes came from Mastro Martino, a cook from Como who worked for the Patriarch of Aquileia. In almost every restaurant I went to where they served regional dishes, chefs brought out facsimiles of books written by men who cooked at the courts, from which they picked ideas for their menus. The most commonly used is *L'Arte di ben cucinare*, published in 1662 by Bartolomeo Stefani, a Bolognese who was chef at the Gonzaga court in Mantua. But the chefs also gave me lyrical accounts of the poor food of the old peasantry; of the offal (tripe, heads, tails, feet, lungs) and cured meats and sausages they ate only a few times a year; of the one-pot *piatto unico* in which the poor combined meat and vegetables; of the pheasants and partridges and birds they caught (illegally, as they belonged to the landlords); of the eel and trout of the lakes, the chestnuts gathered in the mountains, the wild strawberries with their extraordinary perfume; and the mushrooms and truffles they found in the woodland.

It is impossible to speak in general of the cooking of Lombardy because, apart from these rich and poor traditions, and differences in the cooking of the plain, lakes, hills and mountains, each town is different and does not know the dishes of the next. It is, more than in any other region of Italy, a real mosaic. Bergamo, once part of the Serenissima, is still more Venetian; Mantua, which was the seat of the Gonzagas and has refined aristocratic cooking traditions, is more like Emilia to the south; the Valtellina has the resources of the mountains, including game. But they do have things in common: they use enormous quantities of butter, lard and cream, and all the cuisines are based on risotto, polenta and soups.

Lombardy is the region that grows and consumes the

most rice. Cultivation of the grain expanded throughout the plain in the sixteenth century, but not without difficulties; it was blamed for the malaria which prevails in the watery areas, and fields were constantly destroyed by edict. Before it was mechanised, rice-picking was the work of women, the *mondine,* who spent their days wading in the marshy waters, their dresses stuffed into their drawers. The rice is short-grain and there are many varieties: the round Originario and Padano, which fall apart and stick together quickly, are preferred for soups and for stuffing vegetables. Of the rice used for risotto the most prized are Carnaroli, Vialone Nano, Razza 77 and the famous Arborio, which retain a certain firmness and bite. In the past, rice was the food of the urban rich; and even now, in some parts, risotto is a wedding dish, and Sunday is not Sunday without it. As in the Veneto, almost every ingredient you can think of – vegetable, fish and meat – is made into a risotto. But here the risotto is dry (*asciutto*), not almost liquid as in Venice. *Risotto alla milanese,* made with saffron and also called *risotto giallo*, or yellow risotto, is the most famous. *Risotto alla certosina*, a speciality of Pavia, which takes its name from the Carthusian monks who were not allowed to eat meat and so devised many rice dishes using the freshwater fish, crayfish and frogs they farmed in great pits near the abbeys, is one of the most delightful. Rice is cooked in broth (most people in Italy nowadays use stock cubes) and sometimes also in wine, with plenty of butter and sometimes cream; except when it is made with fish and seafood, it is served with grated parmesan.

Polenta, the porridge made with maize flour and water, was the food of the rural poor. Before maize arrived, peasants made it with wheat, barley, oats, millet and buckwheat. Maize flour polenta was introduced relatively late, spreading inland from Venice, but by the beginning of the eighteenth century, maize cultivation was widespread in Lombardy, and polenta was the staple food. It remained that way until the 1930s, and many rural workers in the area ate little else.

In Lombardy polenta is made in many ways: with water, with milk, and mixed with other grains including buckwheat and black flour (*fraina*). It is served as it is, a sort of porridge, or allowed to cool and then sliced and fried or grilled. Polenta can be mixed with butter, cheese, tomatoes or pork fat, and can be served with beans and other vegetables (in Rogaro, a village near Lake Como, it is served with asparagus) or with sausages and stews of all kinds, including some made with game, pork and veal. Bergamo is said to make the best: its speciality is *polenta e osei,* for which a mound of polenta is topped with small roasted birds threaded on skewers. Pasta has largely taken the place of both rice and polenta, because they take so long to make and must be stirred constantly. But polenta – once called *stramaledetta* (the cursed) and *il cibo della miseria* (the food of poverty) – is still an important part of mountain cooking, and it has now become fashionable, presented in elegant portions and crisp little grilled rectangles.

The third staple food to be found throughout Lombardy are the *minestre*, rich soups of peasant origin made with dried beans, rice or pasta (sometimes all three) and vegetables, and sometimes including bacon or sliced sausage – a little lard or pork rind gives them the old country flavour. *Minestre di riso* are based on rice, and there are versions with vegetables such as turnips, leeks and cabbage, with fish and also with sausages and chicken livers. Many soups include fried or toasted bread, which goes at the bottom of the bowl.

Lombardy is the most important livestock and milk-producing region in Italy, although you never see the cows because they never leave the sheds. Their milk is used to make every kind of cheese, including those traditional to the south, but the region has its own cheese repertoire: bitto comes from the Valtellina and Val Gerola near Morbegno; bransi, from the Val Brembana; hard, semi-matured bagoss, which has a powerful flavour and aroma, is made in the mountains of the Val Caffaro near Bagolino; furmai maioch is from the Val Chiavenna; formagella is from Brescia; and scimud is made in Valmalenco. Other cottage-industry cheeses are caprini, certosa, straness and quartirolo, crescenza, uso monte, zincherlino, fiorett and cupeta. Four great cheeses, stracchino, robiola, runny taleggio and tartufelle, are matured in caves in the Valsassina. Rich creamy mascarpone is eaten as a sweet. More commonly found in British supermarkets are gorgonzola, made in the province of Novara around Mortara, and Bel Paese. The hard and sharp grana padano, made into huge wheels and aged between ten months and two years, is used like parmesan for grating.

There is plenty of meat throughout Lombardy. Veal, pork, chicken, rabbit, even lamb and their offal go into making the *bolliti misti* (boiled meats), *arrosti* (roasts), *stracotti* (stews) and *fritti misti* (breaded and fried morsels) that are characteristic of the land along the valley of the Po.

Lombardy is pig country, and the areas of Brianza and Cremona are famous for their sausages. They manufacture specialities from other regions, but their own are the fine-cut pork and beef *salame di Milano*;

bastardei, also with pork and beef; coarse-cut pure pork *salamella di Cremona*; and *varzi*, which is pork flavoured with salt, pepper, garlic and wine. Luganega needs to be fried or grilled; *mortadella di fegato*, made with liver, and *sanguinaccio*, black pudding, are cooked and eaten hot. *Bresaola* is air-dried spiced beef. Red *culatello* and *fiocchetto* are salted and spiced lean hams in sausage casings which are matured for up to a year. Other meats are used: in the Lomellina, where geese are reared, there is goose salami and goose liver pâté, while *violin* is cured goat's meat. It is no wonder that the favourite antipasto of the region is a selection of cured meats and salami served with pickles.

Lombardy is not vegetable country, but there are a few: the potatoes, which are very good, came in Napoleon's time, were grown by priests and moved up from the peasants' kitchens to the grand tables; cabbages, once kept buried during the winter in pits lined with maize stalks; turnips, beans and asparagus, which grow between the vines; very sweet peppers and a delicious variety of yellow pumpkin. In the hills apples and pears, apricots and peaches, strawberries and raspberries are grown; in the mountains, chestnuts, white truffles and many different kinds of wild mushrooms including porcini, ovoli (Caesar's mushrooms), *gallinacci* (chanterelles), and *prataioli*, are found.

Fish from the lakes – eel, trout, sturgeon as well as humbler perch, carp and whitefish – are treated simply, mostly grilled or poached. Shad is salted and dried in the sun and becomes *missoltitt* which can be grilled.

Two centuries of Spanish rule, which began in 1535 when Charles V made his son Philip Duke of Milan, brought saffron and rice-growing to the Po Valley and dishes such as risotto and *cassoeula* – a stew made with sausages and pig's trotters, ears and ribs that derives its name from the Spanish clay pot in which it is made. The other main foreign influence is Germanic, and it is evident in the heavy dishes of meat and cabbage, the schnitzel-like *costoletta milanese* and the range of panettone and other brioche-type cakes. It comes not from the Teutonic Longobards who ruled Lombardy for two hundred years and gave the region its name, but from the Austrians who took over from the Spanish in 1713 at the end of the War of the Spanish Succession. Austria also introduced a land tax in 1760 that encouraged small landowners and led to a fairer division of wealth and agriculture. There is a French connection in Lombardy, mainly through Turin and the House of Savoy.

Lombardy's chief city, Milan, which has led the country into industrialisation and modernisation, is a European city in the centre of Europe and it has lost its culinary traditions almost entirely. No one in Milan wants to cook Milanese dishes (which survive in the Bassa, south of Milan). The Milanese say they have no time for lengthy cooking and prefer the healthier Mediterranean diet of southern Italy. After the war they ate steak and salad. Now many have become hardened eaters of sandwiches and pizza. Milan is a world of fast foods, of sandwich bars, hamburger stands and pizzerias (in 1956 there were six, now there are five hundred), but it is also the city where you can eat the best food – at Tuscan, Apulian and other regional trattorias, as well as at restaurants that serve international cuisine and *cucina creativa*. And Peck, perhaps the greatest food shop in Europe, is here.

The mountains and lakes of Lombardy are now resorts for city people. The harsh life of villagers has gone and, with the sub-alpine civilisation practically dead, traditional variety is hard to find. But around Cremona and Mantua and in other centres of the more leisurely life lost long ago in Milan, people are still attached to the good things of the past.

The Wines of Lombardy

Oltrepò Pavese (which means 'south of the river Po in the province of Pavia') is the leading wine area of Lombardy, and much of the wine production consists of sparkling wines. These include slightly sweet, semi-sparkling reds with curious names like Barbacarlo, Sangue di Giuda and Buttafuoco, and some truly magnificent sparkling whites, based on Pinots Grigio and Bianco, Riesling, Cortese and Moscato grapes, which are made by the champagne method and are said to rival fine champagne.

In the Valtellina, a valley between Lake Como and Lake Garda, Nebbiolo grapes, like those used for Barolo in Piedmont, are used with other native grapes to make good, hearty, light, everyday reds. Valtellina Superiore, known by the names of localities such as Grumello, Inferno, Sassella and Valgella, are similar to their Piedmontese cousins – full-bodied, slightly tannic, long-ageing and aromatic, but softer on the palate and not as rich in flavour. Sforzato (or Sfurzàt) is an extraordinarily full, strongly flavoured and highly alcoholic Valtellina wine made from grapes which have been allowed to shrivel in the sun.

The provinces of Brescia and Lake Garda offer the greatest variety. Among their wines are gems like the Riviera del Garda Bresciano Rosso, a luscious, slightly bitter red; the lovely pink Chiaretto, which has a taste of bitter almonds; the delightful warm, intense Botticino; the fine white Tocai di San Martino della Battaglia; the delicate white Lugana; and the hugely popular Franciacorta reds, whites and brilliant champagne-method bubblies.

CAPON OR CHICKEN SALAD
Insalata di cappone

This salad is from a book published in 1662 by Bartolomeo Stefani, chef at the court of the Gonzagas in Mantua. It is one of the ancient recipes that Franco and Silvana Colombani have on their menu at the Albergo del Sole at Maleo which has been in the family for 100 years. Franco has a rare collection of antique Italian cookery books and manuscripts, and also collects cooking utensils, which are in a gigantic tangle in the attic. (When Mussolini asked the Italian people to give their pots and pans for the manufacture of armaments, many hid them in their attics and forgot all about them.)

SERVES 4

500g (1lb) cooked capon, chicken or turkey
2 tablespoons sultanas, softened in water
1–2 tablespoons finely chopped candied
    lemon peel
Salt and pepper

6 tablespoons fruity olive oil
1 tablespoon wine vinegar
1 teaspoon balsamic vinegar, or 1 tablespoon red
    wine vinegar with a pinch of sugar

Remove the skin and bones and cut the meat into very thin strips. Put in a bowl, add the sultanas, candied peel, salt and pepper to taste, and stir in the oil, wine vinegar and balsamic vinegar. The balsamic vinegar available, unless very aged, is probably not as strong as the one the Colombanis use, so you may want to use more. Arrange on individual plates on a bed of lettuce leaves dressed with oil and vinegar. Franco suggests serving the chicken salad with crisply cooked green vegetables, such as green beans.

VEGETABLE SOUP WITH BEANS AND RICE
Minestrone alla milanese

There are many versions of this heartwarming winter soup, which becomes a cold soup (served at room temperature) in the summer.

SERVES 10

250g (8oz) pancetta or unsmoked bacon, cut
    into small pieces
1 large onion, finely chopped
1 clove garlic, finely chopped
Small bunch of parsley, finely chopped
4 carrots, diced
4 stalks celery, thinly sliced
4 all-purpose potatoes, diced
500g (1lb) tomatoes, peeled and chopped

250g (8oz) *borlotti* or dried white beans, soaked
    overnight and drained, or about 500g (1lb)
    canned beans, drained
Salt
1 small white cabbage, shredded
250g (8oz) fresh or frozen peas
4 small courgettes, diced
200g (7oz) Arborio rice
Good bunch of basil, cut into strips
Grated grana or parmesan

In a very large saucepan, heat the bacon until some of the fat melts, then fry with the onion until the onion is pale gold. Add garlic and parsley and stir until the aroma rises. Add the carrots, celery, potatoes, tomatoes and dried beans (soaked and drained). (If you are using canned beans, these must be added at the end.) Cover with plenty of water; bring to the boil and simmer, covered, for about $2\frac{1}{2}$ hours, adding salt, when the beans have begun to soften, and water if necessary (the soup should be thick, but not too thick). Add the cabbage, canned beans if you are using them, peas and courgettes, and simmer 15 minutes more. About 20 minutes before serving, add the rice. At the end of the cooking, stir in the basil. Pass the grated cheese at the table.

PASTA STUFFED WITH PUMPKIN PUREE
Tortelli di zucca

On the road between Mantua and Cremona is a huge stall selling pumpkins of every size, shape and colour. Pumpkins have always prospered in the plain around those two cities and they have always been exceptionally sweet and yellow.

These large pumpkin tortelli are a speciality of Mantua and well represent aristocratic cooking traditions that go back to the court of the Gonzagas. They are traditionally made for Christmas Eve, but they are eaten all year round.

Although this is a fashionable dish, not everybody in Italy likes it. In Parma, Mantua and Cremona, where I found it, there were always great discussions about whether crumbled amaretti and mostarda (fruit in syrup with mustard essence) should be used. Also controversial is whether the pumpkin should be boiled, baked or fried in butter. I liked all the versions I tried. The important thing is to find a pumpkin with a really good sweet taste.

SERVES 6

For the filling

1.5kg (3lb) pumpkin	2 eggs
125g (4oz) mostarda di Cremona, finely chopped	Freshly grated nutmeg
125g (4oz) amaretti biscuits, crushed	Salt
125g (4oz) fine dry breadcrumbs	Grated rind of $\frac{1}{2}$ lemon
50g (2oz) grated parmesan	

For the dough

500g (1lb) plain flour	Salt
4 eggs	1 egg yolk, lightly beaten

For the garnish

75g (3oz) or more butter	50g (2oz) grated parmesan

To make the filling, peel and seed the pumpkin. Wrap in foil and bake in the oven at 200°C (400°F, gas mark 6) for 1 hour. Mash to a purée and add the mostarda, amaretti, breadcrumbs, parmesan, eggs, nutmeg, salt and lemon rind. Stir well and leave to rest for at least a couple of hours.

To make the tortelli, work the flour, eggs and a pinch of salt into a soft dough and roll out very thinly into two equal rectangles. Place small mounds of filling the size of a walnut on one of these. Brush in between and around the mounds of filling with egg yolk. Cover with the second layer of dough and press the edges down well to make sure they are completely sealed and there are no air pockets. With a pastry cutter, cut the tortelli into squares. Let them rest.

Cook a few at a time in boiling salted water for about 3–4 minutes until al dente. Drain and serve with plenty of butter and parmesan.

Variation
Finely chopped almonds with a few drops of almond essence may be used instead of amaretti.

PUMPKIN SOUP WITH ALMONDS
Zuppa di zucca con le mandorle

This is a recipe from Jolanda Migliorini, who cooks at her husband Valentino's restaurant at Caorso, south-west of Cremona in the Piacentino.

SERVES 4

500g (1lb) pumpkin, peeled, seeded and diced	Freshly grated nutmeg
900ml (1$\frac{1}{2}$ pints) milk	300ml ($\frac{1}{2}$ pints) single cream
Salt and pepper	4 tablespoons chopped toasted almonds

Put the pumpkin into a saucepan with the milk, and add salt, pepper and nutmeg to taste. Bring to the boil and simmer for about 30 minutes. When the pumpkin is tender, pour into a blender and process until smooth. Pour back into the saucepan, stir in the cream, taste and adjust the seasoning. Reheat and serve, sprinkled with the toasted almonds.

Note

The success of this soup depends on the flavour of the pumpkin. With so many varieties available, it is worth experimenting.

CHEESE AND SPINACH DUMPLINGS
Malfatti

They are called *malfatti* ('misshapen ones') because they are like the filling of ravioli without the dough.

SERVES 6

2kg (4lb) spinach
Salt
500g (1lb) ricotta
2 eggs
125g (4oz) freshly grated parmesan

Pepper
Freshly grated nutmeg
Flour
75g (3oz) butter, melted

Wash the spinach and remove the stems. In a large pan with the lid on, steam the leaves with a little salt in the water that clings to them, turning them over, until they crumple. Strain and squeeze every bit of water out with your hands: this is all-important and is the secret of success (otherwise the dumplings would fall apart). Finely chop the leaves.

Mash the ricotta and stir in the eggs, half the parmesan, salt, pepper, nutmeg and spinach. Work very well, shape into balls the size of a walnut and roll in flour.

Half fill a large saucepan with water, bring to the boil and very carefully drop in the dumplings. Keep the water barely simmering until they rise to the surface – they do so very quickly.

Lift them out very carefully with a slotted spoon and serve very hot with melted butter and the remaining parmesan.

PUMPKIN RISOTTO
Risotto con la zucca

SERVES 4

500g (1lb) pumpkin
1 onion, chopped
1 tablespoon olive oil
Salt and pepper
250ml (8fl oz) milk

1 litre (1³⁄₄ pints) light chicken stock (you may use
    1¹⁄₂ stock cubes dissolved in 1 litre (1³⁄₄ pints)
    water)
350g (12oz) Arborio rice
50g (2oz) butter
Grated parmesan

Peel the pumpkin, remove the seeds and stringy bits and cut into small cubes. Fry the onion in the oil until soft, add the pumpkin, season with salt and pepper and cover with milk. Simmer gently for 5–15 minutes until the pumpkin is tender. Bring the stock to the boil in a large saucepan, add the rice and let simmer gently for 18 minutes, stirring occasionally and adding salt, pepper and stock or the milk in which the pumpkin cooked or water, if necessary, until the rice is tender and the liquid absorbed. Stir in the pumpkin mixture and the butter and heat through. Serve with grated parmesan.

SAFFRON RISOTTO
Risotto alla milanese

You find this yellow risotto everywhere in Milan, but I wonder how often it is made with real saffron, real stock and bone marrow: that is how chef Fulvio de Santa makes it at the new restaurant Peck in Milan. Peck offers two menus – a modern one and one offering the old traditional classics of Milanese home cooking.

This is the traditional partner to ossobuco.

SERVES 4

1 small onion, chopped

Small piece of marrow from a beef bone (optional)

50g (2oz) butter

1 litre (1$\frac{3}{4}$ pints) meat or chicken stock

150ml (5fl oz) dry white or red wine

300g (10oz) Arborio rice

Salt

$\frac{1}{2}$ teaspoon saffron threads, or $\frac{1}{4}$ teaspoon powdered saffron

50g (2oz) grated parmesan

In a large saucepan, fry the onion and marrow, if using, in half the butter until the onion is soft and transparent. In a separate saucepan, heat the stock. Add the wine to the fried onion and boil until much reduced. Add the rice and stir to coat the grains well. Add the salt and the boiling stock gradually, ladleful by ladleful, stirring constantly as it becomes absorbed. After about 17 minutes add the saffron diluted in some of the stock. When the rice is done – there should be enough liquid to make it creamy, but the grains must still be firm – add the rest of the butter, and the parmesan.

RISOTTO WITH ASPARAGUS
Risotto con gli asparagi

SERVES 6

1kg (2lb) asparagus

1.25 litres (2$\frac{1}{4}$ pints) chicken stock made with 1 stock cube

Salt

1 onion, chopped

50g (2oz) butter

350g (12oz) Arborio rice

1 bottle (750 ml) dry white wine

Pepper

3–4 tablespoons grated parmesan (optional)

Wash and peel the asparagus. Cut off about 7.5cm (3in) of tips and set them aside. Boil the stalks in the stock until very tender. Lift them out and put them through a food processor with a little stock. Strain out the hard stringy bits and return the purée to the pan with the stock. In another saucepan, cook the asparagus tips in salted water for a few minutes only until just tender.

In a large frying or shallow pan, fry the onion in half the butter until soft. Add the rice and stir to coat the grains well. Pour in the wine, bring to the boil, add salt and pepper, and simmer gently, stirring. Add the stock containing the puréed asparagus gradually as it becomes absorbed, stirring often. Continue adding water as required – you may need as much as 600ml (1 pint) – until the rice is al dente and creamy. Stir in the rest of the butter and the grated parmesan, if using, and serve at once, garnished with the heated asparagus tips.

BAKED POLENTA WITH GORGONZOLA
Polenta e gorgonzola

SERVES 4

300g (10oz) maize flour (meal)
Salt
75g (3oz) butter

Pepper
250g (8oz) gorgonzola

Make polenta as described on page 86 with the maize flour and 1.5 litres (2½ pints) salted water. When it is done, stir in the butter and pepper. Pour a layer of hot polenta into a buttered ovenproof dish, cover with a layer of cheese pieces, then continue with another layer of polenta, another of cheese and finish with polenta. Bake in the oven at 220°C (425°F, gas mark 7) until browned.

Variations

Use taleggio instead of gorgonzola, or fontina as they do in the Valle d'Aosta.

For a *pasticcio di polenta*, add alternating layers of a reduced and thick tomato sauce (page 19).

FROGS' LEGS IN WINE
Rane in guazzetto

I went with another frog enthusiast, Lucia Alberini, wife of distinguished culinary historian Massimo Alberini, to try several dishes at Piero Bolfo's elegant Ristorante Canoviano in Milan. We had frog soup, frog stew and frog risotto – all marvellous.

SERVES 4

800g (1¾lb) frogs' legs
75g (3oz) butter
250ml (8fl oz) dry white wine
4 tomatoes, peeled and chopped

Salt and pepper
4 tablespoons chopped parsley
Juice of ½ lemon

Rinse the frogs' legs and fry quickly in half the butter. Add the wine and tomatoes, season with salt and pepper, and simmer vigorously for at least 20 minutes to reduce the wine sauce. Add the parsley towards the end. Just before serving, stir in the rest of the butter and the lemon juice.

VEAL CHOPS IN WINE
Rostin negàa

This is a recipe from Sergio Torelli, the head chef at Savini in Milan.

SERVES 4

4 veal chops
1 tablespoon flour, seasoned with salt and
    pepper
1 tablespoon diced bacon

50g (2oz) butter
1 tablespoon chopped rosemary
120ml (4fl oz) dry white wine
Salt and pepper

Dip the chops in seasoned flour. Fry the bacon in butter with the rosemary and add the chops. Brown on both sides. Add the wine, season, cover and cook slowly for 35 minutes, until tender. Uncover and reduce the sauce to a glaze. Serve immediately.

BRAISED SHIN OF VEAL
Ossobuco alla milanese

SERVES 4

4 thick slices of shin of veal, cut with a piece of
    marrow bone
Flour
50g (2oz) butter

120ml (4fl oz) white wine
250g (8oz) tomatoes, peeled and chopped
Meat stock or water
Salt and pepper

For the gremolata

4 tablespoons finely chopped parsley
1 tablespoon finely grated lemon rind

1 small clove garlic, crushed
1 anchovy, finely chopped (optional)

Coat the meat with flour and brown in butter on both sides. Add the wine and simmer for 10 minutes, then add the tomatoes and stock or water to cover and season with salt and pepper. Cook, covered, for $1\frac{1}{2}$–2 hours, stirring occasionally to make sure the meat does not stick, until it is so tender it comes away from the bone. Add stock or water to keep the meat covered at first. The sauce should be thick at the end.

Make what is called a *gremolata*: mix together the parsley, grated lemon rind, garlic and anchovy, if you like. Place a little on each piece of meat and cook a few minutes longer. Serve with *risotto alla milanese* (page 60) or plain white rice.

SWEET AND SOUR SWEETBREADS
Animelle in agrodolce

We cannot use sweetbreads from Britain at the moment, but hopefully we will be able to in the near future.

SERVES 6

2 tablespoons capers
4 tablespoons olive oil
$1\frac{1}{2}$ tablespoons sugar, or to taste
4 tablespoons wine vinegar
800g ($1\frac{3}{4}$lb) calf's sweetbreads
50g (2oz) butter

50g (2oz) prosciutto, diced
1 large onion, peeled and diced
1 large carrot, peeled and diced
1 stalk celery, diced
Salt and pepper

First make the sauce: strain and squeeze the capers well and chop them finely. Put them in a small bowl, add the oil and beat well. Heat the sugar in a small saucepan with the vinegar to dissolve it, then add the oil and caper mixture, stirring constantly. Take the sauce off the heat before it boils, pour it into a bowl and leave to cool.

Heat plenty of water in a saucepan and plunge the sweetbreads into it as soon as it comes to the boil. Simmer for 6 minutes, then plunge into cold water and remove the outer membrane. Cut into 2.5cm (1in) chunks.

Melt the butter in a frying pan, add the prosciutto, onion, carrot and celery, and cook over medium heat until they begin to brown and soften. Add the sweetbreads, stir, season with salt and pepper and cook gently for 15 minutes more. This dish should be served very hot, with the sweet and sour sauce poured over.

CHRISTMAS TURKEY
Tacchino di natale

SERVES 8

For the filling

4 Golden Delicious apples, cut into pieces
200g (7oz) pitted prunes, chopped

350g (12oz) luganega sausage, skinned and cut
    into small pieces

350g (12oz) chestnuts, roasted and peeled, or 250g (8oz) canned unsweetened chestnuts

Salt and pepper
75g (3oz) butter, cut into pieces

1 small turkey, about 4.5kg (10lb)
Salt and pepper
2 sprigs of sage, chopped

2 sprigs of rosemary, chopped
50g (2oz) butter, shaved

Mix the filling ingredients and stuff the turkey with them – the cavity as well as the skin at the neck. You may add the heart, gizzard and liver, cut into pieces, but I prefer not to, as the liver sometimes tastes bitter and the gizzard always remains tough. Sew up the openings with thread and sprinkle the turkey with salt, pepper, sage, rosemary and butter. Place the bird, breast side down, in a roasting tin and bake in the oven at 150°C (300°F, gas mark 2) for about 3 hours, or until done to your liking, turning it over for the last 30 minutes to let the breast become crisp and brown.

DUCK BREASTS WITH BALSAMIC VINEGAR
Anatra all'aceto balsamico

At the restaurant Dal Pescatore in Canneto sull'Oglio, Antonio Santini has introduced some of the grand old dishes of nearby Mantua in addition to local peasant dishes.

SERVES 4

1–2 tablespoons sunflower oil
4 duck breasts
1–2 tablespoons balsamic vinegar, or red wine vinegar with a pinch of sugar

Salt and pepper
$\frac{1}{4}$ teaspoon cinnamon
4 tablespoons blueberries or cranberries

Heat the oil in a frying pan. Put the duck breasts in, skin side down, and cook on low heat. Turn over when the fat under the skin has melted and the skin is golden. Add the vinegar, salt and pepper, cinnamon and berries. Cover and cook for 10–15 minutes more (the duck breasts should be juicy inside). The berries will have melted to make a delicious sauce. Spoon off any excess fat and serve the breasts with the sauce poured over them.

RISOTTO WITH QUAIL
Risotto con le quaglie

SERVES 6

6 quail
1 onion, chopped
3 tablespoons sunflower oil
125g (4oz) butter
Salt and pepper
2 sprigs of sage

300ml ($\frac{1}{2}$ pint) dry marsala
500g (1lb) Arborio rice
1.5 litres ($2\frac{1}{2}$ pints) light chicken stock seasoned with salt and pepper (you may use 3 stock cubes)

Rinse the quail. In a large frying pan, fry the onion in the oil with 25g (1oz) butter until soft. Put in the quail and turn to brown them all over. Add salt and pepper and the sage leaves, pour in the marsala and cook gently for about 20 minutes, until the quail are done, turning them over a few times.

In the meantime boil the rice in plenty of stock seasoned with salt and pepper for about 18 minutes, until cooked al dente, then drain quickly. Stir in the remaining butter and serve with the quail on top and the sauce poured over.

PEACHES IN WINE
Pesche al vino

SERVES 6

6 large ripe peaches or nectarines
About 400ml (14fl oz) red wine

2 tablespoons sugar, or to taste (optional)

Pour boiling water over the peaches or nectarines and skin them. Slice them into a bowl or individual wine glasses and pour the wine over them. Add sugar if the peaches are not sweet enough, and leave to macerate for 1 hour.

STUFFED PEACHES
Pesche ripiene

There are not many old Italian desserts, but this is one of the classics. The recipe is from Sergio Torelli, head chef at Savini, Milan's famous restaurant in the Galleria, near the Duomo. It appears in *Le migliori ricette della scuola del Gritti*, edited by Massimo Alberini.

SERVES 6

12 yellow peaches
50g (2oz) butter
12 macaroons (amaretti, the small, slightly bitter
    ones)
2 egg yolks
2 tablespoons maraschino, marsala or
    amaretto

50g (2oz) finely chopped almonds
125g (4oz) granulated sugar
1 teaspoon cocoa powder
Grated rind of $\frac{1}{2}$ lemon
White wine
Butter
Caster sugar

Cut the peaches in half, remove the stones and hollow out some of the flesh. Lightly grease an ovenproof dish with butter. Place the peach halves in it, cut side up. Chop the peach pulp, crush the macaroons and stir together in a bowl with the egg yolks, maraschino or liqueur, almonds, sugar, cocoa and grated lemon rind. Mix well. Fill the peach halves with this mixture, sprinkle with white wine, dust with sugar and put a shaving of butter on each. Put the dish in the oven at 180°C (350°F, gas mark 4) for 20–30 minutes, until golden. Serve dusted with caster sugar.

STUFFED APRICOTS
Albicocche ripiene

SERVES 6

For the filling

4 apricots, peeled, halved and stoned
1 egg
125g (4oz) ground almonds

125g (4oz) sugar
A few drops almond essence

700g ($1\frac{1}{2}$lb) apricots
25g (1oz) butter

6 tablespoons marsala

To make the filling, blend the apricots and egg together and mix with the almonds, sugar and almond essence into a paste.

Cut the apricots in half and remove the stones. Lay them close to each other, cut sides up, in a lightly buttered baking dish. Cover each half with almond filling, sprinkle a few shavings of butter on top, pour the marsala into the dish and bake in the oven at 200°C (400°F, gas mark 6) for 25 minutes, or until lightly browned.

DOLCI DI MASCARPONE
Mascarpone Desserts

This delicious rich creamy cheese made by curdling thick cream with citric acid originates in Lodi, but it has become so popular in Italy that many regions produce it. It is served with the cheese course, spread on a slice of bread or mixed with sugar and cognac or rum in an emptied wine glass or coffee cup.

Mascarpone is used instead of cream to sauce fruits and pastries. The classic *crema di mascarpone* has 2 egg yolks, 150g (5oz) sugar and 3 tablespoons rum mixed into 250g (8oz) mascarpone. Two stiffly beaten egg whites are folded in and the fluffy cream is chilled.

A favourite way of serving mascarpone is *al caffè*. Take 250g (8oz) mascarpone and stir into it about 2 tablespoons very finely ground or pulverised coffee (a dark roast is good), 3 tablespoons or more caster sugar and 2–4 tablespoons rum. Let the flavours infuse for a while, and serve chilled.

BAKED PEARS
Pere al forno

SERVES 6

6 large firm pears
250g (8oz) caster sugar
250ml (8fl oz) or more dry marsala or red wine

1 stick cinnamon
1 vanilla pod or a few drops vanilla essence
120ml (4fl oz) or more water

Stand the pears, unpeeled, in a large ovenproof dish with the rest of the ingredients. Bake, uncovered, in the oven at 150°C (300°F, gas mark 2) for $1\frac{1}{2}$–2 hours. Serve hot or cold.

CHOCOLATE DESSERT
Torta di cioccolato

Turin had a dominating influence on Lombardy in the nineteenth century, and this dessert is a legacy. The recipe comes from Franco and Silvana Colombani's delightful *Cucina d'amore*.

SERVES 8

200g (7oz) fine quality dark chocolate
125g (4oz) unsalted butter, softened
4 eggs, separated

200g (7oz) granulated sugar
3 tablespoons flour
Icing sugar (optional)

Melt the chocolate and butter in a bowl placed in boiling water. Mix the egg yolks with the sugar and 2 tablespoons of the flour, then mix well with the butter and chocolate. Beat the egg whites until stiff and fold them in. Butter a 30cm (12in) round baking dish and dust with the remaining flour. Pour in the chocolate mixture and bake in the oven at 140°C (275°F, gas mark 1) for 45 minutes. Serve cold in the baking dish, dusted if you like with icing sugar. The dessert is soft and best served with a spoon.

Variation

A *torta* both incredibly easy and incredibly delicious is made by beating 420ml ($\frac{3}{4}$ pint) double cream until very stiff, then beating in 250g (8oz) semi-sweet or Menier chocolate which has been melted then cooled a little. Chill it or put it in the freezer. I discovered it at the River Café in London. It serves eight.

Trentino-Alto Adige

Trentino-Alto Adige

There are two different worlds in this spectacular region of dark forests, mauve-coloured mountain peaks and valleys, which below Bolzano turns into gentle slopes and terraces: German-speaking Alto Adige in the north and Italian-speaking Trentino in the south. Salorno, a village above Trento, represents the dividing line.

Alto Adige takes its name from the river Adige and is a prosperous tourist region full of old castles, turreted houses and fortified convents, many of which have become hotels and restaurants for people going skiing and taking local health cures. It attracts mainly German and Austrian tourists. The region produces some of the best white wines in Italy and a great variety of fruit including apples, pears, plums and grapes. Until the First World War it was the Austrian South Tyrol, and the people have clung fiercely to those traditions.

The cooking is Tyrolean and based on the pig. Its heart and soul is *Speck*, a delicious salted and smoked pork which is eaten for breakfast, as an appetizer and as an afternoon snack and is also used in cooking. Shops in Alto Adige are full of the great blackened chunks. The best *Speck* is made in old wooden farmhouses that have just the right ventilation and no central heating. Pigs are killed in winter and the hams are boned, opened like a book, covered with a mixture of salt and saltpetre, with pepper, bay leaves and juniper berries and left to rest for three weeks while the liquids run out. After that the meat is hung in the fireplace and smoked with fruit wood and juniper for a few hours a day and allowed to get cold after each smoking. This continues for up to three months; then it is left to mature in well-ventilated attics for six months more.

The repertoire of Tyrolean dishes includes *Knödel*, bread dumplings the size of small oranges, which are dropped into soups and stews or eaten with roasts and boiled meats; *Gulasch*; trout from the lakes and streams and game cooked in wine and vinegar. The main vegetables are cabbage (especially as sauerkraut) and potatoes. Red cabbage is cooked in red wine with onions and bacon. Apple sauce, bilberry jam and sour cream and all kinds of sausages and salami are typical to the region.

Bread is all-important. There are many different kinds, some dark, with mixtures of wheat, rye and barley flour. Every village has its own.

Sweets are Austrian yet with a difference: *Krapfen* (doughnuts) are filled with jam and poppy seeds or with cream; strudel is filled with apples, raisins and pine nuts, or with poppy seeds, honey and cream, or with ricotta and sour cream. There are plum tarts, prune dumplings, chestnut cakes and puddings, stuffed pancakes and pastries filled with nuts and marzipan.

The cooking of Trentino is a mixture, similar to that of the Veneto mountains but with a German and mid-European influence because of neighbouring Alto Adige; Trentino was once part of the Austro-Hungarian Empire, and there are pockets of ethnic communities whose ancestors came to mine coal in the eleventh century and who still speak an old German dialect. The cooking is based on polenta, which is made differently in every valley, with water, milk or even wine, sometimes combined with mashed potatoes. A dark *polenta nera* is made from a mixture of maize and buckwheat flour. They also have rice and pasta, and they sauce their pastas with veal stew and thick cream, and with mashed sardines.

In Trentino they make all kinds of gnocchi including a German-inspired *gnocchi di prugne*, filled with prunes, and their *canederli* are the same as German bread dumplings. They poach trout and eel in white wine and vinegar, and fry frogs' legs in batter. *Baccalà dei frati* (salt cod cooked in broth and milk with mashed anchovies and tomato paste) is so called because it was made by monks (*frati*) and sold with steaming polenta at monasteries on Fridays. Salted and smoked herring from the North Atlantic are soaked in milk and cooked with onions in vinegar. Meat is simmered long and slowly with wine, vinegar or milk; rabbit is prepared Hungarian style with white wine, paprika and juniper berries; and *Gulasch* and *crauti* (sauerkraut) are also common. Potatoes are a favourite vegetable – they are grated raw for tarts, cakes, pancakes and omelettes.

During the mushroom season there is a little market in the heart of the old centre of Trento that sells nothing but mushrooms and a few other wild things. Gatherers arrive from the hills and valleys to sell what they have found – the familiar porcini, as well as *porcinelli*, *chiodini*, *finfireli*, *vescie*, *russole* – as many as 250 different types have been seen. The commune employs experts to vet them. A speciality of the Trentino region is *misto di funghi*, a mushroom stew with wine, which accommodates the unremarkable and is served with polenta, risotto or pasta.

The Wines of Trentino-Alto Adige

Alto Adige is the great wine-exporting area of Italy. Its international reputation is built on magnificent whites. The reds produced in the high alpine vineyards are mainly for neighbouring Switzerland, Germany and Austria.

Wine production in Sudtirol (the German name for Alto Adige) is an exciting mixture of German, Italian and French traditions with new technology and both native and foreign grapes. Vineyards boast a splendid mix of grapes – Germanic, French and Italian – and almost every variety is capable of giving a unique flavour.

Among the red wines are fine examples of Cabernet, Merlot and Pinot Nero. The popular Lago di Caldaro (or Kalterersee), made from the local Schiava grape, is a light soft wine with the flavour of strawberries and almonds. Santa Maddalena has depth of flavour and a delicate fragrance with a hint of violets and almonds. A pleasing Malvasia and some reds and rosés made from the native Lagrein reveal how Alto Adige combines the strength of Italian reds with the fresher, brighter tastes of France.

In making the whites, Alto Adige has learned from the French how to produce searing dryness; and from the Germans how to make dry, light and delicate wines that are sweet enough for the wine to have perfume and fruit, soft edges and gentleness. They make a vigorous, fruity Chardonnay and an Italian-style light, fruity, ripe Sauvignon. Their Riesling Renano is a sharp, steely dry, lean, crisp and tingling white with a densely fruity bouquet which can have a remarkable flavour of honey when it grows older. Their Sylvaner is dry, crisp and lemony, and a Muller-Thurgau, which is a mixture of Riesling and Sylvaner, is soft, sharp-scented and herby.

But Alto Adige's greatest glory are the heady, perfume-packed varieties: dry yet nutty and full of honey and raisins Pinot Grigio with a fragrance of flowers, peaches and angelica; dry but creamy Pinot Bianco with a nutty, honeyed flavour and a crowd of fruity, flowery aromas; seductively exotic, spicy Gewürztraminer; and the white dry Goldmuscateller and sweet rose-scented Rosenmuscateller made from Muscat grapes, which give unbridled pleasure with their pure and lovely flavours and perfumes.

Trentino's red wines are generally light, with good flavour but not much character. There are some good Cabernets, Merlots and Pinot Neri, but the best reds are the local Marzemino and Lagrein and the prestigious dark, tart, slightly bitter Teroldego Rotaliano, important in Trentino but hardly known elsewhere. Some of Italy's best white Pinot Bianco and Chardonnay, and sparkling wines from these grapes and others, such as the native Nosiola, are made here. The sparkling champagne-method wines are impressive. There is also a pleasant, sweet vin santo.

WINE SOUP
Weinsuppe

This is one of my favourites from this region. The recipe is from Andreas Hellrig, owner-chef of the restaurant Andrea in the mountain resort of Merano. Andreas uses old traditional recipes from local families as well as his own creations.

SERVES 4

4 egg yolks

500ml (18fl oz) meat broth (you may use a beef stock cube dissolved in 500ml/18fl oz water)

250ml (8fl oz) or more white wine

120ml (4fl oz) double cream

Salt

1 teaspoon cinnamon

Small bunch of chives, finely chopped

Beat the yolks, broth, wine and cream with salt and a pinch of cinnamon in a saucepan and stir vigorously over very low heat until the mixture thickens slightly and becomes creamy. Serve hot with a sprinkling of cinnamon and chives.

TYROLEAN DUMPLINGS
Canederli tirolesi

These dumplings are called *Knödel* in German-speaking Alto Adige. They are served with melted butter or grated cheese or in a soup of delicate meat or chicken broth.

They are very large and very filling; one or two are enough per person.

SERVES 6

3 eggs
250ml (8fl oz) milk
275g (9oz) stale white bread, crusts removed and crumbled
125g (4oz) *Speck* or smoked ham, diced
1 tablespoon chopped chives

2 tablespoons chopped parsley
Salt and pepper
A pinch of nutmeg
200–250g (7–8oz) plain flour
1.5 litres (2½ pints) stock

Beat the eggs with the milk, add the bread, the *Speck* or ham, chives, parsley, salt, pepper and nutmeg. Stirring continually, add enough flour to make a dough that will hold together. Mix it well, then with wet hands make balls a little larger than an egg.

When all are ready, flour lightly and simmer in the stock for about 20 minutes.

BREAD DUMPLINGS WITH MUSHROOMS
Canederli ai funghi porcini

These dumplings are served with melted butter and grated parmesan or in chicken or meat broth as soup.

SERVES 6

200g (7oz) white bread, crusts removed
120ml (4fl oz) milk
1 onion, chopped
40g (1½oz) butter
250g (8oz) mushrooms

2 eggs
2 tablespoons flour
Salt and pepper
4–6 tablespoons finely chopped parsley

Break up the bread, sprinkle with milk and mix it well with your hands.

Fry the onion in butter until soft, then add the mushrooms, cut into pieces, and cook until they are done and the moisture is absorbed. Put through a food processor and mix with the crumbled bread (squeezed dry) and the rest of the ingredients. Work into a dough and let it rest for a few minutes.

With wet hands, roll the dough into little balls the size of walnuts (in Alto Adige they sometimes make balls as big as tangerines, but smaller ones are better). Drop a few at a time into boiling salted water and simmer for about 2 minutes, until they rise. It is good to test one for consistency at the beginning so that if it falls apart you can add a little more flour to the rest. Lift out with a slotted spoon.

RAVIOLI WITH SPINACH AND RICOTTA
Schlutzkrapfen o ravioli della Pusteria

A version of ravioli with spinach and ricotta, a speciality of northern Italy, can be found in almost every corner of the country. In this region they make pasta dough with eggs and milk. But you can also make it with the usual flour and egg mixture (page 110).

SERVES 4–6

For the filling

700g (1½lb) fresh spinach leaves, or 350g (12oz) frozen spinach

½ onion, chopped

15g (½ oz) butter

2 tablespoons or more grated grana or parmesan

Salt

½ teaspoon freshly grated nutmeg

300g (10oz) ricotta

For the dough

2 eggs

500g (1lb) plain flour

Pinch of salt

Salt

75g (3oz) butter, melted

150ml (5fl oz) milk, warmed

I egg yolk mixed with 1 teaspoon water

Grated grana or parmesan

To prepare the filling, wash the spinach and boil until the leaves crumple, in very little water. Drain, squeeze out all the water you can and finely chop. Fry the onion in butter until soft. Add the spinach and stir well. Add the grana or parmesan, salt if necessary and nutmeg. Take off the heat and mix with the ricotta in a bowl.

To make the dough, mix the eggs into the flour and salt, add the milk gradually, just enough for a firm dough, and knead well for about 10 minutes until the dough is smooth and elastic. Leave it for 15 minutes wrapped in clingfilm. Roll it out as thin as you can (it is easier to divide the dough in half and roll out smaller amounts).

Cut into 7.5cm (3in) rounds with a pastry cutter. Brush around the edges with the egg yolk-water mixture so that they stick more easily. Place a tablespoon of filling in the centre of the dough, fold over to form a half-moon and press the edges firmly together (or use the methods given for ravioli on page 111).

Drop into plenty of boiling salted water and cook for 3–4 minutes, until tender. Drain well and serve with melted butter and grated cheese.

RAVIOLI WITH MUSHROOM FILLING
Schlutzkrapfen con funghi

This is an alternative and most delicious filling for the preceding recipe.

1kg (2lb) shiitake or other mushrooms

40g (1½oz) butter

1 tablespoon oil

3–4 cloves garlic, crushed

Large bunch of parsley, finely chopped

150ml (5fl oz) double cream (optional)

Salt and pepper

Fry the mushrooms in a mixture of butter and oil with the garlic until they are tender and the liquid has disappeared. Finely chop (in a food processor if you like), and then add parsley and cream, if using. Season to taste with salt and pepper.

Make the ravioli and fill them according to the instructions for the preceding recipe.

TROUT WITH SOUR CREAM

Trote alla panna acida

Trout is a favourite freshwater fish all over Italy. In many parts farmed trout are used, but here the fish come from mountain streams. Fresh cream is sometimes used instead of sour cream.

SERVES 2

2 trout, cleaned, heads left on
Juice of $1/2$ lemon
120ml (4fl oz) wine vinegar
Salt

25g (1oz) butter
150ml (5fl oz) sour cream
A few sprigs of parsley, chopped

Into a large sauté pan put just enough water to cover the fish. Add lemon juice, vinegar and salt and bring to the boil. Put in the trout and poach, covered, the heat turned down as low as possible so that the water barely trembles, for about 6–8 minutes.

Melt the butter in a small pan, add the sour cream and heat through, stirring.

Lift the trout out of the pan and serve with the sauce poured over, sprinkled with parsley.

GRILLED VENISON

Grigliata di cervo

The venison available in shops and supermarkets now is young tender meat, which you can grill as you would beef.

SERVES 6

6 venison chops or steaks
$1/2$ bottle red wine
3 tablespoons olive oil
1 onion, chopped
2 cloves garlic, finely chopped
5 cloves

1–2 teaspoons cinnamon
Grated rind of I lemon
Salt and pepper
1 bay leaf
10 juniper berries, crushed

Put the venison chops in a bowl with the rest of the ingredients, well mixed, and leave, covered, for a day in the refrigerator, turning the meat over once or twice.

Cook the meat under the grill for about 10 minutes, until done, turning it over once.

Pour the marinade into a saucepan and boil to reduce it to a rich sauce. Serve the meat, with the strained sauce, accompanied by polenta if you like and *salsa di cren* (horseradish sauce; recipe follows).

HORSERADISH SAUCE

Salsa di cren

This strongly flavoured sauce of Alto Adige (it is found also in Friuli) is served with all kinds of boiled and roast meats. It varies greatly and is the kind of sauce you make up to taste.

You can start with 250ml (8fl oz) whipped double cream, add a pinch of salt and 1–2 teaspoons sugar, and grate in as much peeled and washed horseradish root as you like.

Alternatively, grate about 125g (4oz) horseradish and add 3 tablespoons fresh breadcrumbs soaked in about 5 tablespoons milk, a pinch of salt and 1 teaspoon sugar.

Serve the sauce as is or add 4 tablespoons white wine vinegar or the juice of $1/2$–1 lemon or a little mustard or a pinch of cayenne. There are those who simply mix the horseradish with unsweetened stewed apple.

FRUIT PUDDING
Früchtepudding

SERVES 8

175g (6oz) white bread, crusts removed
600ml (1 pint) milk
65g (2½oz) butter, softened
3 large eggs, separated
65g (2½oz) almonds, finely chopped

125g (4oz) sugar
1 teaspoon cinnamon
Grated zest of 2 lemons
1kg (2lb) fruit, such as apples, pears, seedless
   grapes and plums, cubed

Break up the bread, put it in a bowl and pour in the milk, working it in with your hands and crumbling the bread.

Beat the butter with the egg yolks, then add the almonds, sugar, cinnamon and lemon zest, and beat into the soaked bread. Beat the egg whites until stiff and fold them into the mixture. Finally, fold in the fruit (apples and pears should be peeled).

Pour into a wide baking dish and bake in the oven at 180°C (350°F, gas mark 4) for 1 hour or more, or until firm and golden on top.

Serve hot or cold. The plums give a beautiful red colour where they touch the surface.

APPLE AND NUT CAKE
Apfelnusstorte o Torta di mele

100g (3½oz) blanched hazelnuts or almonds or
   a mixture of both
6 apples, such as Golden Delicious
4 eggs, separated

140g (4½oz) sugar
Juice of 1 lemon
140g (4½oz) flour
25g (1oz) butter, melted

Chop the hazelnuts or almonds (or both) and toast them in a dry frying pan, shaking the pan so that they brown all over. Peel, core and slice the apples; set aside. Beat the egg yolks with the sugar. Add the lemon juice, then the flour gradually, beating well. Beat the egg whites until stiff and fold them in, then fold in the nuts.

Grease a 23–25cm (9–10in) springform tin with butter and dust with flour. Pour in half the cake mixture, arrange a layer of apples on top, and pour the remaining cake mixture over them. Arrange the rest of the apple slices in circles on top, brush with melted butter and sprinkle with sugar.

Bake in the oven at 180°C (350°F, gas mark 4) for 1 hour and 25 minutes, or until a skewer pushed into the cake comes out clean. You can put the cake under the grill for a minute at the end to give the top a caramelised look.

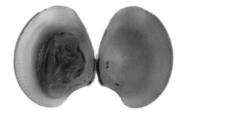

Veneto

Veneto

Italians describe the cooking of the Veneto as delicate and colourful. They compare it to Venetian mosaics and tinted marbles, use words such as 'poetic' and 'spiritual' and explain that Venetians have Venice and the paintings of Bellini and Titian to inspire them. They talk of the Middle Ages and Venice's central role in the spice trade, of the dried fruit and nuts that came from the East, of the Saracens and Byzantium and the feasts of the Doges.

But the people I met in the Veneto, in Verona and Vicenza, Padua and Treviso, and in Venice too, said their cooking was *la fantasia dei poveri* (the fantasy of the poor), and stemmed from the days when the region lived (meagrely) off the land. There is no trace, they claim, of the grand dishes of the old noble families, *i signori*, such as the Della Scala of Verona.

The Veneto consists of the plain between the rivers Po and Tagliamento, bounded in the north by the spectacular Dolomite Mountains. The plain is a region of small industries: factories are dotted amid fields and woodlands, and busy modern agglomerations contrast with ancient villas and palazzi, noble cities and serene villages. Most people have either moved to the nearest town or remained in the village and gone to work in the nearby factory, so there has not been a complete break with the countryside.

The main feature of the cooking in town and country is the all-important influence of Venice, the lagoon city, which developed as a refuge for mainlanders fleeing the northern invaders and became the ruling economic and political power of the Venetian republic, which remained independent for a thousand years. Venice was once the richest, most powerful city in the world, mistress of the Mediterranean, an international market and a great mari-time power, with her own fleet and her own trading posts in the Levant. She was like a bazaar city, with foreign communities – there were Germans, Turks, Greeks, Arabs, Jews and Armenians, each with their own quarters – traders from everywhere at her quayside and her own merchants and seamen in the four corners of the world. Marco Polo was Venetian.

Venice was Europe's point of contact with the East, and Venetians absorbed culinary ideas from the Arabs and Byzantium (Arab-style *pesce in saor*, sweet and sour fish with raisins and pine nuts, is typical of the region). But they translated everything into their own, very simple, style. When I asked the owner of the popular Madonna restaurant in the Rialto why, despite the sumptuous past and the spice trade, the cooking of Venice was so uncomplicated, he explained that their cooking was simple because it was based on fish.

If you could see the fish come in live at dawn in barges on the Grand Canal straight on to the market stalls around the corner from the Madonna you would understand why all they want to do is lightly fry, poach or grill it.

The entire Veneto is a region of water with rivers and streams, lakes, canals and lagoons, so much of the cooking revolves around fish. The best antipasto is seafood. Large and small prawns, crab, squid, cuttlefish, baby octopus, and all kinds of shellfish are served simply dressed with olive oil, chopped parsley and lemon, but the lemon seems superfluous. My own favourites are moleche, the tiny soft-shelled crabs of Murano, netted when they change their shells in the spring and autumn, dipped live in egg batter with garlic and parsley, and fried.

Shellfish soups are simple, made with olive oil, white wine and garlic. Mixed fish soup, *broeto*, is served with fried bread. Scampi are dipped in batter and fried; eel is cooked in marsala, mackerel in white wine. One of the most famous Venetian dishes is *seppioline nere*, baby cuttlefish cooked in their ink. As everywhere in the Mediterranean, salt cod and stockfish are adored. There is a great variety of fish and seafood risottos variously called *bianco, di pesse* (dialect for 'fish'), *di mare, ai frutti di mare, alla marinara* or *dei pescatori*. Recently, pasta with seafood has become very popular.

Although most dishes in the Veneto are variations of Venetian ones, each city also has specialities of its own.

Horsemeat stew is a speciality of Verona, an old garrison town where, once upon a time, when they were surrounded, they ate their horses. Also from there is *peara*, a peppery sauce made with bone marrow and breadcrumbs, the secret of which Veronese girls are supposed to receive when they marry. Verona is also the city of potato gnocchi. Every year on Good Friday the Veronese celebrate a *baccanale del gnocco* with a procession in fourteenth-century clothes, and they elect a *papà del gnocco*, who rides on a donkey holding a dumpling on the end of a fork. Padua is known for mutton with a wine sauce called *piperata*, Treviso for a pigeon stew, Vicenza for stockfish, Belluno for bean soups and ice cream. Every city is famous for something.

What is special about the cooking of the Veneto is the cosmopolitan and exotic touch. Meat is marinated in wine, then simmered in milk; turkey is bathed in pomegranate juice; fish is garnished with pine nuts and raisins. It is the result of Venice's old connections with both Germany and the Orient.

Spices were much used in the Middle Ages: the old cookery books are full of ginger, saffron, cumin, cloves, cinnamon and nutmeg. By the beginning of the nineteenth century, under the influence of the French after Napoleon had conquered Venice, they went out of fashion in favour of herbs. But Venetians never forgot that pepper was once worth its weight in gold. They also have great respect for the salt from their marshes, which has a special flavour.

The Veneto is in the polenta, bean soup and risotto belts that run right across the north of Italy. Polenta was once eaten for breakfast, lunch and supper, and is an accompaniment to many foods. (It was blamed for pellagra because many of those who suffered from the disease ate hardly anything else.) Maize was brought from America to Venice in the sixteenth century; it was called *granoturco* because it was believed to come from Turkey. In Venice they like polenta soft and creamy and use a coarser grind of maize flour which is supposed to keep better by the sea. In other parts of the Veneto they make it firm, turn it out on a board, cut it into slices, then grill or fry it. Some cooks mix milk with the water, and there are various refinements such as alternating layers with bits of butter and gorgonzola or with stew.

Minestre (soups) are a strong point of the cooking of the Veneto, and *pasta e fagioli* (pasta and beans) is the queen of soups. This chocolate-coloured soup is made with borlotti beans, which came originally from Mexico straight to Belluno in the region of Lamon, where they are still grown.

The rice dishes of the Veneto are among its glories. Rice was introduced by the Arabs, and many short-grained types grow in the marshlands around the river Po. Other Italians have their way of cooking risotto with stock and also sometimes with wine, gradually adding liquid and stirring as it becomes absorbed, so that the risotto attains an almost creamy consistency while the grain remains firm; but Venetians make their risottos *all'onda*, almost liquid, with a velvety consistency, and eat them cold as soups, *minestre di riso*. The merit of the Veneto risotto lies in its delicate flavour, its jewel-encrusted look and most of all in its versatility, for every possible seasonal ingredient is used. Peas, green beans, artichoke hearts, asparagus tips, mushrooms, spinach, fennel, celery, carrots, potatoes, cabbage, cauliflower, leeks, courgettes, pumpkin and courgette flowers – all these go in. There is risotto with herbs, with chicken livers, with cubed chicken or mutton, with quail, sausage, tripe, snails or frogs' legs. A risotto with raisins and pine nuts is a legacy of the Arabs. Most famous of all is *risi e bisi*, made with tiny, sweet, tender peas; most dramatic is *riso nero*, which is black with cuttlefish ink.

The Veneto is richer in vegetables than any other region of Italy, and this is why Venetian food is so colourful. There are five types of their famous radicchio. The most popular are the long-leafed variety of Treviso (Trevisans have a radicchio festival in November, when they make everything, even puddings, with it) and the round kind with variegated leaves from Castelfranco. Radicchio is used raw in salads, or grilled or cooked with onion and bacon.

The asparagus of Bassano del Grappa is served with a beaten egg sauce; glazed baby onions are cooked with wine and a touch of vinegar and sugar; artichoke hearts are simmered in broth with oil and lemon; green beans are flavoured with a touch of anchovy; pumpkin is deep-fried or baked with garlic, vinegar and basil; cabbage is cooked slowly with rosemary and white wine; spinach, nettles and all kinds of wild greens are boiled together and dressed with oil; and courgette flowers are made into fritters or stuffed. During the mushroom season half a dozen wild varieties appear at the market. They are sliced raw into salads, grilled, fried or stewed.

Venetians do not eat much meat, but they like offal, and liver is their favourite. They cook chicken and many types of migrating birds that are trapped when they alight on beaches and marshes. Inland there is plenty of game, and farmyard animals such as rabbits, geese, ducks, guinea hens and turkeys.

In the hills and mountains in the north cows and pigs

are raised, and cheeses, hams and sausages are produced. The most famous cheeses are the hard, strongly flavoured asiago and vezzena, which are aged from six to eighteen months. Smoked ricotta is also made in the Veneto. Venetian hams are lean and savoury, and each mountain province has its own special recipes for making salami and sausages (you can still occasionally find them hanging in cellars in country homes). There is a Venetian saying, 'Chi no ga' orto ne' porco, porta el muso storto' (he who has no vegetable patch and no pig has a sad twisted face). It was said that the pig was the king of the peasant table and that polenta was the queen. One accompanied the other. Special Venetian sausages include the soft *soppressa*, fatty *ossocollo*, *musetto* (made from head meat), fat cotechino for boiling, and luganega, which is grilled, fried or stewed in broth. *Bondola*, a smoked and seasoned speciality of the plain near the river Po, is coarsely minced pork with red wine and plenty of pepper stuffed in a turkey bladder. The making of salami, sausages and ham has been governed by Venetian statutes since the Middle Ages, and today it is guaranteed by an association that uses a roaring lion of St Mark as a trademark.

Cakes and pastries here have always been for special occasions, such as weddings, baptisms and anniversaries, and many are attached to religious holidays. Every town has its own specialities which are made by bakers. Venice has an Easter yeast cake in the shape of a dove. The town of Este has one too, highly esteemed in all of Italy for its delicate flavour, a secret of the family which has been making it for generations. Vicenza has the marsala-flavoured sponge cake called *bussolano,* and Padua has *pinza*, which is packed with dried and candied fruit. Verona became a capital of industrial pastry-making before the Second World War with yeast cakes in the Viennese tradition, which were introduced when Napoleon handed Venice over to Austria. *Pandoro* and *nadalin* are Veronese Christmas specialities, rivals of the Milanese panettone. Verona has also *brassadela*, flavoured with grappa, and the famous *mandorlato*, also called *il miracolo del miele*, made with almonds and honey and produced by the same family for 150 years; the *festa del mandorlato*, with flags, tastings and banquets, is held in Verona the last week in November. The *torta sabbiosa*, a light sponge cake made with potato flour and perfumed with vanilla and anise-flavoured alcohol, is one of the most popular cakes; people sometimes embellish it with zabaglione or mascarpone cream.

There are many old traditional sweets, such as *crema fritta* (fried cream), *fagottini di riso* (rice fritters) and *frittelle* (carnival fritters) with pine nuts, raisins and candied fruit peel or with apples and wine, as well as *crema di riso* (creamed rice) and other milk puddings. Sweet lasagne with nuts and poppy seeds, a bread pudding called *torta Nicolotta* and a tagliatelle cake are other old specialities, but it is the new ones that are the stars in the Veneto today. Treviso claims to have invented tiramisù (literally, 'pick-me-up'), perhaps the most popular dessert in all Italy, made with mascarpone and sponge fingers; and the men of the Valle del Zoldo near Belluno, who are professional ice cream makers, have developed some of the best ice cream I have eaten.

After dinner, in the Veneto, they bring out a bottle of homemade grappa – a powerful spirit made from grape skins – sweet wines and hot chocolate or coffee, and biscuits for dunking, from the famous yellow maize flour *zaleti* to the *bigaroni* of Bassano del Grappa and the Venetian *baicoli*, hard biscuits perfumed with cinnamon, nutmeg and orange zest which, many years ago, were taken on long sea voyages because they kept so well.

The Wines of the Veneto

The wines of the Veneto are the most widely available of all Italian wines abroad. The three most famous – Valpolicella, Bardolino and Soave, produced in the hills around Verona – are 'party' wines, often unpalatable (especially Soave) as a result of too much pressure to produce too much at the lowest possible price, and they have not done much for the image of Italian wines as a whole.

But there are some good examples. At their best, Veneto wines are quaffable, very pleasant everyday wines, light, dry, fruity and refreshing with a slight acidity – the reds with a cherry and bitter almond aftertaste. Bardolino especially is delightfully easy to drink, both in the light red, and in the dark pink *chiaretto*. You can serve them as aperitifs as well as with simple antipasti and primi and with secondi such as poultry, pigeon, rabbit and white meat.

The area is also capable of high quality. Of the fine whites, Bianco di Custosa is clean, light, aromatic, slightly bitter and acidic; Gambellara is fresh and dry and sometimes slightly sweet and bitter; Prosecco, a favourite of Venetians, is bright, clean, fruity, highly scented, and it can be still or sparkling, dry or semi-sweet (when it is known as *amabile-dolce*). All are good with antipasti, pasta and light secondi of fish or white meat.

Of the reds, Colli Berici Tocai Rosso and Colli Euganei

Rosso are exceptional, Breganze-Cabernet is outstanding and Venegazzu, made from a blend of Bordeaux grapes, is one of the most admired of Veneto wines. The most highly prized wines of the Veneto are the Recioto wines. They are based on Valpolicella, both dry and sweet, and are made from partly dried, shrivelled grapes (*recioto* means 'ears' in dialect – the ears are the grapes that protrude on the outside of the bunch which catch the sun and ripen faster) and are quite different from any others in the Veneto. Amarone is a dry Recioto, and the only slow-ageing big red wine in the Veneto. It is great and memorable, with exceptional robustness; when it is allowed to age a really long time it attains a great elegance with a rich and totally dry fruitiness. It is bitter, as its name implies, but also has an incredible array of flavours, from cherry, chocolate, plum and woodsmoke to a penetrating bruised sourness. It is so deep and complex that it is best partnered with red meat or game and rich sauces, or it can be served at the end of the meal with strong cheeses such as gorgonzola forte or Parmigiano. The sweet Recioto della Valpolicella is full, warm, velvety and almost port-like with a marvellously rich intensity of flavour and high alcohol content. Torcolato and Vin Santo di Gambellera are other much appreciated dessert wines.

ASPARAGUS WITH ZABAGLIONE SAUCE
Asparagi con salsa zabaione

Bassano del Grappa in the Venetian Alps is famous for fat, white, wonderfully flavoured asparagus, which grows on the banks of the tumultuous river Brenta. A green sauce (page 115) and this very delicate one are the best accompaniments I have found.

SERVES 4

700g (1½lb) asparagus
4 egg yolks

120ml (4fl oz) dry white wine
Salt

Rinse the asparagus, peel away any hard skin and snap off the tough ends. Tie them up in bundles and simmer in salted water for 10–12 minutes, or until you can pierce the stalks with a pointed knife, being careful not to overcook. Lift out carefully, drain well and keep warm.

To make the sauce, beat the egg yolks with the wine and a little salt in a heatproof bowl in a pan of boiling water and continue beating until the sauce is thick and smooth. Serve at once with the asparagus.

PEPPERS, VENETIAN STYLE
Peperonata alla veneta

Peperonata is originally Neapolitan, but the Veneto has its own version, from Treviso, where the peppers are so good they hold a festival for them each year.

SERVES 4

375g (12oz) aubergine, cubed
Salt and pepper
4 tablespoons oil
1 clove garlic, peeled
250g (8oz) small onions, peeled

3 large sweet yellow or green peppers, seeded and
   sliced
150ml (5fl oz) white wine
5 tomatoes, peeled and chopped

Sprinkle the aubergine pieces with salt and leave for 1 hour to draw out the juices. Wash and dry them.

Heat the oil in a sauté pan with the garlic (remove it as soon as it browns). Add the onions, and cook over a low heat until soft and golden, shaking the pan every so often. Add the aubergine and the peppers.

Pour in the wine, cover and cook gently for 20 minutes, or until tender. Uncover, add the tomatoes, turn up the heat and boil rapidly for 10 minutes, or until most of the liquid has evaporated. Season to taste. Serve cold or warm.

DRESSED CRAB IN THE SHELL
Granseola alla veneziana

There are many types of crabs in Venice. Only one, the *granseola*, is large enough (like our own) to cook in this way.

SERVES 4

4 medium crabs, cooked or live, or 500g (1lb) fresh crabmeat, drained	Pepper
	2 tablespoons finely chopped parsley
Olive oil	1 lemon, quartered

If you are using cooked crabs, open them (or have the fishmonger open them for you) and remove the inedible parts. Plunge live ones into boiling salted water and boil for 6 minutes with the lid on, then simmer until the shells turn red. (A 900g–1.1kg/2–2½lb crab needs 10–12 minutes.) Drain and let cool.

Twist off the claws and legs, crack them with a nutcracker or hammer and remove the meat. Holding the crab upside down, pull the shell away from the body with the help of a rounded knife. Pick out the meat from the body with the knife. Throw away the mouth and the grey stomach sac along with the intestine, attached to the top of the shell, and the long pointed white gills, attached to the bony body. The soft tomalley (liver) is a delicacy, as is the coral roe found in the female crab. Break away the inner rim marked with a line and scrub and rinse the shell. Chop the meat, including that from the claws, and dress with olive oil, pepper and a sprinkling of parsley, then return it to the empty shell.

Serve the shell on crushed ice accompanied by lemon wedges.

DEEP-FRIED SQUID AND PRAWN
Calamaretti e gamberoni fritti

The Adriatic has the tiniest squid and the largest prawn. The most popular way of doing them is deep-frying in oil. One or the other can be served alone but often they come together as a little appetizer.

SERVES 4

250g (8oz) small or medium squid	Flour
250g (8oz) large prawns	Olive oil
Salt	1 lemon, cut in wedges

Clean and rinse the squid (see page 18). If they are small leave them whole; if they are medium cut the bodies into rings. Peel and devein the prawns.

Roll both in salted flour. Deep-fry briefly in not-too-hot oil and, with a slotted spoon, lift them out quickly when golden. (Squid become hard if overcooked.) Drain on absorbent paper towels, and serve at once, accompanied by lemon wedges.

SCALLOPS IN WHITE WINE
Sopa di cape sante

SERVES 4

400ml (14fl oz) dry white wine	½ clove garlic, crushed (optional)
12 scallops	Salt and pepper
25g (1oz) butter	2 tablespoons finely chopped parsley
2 tablespoons olive oil	

Simmer the wine in a pan for 10 minutes to reduce it (it will acquire a mellow flavour).

Cook the scallops, only for a moment, in a mixture of butter and oil with a little garlic if you are using it, in a large sauté pan, turning them over carefully. Add salt and pepper and pour in the reduced wine, then simmer for 1–2 minutes only, until the scallops become translucent. Be very careful not to overcook them as they quickly become tough.

Add the parsley and serve in soup plates.

FISH IN SWEET AND SOUR SAUCE
Pesce in saor

Saor is dialect for *sapore*, which means 'flavour'. Marinating in vinegar was an old Italian way of making fish last in the days before refrigeration, but this recipe has a particular Arab flavour.

Around the end of the twelfth century in Venice, an Arab treatise on dietetics, including 83 recipes, written by a Baghdad doctor, Gege son of Algazael, was translated from the Arabic into Latin by a certain Jambobinus of Cremona, who called it *Liber de coquina* (cookery book). Much later, in the sixteenth century, a scholar from Belluno, Andrea Alpago, who spent 30 years in Damascus and later became professor of medicine in Padua, published, in Venice, a translation of the works of the famous Arab physician and philosopher Avicenna (Ibn Sina), a great part of which was devoted to dietetics and cooking. Quite a few of the dishes described were embellished with raisins and pine nuts.

According to an old Venetian saying, social class is characterised by what fish is used for *pesce in saor*: the poor use sardines, the middle class use fish called *passarini*, and the rich use sole.

SERVES 6

500g (1lb) onions, finely chopped	2 bay leaves
2 tablespoons olive oil	Salt and white pepper
120ml (4fl oz) white wine vinegar	Flour
250ml (8fl oz) dry white wine	6 small fish, such as sole, lemon sole, sand-dabs or
2 tablespoons raisins	other delicate fish
2 tablespoons pine nuts, toasted	Oil for frying

Fry the onions in the olive oil until lightly browned and very soft. Add the vinegar and wine, raisins, pine nuts and bay leaves, season with salt and pepper, and let the sauce simmer for about 15 minutes.

Lightly salt and flour the fish and fry quickly in hot oil, turning them over once. Drain well and place in layers on a serving dish, pouring some of the sauce over each fish. Allow to rest and absorb the marinade for several hours before serving cold.

PASTA AND BEAN SOUP
Pasta e fagioli

Pasta e fasioi (dialect for 'beans') is an old peasant dish that is now so popular it is served at elegant parties and appears on every restaurant menu in the Veneto. The soup varies from one city to another. There are small differences – wide tagliatelle is used in Vicenza, wholewheat noodles called bigoli in Verona, lasagne in Este and Padua, and thin fettuccine in other parts.

This recipe comes from the family of a Verona lawyer and famous *buongustaio* (food lover), Vito Quaranta.

SERVES 4

200g (7oz) dried borlotti or haricot beans, soaked overnight, then drained	2 tomatoes, peeled and chopped
	Salt and freshly ground pepper
125g (4oz) bacon, rinds removed, chopped	25g (4oz) bigoli (wholewheat noodles), small, tubular
1 stalk celery, finely chopped	macaroni or tagliatelle
1 onion, finely chopped	Extra-virgin olive oil
1 carrot, peeled and finely chopped	Grated parmesan or grana padano
1 medium potato, peeled and chopped	

Put the drained beans, bacon and vegetables into a saucepan. Cover with water and simmer for about 2 hours, or until the beans are tender. Take out a few tablespoons of beans and put them through a blender, then return them to the soup. Add salt and pepper and the pasta and cook for 10 minutes until it is tender.

Serve the soup warm, with a little freshly ground pepper and a dribble of olive oil on each serving, and pass the cheese.

PAPPARDELLE WITH CHICKEN LIVERS
Pappardelle e figadini

The Veneto is not a region of pasta, yet, like every part of Italy, they like to claim that pasta originated there. The basis of their claim is that Marco Polo brought noodles back from his voyages to the East. The typical pasta of the Veneto are bigoli (wholewheat noodles), pappardelle (wide tagliatelle known locally as *paparele*) and *maltaja* or *maltagliati*, which are cut into uneven triangles. In this lovely speciality of Verona there should be some liquid but not so much that it becomes a soup. *Maltagliati* are sometimes used instead of pappardelle.

SERVES 4

250g (8oz) chicken livers
20g ($^3/_4$oz) butter
Salt and pepper
250g (8oz) tagliatelle

1 litre ($1^3/_4$ pints) light beef or chicken stock
   (you may use 2 stock cubes)
Plenty of grated parmesan or grana

Clean the chicken livers and cut a few into pieces, leaving the rest whole. Fry them quickly in the butter for less than a minute, stirring, so that they are brown outside but still pink inside. Season with salt and pepper and take off the heat.

Drop the pasta into the boiling stock, stir well and after 2 minutes add the livers. When the pasta is cooked al dente, serve hot with the stock in which it has cooked, with plenty of grated cheese.

GORGONZOLA DUMPLINGS
Gnocchetti di ricotta al gorgonzola

This recipe from *Le migliori ricette della scuola del Gritti* was contributed by brothers Celeste and Giuliano Tonon, owners of Da Celeste alla Costa d'Oro at Venegazzù in Volpago del Montello, near Treviso.

SERVES 6

275g (10oz) ricotta
2 tablespoons grated parmesan
3 egg yolks
1 tablespoon semolina
A good pinch of nutmeg

Salt and pepper
15g ($^1/_2$oz) butter
2 tablespoons double cream
125g (4oz) gorgonzola
2–3 tablespoons chopped parsley

Mash the ricotta with the parmesan, egg yolks, semolina, nutmeg, salt and pepper, and mix well. On a lightly oiled surface, roll this mixture into thin rolls about 1cm ($^1/_2$in) in diameter, then cut with a sharp knife into pieces about 2cm ($^3/_4$in) long.

Melt the butter with the cream in a pan, add the gorgonzola and cook over very low heat, crushing and stirring the cheese until you have a homogeneous sauce.

Drop the *gnocchetti* into plenty of boiling water and let them simmer for about 2 minutes, or until they rise to the surface. Serve hot with the sauce and sprinkled with parsley.

RICE WITH PEAS
Risi e bisi

This is one of Venice's great loves. They make it in the springtime with tiny, tiny young tender peas. The dish is moist, with a little liquid, and they call it a *minestra*, or soup, but it is something between a soup and a risotto. Like any risotto, it is served as a first course. Unless you can get really tiny young peas it is best to use frozen petits pois.

SERVES 4

1kg (2lb) tender young fresh peas in the pod, or
   250g (8oz) frozen petits pois
2 slices pancetta or unsmoked bacon, chopped

1 small onion, chopped
40g ($1^1/_2$oz) butter
1 tablespoon olive oil

1.5 litres (2$\frac{1}{2}$ pints) light meat or chicken stock or stock made by boiling the pea pods
250g (9oz) Arborio rice
Salt and pepper

1 teaspoon sugar
2 tablespoons finely chopped parsley
4 tablespoons or more grated parmesan

Shell the peas. Fry the pancetta or bacon with the onion in half the butter and the oil until the onion is soft. Add the fresh peas (see note below), cover with a little hot stock and simmer for 5–15 minutes, depending on how tender the peas are.

Pour in the rest of the stock and bring to the boil. Add the rice, season with salt and plenty of pepper and a little sugar if the peas are not sweet enough, and cook gently, stirring occasionally until the rice is tender. Stir in the rest of the butter, the parsley and cheese, and serve.

Note

With frozen petits pois, cook the rice first and stir the peas in, defrosted, when the rice is almost cooked.

SEAFOOD RISOTTO
Risotto ai frutti di mare

Every region of Italy has its own way of cooking rice. In the south, where rice dishes are a festive and not an everyday food, they appear in the form of little balls called *arancini* ('little oranges') or the large cakes *gattò* and *sartù*. The famous risotto of the north is soft and creamy (they call it velvety), the grains remaining firm to the bite, or al dente. But even risotto in the north differs according to region. In Lombardy and Piedmont, first the rice is fried in butter, then stock is added gradually, as it becomes absorbed; in the Veneto the rice is cooked from the start in plenty of stock, often with the addition of wine, and sometimes milk. And in Venice it is made almost liquid and called *minestra*, or soup.

There are dozens of fish and seafood risottos using only one kind or, as restaurants now mostly offer, a variety of fish and seafood.

SERVES 4

500g (1lb) mussels, scrubbed and beards removed
250ml (8fl oz) dry white wine
About 1 litre (1$\frac{3}{4}$ pints) water or light fish or vegetable stock
350g (12oz) Arborio rice

1 small onion, finely chopped
50g (2oz) butter
125g (4oz) prawns, peeled and deveined
250g (8oz) scampi or king-sized prawns, peeled and deveined
Salt and pepper

Place the mussels and wine in a saucepan and cook, covered, until the mussels open. Remove them from the pan. Strain the cooking liquid and reduce to about 150ml (5fl oz) by simmering for 10 minutes. Take the mussels out of their shells.

Bring a large saucepan of salted water or fish or vegetable stock to the boil. Take some out to add later as needed (because rice varies so much, it is impossible to know how much liquid it will need). Add the rice, stir and simmer for about 10 minutes. Pour in the reduced wine used to cook the mussels and cook for 5–10 minutes longer, adding a little stock if necessary, until the rice is tender but firm and there is still a little liquid left.

In the meantime, fry the onion in 15g ($\frac{1}{2}$oz) butter until soft, add the prawns and cook for 1–2 minutes until they turn pink. Add the mussels and mix into the rice. Season with salt and pepper. Stir in the rest of the butter before serving.

It is heresy to serve parmesan with fish or seafood risotto. I saw a cook adding some in a restaurant kitchen who said with a smile, 'We are all heretics!'

Variations

Add squid or baby octopus, cut into small pieces and cooked in the wine mixture, or, if you like, clams and other shellfish.

CUTTLEFISH IN INK
Seppioline nere

The Veneto is famous for cuttlefish cooked in their own ink served with creamy polenta and *risotto nero* where rice is cooked in the black sauce. The legendary Harry's Bar has been serving it with tagliatelle for some years and started a fashion. Most of the cuttlefish sold in Britain have had their ink sacs removed because they crush easily with messy results. The dish can be made without the ink and it will be good, though lacking in the distinctive extra flavour from the ink and in the dramatic visual effect. The dish can also be made with squid.

SERVES 4

1kg (2lb) cuttlefish with ink sacs
½ onion, finely chopped
2 cloves garlic, finely chopped
2–3 tablespoons olive oil

120ml (4fl oz) dry white wine
1 tablespoon tomato paste (optional)
Salt and black pepper
4 tablespoons finely chopped parsley

Pull off the head and tentacles, then carefully remove the ink sacs from the cuttlefish without breaking them, and put them aside. Wash the cuttlefish in running water and remove the soft innards and the cuttle bones from the bodies. Cut each into short, thin strips and the tentacles into pieces.

In a large saucepan, fry the onion and garlic in oil until the aroma rises. Add the cuttlefish and cook, stirring and turning the pieces over, for a few minutes. Pour in the wine, the ink from the sacs, and the tomato paste, if using. Season with salt and pepper and simmer gently for 20–30 minutes, adding a little water if necessary to have enough sauce. Add the parsley. Serve hot with soft polenta or with tagliatelle or fettuccine.

Note

For *risotto nero*, stir 275g (10oz) Arborio rice into the sauce when it has cooked for 20 minutes; continue to cook, stirring and adding water or fish stock (you may need about 1 litre/1¾ pints) until the rice is done. There should be a little liquid left at the end.

CREAMED STOCKFISH WITH OLIVE OIL AND MILK
Baccalà alla vicentina

It seems strange that a country that juts out into the sea and has so much coast should adore *baccalà*, cod dried and preserved in salt, and stockfish (*stoccafisso*), cod dried in the sun and the wind until it is rock-hard, both imported from North Sea countries, and that coastal towns should have adopted them even more than inland towns. But although the variety of fish is great in the Mediterranean, it has always been scarce and expensive. And in the days when preservation was difficult and Lenten meatless dishes were obligatory, this dried cod was a certain and cheap source of fish. Now that it is no longer cheap it is a much-loved delicacy. The best quality of stockfish is the smallest and least hard, called *ragno* in Italy.

Every region has its special ways of preparing *baccalà* and *stoccafisso*, and the Veneto and Liguria have the most (at least 150 dishes). Vicenza is especially proud of its *baccalà alla vicentina*, the local glory. It is the dish everyone there wanted me to taste, and when I did, everyone looked at my face to see my reaction.

SERVES 8

1kg (2lb) stockfish (you can substitute salt cod
    if stockfish isn't available)
1 large onion, chopped
500ml (18fl oz) olive oil
1 clove garlic, crushed

6 anchovy fillets, finely chopped
500ml (18fl oz) milk, or as needed
Salt and white pepper
Small bunch of parsley, finely chopped

Break up the stockfish (or salt cod), then soak it in cold water for 2 days, changing the water a few times. Drain, put in a large pan, cover with cold water, bring to the boil and poach (the water must barely tremble) for 18 minutes, then drain. Carefully remove the skin and bones and chop the fish very finely in the food processor.

In a heavy-bottomed pan over very low heat, fry the onion in a few tablespoons of oil until golden. Add the garlic and anchovies and, when the aroma rises, stir in the stockfish or salt cod. Add the rest of the olive oil, a little at a time, working it in very hard with a wooden spoon. Add the milk very gradually, as it becomes absorbed, beating vigorously all the time as if making mayonnaise, until the *baccalà* has the consistency of creamy mashed potatoes. Add salt, pepper and parsley, pour into a baking dish and bake in the oven at 200°C (400°F, gas mark 6) for 15 minutes.

Serve with polenta or with pieces of fried or toasted bread.

Variation

In Venice they make *baccalà mantecato*, with olive oil and no milk, although I have seen some people add cream flavoured with garlic. It is served with a squeeze of lemon.

PORK BRAISED IN MILK
Maiale al latte

Pork is traditional country fare in the Veneto. This exquisite way of cooking it makes it an elegant dish.

SERVES 4

1kg (2lb) boneless leg or loin of pork, rolled and tied	Salt and pepper
	A few sage leaves
3 tablespoons white wine vinegar	Sprig of rosemary
350ml (12fl oz) white wine	600ml (1 pint) milk
2 tablespoons oil	

Put the meat into a deep dish, cover with vinegar and wine and leave to marinate overnight.

The next day, remove the meat, dry it and brown it in oil in a flameproof casserole. Season with salt and pepper, add a few leaves of sage and a sprig of rosemary and cover with milk. Cover and place the casserole on low heat to cook very slowly for about 2 hours. When the meat is very tender, remove the lid and increase the heat to reduce the liquid.

Take out the pork, slice (not too thinly) and put on a warm plate. Strain the sauce if you like (it always curdles), putting a little on the meat and serving the rest in a sauceboat.

LIVER, VENETIAN STYLE
Fegato alla veneziana

This famous Venetian dish is always popular.

SERVES 4

4 tablespoons olive oil	550g (1¼lb) calf liver, very thinly sliced
50g (2oz) butter	2 tablespoons finely chopped parsley
2 large onions, halved and thinly sliced and cut into pieces	Salt

Heat 2 tablespoons of the oil and all the butter in a sauté pan. As soon as the butter is melted, add the onion and stir. Cover the pan and cook the onion on low heat, stirring occasionally, for about 1 hour; until very soft and creamy.

Heat the remaining oil in another sauté pan, add the liver and fry very quickly until brown on all sides, then add the onions. When the liver is cooked (it takes less than 5 minutes), take it off the heat, stir in the parsley, season to taste and serve at once.

ROAST CHICKEN STUFFED WITH CHEESE AND HERBS

Pollastri pini e boni

I am not sure if this dish originated in the region, but it comes from the celebrated Ristorante Cipriani in Venice.

SERVES 4

500g (1lb) caciotta, or a bland soft cheese
2 or more tablespoons milk
8 tablespoons finely chopped herbs including
    parsley, rosemary, sweet marjoram, basil and sage

Salt and pepper
1.75–2kg (3$\frac{1}{2}$–4lb) chicken

Blend the cheese to a paste with the milk, then mix in the herbs, salt and pepper.

Starting at the neck, work your hand under the skin of the chicken, separating it with your fingers from the flesh all the way along the breast and legs (the membranes which join them are easily detached). Stuff the pockets with the cheese and herb mixture, pushing it in from the neck and pressing it evenly into place from the outside. Close up the opening at the neck and sew up any tears in the skin with a needle and thread.

Roast the chicken in the oven at 230°C (450°F, gas mark 9) for 10 minutes, then lower the heat to 180°C (350°F, gas mark 4) and cook another 40–50 minutes, basting occasionally with the pan juices.

GOOSE WITH APPLES AND CHESTNUTS

Oca con mele e castagne

Geese were called the 'farmyard pigs' because they ate anything and were easy to keep.

SERVES 6

1 goose, about 5–6kg (10–12lb)
Salt and pepper
1.1kg (2$\frac{1}{2}$lb) eating apples, such as Golden
    Delicious or Jonathans

50g (2oz) unsalted butter
1kg (2lb) chestnuts

Remove the giblets from the body cavity and wash the goose thoroughly inside and out. Sprinkle with salt and pepper and stuff with 2 of the apples, coarsely chopped.

Place the bird in a roasting tin (on a rack if you like) and pierce the skin all over with a fork to allow the fat to run out. Roast in the oven at 220°C (425°F, gas mark 7) for 20 minutes, then cover the bird with foil, turn the oven down to 180°C (350°F, gas mark 4) and roast for another 2$\frac{1}{4}$–2$\frac{3}{4}$ hours. Test for doneness by piercing the thigh with a pointed knife. The juices which run out should not be pink.

Peel the remaining apples and slice them thickly. Fry gently in batches in the butter in a large sauté pan until soft.

Slit the skin of the chestnuts on their flat side with a pointed knife and put them on a tray under the grill (close to the heat) for 10 minutes, turning them over once, then peel them while still hot, making sure that you remove the inside skin. They should not be allowed to brown or they will become too hard. An alternative, resulting in softer chestnuts, is to boil them for about 20 minutes. In this way peeling is slightly more difficult. (I prefer them when they are roasted and firm.) Break the chestnuts into quarters and mix with the apple slices. Put them in a baking dish and heat through in the oven when you are nearly ready to serve the goose.

POLENTA

Polenta

Restaurants were once ashamed to offer polenta. After thirty years of neglect, the old heartwarming maize flour mush, rejected as 'poor food' in the 1950s, has made a triumphal come-back and is now very fashionable in the north of Italy and especially in the Veneto, where it was once a staple. Restaurants serve elegant portions, often in the form of thin toasted slices, *crostoni*, which act as a bed for game birds, sausages, fish and meat stews. Some pour it on to a large board and cut it with a long thread in the old way, or press it in a mould and turn it out.

Polenta is not an easy dish to master, partly because there are so many ways of making it. There are those who like it soft and creamy, those who prefer it firm enough to cut with a knife, those who want a thickness of three or four fingers and those who like it sliced no more than 1cm (½in) thick.

There is white maize flour as well as the more common yellow one in Italy, but they taste the same; there are different degrees of fineness. The fine-ground flour is considered the best, although many people prefer the coarse one.

The difficulty with the traditional way of making polenta is that it must be stirred for about 45 minutes so that lumps do not form. The flour is poured gradually in a thin rain, with the left hand, into boiling salted water, while the right hand stirs vigorously, always in the same clockwise direction. As the thick mass gurgles and splatters you must be careful that the bottom does not stick and burn, or the taste will be spoiled. The traditional polenta pan, or *caldiera*, is heavy copper with a cone-shaped bottom which would fit into a hole in the old hearths; it has a kind of oar, or *caldina*, which makes stirring easier. Although gourmets claim that polenta made in the slow, even heat of a *caldiera* is superior to any other and has another flavour and another smell, people have successfully devised ways of preparing polenta more easily and you can even buy a special polenta pan with a built-in electric oar.

Here is a basic and easy – although heretical – way of making polenta, given by Lucia Alberini, which works very well.

SERVES 4
300g (10oz) polenta (maize flour or maize meal)   1 tablespoon salt
1.25 litres (2½ pints) cold water

Put the maize flour with the water in a very large saucepan (it needs space to grow by more than a third) and stir very thoroughly. Add salt and, stirring vigorously and constantly so that lumps do not form (this is crucial), slowly bring to the boil. Cook for a few minutes, stirring, then pour into a greased baking dish. Cover with foil and bake in the oven at 200°C (400°F, gas mark 6) for at least 1 hour.

To make *crostoni*, turn out the polenta while still hot, let it cool and become firm, then cut into slices, brush them or not with oil, and toast under the grill or over a fire until lightly browned on both sides.

Variations

For a softer; creamier polenta, add more water, or a mixture of milk and water – you can add up to twice as much liquid – with the maize flour. This too eventually becomes firm and can be sliced and grilled; it yields a lovely crisp crust and a soft inside.

For *polenta a bocconi*, serve in deep bowls with plenty of butter and grated parmesan. For sweet *polenta a bocconi dolce*, sprinkle with sugar and cinnamon instead of parmesan. For *polenta conzada* serve with plenty of butter, ricotta and grated parmesan. *Pasticcio di polenta* is a baked pie with layers of pigeon, chicken or veal stew with ham and mushrooms and polenta.

A dramatic traditional way of serving polenta is to pour it out on to the table (you can cover it with foil) and lay on top of it various foods, such as fried sausages, slices of salami or cheese, quail, lightly fried mushrooms, pigeon or hare stew; people can then help themselves. The traditional way of cutting plain polenta is with a thread.

MUSHROOMS IN WHITE WINE
Funghetti al vino

There are many varieties of wild mushrooms in the Veneto. They are fried lightly in butter with garlic and parsley, grilled, deep-fried in batter, and stewed with tomatoes or in wine. When they are in season you find them in everything – soups, tarts, risottos, gnocchi, omelettes, pancakes. I tried them in many different ways at Da Celeste alla Costa d'Oro at Venegazzù in Volpago del Montello, near Treviso. This recipe is good with every kind of mushroom.

SERVES 4

4–5 tablespoons olive oil	Salt and pepper
1 small clove garlic, crushed	120–250ml (4–8fl oz) white wine
700g (1½lb) mushrooms, cut into pieces if large	2 tablespoons chopped parsley
1 tablespoon fresh thyme	

In a saucepan, heat the oil with the garlic. When the aroma rises, add the mushrooms and thyme and cook over high heat for 1–2 minutes. Season with salt and pepper, add the wine and boil vigorously until it almost evaporates. Add parsley and serve hot or cold.

RADICCHIO AND ROCKET SALAD
Radicchio con rucola

Radicchio, the salad leaf that has become popular all over the world because of its beautiful red colour, is in its native Veneto grilled and fried in egg and breadcrumbs, as well as braised and made into risotto. But the type available in the UK is best eaten raw in a salad. A traditional radicchio salad, a speciality of Vicenza, is dressed with hot bacon fat and a sprinkling of fried bacon bits, but the following combination with rocket is now the most popular.

SERVES 4

2 heads radicchio	1 tablespoon vinegar
Bunch of rocket leaves	Salt and pepper
3 tablespoons olive oil	

Dress the salad leaves with oil, vinegar, salt and pepper just before you are ready to serve.

TIRAMISÙ
Tiramisù

There cannot be a restaurant or trattoria in Italy that does not have its stock of individual bowls of tiramisù in the freezer, or a home cook who does not have a favourite recipe cut out of a magazine. This easy dessert, which is still a relatively new dish, has many versions. The following is my own favourite.

SERVES 8

4 tablespoons rum, or to taste	2 eggs, separated
120ml (4fl oz) strong black coffee	5 tablespoons icing sugar
2 tablespoons brandy	75–125g (3–4oz) dark bitter chocolate, pulverised
16–20 sponge fingers	in a blender
500g (1lb) mascarpone	

Mix 2 tablespoons of the rum with the coffee and brandy. Dip sponge fingers in this mixture and lay in a shallow dish. Pour over them any remaining coffee mixture, but not so much that the sponge fingers become soggy. Beat together the mascarpone, egg yolks and icing sugar, and add the remaining rum. Beat the egg whites until stiff but not dry, and fold into the mascarpone mixture. Spoon over the sponge fingers; sprinkle with chocolate. Refrigerate overnight.

HONEY ICE CREAM
Semifreddo al miele

The Valle del Zoldo near Belluno in the northern Veneto is known for its creamy, delicately flavoured s*emifreddo*, which is quite different from the legendary Sicilian and Neapolitan ice creams. The men of the region – like Sicilians and Neapolitans before them – have brought their trade all over Italy and abroad (they go to Germany especially). They are constantly bringing out new flavours like this one.

SERVES 4–6

1 egg
4 egg yolks

100g (3^1/$_2$oz) scented honey, such as acacia honey
300ml (^{1}/$_2$ pint) double or whipping cream

Beat the egg and the egg yolks with the honey in a bowl over boiling water until the mixture becomes thick and pale. Beat the cream until stiff and fold it in. Pour into a serving bowl and freeze overnight.

The whipping cream gives a fluffier, lighter ice cream.

CHOCOLATE ICE CREAM
Semifreddo di cioccolato

SERVES 6

250g (8oz) bitter or dark chocolate
3 tablespoons milk
6 eggs, separated

4 tablespoons cognac
300ml (^{1}/$_2$ pint) whipping cream

Melt the chocolate with the milk over boiling water. Beat in the egg yolks vigorously, one at a time, and add the cognac. Whip the cream and fold it in. Whisk the egg whites until stiff and fold them in gently. Pour into a bowl and put into the freezer for several hours until the mixture hardens. Take it out about 1 hour before serving.

Note

If you want to serve the ice cream moulded, line a mould with clingfilm so that you can easily turn it out.

WINE-FLAVOURED ICE CREAM
Semifreddo al vino

SERVES 6

2 eggs
125g (4oz) sugar

175ml (6fl oz) sweet white or red wine
300ml (^{1}/$_2$ pint) double or whipping cream

Beat the eggs with the sugar in a double boiler. Gradually add the wine, beating well until the mixture thickens. Let cool. Beat the cream until stiff and fold into the cooled egg and wine mixture. Freeze overnight.

COLD ZABAGLIONE
Zabaione freddo

This recipe comes from Giorgio Gioco, chef-owner of the Ristorante 12 Apostoli in Verona.

SERVES 6

6 egg yolks
150g (5oz) sugar
200ml (7fl oz) marsala
Grated rind of ^{1}/$_2$ lemon

1 teaspoon cinnamon
A few drops of vanilla essence
200ml (7fl oz) double or whipping cream

Put all the ingredients, except the cream, in the top of a double boiler or in a bowl placed in a pan of boiling water, and beat vigorously until the mixture is frothy. Put directly on the heat and beat constantly until the mixture is thick and creamy. Take off the heat and let cool. Beat the cream until stiff and fold into the egg mixture. Pour into a bowl or wine glasses and serve chilled with biscuits.

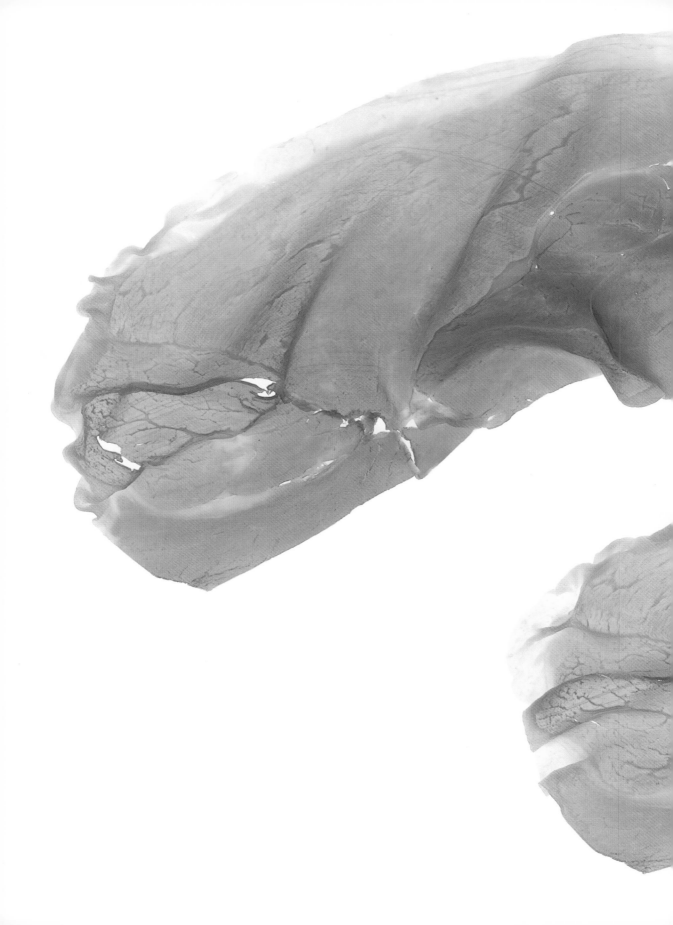

Friuli – Venezia Giulia

I was brought up in Egypt by a woman who came from a village near Gorizia on the Yugoslav border. She taught me Italian and introduced me to polenta, and because of her this eastern corner of Italy is magical for me. Friuli covers most of the region since a great part of Venezia Giulia was given to Yugoslavia after the Second World War. The Friulians are a quiet, reserved people who speak a language of their own; they complain that no one knows they are there and that everyone thinks Italy stops at Venice. Life has always been harder and the people poorer here than anywhere else in the north – many of the men go to work in Switzerland and Germany – yet the area produces the best white wines in Italy (they rival those of Alto Adige) and the sweetest, most tender pinkest prosciutto. San Daniele, a little town on a hill, has fifteen *prosciuttifici* and just the right air and humidity to dry the hams without needing too much salt to preserve them.

In this modest backwater you can still find good homemade foods. In the village of Sauris in the Carnia Mountains in the north, the people smoke the hams of their little brown pigs over the fumes that come up through the floorboards from juniper and fruit wood burning in the room below. In the Carso hills above Trieste the cured hams have hardly any fat but a great deal of flavour, and goose too is smoked. Spicy sausages such as *lujanis* and *muset* (the latter is meat from the head of the pig flavoured with cinnamon, coriander and other spices) are also produced. Mountain cheeses, called *formaggi di malga*, are made in the alpine huts used in the summer, when cows are brought to graze in the mountains; they include montasio, pendolon, tegolino and fresh-smoked ricotta, blackened, pear-shaped and with herbs. Tolmezzo is famous for these and for a much-prized breed of veal called Pezzata Rossa.

Friuli-Venezia Giulia has a fascinating and complex gastronomy because it was a zone of passage, invaded by 'tutti, tutti, tutti', where three cultures meet – Venetian, Austro-Hungarian and Yugoslav. The cuisine is further divided into primitive mountain food, the simple cooking of the plain, sophisticated city dishes and the cooking of the sea.

In the mountains, the heart of the cooking is polenta, which 'sings, snores, blows and smokes' on the fire. It is white here, from the special white maize that grows on the Friuli plain. The people pour the cooked polenta out on to a board, cut a cross on it with the ladle and eat it with salami (hot and sprinkled with vinegar), spit-roasted birds, pork, game, fish and *frico*, grated cheese cooked in a pan until it is crisp and crackling. In the autumn they live on game such as hare, partridge, pheasant, wild boar and deer, and on trout, mushrooms and wild salad leaves such as rocket and lamb's lettuce.

In the plain, people eat roast chicken, duck, goose, turkey stuffed with chestnuts and tiny pork chops, a legacy from the days when small farmyard animals, *animali di cortile*, were considered a woman's job and were raised for the family table; the men took care of the cows and sheep.

In town, pork cooked in milk and *bollito misto* (boiled meats) are eaten with *brovada*, a kind of relish of turnips fermented in marc. This relish is the most typical food of the area. Like the grand villas in Udine (the last doge, Manin, had one just outside), many dishes are a testimony to the long domination of Venice.

Soups are as important here in the north as spaghetti is in the south, and they are made with root vegetables, barley and rice and, the most popular, beans. They have risottos with herbs and vegetables, pumpkin and sausage, chicken livers and quail, frogs and snails. Little omelettes called *frittatine* are thick with vegetables and bits of sausage.

Gnocchi are part of the Austrian heritage. They are made large or small, round, square or oval, and are usually made with potatoes combined with smoked ricotta, pumpkin or aubergine and stuffed with prunes or ham. Other Germanic touches are fruit sauces with red and black currants and combinations of fruit and meat such as apples, prunes and bilberries with pork.

Throughout Venezia Giulia you get surprising taste

combinations, including marriages of sweet and sour flavours. The most stunning are to be found in the many variations of a local stuffed pasta called *cjalzons*, which is shaped like a large halfmoon. The pasta is served in broth or with melted butter and a sprinkling of grated smoked ricotta or stravecchio, and sometimes with a touch of sugar.

Near the border, towards Gorizia and Trieste, where Slovene is spoken (the area was annexed to Italy in 1918), the Austro-Hungarian influence is strongest. *Gulasch* with sauerkraut is served in beer cellars. Hare with sweet and sour sauce is another Bohemian dish. Boiled pork is cooked with mustard, and Vienna sausages with sauerkraut. At Eastertime people eat ham baked in bread with horseradish sauce. And because Trieste was a great centre for trade with the Levant (and southern Yugoslavia was part of the Ottoman Empire), it has dishes such as the Greek rice with egg and lemon sauce and pastries stuffed with dried fruit and nuts, spices and honey.

By the sea in Trieste and Grado, the cooking is very Venetian. These towns are famous especially for scampi, oysters, eels, sole, turbot and crab and their fishermen's stews. Grado's *broeto* (fish stew) is turbot and eel cooked in wine.

For dessert, pastries are popular, Austrian in style and often made with apples and cherries. The most famous are *gubana*, a crusty strudel, and *putizza*, a yeasty roll, both stuffed with walnuts, pine nuts, raisins and chocolate. And to end the meal, one of the oldest traditions in this country of fine wine, where everyone seems to make grappa (a strong alcohol spirit made from the distillate of grape pressings – skins and pips – which is sometimes here flavoured with pears, plums and peaches) at home, is to dunk little hard biscuits called *pandaluts* in your drink.

The Wines of Friuli-Venezia Giulia

Friuli-Venezia Giulia has undergone a wine renaissance that began a decade or so ago when it started producing really great wines reliably, in competition with Alto Adige.

The vine-covered hills of Friuli produce wines of the most varied types, but elegant white wines are gaining ground in response to international demand. Under a marked French influence and with new high-tech methods, producers of Collio and Colli Orientali del Friuli have developed exquisite fashionable wines that combine freshness and fruitiness with exuberant fragrance and flavour.

To the native wines – a lemony Malvasia and crisp Ribolla, the gently astringent popular Verduzzo and a personable Tocai much loved by the Friulians for its scent of flowers, liquorice and almonds and its gently acid and slightly bitter aftertaste – the producers have added some Chardonnay, Sauvignon, Pinot Grigio and Bianco, a Muller-Thurgau and a Riesling Renano of exceptional quality. Of these, the Friulians are most proud of their splendidly fruity and aromatic Pinot Grigio.

Friuli also produces two reputed dessert wines: the delicately sweet Verduzzo di Ramandolo and the legendary Picolit, which is the most expensive dessert wine of Italy.

On the plains, Grave, Aquileaia, Colli Orientali and Latisana make mellow red wines to drink young, such as Merlot, Cabernet, and the local plummy, slightly bitter red Refosco, which ages well.

FRITTATAS
Frittate

The frittata is common throughout Italy, except in Sicily and Sardinia. Piedmont is famous for its truffle frittata, Trentino for its mushroom and artichoke ones. In Trieste they are sweet, filled with fruit or jam and cream. The frittata is especially popular in Friuli, where people make great use of eggs. There, frittatas are taken to work for lunch and served as a snack in *osterie*. In most regions they are thin and pliable like French omelettes, but in Friuli they make them two fingers thick, crusty and brown outside and creamy inside. And, whereas in central Italy they are cooked in oil, here butter and sometimes still pork or goose fat are used.

ONION FRITTATA WITH HERBS
Frittata di cipolle

SERVES 4

2 large onions, coarsely chopped
3 tablespoons oil
Salt and pepper
4 eggs

4 tablespoons chopped herbs, such as oregano, marjoram, thyme, sage, parsley, mint and basil (choose 2 or 3)
15g (½oz) butter

Fry the onions gently in 2 tablespoons of oil for 20 minutes, adding salt and pepper and stirring often, until very soft and golden. Put them in a bowl with the eggs and herbs (in Friuli they use every kind of edible plant that grows wild in the fields, including nasturtium and poppy), a little more salt and pepper, and beat well.

Pour the mixture into a large non-stick frying pan with the sizzling butter and remaining oil. Cook until the bottom is set and browned and then turn over or put under the grill to brown the other side.

Variations
Use vegetables such as spinach, chard, leeks, courgettes, asparagus, peas and cabbage, previously boiled, or fried bacon, salami or pork sausage cut into pieces. Fold into the eggs with herbs and seasoning and cook in the same way.

POTATO FRITTATA
Frittata di patate

SERVES 4–6

500g (1lb) all-purpose potatoes
4 eggs
1 large beef tomato, peeled and chopped
Salt and pepper

2 tablespoons finely chopped mint
15g (½oz) butter
1 tablespoon oil

Boil the potatoes until tender, then peel and mash them. Beat in the eggs, tomato, salt, pepper and mint. Heat a mixture of butter and oil in a large non-stick frying pan and pour in the potato and egg mixture. Cook until the bottom is set and lightly browned, then do the other side by slipping the frittata on to a plate with a spatula and slipping it back into the pan upside down. Or put it under the grill to brown.

CREAM OF MUSHROOM SOUP
Zuppa di funghi

This is the way they make mushroom soup with wild porcini and ovoli up in the hills around Gorizia. A few dried porcini (which need to be soaked) give a special flavour. Out of season, the soup is made entirely with dried mushrooms. The recipe comes from Gianna Modotti, who occasionally gives cooking classes in Udine and puts people who come from abroad up at an old castle at Coloredo di Monte Albana, near San Daniele. The touch of wine and brandy is an addition suggested by the restaurant Da Toni, at Gradiscutta di Varmo outside Udine. Sour cream is part of the Austro-Hungarian influence. Gianna says you can use any mushrooms. I find that shiitakes give the best results, but ordinary mushrooms also make a good soup.

SERVES 6

350g (12oz) porcini or shiitake mushrooms
250g (8oz) potatoes
25g (1oz) butter
2–3 tablespoons olive oil
Salt and pepper
1 clove garlic, crushed
1 tablespoon flour

175ml (6fl oz) white wine
1.5 litres (2½ pints) light chicken stock (you may use 2 stock cubes)
Sprig of marjoram, finely chopped
2–3 tablespoons brandy (optional)
2 tablespoons finely chopped parsley
350ml (12fl oz) sour cream (optional)

Chop the mushrooms and potatoes very finely (I put them separately through the food processor). Sweat the mushrooms in a large saucepan in a mixture of butter and oil for 5–10 minutes, adding salt and pepper. Add the garlic and, when the aroma rises, stir in the flour. Add the wine, potatoes and stock, and stir in the marjoram. Simmer for 25 minutes, or until the broth is creamy and tastes cooked, adding more salt and pepper, if needed, and brandy, if desired, towards the end. Serve sprinkled with parsley and pass the sour cream to be stirred into each serving to taste.

PUMPKIN TAGLIOLINI
Tagliolini di zucca

Pumpkin has never found favour in Italian gastronomy until today. In the past culinary writers always seemed to deprecate this vegetable, commenting that the flavour was insipid and that it upset the humours.

It has now been 'discovered' and is very popular and fashionable in Venezia Giulia, the Veneto and Lombardy, and also in Sicily.

There are many varieties of pumpkin, with different shapes and colours, and their flavour varies, so it is important to find a good one. The toasted seeds are eaten as *passatempi*, to pass the time.

This recipe also comes from Da Toni.

SERVES 4

500g (1lb) pumpkin, weighed with the seeds and skin removed
Salt and pepper
250g (8oz) flour, or more as needed

4 egg yolks
½ onion, chopped
15g (½oz) butter
Grated ricotta salata, grana or parmesan

Wrap a quarter of the pumpkin in foil and bake in the oven at 200°C (400°F, gas mark 6) for 1 hour. Mash to a purée and season with salt and pepper.

Put the flour in a bowl with the egg yolks and pumpkin purée. Mix well and knead for about 10 minutes, until the dough is soft and elastic, adding flour if it is too sticky (the amount will depend on how moist the pumpkin is).

Wrap in clingfilm and leave to rest for 30 minutes, then roll out as thinly as you can on a well-floured surface with a generously floured rolling pin, and proceed as indicated on page 111, cutting the sheet into very thin ribbons.

For the sauce, dice the remaining pumpkin and simmer in a little salted water to cover for about 5 minutes, until just tender, then drain. Fry the onion in butter until soft and add the diced cooked pumpkin.

Boil the tagliolini in plenty of boiling salted water until al dente. Drain, mix with the sauce and serve with the grated ricotta, grana or parmesan.

POTATO DUMPLINGS
Gnocchi di patata

Potato gnocchi are a speciality of the north of Italy, and they are especially popular in Friuli, where they come in all shapes and sizes – in little balls the size of peas or large walnuts, and also in square, oval and finger shapes. Having failed more than once to make them years ago – they either fell apart in the cooking water or tasted of uncooked flour – I asked everyone on my recent trips for the secret of success, and after much experimenting I found that baking, not boiling, the potatoes results in perfect gnocchi which never fail. Because there is less moisture they need less flour and taste purely of potato. Choose mature baking potatoes which have a flaky quality. They should be of the same size.

SERVES 4

800g (1^3/$_4$lb) baking potatoes

Salt

2 egg yolks

100g (3^1/$_2$oz) plain flour

For the dressing

50g (2oz) butter, melted

Grated parmesan or grana

Wash the potatoes and bake them in their skins in the oven at 200°C (400°F, gas mark 6) for 1 hour, or until tender.

Peel and mash them while still hot, so that they are very smooth, with no lumps. Add salt, work in the egg yolks and flour, and knead well to a smooth, elastic dough.

Shape the dough into little balls: the usual way is to make long rolls the thickness of a thumb and cut them into 2cm (3/4in) segments. Press these against a grater or the prongs of a fork to mark them, so that they hold the dressing better. Place them, not touching, on a floured cloth.

Cook the gnocchi in batches in barely simmering, slightly salted water (take into account they are already salted) for at least 10 minutes. Lift them out of the water with a slotted spoon, drain well and serve with melted butter and a sprinkling of cheese.

Variations

A teaspoon of cinnamon is sometimes dusted on.

Gnocchi are often served with the sauce from a meat or duck stew.

Veneto-style gnocchi are served with 500g (1lb) peeled and chopped tomatoes heated in a pan with 2 tablespoons of butter, seasoned with salt and pepper, and finished with a sprinkling of chopped parsley. And, of course, grated cheese is passed around.

For Piedmontese *gnocchi alla bava*, put the cooked gnocchi in a very hot oven with butter and thinly sliced fontina until the cheese melts.

PUMPKIN DUMPLINGS
Gnocchetti di zucca

SERVES 4

800g (1^3/$_4$lb) pumpkin flesh

1 egg

Salt and pepper

200g (7oz) plain flour

75g (3oz) butter, melted

Grated ricotta salata, grana or parmesan

Cut up the pumpkin, wrap the pieces in foil and bake in the oven at 220°C (425°F, gas mark 7) for 1 hour, or until very tender. Mash to a paste, or blend briefly in a food processor (do not overblend). Add the egg, salt (it needs plenty) and pepper, and work in enough flour to make a firm dough.

Make dumplings by dropping the dough by the tablespoon (using another tablespoon to push it off) into barely simmering salted water. When the dumplings rise to the top, let them cook a few minutes longer, then lift them out carefully with a slotted spoon.

Drain well and serve with melted butter and grated cheese.

EELS WITH WINE AND VINEGAR
Anguilla in tegame

Eels abound in the lakes and rivers and lagoons around the coast in Friuli (they are less fatty and at their best in the winter months). They are grilled over charcoal, dipped in egg and breadcrumbs and fried, and stewed with tomatoes. This recipe is usually served with a creamy polenta.

SERVES 4

4 small eels, about 700g (1½lb), cut into 5cm
    (2in) pieces
Flour
1 onion, chopped
15g (½oz) butter
1 tablespoon olive oil
2 cloves garlic, finely chopped

3 tablespoons white wine vinegar
600ml (1 pint) dry white wine
Salt and pepper
2 bay leaves
Sprig of sage
4 tablespoons chopped parsley

Have the fishmonger gut and clean the eels, skin them if necessary and cut them into pieces. Roll the eels in flour. Fry the onion until soft in a mixture of butter and oil, then add the garlic and the pieces of eel. Turn the eel to brown it all over and add the rest of the ingredients, except the parsley. Simmer for about 20 minutes, or until the eel is tender, add the parsley and serve hot.

ROAST DUCK
Anatra arrosto

Herbs and grappa give this simply cooked duck an Italian flavour.

SERVES 4

1 duckling, about 2.3kg (5lb)
Salt and pepper
Juice of 1 lemon
1 onion, peeled

3 bay leaves, broken into pieces
Sprig of sage
2 sprigs of rosemary
4 tablespoons brandy or grappa

Sprinkle the duck inside and out with salt, pepper and lemon juice. Put the onion inside the cavity with a bay leaf and a few sage and rosemary leaves and sprinkle the rest of the herbs outside.

Bake in a roasting tin, breast side down, in the oven at 200°C (400°F, gas mark 6) for 30 minutes, then take it out and turn it over, and prick the skin all over with a fork to allow the melting fat to escape. Bake for 30 minutes longer. Remove from the oven, pour off all the fat, sprinkle with brandy or grappa and return to the oven for a further 1¼–1½ hours, until done.

APPLE PIE

Pita di mele

I ate this at Gianni Gosetti's Ristorante Roma at Tolmezzo in the mountains.

For the biscuity pastry

250g (8oz) flour

50g (2oz) sugar

Grated rind of $\frac{1}{2}$ lemon

75g (3oz) unsalted butter

1 tablespoon rum

1–2 tablespoons milk, if necessary

For the filling

700g (1$\frac{1}{2}$lb) apples, such as Golden
   Delicious, peeled and coarsely grated

75g (3oz) sugar

50g (2oz) raisins

4 tablespoons rum, or 3 tablespoons grappa

2 teaspoons cinnamon

Juice of 1 small lemon

100g (3$\frac{1}{2}$oz) walnuts, hazelnuts or almonds,
   coarsely ground

Icing sugar

To make the pastry, mix the flour, sugar and grated lemon rind. Cut the butter into small pieces and rub it into the flour until you have a crumb texture. Add the rum and work briefly with your hands into a soft dough, adding milk only if necessary. Wrap the pastry in clingfilm and let it rest for 30 minutes.

Mix all the filling ingredients together.

Divide the pastry into two pieces and make each into a ball, one of them slightly larger. Roll the larger one out on a generously floured board with a floured rolling pin and use to line the base and sides of a 25–30 (10–12in) tart pan or flan dish. Spread the filling on top and cover with the rest of the pastry, rolled out thinly. Prick a few holes with a fork and bake in the oven at 180°C (350°F, gas mark 4) for about 45 minutes, until it is a light golden colour. It will firm as it cools. Serve sprinkled with icing sugar.

CHESTNUT CAKE
Torta di castagne

I found many chestnut recipes in different regions and liked this one best. It is moist and delicious.

500g (1 lb) fresh chestnuts or 400g (14oz) frozen
   or vacuum-packed ones
300ml (½ pint) milk
125g (4 oz) best-quality bitter chocolate
100g (3½ oz) blanched almonds or walnuts

125g (4oz) unsalted butter
250g (8oz) sugar
5 eggs separated
Grated rind of 1 lemon
3–4 tablespoons strega or cognac

If using fresh chestnuts, make a long slit on the flat side of each and put them under the grill, turning them over to brown both sides, then peel them while still hot.

Simmer the chestnuts in the milk for about 10 minutes until soft, then drain and throw away the milk.

Chop the chocolate and almonds together coarsely in a food processor. Add the chestnuts and blend to a soft mass. Pour this into a bowl.

In the same food processor, cream together the butter and sugar. Add the egg yolks, lemon zest and strega or cognac, and blend well. Pour the chestnut and chocolate mixture back in and mix thoroughly. Turn out into the bowl.

Beat the egg whites until stiff and fold gently into the cake mixture. Pour into a buttered and floured 25cm (10 in) round, preferably non-stick, spring-release cake tin.

Bake in preheated 180C (350F, gas mark 4) oven for about 50–60 minutes. Let it cool before removing from the tin.

Emilia-Romagna

Emilia-Romagna

The people of Emilia-Romagna eat more, care more and talk more about food than anyone else in Italy. They like nothing better than to get together, eat, drink, tell jokes, sing and discuss the merits of dishes. Other regions describe this feel for the good life as *il culto del benessere*; it requires a strong stomach and a delicate palate. Bologna became famous for gastronomy when its university, the first in Europe, opened in the twelfth century and the city became known as Bologna *la grassa e la dotta* (the fat and the learned). The city's reputation as gastronomic capital of Italy has flourished ever since. Rich, abundant, robust, even opulent, but also elaborate and refined, the cooking of Emilia-Romagna came to represent the ideal Italian cuisine through Pellegrino Artusi's *La scienza in cucina e l'arte di mangiare bene* (The Science of Cooking and the Art of Good Eating), Italy's most famous cookery book, published in 1891 and reprinted more than a hundred times. Now simply called *l'Artusi*, it was the first book to deal with the cooking of Italy as a whole. The author, fired by patriotic fervour and the desire 'to create a national cuisine that would achieve cultural unity', developed a 'common national cuisine' from the multitude of regional ones, 'so that Italians could understand each other at table'. But Artusi came from Forlimpopoli; Emilia was his model, and its dishes, which he describes with special enthusiasm, form the bulk of his recipes. (Romagna is a separate entity from Emilia, with a different character, although for administrative purposes the two are united as one of the twenty regions of Italy.) As for the Italian south, Artusi transformed southern dishes by reducing or eliminating garlic, onion, spices and peppers and increasing the quantities of meat (he wrote for an emerging middle class who could afford it) and by adding butter and velvety sauces. He told his readers to 'make a deep bow when you meet Bolognese cooking, it deserves it'.

In the 1950s and 1960s Bolognese cooks won international prizes, but today some Bolognese gastronomes feel their cooking should be less famous. In this age of health and cholesterol awareness and dieting, there is too much emphasis on meat, charcuterie and cheese, too much use of pork fat, butter and oil and too few vegetables. Today in Emilia they are pulling out from the past dishes that Artusi would have ignored.

Emilia, with its long plain in the valley of the river Po and its rich alluvial soil, has always been the greatest food-producing area of Italy. Huge quantities of soft wheat and tomatoes are grown there, as are maize, sugar-beet, rice, onions, apples, pears, plums, quince, sweet melons, watermelons and cherries. Emilia too is the home of the biggest pasta-making, tomato-preserving and fruit- and vegetable-canning plants. But her reputation as the great gastronomic centre of Italy is based mainly on two items: *prosciutto di Parma*, the most popular antipasto in Italy, whose special tenderness, sweet delicate flavour, enticing perfume and pale pink flesh marbled with pure white fat have made it famous all over the world; and parmesan cheese, the most essential ingredient in Italian cooking.

According to legend, Hannibal, on his way to fight the Romans, was served raw cured ham at a banquet in Parma in 217 BC. Now it is a large industry involving about 250 firms, but the old artisan methods of treating and curing continue. The pigs, a cross between an English and a Danish breed, grow voluminous legs in eleven months on a mixture of whey and maize, barley and soya flour. By law, hams can be branded with the ducal crown of Parma only if they are taken from this variety of pig raised in northern Italy and fed on controlled foods and if they are cured in the traditional manner in a strictly defined zone.

The hams are trimmed, brushed and polished; a few, especially those for export, are also boned. Otherwise, retailers do this themselves in order to slice the ham very thinly by machine. The hams are salted and left for a few weeks in a very cool atmosphere while much of their liquid drains away; then they are washed and allowed to dry out and mature for ten to twelve months. Only just enough salt to draw out the water and prevent fermentation is used, so the hams are only slightly salty. At a certain height, the hills of Langhirano outside Parma have the ideal climate, neither too dry nor too humid, with cool winters and breezy, perfumed air. The cool ventilated environment, once controlled by the opening and closing of special long thin windows, is now technologically reinforced.

Apart from prosciutto, there is a whole world of cured meats and salamis to be discovered in Emilia. Zibello and Busseto make the highly prized *culatello*, from the best part of the buttock, matured in the bladder of the animal; *fiocco* or *fiocchetto*, from the top of the leg; and *spalla cotta*, boiled shoulder. *Coppa*, fillet in sausage skin, and pancetta, unsmoked bacon, are specialities of the region around Piacenza. Bologna is known for mortadella. Zampone, stuffed pig's trotters; *cappello da prete*, the lower part of the leg, treated with salt, garlic and spices and sewn up in the shape of a triangle; and cotechino, a strongly flavoured boiling sausage, are specialities of Modena. One of the best salamis comes from Felino. Ferrara is known for a *salame da sugo* made with ground pork, liver and tongue, enriched with spices and red wine. It was thought to have aphrodisiac qualities and it is still served at wedding parties. A selection of salamis and cured meats served with bread or grissini or a plate of prosciutto accompanied by slices of melon or ripe figs is the usual way to start a meal.

For years Parma and Reggio nell'Emilia, the two great centres of parmesan cheese, battled over the name. (In reality the cheese was born in the Val d'Enza in the province of Reggio but it was first sold through Parma.) The controversy was finally settled with the official, double-barrelled Parmigiano-Reggiano. The king of the hard grana-type cheeses, it holds its lofty position by keeping the highest possible standards. Here, too, there is a defined and jealously protected production zone, with requirements specified by law and a consortium to control and guarantee quality.

The production method has not changed for seven centuries. The cheese is made from a mixture of morning and evening milk from cows fed on fresh green grass and clover between mid-April and November. (The rest of the year, when the cows eat hay, they produce a paler cheese of slightly lesser quality called vernengo.) The evening milk is left in shallow basins overnight to allow the cream to rise. This is removed (it is used for making butter) and the skimmed milk is mixed with the full-fat morning milk (that is why parmesan is a semi-fat cheese) and boiled in huge copper vats with kid rennet as the curdling agent.

No preservative or antifermenting substance is used. When it separates, the whey is sent off to the pigs and the curds are broken, then drained in large cloths and pressed into great rounds. As soon as it is firm the cheese is left to float in brine until it has absorbed the right amount of salt, then the huge drums of cheese, weighing up to 40kg (88lb), are aged for two or three years. They are regularly turned and cleaned so that each side is properly aired.

The cheese can be eaten after a year, when it is *nuovo*. It is 'opened', not cut, so as not to spoil the grainy texture, and is chipped at with a small knife. It is golden, with a delicate fragrance and a rich, delicious flavour. Only recently has parmesan been discovered as a dessert cheese and appetizer – one of the best in the world. For its traditional role, grated over pasta, soups and rice (its special quality is that it melts without producing threads), and to take on a more piquant flavour, it must wait another year to become *vecchio*, or old, and another to be *stravecchio*. At Peck, a Milan food shop, there is parmesan aged for seven years, but many Emilians don't approve, believing that the cheese goes downhill after the third year. Grated parmesan is used so much that it has been called the vice as well as the backbone of Italian cooking.

One of Emilia's great strengths is a vast range of pasta first courses. This is the land of fresh egg pasta. Purists roll it out by hand, as machines make the dough too smooth for the pasta to hold sauce well. About 500g (1lb) of flour is worked with four eggs (saffron-yellow yolks in spring give the prized golden look), first with the fingertips and then with the palms of the hands, into a ball. The dough is rolled out with a long slim rolling pin into a sheet, or s*foglia*, which should be so thin you can see through it. The sheet is folded and cut into thin ribbons to make tagliatelle or into rectangles for lasagne. The pasta is sometimes made green with spinach or nettles, which have become fashionable (in the past they were used by the poor in the countryside). Stuffed pasta is a world in itself, with different shapes – little hats, scarves, rings, twists, butterflies, little squares, big squares, triangles, rounds, half-moons – different names and an astonishing variety of fillings.

For Bolognese tortellini, the king of this world, a square is folded into a triangle, then the triangle is wound into a ring on the end of the little finger and the points stuck together so it resembles a tiny headscarf. The filling is a mixture of veal and pork cooked in white wine with added ham and mortadella, garlic, rosemary and pepper, all finely minced and worked into a paste with a little egg, grated parmesan and a pinch of nutmeg. I have watched women prepare millions of these in restaurants – it is always women, standing up, laughing and gossiping, making an art of each one. The tortellini are served *in brodo* (in a meat or chicken broth) or with meat sauce, the famous Bolognese ragù (the origin of our Bolognese sauce, which is never, ever served in Bologna with spaghetti).

Here are descriptions of a few other fillings, as examples of just how elaborate, refined and varied Emilian cooking can be. Parma's anolini are filled with the sauce from *stracotto*, a beef stew cooked for hours in red wine, mixed with breadcrumbs, egg and grated parmesan; its *tortelli alle erbette* have a mixture of ricotta with beet greens, spinach or Swiss chard; and its *anolini di magro* are filled with cheese and egg and perfumed with herbs and spices. Modena's ravioli are filled with a variety of roast meats, finely minced and delicately flavoured. The cappellacci of Ferrara are stuffed with pumpkin, potato and cheese; the cappelletti with brains and minced turkey breasts. *Tortelli di zucca* are filled with pumpkin, parmesan and crumbled amaretti biscuits. You also find tortelli filled with game, pork, raisins and cheese, with mushrooms and with a mixture of chestnuts and carrots flavoured with mustard. All are marvellous and none is new: a fourteenth-century cooking manual discovered in Bologna University's library contains a description of *ravioli alle erbe*.

The various stuffed pastas are served in broth, with meat sauce or simply with melted butter (sometimes a few sage leaves are thrown in when the butter is heated, to give a faint aroma). In recent years, fresh cream has been used frequently as a pasta sauce, but purists believe it deadens the delicate flavours. Parmigiano-Reggiano is always passed around. Any cheaper grana padano is detected and spurned. In Modena tortellini go into a *pasticcio*, a sweet-crusted pie, with a meat sauce, a light béchamel and sometimes wild mushrooms and truffles. The combination of sweet with savoury is a legacy of the Renaissance.

Another triumph of Emilian cooking is the *fritto misto*, a grandiose assortment of morsels breaded then deep-fried, which is served as an antipasto in winter. There can be sweetbreads, liver, brains, veal, chicken pieces, chicken livers, slices of cheese, and prosciutto sandwiches soaked in milk and called *bocconcini*; extraordinary mixtures of liver, ham and cheese with truffles, bound together with a thick béchamel sauce, rolled into balls and threaded on to skewers; and vegetables such as artichokes and cardoons made into fritters, courgettes cut into sticks, and sweet things such as apple slices, macaroons, and cream croquettes. After this there can be little room for anything else.

But traditionally an antipasto is followed by a *minestra* (soup), then by a pasta dish such as tagliatelle or lasagne (Emilians are masters of this famous classic). There may also be a risotto. Emilia does not have many, but the *riso e tardura*, rice cooked in meat broth dressed with beaten egg and parmesan, and the *bomba di riso*, which is turned out of a mould and has a filling of chopped pigeon in mushroom sauce, are very popular.

Then come the meats. The *costoletta alla bolognese*, the famous veal cutlet, is stuffed with cheese and thin slices of truffle, floured or breaded and fried in butter, then covered with a layer of raw ham and a layer of cheese, and finally baked, sometimes with tomato sauce. *Filetti di tacchino* or 'Duchessa di Parma' are turkey breasts treated in the same way.

Stracotto is in the great tradition of Italian stews. The meat is cooked for up to five hours until it practically falls apart; it is rich with the flavours of gentle spices such as cinnamon, cloves and nutmeg and constantly replenished (because evaporated) red wine. *Arrosti* (roasts) may be pheasant, duck, chicken, veal, rabbit or hare, wild boar or baby pig, flavoured with garlic and rosemary and doused with white wine. Some meats are cooked *in due tempi*, first boiled then roasted. *Bollito misto* (mixed boiled meats), a speciality of Modena, is a great dish served with pomp. Few now make it at home because families are just not large enough for the amount of meat it requires. In restaurants *bollito misto* is brought to the table on a silver trolley; here you'll find boiled beef, chicken, ham, veal tongue, calf's head, zampone (pig's trotter) and cotechino (pork sausage), all left soaking in their broth to keep juicy and tender. They are served in good hearty slices, accompanied by an assortment of sauces and pickles; these include *salsa rossa*, made with tomatoes; *salsa verde*, a piquant green sauce with garlic and parsley; *mostarda di Cremona*, fruits preserved in syrup with a little mustard essence; *peperonata*, made with fried peppers; and *cipolle all'agro*, onions cooked in vinegar. Also served is *savor* (the name comes from *sapore*, flavour), a mostarda made in Carpi in the province of Modena; it contains pears, apples and quince cooked in boiled-down fermented grape must.

Favourite vegetables of the region are spinach, beet greens, Swiss chard, cardoons, cabbage, courgettes, pumpkin and potatoes; a usual way of preparing them is *alla parmigiana*, baked with parmesan. There are sweet onions, greenish radicchio, green beans, spinach and more tomatoes than anywhere else in Italy. *La vecchia* (literally, the old woman) is a dish of roasted peppers; asparagus is eaten with oil and lemon; artichokes are eaten raw, boiled or fried; cauliflower is dressed with vinegar; courgettes are stuffed. Chestnuts, which grow wild in the Apennines, are eaten boiled or roasted; *la pattona* is a cake made with chestnut flour. In the area around Piacenza, walnuts are used to make a sauce for pasta.

Emilia-Romagna is mushroom and white truffle country, and in season their perfume pervades many dishes. Dried mushrooms, which have a stronger flavour than fresh ones, are used for sauces throughout the year. The Apennine hills have some of the best mushrooms in Italy and in the autumn great feasts are held featuring them. The mushrooms are eaten raw, marinated with oil and lemon juice and sometimes sprinkled with truffle shavings, grilled, fried with garlic and parsley or stewed with tomatoes or wine. Porcini (*cèpes* or boletus) and the egg-shaped ovoli (Caesar's mushrooms), white outside and red inside, are local favourites. Dried mushrooms are used for pasta and meat sauces and for risottos.

In the old days, despite the rivers, there was never much fish cooked. As I was told, 'Who had time to fish?' The really poor ate polenta, sliced and then grilled on the fire, pork fat, also grilled on the fire, salted herrings, snails, frogs, chestnut cakes and fritters.

Gargantuan banquets that lasted days, with songs, dances, music and games, are constantly featured in tales of Bologna's past. Great feasts, with thirty different dishes and an extraordinary, even bizarre presentation (game birds dressed to look alive, their beaks set alight), were at their peak during the Renaissance and in the baroque period, when table setting and table manners were a refined art. The table remained a symbol of power and status, and there was always a ceremonial dimension to Bolognese cooking.

Now, most people want to make life easy for themselves and to lighten things, and they go out to the trattorias to eat what they can no longer be bothered to make. But civic events still have the old-style pomp and grandeur. I attended one that seemed to have come out of a Renaissance print – there were long tables set in a square with a fantastic display of lemons and arrangements of feathered game and all kinds of foods in the centre of the hall. Restaurants have a double menu, one for 'creative cooking' and one for Bolognese dishes. There are a hundred confraternities of people whose purpose, apart from conviviality, is to uphold the standards of one particular food, such as *fritto misto* or tortellini. Members go on group tastings and complain if, for example, the broth in which the tortellini are cooked does not have golden globules of fat swimming on the surface (some restaurants remove fat).

In today's Communist-governed Emilia-Romagna, the great old dishes are offered at a subsidised price at the annual Communist Festa dell'Unità. The feasts are held by all the political parties for a week each summer in the parks and streets of every district and are as much gastronomic as political events. Members donate their skills and their produce and, so they say, the same people can be spotted at the Christian Democrat Festa dell'Amicizia, the Socialists' Festa dell'Avanti and the Fascists' Festa del Tricolore as well as the Festa dell'Unita', savouring the cappellini and tortellini, lasagne, *bolliti misti* and *arrosti* dished out from movable kitchens or prepared on open fires.

At a banquet in a trattoria outside Bologna, a large crowd, including Communist Party officials, industrialists, a journalist and an army general, recalled for me the daily ritual observed up to the last war, as it had been for hundreds of years. Lunch on Monday, Tuesday, Wednesday, Thursday and Saturday was always a mountain of tagliatelle with meat sauce that had simmered away all day, followed by fruit. For supper there was sausage or meat, mostly pork, usually cooked with onions, garlic and tomatoes. Those who sold ham cut it for themselves on summer evenings. Friday, when people could not eat meat, was bean day: the smell of boiling borlotti wafted out of every kitchen window. For lunch some beans were mashed and turned into a soup with maltagliati, odd-shaped pasta, and tomato sauce. In the evening the rest of the beans were dressed with oil and vinegar and served with hard-boiled eggs. Once in a while Friday featured salt cod in tomato sauce or dipped in batter and deep-fried.

For Sunday lunch, people boiled a piece of beef with a bone and a tomato. Those who could added a chicken. Tagliolini, little pasta squares, were added to the broth for the first course, and the boiled meat was the second. Only on Sunday was there dessert. It was always a *ciambella*, a sweet shortcrust shaped in a ring or made into a tart and filled with jam. For the evening meal, homemade tomato sauce was added to any left-over meat; in winter cardoons were boiled, then dipped in batter and deep-fried. *Fritto misto* was a Saturday or Sunday dish for the well-to-do, who might also enjoy an occasional rabbit or hare, duck or chicken, roasted or cooked *alla cacciatora* with the same ('blessed', they called it) tomato sauce flavoured with rosemary and parsley, the favourite local herbs.

On festive days such as Christmas, New Year's, Easter and Ferragosto (15 August), people made the famous tortellini in broth. The meat and capon that had been boiled to make the broth were then roasted in the oven with garlic and rosemary. Dessert would be a *ciambella* or half-moon-shaped *ravioli di San Giuseppe*, made with the same shortcrust and stuffed with the same jam as the *ciambella*; the sweet ravioli were baked and immersed, straight out of the oven, in liqueur, or a thick syrup of boiled-down grape must, and then sprinkled with sugar. Apart from these, fresh fruit or dried fruit and nuts were always served. Such sweets as *torta di riso*, a rice cake made with milk, almonds and crystallised fruit; *zuppa inglese*, layers of sponge cake soaked in liqueur; custard; chocolate pudding; and *fior di latte*, a crème caramel in which the caramel is absorbed right through the cream, were made for weddings and baptisms. At wedding and baptism celebrations, people ate until they 'almost died'.

The provincial cities of Emilia-Romagna – apart from Ferrara and Ravenna, they are all on the Via Emilia, which was built by the Romans and runs through Bologna, Modena, Reggio nell'Emilia and Parma, all the way to Piacenza – have kept their own traditions, a mixture of grand style and simple farmhouse cooking. Their history was one of Roman and Byzantine domination, rule by Longobards and Franks, episcopal domination and a long period of free communes until these gave way, around the fourteenth century, to *signorie*, rulerships by a single family. They were not all-powerful families as in Tuscany and Lombardy, but small local nobility. The most important were the Este and the Farnese families. In this period of Renaissance splendour cooking also reached great heights of magnificence. Dishes were recorded by Cristoforo de Messisburgo, who was in charge of the Este household, in his sixteenth-century treatise *Banchetto, composizione di vivande e apparecchio generale* (Banquet, Composition of Dishes and General Utensils).

Ferrara has many elegant, delicate dishes that originated in the princely court of the Este family: *pasticcio*, a pasta pie filled with meat sauce, wild mushrooms and white truffles; prawns cooked in a delicate wine sauce; and courgette-flower fritters. Ferrara's bread, *coppietta*, is said to be the best in Italy. But what really makes Ferrara's cuisine distinctive is a range of dishes originating from her once-important Jewish community: *prosciutto d'oca*, smoked goose;

buricchi, large ravioli stuffed with minced chicken (without the usual pork); *ciccioli d'oca*, deep-fried goose scraps and crackling; *l'hamin*, egg noodles dressed with goose fat, raisins and pine nuts; *polpettone di tacchino*, turkey loaf; and a vast range of marzipan sweets and deep-fried holiday desserts such as *coppette* and *pignolate*. It is from the Jews that the Ferrarese learned to make sturgeon's caviar.

Parma was capital of a duchy under the Farnese family lordship and briefly under Bourbon princes with Spanish and French connections; the duchy was given to Maria Luigia (Marie Louise), the estranged second wife of Napoleon, after the Congress of Vienna in 1815. It is a noble city, an artistic city (Antelami and Correggio worked here), a musical city (Verdi and Toscanini were here) and an industrious city. Its culinary traditions are born of its produce, butter, ham and cheese. Cooking *alla parmigiana* means with cheese and sometimes with cured ham; this method has been adopted all over Italy. Asparagus, artichokes and aubergine are cooked with cheese, and truffles are warmed in oil with shavings of cheese. The pig is almost sacred. Pork is grilled, roasted, boiled, stewed with tomatoes and cooked in milk. Everything is used – feet, ears, liver, bladder, guts. There is a saying in Parma, 'The pig is like Verdi's music, there is nothing to throw away'.

Game dishes such as hare *in salmì*, quail cooked in rice, pheasant, woodcock, partridge, thrushes – roasted, stewed or cooked with cream – are part of Parma's court traditions. The nobility turned the hills into a game reserve. Many dishes, such as turkey breasts *della duchessa* and *tagliatelle della duchessa*, with fried chicken livers and beaten eggs and cheese stirred in at the end, are named in honour of Maria Luigia, who is said to have been as fond of food as she was of men. The duchess, who was Austrian (her father was Emperor Francis I), brought chefs from France and pastry cooks from Austria, so now Parma has pastries such as *bignè*, *millefoglie*, *St Honoré*, *bavarese*, *charlotta* and *Krapfen*.

From the countryside come dishes such as *torta fritta*, bread cooked on a griddle, eaten hot and crisp with raw ham; polenta, which is poured out on a wooden board, cut with a thread and served with fried onion and cheese or with salami heated up with vinegar; *caval pist*, raw minced horse meat; snails boiled with lemon and vinegar, then fried in butter with tomatoes, garlic and herbs; frogs' legs cooked in tomato sauce, deep-fried or marinated in vinegar and preserved in oil; kidneys sautéed in butter with a little wine vinegar; tripe cut into thin ribbons and cooked with tomatoes, onion and garlic; and rabbit and chicken, roasted or stewed with tomatoes.

Parma's most famous dish, *tortelli alle erbette*, is special to the night of 24 June, when the *rugiada di San Giovanni* (dew of St John the Baptist), a feast commemorating witches, is held. The great liqueur of the Po valley, dark brown *nocino*, slightly bitter and made with green walnuts, is also linked with the *rugiada*. By tradition the nuts are picked on 24 June at dawn, when they are still damp with dew. They are marinated in pure alcohol with cinnamon, cloves and lemon peel for forty days, then the liquid is filtered, mixed with sugar syrup and left to age for a year.

Modena is famous for its zampone sausage, the emblem of Modenese cooking; for amaretti; for cherries in alcohol made in nearby Vignole; and for *aceto balsamico*, balsamic vinegar. In the past, balsamic vinegar was made at home by wealthy landed families who had vineyards, people to boil up the grape must, attics to keep the barrels (they need to be in a ventilated place, not a wine cellar, so that the vinegar can reduce by evaporation) and who could sit on their capital. It took at least twelve years to produce a good vinegar, and it was the kind of thing you passed on to your children and grandchildren and started as a dowry for your daughter when she was born. The habit was almost lost when the system of *mezzadria* (sharecropping) was abolished and country life was transformed. But a competition for the best balsamic vinegar at the Fair of San Giovanni in the village of Spilamberto in 1966 reawakened the passion the people of Modena still kept in their hearts. Now the vinegar industry has become important, with exports all over the world, especially to America.

To make balsamic vinegar, grape juice with crushed skins and seeds is allowed to ferment just long enough for the right amount of alcohol, sugar and acidity to develop; the juice is then filtered and boiled down in huge copper vats to a third or a half of its original volume. A little caramel is produced in the process, which gives a bittersweet flavour and an amber colour. The boiled-down grape must (*vin cotto*) is then mixed with strong wine vinegar and starts a long ageing process (I tasted some that were thirty and eighty years old) and a voyage from one wooden barrel to another. There should be at least five barrels of different woods – the more the better – so that each can give its own special aroma. Oak, chestnut, juniper, ash, locust, acacia and fruit woods such as cherry, apple, pear and mulberry are used. People starting an *acetaia* sometimes look for old marsala or cognac barrels. Every year part of the vinegar from each barrel is transferred to another, and gradually it becomes more concentrated, darker (the dark luminous brown can get almost black), denser, almost like a syrup, and develops a rich sweet and sour flavour and seductive perfume.

It is said that balsamic vinegar was made in Roman times and that the Este court raised it to the level of an art. It was thought to have medicinal properties. That is why it is called *balsamico*. A drop goes in an olive-oil dressing; on strawberries; with fried liver, kidney, pork, veal or duck; into frittatas. What you find cheaply on the market is a far cry from the real thing. There is not yet a consortium to guarantee standards.

Romagna is very different from Emilia: the people speak differently, for one thing. On a train journey some Romagnols explained to me that it was because they had been part of the Papal States from 1278. They were poor while Emilia was rich. The popes in the old days had been tyrants, so traditionally the people of Romagna are anticlerical. All in the carriage revealed they had not had their children baptised. In contrast, the predominantly Communist Emilians are said to be ecstatic when the Pope visits. Culturally, Romagna is more like the neighbouring Marches.

It is a small world of wooded mountains, fertile plain and sea coast where foothills gradually give way to harsh rocky mountains. Villages sit on top of hills. Towns such as Rimini, Cesena, Forlì and Faenza stand on the Via Emilia, where five rivers flow down the mountains to meet them. There is a sense of lost greatness and ancient glory about them and about Ravenna, port of entry for the Eastern Roman Empire. Gleaming mosaics, mausoleums, basilicas and convents testify to the Greek, Roman and Byzantine presence. The words of Boccaccio and Dante echo here. Romagna made a special impression on Dante, and his poems have given the petty nobles, the brigands of the Apennine passes and the corrupt *signori* immortality.

Now the tourist industry on the coast has brought prosperity, but Romagnols remember working hard in the fields only thirty years ago, and they know the harsh life of the mountains. Where the Emilians are peaceful, the Romagnols are rebellious fiery, prickly. Their traits are reflected in their cooking. Emilia's dishes are buttery and velvety, with delicate flavours. Romagna's are rough and simple with strong earthy flavours: they use plenty of onion and garlic, masses of herbs and hot red pepper, and olive oil, not butter. Romagnols enjoy many Emilian dishes and they do have their own dainty dishes, such as tortelli stuffed with mashed pumpkin and potato, and cappelloni filled with local squaquaron or raviggiolo cheese or with chopped turkey and supposed to look like the headgear of the nuns of San Vincenzo. *Frittelloni*, served in the area around Ravenna, are little tortelli filled with spinach, raisins and cheese, deep-fried and served hot, sprinkled with icing sugar.

But theirs is really poor peasant food: *piadina*, unleavened bread made of flour water and lard, baked on a metal sheet over a fire; beans with maltagliati, so-called 'badly cut' pasta; handmade flour-and-water pasta and *minestre*, soups. Garganelli are squares of pasta rolled around a stick and patiently pressed one by one *sul pettine* (literally, on a comb), which gives them a ribbed surface. *Passatelli* is a dough made with fine breadcrumbs, eggs and cheese that is turned into curly, thickish vermicelli and cooked in broth.

The Romagnols have made an art of the grill; everything goes on it – fish, chicken, veal chops, rabbit, game, meat, sausages and *castrato* (castrated mutton whose flesh becomes extraordinarily fat and tender). *Porchetta* (roast baby pig) has come from the other papal states.

In a large expanse of salt marshes in the northern hinterland is Comacchio, a little town built on a group of thirteen islands intersected by canals and bridges; it is a centre of eel fishing and eel cooking, and splendid eel soups and stews are made here.

And there is the cooking of the sea. The Romagnols have a great variety of fish and are famous for their *mistigriglia* (a mixed grill) and fish soups that contain just about everything from the sea. Romagnol dishes such as flour-and-water pasta and cakes and fritters made with mountain chestnuts, which people stopped eating in the 1960s because they were considered too poor, are now back in fashion.

The Wines of Emilia-Romagna

The wines of Emilia-Romagna are not the most outstanding nor the most varied, but they are pleasing and refreshingly easy to drink and they have a digestive quality (it is said they also reduce cholesterol) which makes them well suited to the rich, heavy local cooking and to meals with many courses. They are mainly bubbly *frizzante* wines; whites are made from the local Malvasia, Trebbiano and Ortrugo grapes and the reds with Lambrusco, Barbera and Bonarda.

Emilia's jewel is the greatly produced and much exported Lambrusco. An unpretentious, simple rustic wine which must be drunk young, it is fresh, vivacious and scented. Lambrusco is a family of vines which produce wines of widely varying styles from slightly petulant to sparkling, from dry to semi-sweet, from dark purple to light pink. Modena is their capital and there are zones for varieties called Sorbara Grasparossa di Castelvetro, and Salamino di Santa Croce (it is called *salamino*, small salami, because of the thin cylindrical shape of the bunch of grapes). Lambrusco Reggiano produced in Reggio Emilia accounts for most of the exports. Lambrusco has become famous in its frothy, *amabile* (semi-sweet) variety, but locally they prefer the dry ones.

Romagna's best wines, from the plains of the Po basin, are still. Sangiovese di Romagna is a good earthy grapey red that ends in a bitter bite which can be aged. Albana di Romagna, considered one of Italy's best whites, has a hint of almonds in its delicate mellow flavour and can be dry or semi-sweet, *frizzante* or *spumante*.

A PLATE OF PROSCIUTTO AND SALAMI
Antipasto di salumi

Emilians are not keen on antipasto generally. Old sayings condemn them as *la morte del pranzo* (the death of the meal) and *la malizia degli osti* (the hosts' trick), implying that a host who fills his guests with antipasto may not have much to offer in the way of main courses. But a few slices of prosciutto or local salami are a must.

For a party, have a well-chosen selection of two or three of these arranged on a large plate, accompanied by bread and butter and grissini.

PROSCIUTTO WITH FIGS OR MELON
Prosciutto con fichi o melone

SERVES 4

12 paper-thin slices prosciutto

4 ripe figs, or 1 ripe melon, cut into wedges and with seeds removed

Lay the slices of prosciutto out on a large platter and arrange the figs or melon beside them. Serve with grissini or bread.

MUSHROOM SALAD
Funghi crudi

This salad is made with different types of wild mushrooms such as porcini and ovoli, but you can try it with other mushrooms.

SERVES 4

500g (1lb) mushrooms

6 tablespoons olive oil

Juice of 1 lemon

Salt and pepper

Clean the mushrooms and slice them thinly. Beat the oil with the lemon juice, salt and pepper, pour over the mushrooms, mix well and let them macerate in the dressing for 30 minutes before serving.

Variations

Sprinkle with finely chopped parsley or with truffles or parmesan shavings.

In Piedmont they add crushed garlic and finely chopped anchovies to the dressing.

TOMATOES STUFFED WITH ONIONS AND HERBS
Pomodori ripieni alla cipolla

Emilia is the greatest producer of tomatoes in Italy. Most of them go into cans. This antipasto is one way they use them in the countryside to make the most of their sweet, fresh flavour.

SERVES 4

8 small tomatoes

2 medium sweet onions, red or white, or 12 spring onions, very finely chopped

1 clove garlic, crushed

3 tablespoons finely chopped parsley

3 tablespoons finely chopped basil

2 tablespoons or more olive oil

Salt and pepper

Wash the tomatoes, cut a slice off the top of each to form lids, scoop out the seeds with a teaspoon and discard. Mix together the onions, garlic, parsley, basil and olive oil, and season to taste. Fill the tomatoes with the mixture and cover them with their lids.

SPINACH SOUP
Minestra di spinaci alla modenese

SERVES 6

700g (1½lb) fresh spinach, or 275g (10oz) frozen spinach, defrosted

50g (2oz) butter

Salt

Pinch of nutmeg

4 eggs

5 tablespoons grated parmesan

1.75 litres (3 pints) stock

Wash the spinach and remove the stems. Cook the leaves in the butter in a saucepan with the lid on, adding a little salt and nutmeg and turning them over occasionally, until they crumple. Cook frozen spinach in the same way for 5 minutes until tender. Chop finely by hand or in a food processor. Beat the eggs together with the grated parmesan and add to the spinach.

Bring a well-flavoured stock to the boil, turn down the heat and, just before serving, beat in the spinach and egg mixture. Leave the soup on the heat for 1–2 minutes, beating in the mixture vigorously until the soup turns creamy: the eggs must not be allowed to curdle and spoil the texture.

Serve accompanied by toast.

FRESH EGG PASTA
Pasta fresca all'uovo

Fresh pasta, rolled out by hand or made industrially (*pasta sfoglia*, or sheet pasta), belongs traditionally to Emilia-Romagna, Tuscany, Liguria, Piedmont and Lombardy. Despite the industrial production of fresh and dried pasta, and although young women will not do it now, the tradition of rolling pasta out by hand continues – and nowhere more than in Emilia, which is the true home of egg pasta. It is so appreciated there that most restaurants employ a *sfoglina* – a woman who rolls out the pasta and makes tagliatelle, tagliolini, lasagne, tortellini and pappardelle once, or even twice, a day.

Until recently all the regions had different ways of making pasta dough with varying ratios of flour and eggs, more or less water, and a little oil or milk. Piedmont used egg yolks with the flour while Romagna in the south used only flour and water. In Alto Adige they add milk instead of water. Although the old differences persist in some places and the old 'poor way' of making dough with only flour and water has come back into fashion, the richer flour-and-egg dough, in the manner of Emilia, has been adopted all over Italy.

Their old cookery books give the quantity of dough by the number of eggs, adding 'as much flour as it takes'. Nowadays the quantity given per egg is 75g (3oz) flour, but in reality this varies according to the type of flour, the size of the eggs and their freshness.

The manner of rolling out and cutting the dough also differs. In Mantua they use a rolling pin 1.2 metres (4 feet) long, the *matterello mantovano*. Around Alba and the Langhe in Piedmont, they cut their sheet of dough very thinly with a knife to make *tajarin*, while in Tuscany they cut it into wide strips to make pappardelle. Apulians cut it with a *ferro da maccheroni*, a metal roller with cutting disks. In the Abruzzi they cut the sheet by rolling it on top of a *chitarra*, a kind of loom with wire threads. Apulia, Basilicata and Calabria all make the same triangular lagane, but maltagliati vary from place to place. They are long, thin diamonds in Mantua, while in Emilia, Lombardy and the Veneto they are small and rhomboid. In the manner of cutting, too, Emilian ways have won over the country because Emilia is considered mistress in the field.

Many people now roll the dough out with a machine. Rough rollers are preferred: the pasta does not come out too smooth and it holds the sauce better. There are many kinds of manual and electric pasta machines that roll out and also cut pasta very well that you might like to try.

SERVES 4–6

400g (14oz) flour

Pinch of salt

4 eggs

Put the flour and salt in a bowl (traditionally it is piled in a mountain on a marble slab, but it is easier to use a bowl). Make a well in the centre and break in the eggs. Work the flour into the eggs with a fork and continue with your hands until the ingredients are well mixed, adding a tablespoon or more extra flour if necessary, so that the mass holds together well.

Knead for 10–15 minutes until the dough is smooth and elastic, adding a little more flour if it is too sticky. Wrap in clingfilm and leave to rest for 15–30 minutes at room temperature before rolling out.

Divide the dough into two balls for easier handling. Roll each out as thinly as possible on a lightly floured surface with a lightly floured rolling pin, working from the centre outwards. With experience you should be able to roll it out evenly, almost paper-thin, without breaking it.

Leave to dry for 20 minutes before cutting.

To prepare noodles such as tagliatelle, tagliolini, fettuccine and pappardelle

Fold the sheets of pasta over and over. With a sharp knife cut into ribbons about 0.5cm (¼in) wide for tagliatelle, narrower for tagliolini and fettuccine and wider for pappardelle. Open out the rolls of noodles and let them air for 5–10 minutes. Cook in plenty of boiling salted water (see page 18).

To prepare ravioli and other stuffed pasta

In various recipes for stuffed pasta you'll find throughout my book, I have given different methods for making them, but the following are the most common and you can use them for all the recipes.

Roll out two fairly thin sheets of dough. Dot one with evenly spaced mounds of filling. The amount of filling is a matter of preference: these days people like to make rather large stuffed pasta with plenty of filling. Brush the spaces in between with egg yolk beaten with a drop of water, and cover with the second sheet. Press with your fingers around the mounds of filling to stick the dough together, and cut the pasta into squares with a pastry wheel by cutting parallel lines between the mounds. If you want to make 'rounds' of pasta, space the mounds of filling a little further apart and cut around them with a round biscuit or pastry cutter.

You can also use a ravioli tray which is like a baking sheet with square hollows. The first sheet of pasta is placed over it and pushed gently into the hollows. The filling goes into these hollows and egg yolk is brushed in between. The second sheet of pasta is placed on top and rolled firmly up and down with a rolling pin. The whole thing is turned out of the tray and cut into squares with a pastry wheel.

Let the stuffed pasta rest for an hour or so, then cook, a few at a time, in boiling salted water for 3–4 minutes.

GREEN PASTA

Pasta verde

SERVES 6

250g (8oz) fresh spinach, or 125g (4oz) frozen
   spinach, defrosted

400g (14oz) flour

Pinch of salt

3 eggs

Wash the fresh spinach and cook in the water that clings to the leaves, turning them over until they are limp and crumple in a soft mass. Drain and squeeze as dry as you can, then reduce to a purée in a food processor.

Put the flour in a bowl with a pinch of salt and make a well in the centre. Drop the eggs in, then the spinach, and work the flour with your hands until you have a soft dough that holds together well. Knead for 10–15 minutes, leave it to rest wrapped in clingfilm for 30 minutes, then roll out thinly as for Fresh Egg Pasta (above).

TORTELLI WITH CHEESE AND SPINACH BEET OR SWISS CHARD
Tortelli alle erbette

This is my favourite Parma dish. The tortelli are ravioli cut quite large with plenty of *code* (literally, tails), that is, with a large border of dough, so they do not take long to make and do not open. The name *erbette*, which means herbs, is mystifying and restaurateurs like to be mysterious about the filling. Actually, it is made with spinach beet, and the name comes from the dialect *arbetta*, derived from the Latin *herba beta* (spinach beet) and not from *erba* or *erbetta* (herbs). If spinach beet or Swiss chard are unavailable, you can use the different kinds of spinach found in supermarkets. You will understand at once the difference between a great dish and industrial ravioli sold by the yard.

SERVES 4–6

Fresh Egg Pasta (pages 110–111) made with 3 eggs
    and 300g (10oz) flour
500g (1lb) Swiss chard, or 300g (10oz) frozen
    spinach, defrosted
250g (8oz) ricotta

1 egg
Pinch of nutmeg
Salt and pepper
50g (2oz) butter, melted
50g (2oz) freshly grated parmesan

Roll the dough out very thinly.

To make the filling, boil the Swiss chard for 4–5 minutes, or until tender, drain thoroughly and squeeze out all the water. If you are using frozen spinach, boil in water to cover for 5 minutes, then drain and squeeze out the water. Chop finely, then blend with the ricotta, egg, nutmeg and seasoning.

Cut the dough into strips about 10cm (4in) wide. Place small balls of filling on half the strips of dough about 5cm (2in) apart, moisten around the filling with water, cover with the rest of the strips, cut into separate squares or rectangles using a pasta wheel and press the edges firmly to seal them. Or use the method for ravioli (page 111) and make them large.

Cook the tortelli in boiling salted water for 5 minutes until al dente, drain and serve with melted butter and grated parmesan.

LASAGNE WITH MEAT SAUCE
Lasagne al forno

SERVES 8

For the meat sauce
1 onion, finely chopped
1 carrot, finely chopped
1 stalk celery, finely chopped
50g (2oz) unsmoked bacon, chopped
75g (3oz) butter
125g (4oz) minced beef

125g (4oz) minced pork
500g (1lb) tomatoes, peeled and chopped
250ml (8fl oz) dry white wine
Salt and pepper
125g (4oz) chicken livers, coarsely chopped
125g (4oz) prosciutto, finely chopped

For the Lasagne
Fresh Egg Pasta (pages 110–111) made with
    175g (6oz) flour and 2 eggs

50g (2oz) grated parmesan

For the béchamel sauce
40g (1½oz) butter
3 tablespoons flour

500ml (18fl oz) milk

Fry the onion, carrot and celery (they can all be chopped together in a food processor) with the bacon in half the butter until the onion begins to colour. Add the minced beef and pork and fry, stirring, for 3 minutes. Add the tomatoes and cover with wine, then season with salt and pepper, and simmer for at least 1 hour, adding water if necessary so as not to let it become too dry. The sauce should be just moist and there should not be any liquid left. Mix in the chopped livers and prosciutto.

Make the béchamel sauce. Melt the butter in a saucepan, stir in the flour, and very gradually add the milk, stirring constantly so that lumps do not form.

Prepare the pasta. Make three balls of dough and roll them out thinly, then cut each into three rounds or rectangles the size of your baking dish. Boil the sheets of pasta one at a time in plenty of salted water and lift out when still very firm. As each is done, drain and lay out on a cloth.

Butter the dish, arrange a sheet of pasta in the bottom, spread with a layer of meat sauce, cover with a few tablespoons of béchamel sauce and sprinkle with a little grated parmesan. Repeat with the second sheet of pasta, sauces and grated parmesan and finish with the third sheet covered with béchamel and dotted with the remaining butter. Bake in the oven at 200°C (400°F, gas mark 6) for 30 minutes, or until browned. Serve very hot.

Variations
For green lasagne use Green Pasta (page 111).

GORGONZOLA SAUCE FOR PASTA
Salsa al gorgonzola

This is not a traditional sauce, but it is very good and very easily made. For four servings, melt 15g (½oz) butter in a saucepan, add 250g (8oz) gorgonzola and crush it with a fork. Add 200ml (7fl oz) double cream or milk and stir until well blended, adding pepper and a touch of nutmeg. Serve mixed well with pasta.

BOLOGNESE MEAT SAUCE
Ragù di carne alla bolognese

SERVES 6

50g (2oz) butter
2 tablespoons olive oil
1 medium onion, finely chopped
1 medium carrot, finely chopped
1 stalk celery, finely chopped
25g (1oz) diced mushrooms (optional)
125g (4oz) pancetta or unsalted bacon, finely chopped

350g (12oz) minced beef, pork or veal, or a mixture
300ml (½ pint) dry red wine
Salt and pepper
4 tablespoons tomato paste
300ml (½ pint) meat stock
150ml (5fl oz) double cream

Heat the butter and oil in a deep saucepan, add the vegetables and fry until they soften and brown lightly. Add the pancetta and minced meat and fry until the meat changes colour. Moisten with wine, simmer until it evaporates, then add seasoning, tomato paste and a little stock. Cook slowly, covered, stirring occasionally and gradually stirring in all the stock.

After 1½ hours, stir in the cream and cook, uncovered, until reduced. Serve with tagliatelle.

FETTUCCINE WITH PROSCIUTTO AND CREAM
Fettuccine con prosciutto di Parma e panna

SERVES 4

400ml (14fl oz) double cream
125g (4oz) prosciutto, cut into thin strips
75g (3oz) freshly grated parmesan
2 egg yolks

Pepper
700g (1½lb) fresh fettuccine, bought or homemade
    (pages 110–111)

Place the cream, ham, half the parmesan and the egg yolks in a large bowl, season and stir until thoroughly blended. Warm the sauce by standing the bowl in a pan of boiling water.

Cook the fettuccine in salted boiling water until al dente, drain, add to the sauce and mix well. Serve with the rest of the parmesan.

EELS IN TOMATO SAUCE
Anguilla in umido

SERVES 4

4 small eels, weighing about 700g (1½lb)
1 small onion, chopped
15g (½oz) butter
1 tablespoon olive oil
1 clove garlic, crushed
500g (1lb) tomatoes, peeled and chopped
300ml (½ pint) dry white wine

Salt and pepper
1 teaspoon sugar
Pinch of nutmeg
1 bay leaf
A few sage leaves
A few celery leaves, chopped
2 tablespoons finely chopped parsley

Have the fishmonger clean and gut the eels and cut them into pieces. All you need to do is wash them in cold running water.

Fry the onion in a mixture of butter and oil until soft and golden, then add the garlic, tomatoes and white wine. Season with salt, pepper, sugar and nutmeg, add the bay leaf, sage and celery leaves and simmer for about 10 minutes. Put in the eel and cook gently for about 10 minutes longer, or until the fish is done.

Serve hot, sprinkled with parsley, accompanied if you like by polenta.

VEAL SCALOPPINE
Lombata di vitello

SERVES 4

700g (1½lb) veal scaloppine
Seasoned flour
1 egg, beaten
175g (6oz) dry breadcrumbs
50g (2oz) butter

4 thin slices prosciutto
25–50g (1–2oz) parmesan, roughly grated or shaved
    with a potato peeler
4 tablespoons double cream
4 tablespoons chopped parsley

Place each piece of meat between sheets of greaseproof paper or clingfilm and flatten with a rolling pin until very thin. Dip in seasoned flour, then in egg, and coat with breadcrumbs. Melt the butter in a frying pan. When foaming, add the breaded scaloppine and cook for 1 minute each side until brown.

Put the meat on a baking sheet. Top each piece with a slice of prosciutto, cover with parmesan, and pour 1 tablespoon cream over each one. Put under the grill until the cheese is melted and golden. Serve sprinkled with parsley.

Variation
Turkey cutlets treated the same way are called 'Duchessa di Parma', named after the duchess who liked them.

ZAMPONE WITH LENTILS

Zampone con lenticchie

Zampone (stuffed pig's trotter) is a speciality of Modena. It is like a coarse boiling sausage and needs at least 2 hours' cooking. Zampone sausages available in the UK are precooked and need to be boiled for only 20 minutes.

SERVES 4

350g (12oz) brown or green lentils, soaked for 1 hour

1 onion, finely chopped

2 cloves garlic, finely chopped

1 stalk celery, finely chopped

1 slice bacon, chopped

2 tablespoons olive oil

A few sage leaves, finely chopped

Salt and pepper

1 zampone

Drain and rinse the lentils. You can finely chop the vegetables in a food processor. Fry the onion, garlic, celery and bacon in the oil until the onion begins to colour, then add the lentils and sage leaves. Cover with water, and simmer until the lentils are tender (the time varies but it generally takes about 20–25 minutes), adding water as it becomes absorbed. Add salt and pepper when the lentils have begun to soften.

Cook the zampone and serve very hot, cut into slices, on a bed of lentils.

Variations

Zampone is served also with spinach and mashed potatoes or with a savoury zabaglione sauce made as for the zabaglione on page 41 but without sugar and using dry white wine with a touch of salt and balsamic vinegar.

BOILED CAPON OR CHICKEN

Cappone lesso

Put a capon or chicken in a large saucepan, cover with water and bring to the boil. Remove the foam, add salt and pepper, 1 stalk celery, 1 carrot and 1 onion, and simmer for 1–2 hours, or until very tender. Keep the capon or chicken covered in broth. Serve hot or cold with the green or red sauce (recipes follow) or both.

EMILIAN-STYLE GREEN SAUCE

Salsa verde emiliana

SERVES 6–8

350g (12oz) flat-leaf parsley

25g (1oz) fresh basil leaves (optional)

One 50g (2oz) can anchovies

3 tablespoons capers

2 cloves garlic, peeled and crushed

1 tablespoon finely chopped shallots or onions

4 tablespoons white breadcrumbs

3–4 tablespoons white wine vinegar

120ml (4fl oz) olive oil, or more as needed

Process all but the oil in a blender or food processor, then slowly trickle in the oil to make a smooth green sauce. If it is too thick you can dilute it with a little more oil.

Variations

You can use lemon juice instead of vinegar; add a teaspoon of prepared mustard; omit the breadcrumbs to make a thinner sauce; add tiny pickled onions or 1–2 finely chopped pickled gherkins after the sauce is blended.

EMILIAN-STYLE RED SAUCE
Salsa rossa emiliana

SERVES 4

1 onion, finely chopped
1 red pepper, chopped
2 tablespoons olive oil

4 tomatoes, peeled and cut into pieces
Salt
Hot chilli powder to taste

Fry the onion and pepper in the oil in a saucepan until very soft but not coloured. Add the tomatoes, salt and hot chilli powder (it should be quite peppery) and simmer for 30 minutes, or until reduced to a thick sauce. Serve cold.

BAKED FENNEL WITH CREAM AND PARMESAN
Finocchi gratinati

SERVES 4

1kg (2lb) fennel bulbs
Salt
Butter to grease the dish

Pepper
2–3 tablespoons grated parmesan
300ml (½ pint) double cream

Remove and discard the tough outer leaves of the fennel, quarter the bulbs and simmer in salted water until very tender but not floppy. Drain well and arrange the pieces in one layer in a generously buttered baking dish. Sprinkle with salt, pepper and parmesan and pour the cream on top.

Bake in the oven at 200°C (400°F, gas mark 6) for 15–20 minutes, or until golden brown. Serve sizzling hot.

APPLE FRITTERS
Frittelle di mele

SERVES 6

175g (6oz) flour
2 eggs
150ml (5fl oz) milk
4–6 tablespoons grappa or rum

Grated rind of ½ lemon
Sugar
6 large dessert apples, peeled, cored and sliced
Sunflower oil for frying

Blend the flour, eggs, milk, grappa or rum, grated rind and 2 tablespoons sugar. Leave to rest, covered, for 1 hour.

Dip the apple slices in the batter and deep-fry until brown, turning them over once. Drain on absorbent paper towels and serve hot, with sugar.

Note

You can marinate the apple slices in a mixture of grappa and sugar for 10 minutes before cooking.

CREAM CUSTARD
Panna cotta

SERVES 4

300ml (½ pint) double cream
2 tablespoons sugar, or more to taste

About 8 drops vanilla essence
1 teaspoon powdered gelatine

Simmer the cream with the sugar and vanilla for 2–3 minutes. Dissolve the gelatine (do not use more, or the cream will be rubbery) in 2 tablespoons cold water and beat well into the cream. Pour into a little serving bowl or 4 small ramekins. As the cream is very rich, small portions are best. Chill for a few hours until set.

RICE CAKE
Torta di riso

1 litre (1³⁄₄ pints) milk
175g (6oz) Arborio rice
Pinch of salt
150g (5oz) sugar
50g (2oz) blanched almonds
2 eggs, separated
Grated rind of 1 lemon
50g (2oz) diced candied orange peel and citron

4 tablespoons pine nuts
1 teaspoon vanilla essence
¹⁄₄ teaspoon almond essence (optional)
Butter to grease the cake tin
Fine dry breadcrumbs
4 tablespoons maraschino (optional)
Icing sugar (optional)

Boil the milk in a heavy saucepan, add the rice, salt and half the sugar and simmer gently for 20–30 minutes, stirring occasionally, until the rice is tender and the milk absorbed. Let it cool. Toast the almonds and chop them finely. Beat together the egg yolks and the rest of the sugar, add the rice, lemon rind, candied orange peel and citron, pine nuts, almonds, vanilla and almond essence, if using. Beat the egg whites until stiff and fold in.

Pour the whole mixture into a 25cm (10in) springform tin, buttered and coated with breadcrumbs. Bake in a preheated oven at 175°C (325°F, gas mark 3) for about 1 hour, or until brown on top. Let the cake cool, then prick it all over and pour on the optional maraschino. Leave for 24 hours, then remove from the tin and dust all over with icing sugar, if desired.

Tuscany

Tuscany

Everyone who has discovered her splendid cities and churches, her art and countryside, has fallen in love with Tuscany and with the dishes that evoke its tender climate and brilliant light, the gentle harmony of contrasting hills and valleys, vineyard and rock, squat silver olive trees and slender dark cypresses and the pastel hill towns we see in the background of paintings by artists such as Masaccio, Uccello, Fra Angelico, Fra Filippo Lippi and Piero della Francesca.

The greatness of Tuscan cooking is an idea deep in Italian minds, bound up with the reverence they feel for the region that produced so many of their geniuses, that generated so many of their ideas about art, literature, science, politics, individual liberty and love, and whose vernacular became their standard language.

In the fifteenth century Tuscany glittered with splendour. Florence dominated the region and stood above all the capitals in other Italian states. She was one of the wealthiest cities: a mercantile city of artisans, bankers and traders (they dyed silk, minted coins, traded in wool cloth, incense, pearls and gems), and also a city of intellect and passions, the powerhouse of the Renaissance, whose influence was felt all over Europe.

The wealth and splendour of the ruling Medici family, the goings-on at Palazzo di Via Larga, Palazzo Vecchio and Palazzo Pitti fascinated Europe. When the French came to Florence for the nuptial celebrations of King Henry IV's marriage to Maria de'Medici in 1599 they were stunned by the embroidered tablecloths, ornate china, sparkling Murano glasses and glittering silver settings, the flowers and golden vines and the sugar sculptures that decorated the table. On the great day, twenty-four different cold dishes were served as a first course, eighteen hot ones as a second, ten more as a third, and as a fourth there were fourteen plates of raw vegetables, cheese and fruit, followed by nine sweets.

It is part of Italian folklore that France learned most of her dishes from the Italians when their future King Henry II married Caterina de'Medici in 1533. Caterina took a retinue of cooks with her to France, and they are supposed to have revolutionised the cooking of the Parisian court. French *canard à l'orange* is said to be Florentine *papero alla melarancia*; the *omelette* none other than the Florentine *frittata*; *pieds de porc* (pig's feet) are *peducci di maiale*; the *vol au vent* is the Florentine *turbanata di sfoglia*; and *caille au raisin* (quail with grapes) is a descendant of *starne coll'uva*. *Pain d'épice*, or gingerbread, was first called *pain de Pise* (literally, bread of Pisa). But Tuscans are among those who are dubious about such claims. Caterina was only fourteen when she married and her mother was French and partly German. The cooking at the Florentine court and in noble houses in the Middle Ages was international, and by the sixteenth and seventeenth centuries French cooking had become the standard and most of the cooks were French. They wrote their menus in French and were called *monsieur*. And France had long-established cooking traditions and was already known as 'the mother of cooking'.

The Italians did have *some* influence in the French kitchen. They brought sorbets and ice creams and fruits preserved in syrup, ideas for pastry-making, like frangipane cream, rice cake and macaroons (pastry-making had just arrived in Florence and Caterina sent for pastry cooks) and also pasta. They made vegetables and fruits such as artichokes, melons and pumpkins fashionable. Forks were introduced, glasses replaced goblets, sugar sculptures (an art developed in Venice, inspired by the glassblowing) appeared. Platina of Cremona's cookery book, *De honesta voluptate* (with many French recipes), translated into French in 1505, was in vogue again during Caterina's reign.

The Florentines also brought manners and refinement to the French court. A sonnet writer, Giovanni della Casa, set out rules of courtesy and good manners in his book *Il galateo*: 'When you are eating do not masticate noisily or crouch gluttonously over the food without raising your head. That is not eating but devouring, and then you soil your hands and even your elbows and dirty the cloth.' He exhorted people to avoid spitting, not to offer a neighbour a morsel already bitten, not to sniff another person's food or point with a fork or put a leg on the table, nor to get drunk. The French considered the Italians too refined (the English traveller Thomas Croyate, who visited Paris in 1608, wrote that forks were almost unknown there, and Louis XIV, who became King of France in 1643, still ate with his hands, while Florentines had started observing table manners in the twelfth century).

But the most important impact the Florentines had was to bring simplicity and frugality to the gothic opulence and disorder of the French court. Tuscans liked natural food undisguised by sauces and elaborate artifice. They hated excess. The Medicis might have offered spectacular banquets and hospitality, but for themselves they were frugal. Dante had described Florence in the fourteenth century as sober and modest, and that is what she was. There was always a streak of austerity in Florence, even during the pleasure-loving and luxurious fifteenth century when sumptuary legislation forbade people from having more than forty guests for dinner and more than three courses. The Florentines never liked extravagance and always liked their own good food. When eventually there was no money and no place for the French cooks in their kitchens, the *monsieurs* went away, leaving little behind but *besciamella* and *maionese*.

As far back as the eighth century BC, the Tuscans' Etruscan ancestors were known for their sobriety. But Etruscan paintings show banquets and revellers with happy smiles; men and women sitting together on beds, eating; game hanging in the kitchen; people cooking steaks and chickens opened out flat on the fire (Tuscans still do this today). You can see they valued the good life.

Because it was enclosed – bounded in the east, north and west by the Apennines and the Tyrrhenian Sea – the region has formed a kind of political entity since Etruscan days. In the fourth century BC the Etruscans were subdued by the Romans. Christianity came in the fourth century AD and in the fifth the Roman Empire crumbled. Despite strict rules and asceticism, convents and monasteries contributed to a flowering of the culinary arts as cultivators and animal farmers; and they gathered a nucleus of cooks and artisans around them. Later Tuscany became part of the Holy Roman Empire which had transferred to the Germans. After that there were continual wars fought by the cities for their independence from the German emperor and the popes. By the eleventh century the cities had become very industrious and also prosperous. Communes came into being and for a time there was intercity rivalry, and wars involving Pisa, Lucca, Pistoia, Siena, Volterra, Florence and Arezzo. Cooking started to become interesting after the twelfth century, and between 1300 and 1600 it reached a golden age.

Tuscany was different from other Italian states in that a kind of equality prevailed. All the people – noblemen, merchants and even peasants – were citizens with political rights, and all more or less shared in public life. The landowning nobility did not live in castles. As soon as a merchant became well-off, he invested some of his money in farmland, often with a small villa where his family spent the hot summer months. The slopes of the surrounding hills were dotted with such villas and there was a perpetual two-way traffic between town and country. Everyone was tied to the land. The farms were run according to the *mezzadria* system, whereby proprietor and cultivator shared the profits. The first contract of *mezzadria* was made between a landed bishop and a peasant in 759 at Lucca and this system survived until the 1960s, by which time the produce was shared half and half.

The estates produced olive oil and wine, wheat, maize and fodder, all kinds of vegetables and fruit trees and small farm animals such as chickens, ducks, rabbits and pigs. There were sheep and in the two large valleys, the Val di Chiana and the Maremma, they raised cows – native breeds, massively built and pure white. Sixteen families, numbering as many as three hundred people (there were several generations), lived as *mezzadri* on some of the large estates.

In the 1960s farm workers began to work regular hours and were paid a regular wage, but most still abandoned the land for the factories. Landowners, finding themselves without workers, sold their properties cheap. People from Milan and Rome, and foreigners, mostly British and American, bought farmhouses as holiday homes. Entrepreneurs from the north came to farm in a modern intensive way. A few cottage industries producing tomato juice, vegetables in oil, jams and fruit preserves developed. Sardinian shepherds purchased a large part of the pasture lands and brought their sheep over from the island on boats. They still produce their own pecorino and ricotta, maintain their traditions and their way of life and keep very much to themselves.

Tractors and machinery were introduced and changed the landscape. The old agriculture of intermingled vines, mulberry and olive trees on the hill slopes (it is called 'promiscuous' agriculture), the little patches of wheat, maize, cereals, legumes and fodder, where the large families of *mezzadri* had spent their days fighting their way through the entanglements to pick everything by hand, were replaced by a more specialised agriculture. Trees were cut down, several fields were made into one, bushes were separated, to allow machines through. A few small farmers continue in the old archaic way of varied mixed cultivation, and their bit of landscape has remained like the background in Renaissance paintings, but the rest has changed.

Country life has changed dramatically, but the old dishes never disappeared and now they are very much in fashion; even the creative innovative cooking is based on them. Tuscan cooking is entirely rustic. The landowners and nobility were always frugal, even austere and parsimonious (many jokes are told about their stinginess), and farmhouse cooking is what they always liked.

The *fattoressa* (farm manageress) cooked for the labourers (usually about twenty-five), who walked for up to one and a half hours to get to the farm each day. During olive- and grape-picking time they slept at the farmhouse. The landowners lived in town, but they would eat only their own produce. Twice a week the farm manager brought them home-grown produce and when they went to the country they ate what the *fattoressa* made: soups, pasta, beans, salad, vegetables, grilled or roast meats.

Tuscan cooking is the simplest in the whole of Italy, but it is not poor; at its best it can be exceptional. What makes it so good is the presence of wine and olive oil, the use of herbs, especially sage, rosemary and basil, and the cooking methods: grilling over chestnut and vine embers and deep-frying in olive oil. Writers describe it as sincere and serene. It is also refined. Everything is produced locally and is of superb quality and the ingredients are always fresh.

Local hams are small, lean and salty, larded with the fat that lies under the skin. They also make boar hams, which have a strong flavour, and *coppiette* (literally, courting couples) made of beef, pork or boar cut into strips, seasoned with salt, ginger and plenty of pepper, dried and smoked, then tied in pairs. A favourite salami is *finocchiona*, flavoured with fennel seeds. It is cut by hand into thick slices and served with Tuscan bread, which is made without salt.

Not much cheese is made in Tuscany (the cows produce hardly any milk) other than sheep's-milk pecorino. The most famous is the oval marzolino produced in the heart of the Chianti region which is eaten fresh or ripened and can be grated. Tomato paste is rubbed on the surface of those that are ripened (once sheep's blood was used), so they have a reddish tinge. The woodland produces a few truffles, both black and white, and plenty of mushrooms. Cutigliano has a market for porcini, ovoli (Caesar's mushrooms) and *spugnola* (morels).

Chestnuts growing wild have been a staple of Tuscan cooking for centuries, and there is a whole tradition of specialities based on fresh and dried chestnuts and chestnut flour. Like polenta in the north, these nuts once provided the food for the very poor, and because of the memories they evoked, they have not been popular in the recent past. But they have made a come-back. Since huge numbers of chestnut trees have been cut down or killed by what is called the 'American disease', chestnuts have acquired the status of a delicacy. In the old days peasants collected them in the woods, put them on latticed shelves and lit a fire to dry them out, and they made their own chestnut flour. Fresh chestnuts were either roasted or simmered whole in salted water with fennel seeds or in milk flavoured with sugar and cinnamon, and then eaten hot. They went into soups with beans or rice. Chestnut flour was used to make a thick mush like polenta and in a whole variety of foods from *necci*, rosemary-flavoured waffles cooked over the fire and eaten hot with ricotta, and fritters, to sweet cakes and the centuries-old *castagnaccio*, born around Lucca, which is made with rosemary, pine nuts and raisins, and no sugar.

The most important ingredient of the region is olive oil, which is used as much for cooking as it is raw and which enters into almost every dish. It is lighter, paler and more delicate than in the south; it can be yellow, gold or green. The spicier, more pronounced piquant flavour is sought when it is to be used raw. This flavour should be intense but mellow and should not grate the throat (it may seem too strong for those who prefer a blander taste). Apart from being used as a dressing for salads, olive oil is poured over bread and vegetables and goes into soups and stews just before serving. For cooking, a blander flavour, which will not dominate the dish, is preferred.

Tuscany produces very little olive oil in comparison to Apulia but it is of very high quality, partly because the olive trees are situated on hillsides and get the full benefit of the sun. In 1985 a great frost and a freezing north-easterly wind, which blew for a week, killed fifty to seventy-five per cent of the olive trees – on the hilltops up to ninety per cent. Snow protected the vines, but the olive trees were more exposed. Now many of the large producers have had to become blenders, using oils from other parts of Italy (and sometimes other countries), striving to find the combination which will reproduce the characteristics of their own lost oil.

Olive oil varies like wine. Its character is determined by the type of tree, the soil on which it grows, the position (on hill, plain or coast), the weather, when and how the olives are harvested and how quickly they are pressed and by which means. Many of the commercial oils are chemically refined and rectified and some are mixed with seed oils. To be sure of their oil, Tuscans go to grower-producers for their supplies. Olive-picking begins around November when the olives are not yet ripe (they are green at first and gradually turn purple-black), and harvesting continues for several weeks. The best oil comes from less ripe olives. It is pea green but turns paler after three months and is more piquant than oil made from riper olives where the yield is greater.

The best way is to pull the olives off by hand. Tuscan trees have huge branches pruned inside so you can climb in. Great nets are sewn together and held up with stakes to catch the falling olives. The branches are sometimes beaten with sticks, and machines like combs, which rip off leaves and twigs, then separate them, are also used (though it is not easy to use machines on slopes). In these last methods the olives get bruised, and since they spoil quickly (oxidation brings acidity), they must be cleaned and washed and pressed within twenty-four hours. Growers take their olives to a local press where they are sure to get their own oil back (at the communal press you wait to make sure you do not get someone else's). Mills used to be stone; now they are steel rollers. The olives (including stones) are ground to a paste which is then processed hydraulically to extract the oil and liquids. These are then separated centrifugally and the pure oil that comes out is what is called a 'first pressing, cold-pressed olive oil'. Factories buy the pulp and press it again, using heat and boiling water: this is called 'second pressing', and the result is fattier and more acidic. Big oil merchants blend this with virgin oils to make branded oils. They can remove the acidity by a chemical process and produce a standard flavour.

The finest oil is cold-pressed extra-virgin. A consortium protects the standard of the extra-virgin label, but it classifies only by acidity and does not specify how the oil was made or whether it was rectified. Extra-virgin must have less than 1 per cent acidity (the best has 0.5 per cent acidity). Then, in descending order of quality, come superfine virgin, fine virgin and virgin. The last can have up to 4 per cent acidity. Tuscans are so concerned with quality that they are prepared to pay very high prices for the best, believing that it makes the dish.

Larger cities in Tuscany were independent city-states in medieval and Renaissance times, and each has its own special dishes. Pisa was a naval power. Its specialities include black cabbage soup, pasta and chickpeas, and a curious dish of newborn eels fried with garlic and sage which is sometimes baked with an egg, lemon and parmesan mixture. Newborn eels are called *cieche* (blind ones) because they are caught on winter nights with lamps that blind them as they start swimming upriver at the mouth of the Arno. Eels are also simply sautéed in olive oil with sage and garlic. Another Pisan speciality, *torta coi bischeri*, a pastry, made on 28 April for the Feast of Pontasserchio, is filled with creamy rice, chopped candied fruit, chocolate, raisins and pine nuts and flavoured with nutmeg and liqueur (the *bischeri*, or fools, are the pine nuts). Lucca is famous for a leavened pastry ring made with milk and marsala. Arezzo features *acquacotta* (literally, cooked water), a soup with fried onion and tomato, and egg and cheese beaten in at the end; *frittata affogata*, a tomato omelette; *fagiano con crema e tartufi*, pheasant sautéed in oil with bacon and a little cognac, and finished with a cream sauce and truffles; and *saporetto*, chicken giblets sautéed with egg, lemon and ginger. Leghorn (Livorno) has *cacciucco*, a soup with a great mixture of fish, tomatoes, garlic, white wine, sometimes a faint taste of ginger, and bread at the bottom; another soup is *bavettine sul pesce*, in which chopped or mashed fish is added to a broth together with thin noodles (bavettine). There are also *bordatino*, a beautiful red bean and black cabbage soup, and *bianchetti coll'uovo*, newborn, jelly-like sardines and anchovies in a creamy mixture of egg and lemon. Specialities of Grosseto are *zuppa di tartaruga* (turtle soup) and *zuppa d'agnello* (lamb soup), which uses the heart, liver and lungs, and plenty of onions and bread.

The cooking of Siena has a link to ancient Etruscan civilisation and to its own medieval past, when *arrosti* (roasts) belonged to the rich merchants and *bolliti* (boiled foods) to the people. The medieval love of spices is still reflected in many Sienese dishes – *panpepato* (spiced or peppered bread), *salsiccia secca* (dried sausage) and *panforte di Siena*, the famous pastry full of nuts and candied fruit, perfumed with spices – the kind of sweet people could take on the Crusades. Siena is also known for simple things such as *pici*, pasta with olive oil and toasted breadcrumbs, and risotto with artichokes.

The main influence in the Tuscan kitchen is the cooking of her chief city. The most famous and most important Florentine dish is *bistecca* (steak) or *costata* (another cut) *alla fiorentina*. It is a thick T-bone steak, weighing about 500g (1lb), grilled over charcoal. Cooking over wood embers is an art in Tuscany. There are those who believe the meat must be salted and peppered and brushed with a drop of olive oil before it is cooked and those who think all that should be done afterwards, but everyone likes the meat *al sangue* (rare). The meat comes from the Chianina breed of cows, native to the Val di Chiana, which is considered the best in the world. It is tender and flavoursome *vitellone* – red meat somewhere between beef and veal, from an animal slaughtered when between sixteen months and two and a half years old. Another, less highly prized meat used outside Florence is of the Maremmana breed. Other Italian regions are fond of white meat; in Tuscany the ideal is red.

Second place belongs to *pollo alla diavola*, chicken split open and flattened, marinated with olive oil and lemon juice or white wine, perfumed with sage or rosemary and sometimes with garlic or ginger, and then grilled. The black chickens from San Giovanni Valdarno and Montevarchi are ideal for grilling, while the white chickens of Leghorn are good for boiling and lay delicious eggs. The Florentines also grill various chops and skewered meat rolls, pork, livers wrapped in caul, sausages and loin prepared with rosemary and garlic.

Soups are very important in Tuscany. The most famous is *ribollita*, which includes a long list of vegetables, among them black cabbage and beans (the beans are often left-over ones and the soup itself is boiled and reboiled – hence its name). *Pappa al pomodoro* is broth with bread, tomatoes and often basil cooked to a porridgy consistency. A less common soup is *cinestrata*, a broth made with marsala, thickened with beaten eggs and dusted with cinnamon, nutmeg and a little sugar. It is said to be a Renaissance soup, as Renaissance cooking featured mixtures of sweet and savoury. There are also chickpea soups made with spinach, beet greens or pasta and tomatoes, and there are many bean soups.

Little white cannellini beans boiled with rosemary and cooked *all'uccelletto* (with tomatoes) or served with olive oil are so common that they are said to be the ambassadors of Tuscan cooking. People in the town of Lari near Pisa claim to have invented *fagioli al fiasco*, beans cooked in a flask in the ashes of a fire. That method is seldom used now; today the beans are cooked in a saucepan.

Favourite pasta dishes are *pappardelle con la lepre*, wide ribbon noodles topped with hare cooked in wine with fried bacon and tomatoes, and *pappardelle aretine*, the same noodles served with duck. *Pasticcio alla fiorentina* is a Renaissance-style sweet-crusted pie filled with short macaroni and meat sauce, sometimes perfumed with truffles.

In the past, game was reserved for landowners. *Mezzadri* and other labourers were forbidden to catch or eat game (at a trattoria in Florence older men remembered how poachers used to be whipped in a public square). Before a hare went to the master's table, the peasants collected its blood and made a sauce for their pasta. *Lepre in dolce e forte* – hare cooked in wine and tomatoes with raisins, pine nuts, candied orange peel and a long list of aromatics – is another Renaissance dish. Game birds are cooked *in salmì*, stewed in broth with marsala and juniper berries. The many tripe dishes, such as *trippa e zampa*, with calf's foot, onions and tomatoes, white wine, garlic and nutmeg, are peasant foods.

Favourite vegetables are artichokes, asparagus, spinach, cardoons, beans, broad beans and peas. They are cooked in oil with tomatoes or with bits of prosciutto or bacon, or are dipped in batter and deep-fried, or used in omelettes. Cooked spinach makes a bed for poached egg and for sole.

Apart from the usual seafood found all around Italy, the Tyrrhenian coast has its own cooking traditions. They say it is because in the past, as was not the case in other parts of the coast, there were colonies of fishermen who had not been frightened away by pirates. The coastline was too straight and the land too marshy (it was reclaimed in the eighteenth century) for pirates, and the Tuscans were able to defend themselves. There are also specialities of the lagoon and freshwater fish, especially trout and eel, in the Arno.

Fruit comes at the end of the meal, along with hard biscuits to dip into sweet vin santo. One of only a few desserts is *zuccotto*, a moulded dessert with an outer layer of sponge cake soaked with brandy and sweet liqueur and a filling of cream mixed with cocoa powder, almonds and hazelnuts.

What gives eating in Tuscany a particular charm is the central Italian habit of eating and chatting together, elbow to elbow, at long tables. I had a taste of it in Florence when I was there one August and all the grand restaurants were closed. I was directed to Da il Latini, via dei Palchetti 6, a *trattoria-fiaschetteria* where everyone knows everyone and where so many of the regulars are poets that they give a poetry prize every year: a meal and a whole ham to take home. It was through the *trattorie toscane* that inundated Milan and the north of Italy after the Second World War that the fresh light Tuscan dishes, so different from the rich, heavy foods of the north, became widely popular in Italy.

The Wines of Tuscany

There has been a great transformation in Tuscan wine-making over the past ten years. Many of the *cantine* are now among the world's best equipped and most dynamic. Ancient traditions, nineteenth-century styles and the most modern oenological experimentation, helped by blessed conditions, have created some of Italy's most exciting wines. In what is sometimes described as Italy's renaissance in wines, the raspy, thin varieties, which decades ago represented Italy in the famous straw-covered flasks, have been replaced by wines of superior balance and depth.

Chianti of course is the archetypal Italian wine. Since 1985 its quality has improved immensely. It is made from a traditional blend of four grapes, the chief one being Sangiovese, which grows profusely all over Tuscany, the others being the local Canaiolo Nero, the white Trebbiano, and Malvasia. Now sometimes a little Cabernet Sauvignon is added. Chianti country spreads through a large area over the Tuscan hills. Chianti Classico is the term applied to wine produced in the historically delimited zone of Central Tuscany beginning just below Florence and ending just before Siena. Chianti wines differ markedly from one another depending on the varied zones, soils and microclimates, and the individual styles of producers. They can be everything from a sharp young rough red, light and easy to drink, which is sometimes slightly prickly on the tongue and has an attractive cherry and raisin taste, to a complex, austere, full-bodied wine of great finesse. These are the *riservas* which are made from the best grapes and aged in the cellars of ancient castles and villas. The wines come out with an intense bouquet reminiscent of violets, iris and tobacco, and a herby flavour which combines pepper, liquorice and raisins. New methods of vinifying and ageing also manage to preserve a fruitiness, which can include strawberry, raspberry and blackcurrant flavours, and to eliminate some of the acidity and tannin.

Other traditional Tuscan reds, based on Sangiovese clones, are made from different grape blends. The most aristocratic and expensive of Italian wines, Brunello di Montalcino, is from a fortified hill town south of Siena, which also makes a younger and very much cheaper Rosso di Montalcino. Vino Nobile di Montepulciano is another rich, strong, velvety, long-ageing wine.

One of the marvellous recent developments in the Chianti region has been the gradual emergence of the Cabernet Sauvignon grape as a component of red wines. Carmignano makes a delicious marriage between the soft, clear blackcurranty fruit and the stark flavours of Sangiovese; and Pomino, from the commune of Rufina, uses Cabernet and Merlot with Sangiovese and Canaiolo to make a soft, velvety wine which becomes increasingly rich and spicy as it ages.

Tuscany is red wine country, but there are a few notable whites. Vernaccia di San Gimigniano, from the multi-towered medieval hill town, is a wonderful modern wine made from an ancient grape, the Vernaccia, which was imported from Greece in the twelfth century. Montecarlo Bianco from the hills east of Lucca is a blend of old Italian and French grapes which can be slightly peppery with hints of hazelnuts and angelica. Moscadello di Montalcino is fresh and delicate with the wonderful flavours and aromas of Muscat grapes. Off the coast, the island of Elba makes the well-known very sharp Procanico.

What has brought most excitement and lustre to Tuscan wine-making in recent years has been the new prestigious unclassified (non DOC) wines, such as the prize-winning Sassicaia made almost entirely from Cabernet Sauvignon grown in the hills by the sea near Leghorn; it has become something of a cult since it won the laurels at a blind tasting in London in 1978 in competition with thirty-three of the best Cabernet Sauvignons in the world. Other prestigious unclassified wines are Tavernelle, also made from Cabernet Sauvignon by Villa Banfi; and the grand Tiganello developed by Antinori in the Chianti Classico area with Sangiovese and Cabernet.

It is not only Cabernet that has been allowed to muscle into Sangiovese territory. Creative Tuscan wine-makers have been experimenting with foreign classics such as Merlot, the Pinots, Chardonnay, Sauvignon, Riesling and Gewürztraminer.

One old classic which is always treated with respect is Vin Santo, the sweet and sometimes dry amber-coloured dessert wine which is made by every estate with their best Malvasia and Trebbiano grapes. The grapes are left to wither on the vine or are hung to dry on slats before pressing. The sugary must is then fermented and aged in small wooden barrels. It is the kind of wine people make at home.

CHICKEN LIVERS ON TOAST
Crostini di fegatini

Everywhere in Tuscany, I have been offered little delicacies – chopped mushrooms, puréed aubergine and other vegetables (they call them *salsine*), even unformed eggs on toast as appetisers. This one is the most popular in Tuscany.

SERVES 8

1 baguette (long French bread), cut into slices diagonally

250g (8oz) chicken livers

3 tablespoons olive oil

2 cloves garlic, crushed

4 tablespoons vin santo or marsala, or more to taste

5–6 small anchovy fillets

2 tablespoons capers

4–5 tiny or 1 medium pickled cucumber

Lay the bread out on a baking tray and toast in a the oven at 190°C (375°F, gas mark 5) until golden. Fry the chicken livers gently in the oil with the garlic for 4–5 minutes, or until they are brown outside and still pink and juicy inside. Add the rest of the ingredients and blend until smooth in a food processor. Spread on the toast and serve at once.

TOMATO AND BREAD SALAD
Panzanella

This very popular country salad needs a firm, coarse-textured, tasty country bread to be good. I found it in many versions. An elegant one has the moist bread mashed finely in a blender, then mixed with very finely chopped raw vegetables and presented like a scoop of ice cream on the plate. I prefer the following, which I ate in a Florentine trattoria.

SERVES 6

250g (8oz) coarse white bread, crusts removed

6 ripe tomatoes

1 red onion

$\frac{1}{2}$ cucumber

2 stalks celery

6 sprigs of basil leaves, shredded

6 tablespoons olive oil

2 tablespoons vinegar

Salt and pepper

Cut the bread into small pieces. Put in a salad bowl and sprinkle with cold water so it is well moistened but not soggy. Add all the vegetables, cut into pieces or slices, and the basil. Dress with oil, vinegar, salt and pepper, stir well and leave for 30 minutes for the bread to absorb the dressing.

RAW VEGETABLES DIPPED IN OLIVE OIL
Verdure in pinzimonio

This is a most delightful central Italian (from Rome to Romagna) way of serving vegetables raw.

SERVES 4

2 fennel bulbs

1 head celery

2 large carrots

2 very small cucumbers

8 spring onions

150ml (5fl oz) extra-virgin olive oil

Salt and pepper

Quarter the fennel and celery and halve the carrots and cucumbers lengthwise. Arrange them on a plate with the spring onions, or serve in a deep bowl so that the vegetables stand up. Accompany them with a bowl of oil with a little salt and pepper beaten in, for dipping, and some bread.

COURGETTE BLOSSOMS FRIED IN BATTER
Fiori fritti

This is the simplest and most popular version of one of the most delightful of dishes.

Courgettes have male and female flowers, and it is the long male ones that are best used for this dish. They must be fresh and firm; very large ones can be cut in half lengthwise.

SERVES 4

150g (5oz) flour
Salt and pepper
Pinch of nutmeg
2 tablespoons olive oil
2 eggs, separated

6 tablespoons white wine
6 tablespoons water
16 courgette blossoms
Oil for deep-frying

To make the batter, put the flour, salt, pepper, nutmeg, oil and egg yolks in a bowl and beat well. Beat in the wine and water gradually until the batter has a light, creamy consistency (you might need a little extra liquid). Leave to rest for about 30 minutes; just before using, beat the egg whites until stiff and fold in. Detach the stem and green leaves from the blossoms, remove the stamens, dip the flowers in batter and deep-fry in hot oil. Serve hot and crisp.

Note
Fresh sage leaves can also be dipped in batter and deep-fried. They are served as an appetiser.

Variations
A Ligurian version has the blossoms stuffed before frying with a purée of mashed potatoes, green beans and courgettes mixed with grated parmesan, chopped basil and marjoram, garlic and pepper, a little melted butter and beaten egg.

A Piedmontese filling for *fiori farciti* is a mixture of minced veal, breadcrumbs dipped in milk and squeezed dry, parmesan, garlic, parsley and basil.

BREAD AND TOMATO SOUP
Pappa al pomodoro

Make this mushy rustic soup (*pappa* means 'mush') only if you have really good country bread, flavoursome ripe tomatoes and fruity olive oil.

SERVES 4

250g (8oz) stale coarse country bread, sliced
   and crusts removed
3 cloves garlic, crushed
4–5 tablespoons olive oil
700g (1½lb) very ripe tomatoes, peeled and cut
   into pieces

1 litre (1¾ pints) light chicken stock (use 1 stock
   cube)
Salt and pepper
3 tablespoons shredded basil leaves

Toast the bread very lightly in the oven so that it dries out but does not colour, then break into pieces. Fry the garlic in 1 tablespoon of oil until it just begins to colour, add the tomatoes and toasted bread and cook, stirring, until the bread falls apart and blends with the tomatoes. Stir in enough hot stock, a little at a time, to get a thick mushy consistency. Season with salt and plenty of pepper, add basil, and simmer gently for about 20 minutes, stirring occasionally. Serve hot with a little olive oil dribbled over each serving.

SHELLFISH SOUP WITH GARLIC TOAST
Tegame di conchigliacci con bruschetta all'aglio

In the UK mussels are the best choice for this soup, but if other shellfish are available it is good to have an assortment.

SERVES 6

2kg (4lb) shellfish, such as mussels and clams

2 cloves garlic, crushed, plus 2 for the garlic toast

5–6 tablespoons olive oil

3 tomatoes, peeled and chopped (optional)

Salt and pepper

150ml (5fl oz) dry white wine

4 tablespoons finely chopped parsley

6 large slices bread, toasted

Clean and wash the shellfish and steam open in a large pan as described on page 18. Take them out of the pan and strain their liquor to remove any sand.

Fry the crushed garlic in 3 tablespoons of the olive oil; when it begins to colour, add the tomatoes, if using, salt and pepper, the wine and the strained liquor from the shells. Simmer for 15–20 minutes, then put the shells in or, for easy serving, turn the sauce and shells into a very large baking dish and heat through. Sprinkle with chopped parsley and serve with garlic toast.

To make the toast, rub the remaining garlic all over one side of each slice. Dip the same side of the toast in the remaining olive oil and sprinkle with salt and pepper.

SPAGHETTI WITH PRAWNS
Spaghetti con gamberetti

This recipe comes from Ristorante La Barca in Forte dei Marmi, in Versilia.

SERVES 4

1kg (2lb) large prawns, in their shells

1 carrot, sliced

1 stalk celery, sliced

1 small onion, cut into pieces

Salt and pepper

2 cloves garlic, crushed

1 small red chilli

2 tablespoons olive oil

A few basil leaves (optional)

2 tablespoons finely chopped parsley

400g (14oz) spaghetti

Boil the prawns in water very briefly until they turn pink. Drain and save the cooking water. Peel the prawns and return the shells to the broth. Add the carrot, celery, onion, salt and pepper and simmer for 30 minutes to get a good stock. Strain.

To make the sauce, fry the garlic with the chilli (leave it whole, or if you want the sauce fiery, remove the seeds and chop it up) in the oil until the aroma rises. Add the tomatoes and cook for 10 minutes, then add the herbs and a little of the fish broth and cook a few minutes more. Put in the cooked prawns and turn off the heat.

Cook the spaghetti in the strained fish stock, adding boiling water if necessary and salt, until al dente, and drain.

Serve with the sauce heated through and poured on top.

Note

You can buy peeled prawns and boil the pasta in salted water.

SOLE, FLORENTINE STYLE
Sogliole alla fiorentina

Cooking with spinach is a style long associated with Florence. For this dish you can use other kinds of white fish besides sole.

SERVES 4

1kg (2lb) fresh spinach or 500g (1lb) frozen spinach

Salt and pepper

125g (4oz) butter

Freshly grated nutmeg

250ml (8fl oz) white wine

8 fillets of sole

40g (1½oz) flour

500ml (18fl oz) milk

Freshly grated parmesan

Wash the spinach, remove the stems and place in a saucepan. Cover and cook for a few minutes with a little salt and only the water that clings to the leaves, turning them over until they crumple. Drain well, return to the pan with 15g (½oz) butter and sauté briefly. Season with salt, pepper and a pinch of nutmeg and set aside. If using frozen spinach, defrost, drain, then stir in butter and seasonings.

Heat the wine with 15g (½oz) butter, salt and pepper in a frying pan. Poach the sole fillets for 30 seconds only, then remove the fish and let the sauce reduce to about 3–4 tablespoons.

Meanwhile, make a béchamel sauce. Melt the remaining butter, add the flour and stir well. Add the milk gradually, stirring all the time until the sauce thickens. Season with salt and pepper and a pinch of nutmeg, and stir in the reduced wine.

Grease a baking dish with butter, line the bottom of the dish with the spinach, lay the sole on top and coat with the sauce. Sprinkle with parmesan and bake in the oven at 200°C (400°F, gas mark 6) for 15 minutes, or until a crust has formed on top.

EGGS FLORENTINE
Uova alla fiorentina

SERVES 4

1kg (2lb) fresh spinach or 500g (1lb) frozen

65g (2½oz) butter

Salt

4 eggs

Pepper

3 tablespoons flour

500ml (18fl oz) warm milk

Freshly grated nutmeg

50g (2oz) grated parmesan

Wash the spinach, remove the stems and put it in a large saucepan with 25g (1oz) butter. Season with salt, and steam, covered, until the leaves crumple to a soft mass, turning them over a few times. (If using frozen spinach, defrost, drain, then stir in salt and butter.) Spread the spinach in a shallow baking dish, make four depressions with the back of a tablespoon and drop in the eggs. Sprinkle with salt and pepper.

Now make a béchamel sauce. Melt the remaining butter in a saucepan, stir in the flour and very gradually add the milk, stirring constantly, and waiting until it boils before adding more. Cook very gently, stirring often, until the sauce thickens. Add salt and pepper, a pinch of nutmeg and half the grated parmesan and pour evenly over the spinach and the eggs. Sprinkle with the rest of the parmesan and bake in the oven at 200°C (400°F, gas mark 6) for 10 minutes, or until the egg whites have set.

BARBECUED MEAT AND GAME
Grigliata mista di carne e selvaggina

Cooking *alla brace*, over a wood or charcoal fire, is popular in central and southern Italy. It imparts a uniquely appetising smoky flavour and a most alluring perfume, so good all you need is bread and salad to accompany and fruit to follow. They say that even an old shoe tastes good if it is cooked in this manner.

For a special occasion offer a *gran misto griglia*, a selection of different meats and young tender game. Choose a few from the following: veal, lamb or pork chops; rabbit, cut into 3 or 4 pieces; chicken or poussin cut up or split open along the breast, pulled out and pounded as flat as possible (for directions see page 133, *pollo alla diavola*). Game birds, such as quail, guinea hen, partridge, woodcock, pigeon, duck and grouse, if they are young and tender, are all excellent cooked over embers. They are sometimes flavoured by being stuffed with a small onion or juniper berries and with herbs such as rosemary or sage. Pork sausages are often part of a mixed grill, as are *spiedini*, kebab-type skewered meats.

Some people marinate their meats in olive oil with rosemary or sage and perhaps wine or lemon juice and garlic, but most find it sufficient to rub the meat with oil, salt and pepper before cooking and to brush it with olive oil or melted butter as it cooks to prevent it from drying out.

It is usual but not always necessary to bard the breasts of game with thin strips of bacon or pork fat tied with string. As the birds are turned over (for 10–40 minutes, depending on their size) the fat melts away, keeping the meat moist and tender and lending it a distinctive flavour. But more simply you can split game birds in half and flatten them (they require much less time).

Start to cook only when the fire has burned down and the smoke has gone and a light powdery grey ash covers the glowing embers. Place the meats on a well-oiled grill and turn them at least once, brushing them with oil or butter or a marinade occasionally. The cooking time will depend on the thickness and type of food, its distance from the fire, the type of embers, the size of the firebed and even on the weather. The best way to find out if the meat is done is to cut into it with a sharp knife.

Serve on a thick slice of bread or toast to capture the juices.

ROAST LEG OF LAMB
Agnello arrosto

SERVES 6

1.5kg (3lb) boned leg of lamb (weight after boning)
2 cloves garlic, crushed
4 tablespoons olive oil

3 sprigs of rosemary
Salt and pepper
250ml (8fl oz) white wine

Lay the boned leg out flat and rub with the garlic and half the olive oil. Sprinkle with rosemary, salt and pepper. Roll up the leg neatly and tie with string. Place in a roasting tin with the rest of the oil and the wine and roast in a preheated oven at 230°C (450°F, gas mark 8) for 20 minutes to seal in the juices. Turn the oven down to 190°C (375°F, gas mark 5) and cook for 45 minutes more, basting occasionally. This will produce lamb with a slightly pink tinge. Allow an extra 20 minutes if you prefer it well done.

CROWN ROAST OF PORK
Arista alla fiorentina

According to legend, this ancient dish acquired its name when Greek bishops, attending an ecumenical council in Florence in 1430, were served the roast and exclaimed *'Aristos!'* which means 'Very good!'

SERVES 6

1.5kg (3lb) loin of pork with rib bones (chine or crown roast)
6 cloves garlic, crushed

Salt and pepper
2 sprigs of rosemary
3 tablespoons olive oil

Ask your butcher to prepare the crown roast, making sure to cut the meat almost but not entirely away from the bone and to break the bones so as to make carving easier.

With a sharp pointed knife make several incisions all around into the meat. Make a paste with the garlic, salt, pepper, rosemary and the olive oil (in the food processor if you like). Press a little into each incision and rub the rest all over the surface of the meat (including where it had been attached to the bone). Tie the meat back on to the bone with string or with skewers and put it in a roasting tin. Bake in the oven at 200°C (400°F, gas mark 6) for 1½ hours, or until done to your taste, basting frequently with the melted fat.

To carve, untie the meat and cut between the rib bones. Serve each person a chop.

Note

About 1 hour before the end of the cooking time, you can put potatoes, cut into small cubes, to cook in the fat.

ROAST SUCKLING PIG
Porchetta

Suckling pig is very expensive but the delicate flesh makes a real event of a meal. In Sardinia, where it is a favourite food, they use no flavouring other than salt and pepper, and they cook it on the spit some 40–50cm (16–20in) from the fire for about 3 hours, or until crusty and brown, greasing it occasionally with a lump of pork fat (melted in the fire) held on the end of a skewer. Sardinians also eat it cold, in which case they wrap the sizzling roast in myrtle leaves so that the aroma penetrates the flesh as it cools.

Roast piglet is also a speciality of Lazio, Umbria, the Marches and Tuscany. For special occasions it is cooked on the spit or in a baker's oven with burning aromatic wood, but people still make it at home. This is the way they make it in Arezzo in Tuscany.

SERVES 6–8

1 suckling pig, about 7.5kg (15lb)
4 cloves garlic, crushed
2 sprigs of rosemary
3 bay leaves
A bunch of wild fennel, or the feathery leaves of a fennel bulb, or 2 teaspoons fennel seeds

4 cloves, crushed
¼ teaspoon freshly grated nutmeg
Salt and pepper
2 tablespoons olive oil
300ml (½ pint) dry white or red wine

Clean the pig. Stuff with a mixture of garlic, herbs, cloves and nutmeg, salt and pepper and rub all over with salt, pepper and olive oil. Roast in the oven at 150°C (300°F, gas mark 2) for 3–4 hours, or until brown and crusty, basting every 30 minutes with the pan drippings and some wine.

TRIPE WITH TOMATOES AND PARMESAN
Trippa alla fiorentina

Tripe is very popular all over Italy, and there are many ways of cooking it. This one may please even those who are squeamish about it.

SERVES 4

1kg (2lb) tripe	A sprig of rosemary
Salt	500g (1lb) tomatoes, peeled and chopped
1 onion, finely chopped	300ml ($^1/_2$ pint) dry white wine
1 carrot, finely chopped	Pepper
1 celery stalk and leaves, finely chopped	A few basil leaves, chopped
4 tablespoons olive oil	A few sprigs of parsley, chopped
1–2 cloves garlic, chopped	4 tablespoons grated parmesan
2 bay leaves	

Tripe is now sold cleaned and needs hardly any advance preparation. Simply rinse and boil in salted water for $1^1/_2$ hours until tender, then drain. Cut it into thin ribbons

In a large pan, fry the onion, carrot and celery in 2 tablespoons oil until they are very soft and the onion is golden. Add the garlic, bay leaves and rosemary and fry until the aroma rises. Add the tomatoes, pour in the wine, season with salt and pepper and simmer until the sauce is reduced by almost half. Put in the tripe and cook gently for 15 minutes longer, adding basil and parsley at the end. Stir in the rest of the oil and the cheese, and serve hot.

CHICKEN PIECES FRIED IN BATTER
Pollo fritto

I ate this in Florence as part of a *fritto misto* that included fried brains, sweetbreads, chicken croquettes, tiny lamb chops and rabbit pieces as well as artichoke hearts, courgette slices, pumpkin blossoms and tomatoes.

Whereas in Piedmont they dip their little morsels in egg, flour and breadcrumbs, in Tuscany they use only flour and egg. The chicken is cut up into 14 small pieces with the bones, but it is easier to use (and eat) boned, skinned chicken.

SERVES 4

1 chicken or boned chicken pieces	Flour
3 tablespoons olive oil	2 eggs, beaten
Juice of 1 lemon	Olive oil for frying
2 cloves garlic, crushed	1 lemon, cut into wedges
Salt and pepper	

Cut the chicken into small pieces with the bones or use boned chicken (the thighs are particularly good for this). Marinate for an hour in a mixture of olive oil and lemon juice, garlic, salt and pepper. When you are ready to serve, roll the drained chicken pieces in flour then soak them in beaten egg seasoned with a little salt, and deep-fry in not very hot oil until crisp and golden, turning them over once. Drain on absorbent paper towels and serve very hot, accompanied by lemon wedges.

Note

Rabbit treated in the same way is also very good.

CHICKEN WITH MUSHROOMS
Pollo ai funghi

Italian dried mushrooms have a strong flavour and firm texture when they are cooked.

SERVES 4

1 chicken, about 1.5kg (3lb), cut up and boned
15g (½oz) butter
2 tablespoons olive oil
120ml (4fl oz) dry white wine

Handful of dried mushrooms, soaked in warm water for 30 minutes, or 500g (1lb) fresh mushrooms
4 tomatoes, peeled and chopped
Salt and pepper

Quickly fry the chicken pieces in a mixture of butter and oil until coloured all over. Add the wine, drained mushrooms (if using fresh mushrooms simply wash them and slice them or leave them whole) and tomatoes, season with salt and pepper, and cook for about 25 minutes, or until the chicken is tender.

GRILLED CHICKEN
Pollo alla diavola

This is a very good way of cooking a whole chicken in the summer on the barbecue.

SERVES 4

1.5kg (3lb) chicken
5 tablespoons olive oil
Juice of 1 lemon

2–3 sprigs of rosemary
Salt and pepper
1 lemon, cut into wedges

Cut the chicken open along the breast and pull it out as flat as you can so that it cooks evenly. Cut the wing and leg joints just enough to spread them flat and pound the chicken as flat as you can. Marinate in a mixture of olive oil, lemon juice, rosemary, salt and pepper for 1 hour.

Place on an oiled grill set 10–12cm (4–5in) above the embers, skin side down. Grill until the skin has turned golden brown, brushing with the marinade from time to time, turning it over more than once, and leaving it longer on the bone side, until the juice coming out of the thigh is no longer pink, usually about 30–40 minutes.

Serve garnished with lemon wedges.

MEAT OR CHICKEN CROQUETTES
Polpette alla fiorentina

Every region of Italy has its own special croquettes made with left-over boiled meats. These are especially soft and creamy inside.

SERVES 4

250g (8oz) potatoes
350g (12oz) boiled meat or chicken
2 eggs, lightly beaten
3 tablespoons finely chopped parsley
1 clove garlic, crushed

1 slice of bread, crust removed, dipped in milk, squeezed dry and crumbled
Salt and pepper
Breadcrumbs
Oil for frying
1 lemon, cut into wedges

Boil the potatoes in their skins, then peel and mash them. Finely chop the meat or chicken (you can do it in a food processor). Put both in a bowl with the eggs, parsley, garlic and soaked and crumbled bread. Add salt and pepper and mix well. Shape the mixture (it will be very soft) into little round cakes or fingers, dip them in breadcrumbs and fry them in oil, turning to brown them all over. Drain on absorbent paper towels and serve very hot, garnished with lemon wedges.

CHICKEN CROQUETTES
Crocchette di pollo

Serve as part of a *fritto misto* or with fried potatoes.

SERVES 4 OR MORE

350g (12oz) boiled boned chicken
25g (1oz) butter
2 tablespoons flour
300ml (½ pint) milk
1 egg

3 tablespoons grated parmesan
Pinch of nutmeg
Salt and pepper
Breadcrumbs
Oil for frying

Finely chop the chicken (you may use a food processor). Make a stiff béchamel: melt the butter in a saucepan, stir in the flour and very gradually add the milk, stirring constantly and waiting until it comes to the boil before adding more. Put the chicken in a bowl with the béchamel, egg, parmesan, nutmeg, salt and pepper. Mix well, shape into little round cakes, dip in breadcrumbs and deep-fry in oil until golden. Drain and serve hot.

PEPPERS STUFFED WITH RABBIT
Coniglio in casseruola nel peperone

This recipe from the beautiful Locanda dell'Amorosa, part of a fourteenth-century village farm estate outside Sinalunga near Siena, is an example of how old traditional recipes are glamorised today. Rabbit cooked with peppers is turned into peppers stuffed with rabbit.

SERVES 4

4 medium peppers, washed
I small rabbit, about 700g (1½lb), boned and
    chopped small
50g (2oz) butter
250g (8oz) mushrooms, sliced

120ml (4fl oz) dry white wine
120ml (4fl oz) chicken stock
1 tablespoon tomato paste
Salt and pepper

Cut the tops off the peppers a third of the way down to make lids, and scrape out the seeds. Bake in a preheated oven at 180°C (350°F, gas mark 4) for about 20 minutes, or until tender, but take care they remain fairly firm.

Meanwhile, fry the rabbit pieces in the butter, add the mushrooms and then the wine, allowing it to evaporate slowly. Pour in the stock, add the tomato paste, season to taste and cook slowly for about 15 minutes. Fill the peppers with the rabbit, cover with their lids and bake for 10–20 minutes, or until the peppers are soft. Be careful that they do not fall apart. Serve hot.

GREEN SALAD
Insalata verde

Green salad accompanies or follows the second course. Lettuce leaves are served alone or mixed with other salad leaves such as endive, chicory, lamb's lettuce and rocket. The last, a native of Apulia, where it grows wild in vast quantities, is so fashionable now that it is offered by itself in restaurants throughout the country. The dressing is simply olive oil and salt, with a drop of vinegar.

Wild leaves and herbs may be added as well.

GREEN BEANS WITH OIL AND LEMON
Fagiolini all'agro

SERVES 4

500g (1lb) green beans
Salt
2–3 tablespoons olive oil

Juice of $\frac{1}{2}$ lemon
Pepper

String the beans (if necessary) and boil in salted water for about 6 minutes, until tender but still crisp. Drain and serve hot or cold, dressed with oil and lemon, salt and pepper.

BEANS IN TOMATO SAUCE
Fagioli all'uccelletto

This is perhaps Florence's most famous dish.

SERVES 6

500g (1lb) small white cannellini beans, soaked
   overnight
2 sprigs of sage
6 tablespoons olive oil

Salt
2 cloves garlic
5 ripe tomatoes, peeled and chopped
Pepper

Drain the beans and simmer in fresh water to cover, with 1 sprig of sage and 1 tablespoon olive oil, for about $1\frac{1}{2}$ hours, or until tender, adding salt when the beans begin to soften.

Heat the remaining oil on low heat with the garlic and the rest of the sage so that the flavours infuse, but do not fry. Add the tomatoes and simmer for 10 minutes, then add the drained beans, season with salt and pepper, and cook for another 5 minutes or so. There should be a good amount of sauce.

PEAS WITH PROSCIUTTO
Piselli al prosciutto

SERVES 4

1 small onion, finely chopped
125g (4oz) prosciutto or bacon, cut into cubes
   or strips
4 tablespoons olive oil
500g (1lb) small shelled fresh peas or frozen
   petits pois, defrosted

Salt
Bunch of parsley, finely chopped
1 teaspoon sugar
120ml (4fl oz) stock

Fry the onion and prosciutto or bacon in the oil. When the onion is golden, add the peas, salt, parsley and sugar and continue to cook slowly, moistening with a little hot stock, for about 15 minutes, or until the peas are tender (frozen ones take only a few minutes).

POTATOES WITH ROSEMARY AND GARLIC
Patate al forno

A simple and most delicious way of preparing potatoes.

SERVES 4

800g (1¾lb) new potatoes

Salt

3–4 cloves garlic, crushed

5 tablespoons olive oil

2 or more sprigs of rosemary leaves

Salt and pepper

Scrub and wash the potatoes well (you do not need to peel them) and boil in salted water until tender. Drain, cut them in half if they are large and put with the rest of the ingredients in a baking dish, turning them to cover well with the garlic, oil, rosemary leaves, salt and pepper. Bake in the oven at 200°C (400°F, gas mark 6) for 20 minutes, or until golden.

CHESTNUT FLOUR CAKE
Castagnaccio

This very ancient cake, which has no sugar, only the sweetness of the chestnut flour, was born in Lucca. The taste is one you acquire.

300g (10oz) chestnut flour

4 tablespoons olive oil

Salt

75g (3oz) raisins, soaked in water then drained

75g (3oz) pine nuts

Sprig of rosemary, chopped

Put the chestnut flour into a blender and gradually blend in about 500ml (18fl oz) water, enough to make a smooth batter. Add 2 tablespoons of the oil, a pinch of salt, the drained raisins, 50g (2oz) of the pine nuts and most of the rosemary. Stir well and pour into an oiled cake tin about 28cm (11in) in diameter; or use a rectangular one, large enough so the mixture is less than 2cm (¾in) high. Sprinkle the top with the remaining pine nuts and a few rosemary leaves and bake in the oven at 230°C (450°F, gas mark 8) for about 30–40 minutes, or until the top is crisp and golden and cracked. Serve warm. It is soft and creamy inside.

FLORENTINE FLAT BREAD WITH GRAPES
Schiacciata con l'uva

This lovely grape bread recipe is from Lorenza de'Medici, who for a few weeks a year is hostess and cooking instructor at her eleventh-century villa at Badia a Coltibuono, the prestigious family estate. Lorenza has written several cookery books.

SERVES 6

2 packages active dried yeast
150ml (5fl oz) lukewarm milk
300g (10oz) flour
150g (5oz) sugar

Pinch of salt
500g (1lb) black grapes, seeded, skins left on
250g (8oz) raisins, soaked in vin santo or other
    sweet dessert wine

Dissolve the yeast in the milk. Mound the flour in a large bowl and make a well in the centre. Add 125g (4oz) of the sugar, the salt and stir in the yeast–milk mixture. Knead for 5 minutes, then cover with a clean cloth and leave in a warm place to rise until double the original size.

Punch down and shape into two rounds about 20cm (8in) across. Place one on a floured baking sheet, cover with half the grapes and half the drained raisins. Cover with the second round of dough and put the rest of the grapes and raisins on top. Leave, covered, to rise again until double. Sprinkle with the rest of the sugar and bake in a preheated oven at 180°C (350°F, gas mark 4) for about 45 minutes.

Umbria

Umbria

The little 'green heart' of Italy is so beautiful, so spiritual, so artistic that one feels that perhaps the people here are less interested in the needs of the body.

Umbria is the only region in central and southern Italy entirely surrounded by land, and the soft, hilly landscape is particularly seductive and familiar, like the background in a Renaissance painting. It is full of history, with Etruscan arches in Perugia, Etruscan tombs in Orvieto, Roman remains in Spoleto, Spello, Gubbio and Norcia, and it feels intensely holy. They say twenty thousand saints were born in Umbria. Saint Francis was. In Assisi I spotted several well-built, even fat, priests, and I waited for the right moment to ask about church cooking and the Vatican kitchen, but it never came.

Umbria is full of splendid churches and stunning religious paintings and frescoes. Every little hill town, with its narrow, twisting streets, grips you and pulls you straight into the Middle Ages. It is an incredible feeling but it does not take away your appetite.

The food here is simple, sober and homely, but it also has great elegance. It is the incredible abundance of truffles that gives it style. The black truffles of Norcia are the most characteristic produce of Umbria, and the most highly prized are found in the Val Nerina, in the Spoleto area, with their main market centre at Scheggino.

Apart from the black knobbly ones (they are black all the way through), there are lighter-coloured truffles, which the Umbrians call *bianchetti*, and white ones. Truffles are so plentiful that they are put into everything – spaghetti, omelettes, scrambled eggs, salads; they are served with fish, cheese, as a garnish for grilled meats and as a spread for toast; and they are in the sauce of almost all the roasts and stews. Great handfuls are used grated, chopped up and in shavings, and not treated too well, as though they were parsley or, as someone has remarked, potatoes. They are even mashed up with garlic and anchovies or with black-olive paste (tapenade) or chopped mushrooms.

There is none of the respectful attitude of the other regions that have truffles, Piedmont and Emilia for instance. There, black truffles are not generally as prized as white ones because they have less perfume, but in Umbria they claim that black ones have a better taste. People use them all year round, keeping them frozen, vacuum-packed, or preserved in jars and cans. But in the autumn, in truffle season, when dogs and pigs are taken to sniff them out and the truffles are pulled out of the ground, it is a time for celebration and festivities.

The seasons are very noticeable in Umbrian cooking, especially the seasons for mushrooms and game. There are hare, pheasant, partridge and guinea hen, quail and pigeons (Assisi is famous for them). The people also catch migratory birds that, twice a year, stop for a month to feed on olives and juniper berries; they make *cappelletti con sugo di tordi*, stuffed pasta with a sauce of thrushes.

One thing that distinguishes the taste of Umbrian food is the extraordinarily fine olive oil from the silver trees that cling to the rocky hills. Green, light, full of flavour and highly scented, the oil is used in all the cooking, while the black olives, marinated in oil with orange peel, garlic and herbs, are served with wine.

Soft wheat and sugar-beet grow here, and also various fruits and vegetables. There are beans at Trasimeno, cardoons and celery at Trevi, peas at Bettona, marvellous tiny lentils (the best in Italy) in Castelluccio. The characteristic strongly perfumed honey is made by nuns; the bees have hundreds of different wild flowers to feed on.

But the most important and interesting feature of the local gastronomy is the pork products of Norcia. Norcia is the gastronomic capital of the region, as much for its cured ham, sausages and salami as for its truffles. In this little medieval town the most brilliant tradition of pork processing in Italy was born. Vittorio Battilocchi, who specialises in local dishes at his trattoria, Dal Francese, thinks it may be because Norcia had the oldest school of surgery (surgeons from Norcia operated at the court of the king of France) and this knowledge of human anatomy may have been applied to the pig. The men of Norcia are artists in the art of preparing the pig. For centuries they have been going to Rome and all over the country, seasonally, to do this work, and *norcino* has come to be the general term used for a pork butcher. Shops selling charcuterie in Rome and Tuscany are called *norcinerie*. The local ham is lean and compact, from small black pigs fed on acorns and chestnuts (although now they do not have enough pigs of their own, so they bring them in from other regions). The ham is stronger, more peppery and garlicky than most.

Other towns have their own specialities and use other breeds of pigs. Recently wild boar has come on to the scene. Umbrians say some escaped from the reserves in Tuscany and reproduced so quickly that they have become a nuisance. The butchers leave a little fur on the hams from wild boar meat so that they can be easily recognised.

Umbria is famous, too, for *porchetta*, a whole roast pig stuffed with garlic and wild fennel, and also with rosemary and sage, the local perfume. This speciality has spread to Rome and elsewhere in Italy. It is sold in the streets from large vans; you get slices of pork and a bit of crisp skin sprinkled with salt and wrapped in a bit of paper. One of the main characteristics of Umbrian cooking is the use of the grill and the spit. Cooking over wood embers gives meat an incomparable flavour. Among the meat prepared this way are steaks of beef and veal, chicken, rabbit, guinea hen, pheasant, partridge and other kinds of game.

Lamb is another speciality. There are villages, such as Capelluccio, an old hill town, inhabited entirely by shepherds. They sell their cheese to the men of Norcia, who age it alongside sausages. The shepherds also exchange the cheese with peasants for wine, olive oil and salami (barter is still a common practice). Freshwater fish – trout from the rivers Nera, Noro and Clitunno, and tench, grey mullet, pike and perch from Lake Trasimeno – is usually grilled. And of course there is homemade pasta, rough tagliatelle called strascinati and umbricci, fat spaghetti pulled out by hand. The best pasta dishes are made with wild mushrooms or olive paste (tapenade), which you can buy ready-made, and – grandest of all – with a rich grating of truffles.

Bakeries sell *tozzetti* and *ciambelloni*, biscuits to dip into sweet wine. Pastries, many of them of Longobard and German origin (the old nobility was of Frank origin, from the time of Charlemagne, and Longobard) and some of which go as far back as the Etruscans, are reserved for festive occasions. Every feast has its speciality. Christmas has *pinocchiatte*, which are biscuits with pine nuts, and sweet tagliatelle with sugar, walnuts, raisins and chopped dried figs. At Easter there is the *crescia di Pasqua*, a savoury brioche baked in a conical earthenware pot and eaten for breakfast with hard-boiled eggs and prosciutto. For All Souls' Day there are *fave dei morti* and *ossi dei morti* (literally, broad [fava] beans and bones of the dead; these sweets with macabre names and shapes were originally made in convents). *Castagnione*, a Carnival speciality, is a mass of round, biscuity fritters (*strufoli*) in the shape of little chestnuts (*castagne*, hence the name), made with leavened dough and wine, dipped in honey with a few drops of liqueur.

Roccio is a brioche with raisins and orange peel. *Rocciata* is a very rich winter speciality of Assisi, Spello and nearby towns. This strudel-type roll is filled with dried figs and prunes, almonds, pine nuts and hazelnuts, as well as fresh apples and pears (now bananas and crystallised orange peel are added), perfumed with nutmeg and cocoa and eaten either hot or cold. A chocolate and apple strudel in the shape of a coil is called *torciolata* because it is like the rolled cloth women used to put on their heads when they carried heavy things. *Torciglione* is a marzipan pastry shaped and painted like an eel. All these are made year-round at Sandri, the famous coffee shop on corso Vannucci in Perugia, which has been run by the Schuani family since 1860.

The Wines of Umbria

Umbria's most famous wine, the white Orvieto, has declined in popularity since it changed twenty years ago from a golden *abboccato* (softly sweet wine) into an anonymous dry, crisp, industrial modern wine with no character. But some producers have brought back some of the old fragrance and honeyed flavour.

Umbria makes simple wines, light, Chianti-like reds, agreeably sharp whites and fresh rosés, but it does also have one or two gems. Red Torgiano from near Perugia is known through the name Rubesco, which is the name of the main producer's *riserva*. Rubesco is a superb aged wine which manages to keep its fresh fragrance and fruitiness. Torgiano Bianco, also known as Torre di Giano, is a lovely, tart, fruity white. Montefalco, made from Sagrantino grapes, is a dark, strong, full-bodied red with a scent of blackberries which can be either dry or bittersweet.

OLIVE TOAST
Crostini di olive

There is a fashion for *crostini* – toast spread with paste – as appetisers in restaurants. This olive spread is delightful, but you must use olives of a very good quality, such as the Greek *calamatas* or the Italian *gaetas*.

1 medium loaf French bread, cut into slices diagonally
150g (5oz) pitted black olives
4 anchovies, chopped

2 tablespoons capers, vinegar squeezed out
1–2 cloves garlic, crushed
2 tablespoons rum (optional)
5 tablespoons olive oil

Lay the bread out on a tray and toast in the oven at 190°C (375°F, gas mark 5) until golden. Put the rest of the ingredients into the food processor and blend only briefly so that the anchovies, capers and garlic are finely chopped but not smooth.

Spread on to the toast.

VEGETABLES WITH OIL AND LEMON DRESSING
Verdure assortite all'agro

Vegetables steamed or boiled to a crisp tenderness, left whole if very small or cut into largish pieces, simply dressed with olive oil and lemon juice, salt and pepper, make a good first course and an accompaniment to most dishes.

For a party, choose a variety of vegetables, from new potatoes, carrots, green beans and cauliflower, fennel, artichokes, chicory and courgettes, broad beans, celery, radicchio and asparagus. Cook them in a large saucepan of boiling salted water, first putting in those, such as potatoes and carrots, which take longer, and those, such as radicchio and asparagus tips, which take hardly any time, at the end, for just 1–2 minutes. Serve hot or cold and be generous with the dressing.

TAGLIATELLE WITH OLIVE AND MUSHROOM SAUCE
Tagliatelle alle olive

Olive paste (tapenade) and mushroom paste are used so much in Umbrian dishes that they are sold already prepared. They are often mixed together. You can sometimes find them in Italian food shops in the UK. This recipe for the sauce is from the restaurant Umbra in Assisi.

SERVES 4

250g (8oz) mushrooms, thinly sliced
2 tablespoons olive oil
1 clove garlic, crushed
175g (6oz) black olives, pitted (choose Greek *calamatas*, Italian *gaetas* or other olives with a rich flavour)

3 tablespoons chopped parsley
500g (1lb) tagliatelle
Salt
¼ teaspoon or more hot chilli powder (optional)
120ml (4fl oz) double cream, whipped
50g (2oz) grated parmesan

Lightly fry the mushrooms in oil until tender, then blend with the garlic, olives and parsley in a food processor.

Cook the tagliatelle in boiling salted water until al dente, then drain.

Meanwhile, heat the olive mixture, adding salt and hot chilli powder, if using. Mix with the tagliatelle and serve with a bowl of cream and parmesan.

TROUT WITH GREEN SAUCE

Trota con salsa verde

Green sauces based on parsley are very popular in northern and central Italy. This one is good with trout.

SERVES 4

4 trout, cleaned, with heads left on

Salt and pepper

For the sauce

1 large bunch of parsley

1 tablespoon capers

2 pickled gherkins

3 anchovies

2 tablespoons olive oil

250ml (8fl oz) dry white wine

6 tablespoons olive oil

Juice of 1 large lemon

Salt and pepper

Wash the trout, season with salt and pepper and place in an oiled baking dish. Pour over the wine and bake in the oven at 230°C (450°F, gas mark 8) for 7–10 minutes, or until the flesh is opaque and flakes when pierced with a pointed knife.

To make the sauce, finely chop and blend all the ingredients in a food processor. Thin, if you like, with a few tablespoons of the cooking wine.

Serve the fish hot with the sauce.

SAUSAGES WITH LENTILS

Salsiccia con lenticchie

This is one of Vittorio Battilocchi's specialities at the trattoria Dal Francese, Norcia. He uses the famous tiny brown lentils of Castelluccio and the equally famous sausages of Norcia.

SERVES 4

350g (12oz) brown or green lentils

50g (2oz) pancetta or unsmoked bacon, chopped

1 small onion, chopped

2 cloves garlic, crushed

2 stalks celery, finely diced

Salt and pepper

4–8 pure pork sausages, such as luganega

Soak the lentils for 1 hour.

Fry the pancetta or bacon until the fat melts, then add the onion, garlic and celery, and fry until soft and coloured. Add the drained lentils, cover with water and simmer for 25 minutes, or until tender, adding water as necessary. Season to taste during cooking.

In the meantime, fry the sausages. Serve the sausages on a bed of lentils.

GUINEA HEN WITH HERBS

Faraona alle erbe al cartoccio

SERVES 2–4

1 guinea hen, about 1.5kg (3lb)

Salt and pepper

Juice of $\frac{1}{2}$–1 lemon

2 tablespoons olive oil

1 clove garlic, crushed

A sprig of rosemary

A few sage leaves

2 bay leaves

Season the guinea hen with salt and pepper and lay it on a large sheet of foil. Sprinkle with lemon juice and olive oil, crushed garlic and herbs and wrap it up in the foil. Bake in the oven at 200°C (400°F, gas mark 6) for about 1 hour, opening the foil for the last 15 minutes to let the meat brown.

FRESH FRUIT TART
Crostata

For the pastry shell

125g (4oz) unsalted butter
250g (8oz) flour
2 tablespoons caster sugar

2 egg yolks
2–4 tablespoons water or milk
1 egg white

For the custard (crema pasticciera)

250g (8oz) sugar
5 egg yolks
75g (3oz) flour
500ml (18fl oz) milk

4 tablespoons kirsch, rum, maraschino or cognac
   (optional)
150g (5oz) blanched almonds, finely chopped or
   amaretti (optional)

For the filling

Choose from cherries, plums, greengages, peaches, nectarines, apricots, strawberries, raspberries,
   grapes, figs, bananas, tangerines, oranges and kiwis
300g (10oz) or more apricot jelly for the glaze

Cut the butter into pieces and rub into the mixed flour and sugar. Add the egg yolks and just enough water or milk to bind it into a soft dough, stirring with a knife, then briefly mixing with your hands. Wrap in clingfilm and leave in a cool place for 1 hour.

Roll out the dough on a floured board with a floured rolling pin. Lift it up with the rolling pin and lay it gently into a 33cm (13in) tart tin or flan dish, pat it into place, and press it into the sides. Trim the edges and prick all over with a fork to prevent puffing. Bake the shell in a preheated oven at 200°C (400°F, gas mark 6) for 10 minutes. Take out of the oven and brush with egg white to seal the crust and prevent it from becoming soggy. Return to the oven for 5–10 minutes longer, or until it is a light golden colour. It will become firm and crusty as it cools.

For the custard, beat the sugar into the egg yolks until light and pale, then beat in the flour. Bring the milk to the boil and pour into the egg mixture gradually, beating vigorously until well blended. Pour into a heavy-bottomed saucepan and bring to the boil, stirring constantly. Simmer for 3 minutes longer, stirring occasionally so that the custard does not burn at the bottom of the pan. Stir in the alcohol and the almonds or amaretti, if using, and let the custard cool before spreading it in the pastry shell.

Pack as much fruit, peeled, seeded, pitted or sliced and skinned where necessary, as you can on top, mixing them if you like and making an attractive pattern.

To coat the fruit with a light glaze, melt the apricot jelly in a saucepan with a few tablespoons of water and spoon it over the fruit.

Note

Poach fruits that discolour in sugar syrup for 5–10 minutes, then drain. For the syrup, boil 500ml (18fl oz) water with 500g (1lb) sugar and 2 tablespoons lemon juice.

Variation

Instead of the custard, use a jam or a fresh-fruit purée. Blend very ripe sweet fruits such as strawberries, raspberries and blackcurrants with a little sugar and spread on the cooled pastry shell.

RICOTTA WITH COFFEE
Ricotta al caffè

For 4–6 people, serve a mound of about 500g (1lb) ricotta, sprinkled with 6 tablespoons caster sugar and 4 tablespoons ground or pulverised coffee (preferably a dark roast). Or, better still, serve individual portions of ricotta and pass around bowls of caster sugar and ground coffee and a bottle of rum for people to help themselves to and stir in to their own taste.

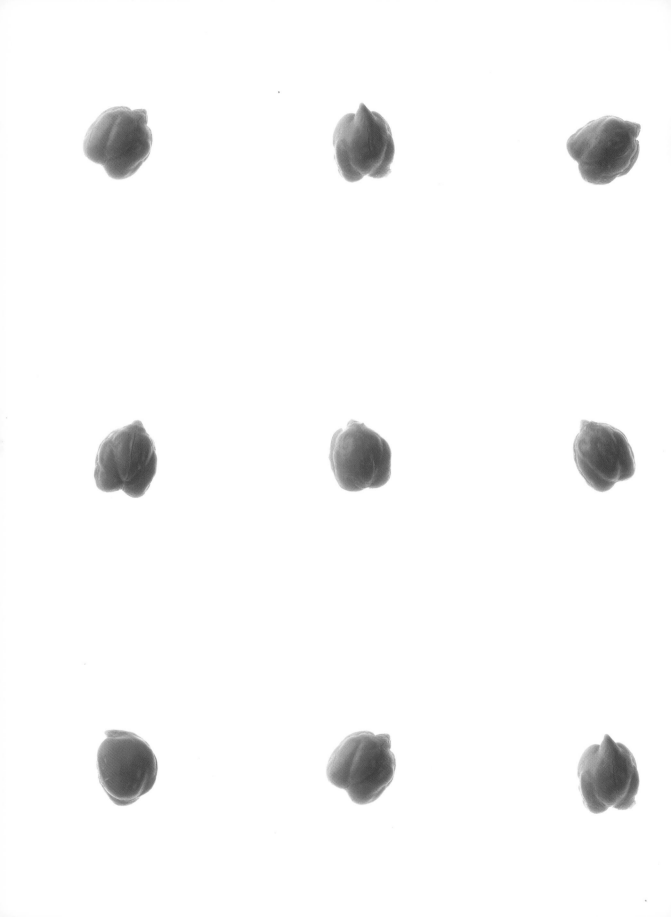

The Marches

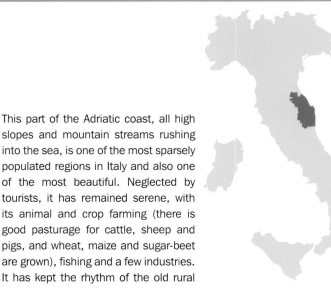

This part of the Adriatic coast, all high slopes and mountain streams rushing into the sea, is one of the most sparsely populated regions in Italy and also one of the most beautiful. Neglected by tourists, it has remained serene, with its animal and crop farming (there is good pasturage for cattle, sheep and pigs, and wheat, maize and sugar-beet are grown), fishing and a few industries. It has kept the rhythm of the old rural civilisation and of the sea, and its people are still involved in the countryside and close to the land, even if they live and work in the city.

This is Etruscan and Roman territory. Feudalism and the ecclesiastical authority were powerful until the thirteenth century; then came a period of free communes followed by the *signorie*, which was rule by families. From the middle of the fifteenth century to 1860 when the region became part of the Kingdom of Italy, the Marches were ruled by the Church. It is a peaceful history compared to that of some of the other regions.

The people of the Marches live entirely on what they produce, which is rare now in Italy. Tomatoes, fennel, tiny artichokes, peppers, cauliflower, peas, broad beans and cardoons grow between the sea and the hills. Vegetables are cooked simply, often boiled and dressed with herbs such as marjoram. The tradition of keeping pigs and making salami and cured ham at home has been kept up.

Cheese is made from sheep's milk here. Pecorino di Monterinaldo is perfumed with a wild herb called *serpillo*. At San Leo they wrap their pecorino in chestnut leaves and leave it to ripen in terracotta jars.

The Marches are important gastronomically as the greatest producers of truffles in Italy, especially in the Metauro Valley. They come in various colours – white, black, grey, brown and hazel – and Acqualagna in the province of Pesaro is the market centre. White truffles, the most strongly perfumed and most prized, compare with the famous truffles of Alba; indeed, many of them find their way to Alba, where they are sold at very high prices. The giant green olives of Ascoli are also famous. They have a wonderful flavour and are so big they can be stuffed with minced meat and cheese, then dipped in egg and breadcrumbs and deep-fried.

There are two sides to the cooking of the Marches: seafood and country cooking. Both are similar to those of neighbouring regions, but there are some distinctive features. The most important is the use of truffles. Another is the use of mushrooms, which lend character to many foods. Much of the cooking is done on the spit or the grill. Umbrian oil rather than lard is used, and the people are fond of cloves and cinnamon. They combine garlic, wild fennel and rosemary in many dishes, and anchovies, chillies, tomatoes and white wine creep into many others.

The great dish is *porchetta*, eaten at all feasts and celebrations. A pig is boned, stuffed with garlic, wild fennel and rosemary, marinated in white wine and finally cooked on a spit in the open. The meat gains a unique flavour from the oak and fruit woods used in the fire. *Porchetta* takes hours to cook, and the enticing aroma of roasting meat pervades an entire village.

The best-known dish is *vincisgrassi*, a specialty of Ancona, named after an Austrian general, Prince Windisch-Graetz, who fought against Napoleon. It is lasagne baked in layers with a béchamel sauce mixed with mushrooms, chicken livers or bits of prosciutto, and truffle shavings.

A delicious speciality is *pizza al formaggio*, which is not a pizza but a brioche filled with ricotta and two different kinds of pecorino, fresh and seasoned. The pizza is herby and can sometimes be slightly sweet.

Pasta is on the table every day. *Macaron' fatt' in casa* (homemade pasta) is usually the classic egg tagliatelle (they call them taglierini) and also pappardelle, and the women prepare pasta with as much passion as the women in Emilia-Romagna. Pasta is served with meat and mushroom sauce or with game or chicken livers. *Tortelli di San Leo* are giant ravioli filled with ricotta, spinach or beet greens, and herbs. Around Pesaro they make cheese ravioli with a fish sauce. Cappelletti, a Christmas speciality, are filled with roast pork and boiled chicken or turkey and marrow-bone, and are flavoured with herbs and cinnamon.

A great deal of seafood is offered in this part of the Adriatic coast. Seaside restaurants serve seafood – giant prawns, squid, cuttlefish, octopus, lobster – and a wide range of fish – sardines, anchovies, hake, red mullet, sole, dogfish and scorpion fish. Every little village has its own version of *brodetto* (fish soup) with a different choice of fish, usually between nine and thirteen types, whole or cut in pieces, cooked with the usual onion, garlic, tomatoes, parsley and a drop of vinegar. South of Porto Recanati they roll the fish in flour and fry it before it goes into the soup, and they add saffron, which lends a delicate flavour and a pale, gentle colour.

Local fish specialities are *arrosto segreto*, which is not a roast, but sardines layered with lemon slices and breadcrumbs cooked in a closed (hence the 'secret') pot; *moscioli*, mussels stuffed with ham, parsley and garlic and put under the grill with a sprinkling of breadcrumbs; *seppie ripiene*, cuttlefish stuffed with breadcrumbs and grated cheese and sautéed in white wine; *triglie al prosciutto*, baked red mullet rolled up in slices of prosciutto with sage and garlic. Otherwise, fish is cooked in simple ways, grilled, deep-fried or baked with wine or tomatoes.

Among the meat dishes are *agnello alla cacciatora* (lamb, hunter's style), with sage, fennel and white wine; *braciola all'urbinata*, a meat roll with a thin cheese omelette and a piece of ham inside, browned in oil and cooked in white wine; and *lombo di maiale al latte*, a pork loin rubbed with cinnamon, stuck with cloves and cooked in milk.

The Wines of the Marches

Verdicchio wines, recognisable in their amphora-shaped, two-handled bottles, are, like the Soave of the Veneto, mass-produced and exported in a big way. But they are better than Soave. They are sometimes said to be the best Italian whites to accompany fish and seafood. Produced on the east coast of the Marches, from Verdicchio grapes with a little Trebbiano and Malvasia, the wines are pale green, extremely dry and refreshingly sharp, yet fruity and with a little nuttiness. And there is also an excellent dry sparkling Verdicchio. Of the two Verdicchio appellations, Castelli di Jesi near Ancona is the well-known one, and Verdicchio di Matlica, which has a little more body and flavour, is rarer.

Other inexpensive but appealing wines of the Marches are the whites – Bianchello del Metauro, Faleno dei Colli Ascolani and Bianco dei Colli Maceratesi, all fresh and lively and good with fish – and the reds – Rosso Piceno, Rosso Conero, Sangiovese dei Coli Pesaresi and Lacrima di Morro.

ADRIATIC FISH SOUP
Brodetto alla marchigiana

The many different dialect names for fish soup – *zuppa di pesce, brodo di pesce, ciuppin, brodeto, broeto, cacciucco, burrida, sburita* – are an example of just how complex and perplexing the world of food in Italy can be. Fish soups are also an example of what Italians call their gastronomic *campanilismo*, or regionalism: every port, every beach claims that its is the best. The many soups, which feature a large assortment of fish cooked together in the simplest possible manner, are basically very similar.

The difference lies in the varieties of fish and shellfish used (in Trieste they put in crabs; in Sardinia, lobster; and so on) and in little touches, such as the use (or not) of onions or garlic, vinegar or white wine, together or not, and the use of tomatoes or not. Tuscan *cacciucco* has ginger; in the Marches there may be a touch of saffron; in Romagna they put in masses of garlic; in the Abruzzi and much of the south, chilli. Very rarely, you detect a new note – a few mashed anchovies, for instance, or pieces of potato or sweet red pepper. And that is all.

Fish soups can be served as a first or a second course or as a one-dish meal.

On the Adriatic coast, where fish soup is *brodetto*, they usually cook it with vinegar and *in bianco*, without tomatoes.

The greater the variety of fish, the better the soup. In the Marches they put in a scorpion fish (unobtainable in the UK) at the start, cook it with the tomatoes for added flavour and remove it before serving the soup.

Buy whole fish, steaks or fillets. It is more sensational to see a whole fish in the soup but more practical to serve when it is already cut into pieces. You may prefer to use cheaper kinds of fish such as cod, cut in steaks or chunks. The result will be just as good.

SERVES 8

1.5kg (3lb) mixed fish and seafood, such as turbot, monkfish, hake, flounder, cod, sole, eels, prawns, squid
500g (1lb) mussels or other shellfish
2 onions, chopped
120ml (4fl oz) olive oil
3 cloves garlic, finely chopped

1kg (2lb) tomatoes, peeled and chopped, or use canned
1 teaspoon sugar
Salt and pepper
6 tablespoons white wine vinegar
4 tablespoons finely chopped parsley
8 slices bread, toasted

Scale and clean the fish and shellfish (see page 18), or ask the fishmonger to do it for you.

In a large shallow pan or flameproof casserole from which you can serve the soup (a terracotta dish which will go on the heat can be used), fry the onions in the oil until soft, then add the garlic and fry until the aroma rises. Add the tomatoes and a touch of sugar. Season with salt and pepper, add 500ml (18fl oz) water and simmer for 10 minutes.

Put in all the fish and seafood in the order of the cooking time they need – first the monkfish, then squid and cod, then prawns. Delicate fish, such as hake and sole, go in last. Add vinegar and a little more water if necessary to half cover the fish, and simmer gently for about 15–25 minutes, or until the fish is done. Open the mussels separately in another pan (see page 18) and arrange them on top. Add the parsley and serve with slices of toasted bread.

Variations

Leave out the vinegar and add 250ml (8fl oz) of white wine after the tomatoes. You may also stir in ½ teaspoon saffron threads, or ½ teaspoon ground saffron dissolved in 2 tablespoons water (in the Marches they use wild saffron, or *zafferanella*) towards the end of the cooking.

CHICKPEA SOUP

Minestra di ceci

SERVES 6

1 onion, finely chopped
1 carrot, finely chopped
1 stalk celery, chopped
1 clove garlic, chopped
3 tablespoons olive oil

300g (10oz) chickpeas, soaked for a few hours
2 litres ($3\frac{1}{2}$ pints) stock
4 tomatoes, peeled and chopped
Salt and pepper
500g (1lb) spinach

Soften the chopped vegetables in oil. Add the drained chickpeas, the stock and the tomatoes and simmer for about $1\frac{1}{2}$ hours, or until the chickpeas are tender. Add salt and plenty of pepper when they begin to soften. Wash the spinach leaves and remove the hard stems. Put them into the soup and simmer for a few minutes until they are soft.

STUFFED PIGEON

Piccione ripieno

Pigeons available in the UK haven't the flavour of Italian pigeons, so use the squabs (young pigeons, or *pigeonneaux*) available here. Alternatively, poussins make good substitutes. This recipe comes from the restaurant Degli Ulivi da Giorgio in the Marches.

SERVES 4

For the stuffing (make double quantity for poussins)

250g (8oz) pork, veal or chicken, chopped
2 chicken livers, cleaned and chopped
4 slices bread, crumbled and moistened with
    2 tablespoons milk

1 small egg
Salt and pepper
Freshly grated nutmeg
2–3 tablespoons cognac

4 pigeons, squabs or poussins
2 tablespoons rosemary leaves
A few sage leaves
1 clove garlic, crushed
4 tablespoons olive oil

Salt and pepper
8 slices pancetta or streaky bacon
120ml (4fl oz) white wine
2 tablespoons cognac (optional)

Mix the chopped meat, chicken livers, breadcrumbs and egg together, season well with salt, pepper and nutmeg, add cognac and stuff the birds. Do not overfill.

Spread rosemary, sage, garlic, oil, salt and pepper over the birds, wrap each in pancetta or bacon and place in a roasting tin. Pour in wine and roast at in the oven at 200°C (400°F, gas mark 6) for 30–40 minutes, basting occasionally and adding more wine or a little stock if needed, until tender but still pink on the breast.

If desired, pour cognac over the birds and flame before serving.

WILD BERRIES

Frutti di bosco

A dish of wild berries (though most are likely to be cultivated, not wild) is one of the joys of summertime in Italy.

Serve one fruit only or a mixture of strawberries (*fragole*), raspberries (*lamponi*), blackberries (*more*) and bilberries (*mirtilli*). Pick over the fruit and rinse briefly or, if garden-fresh, avoid washing them. Serve them on a bed of leaves in a shallow basket or platter, to be eaten with sugar and whipped cream or with mascarpone, ice cream or *panna cotta* (page 116).

An unusual way of preparing berries I discovered is *gratinati* – under the grill, with mascarpone spooned over and a sprinkling of sugar.

Lazio

Lazio

Only Rome counts in Lazio. It dominates the region and eighty per cent of the inhabitants live there; the rest are spread out in very small provincial centres such as Viterbo, Rieti and Frosinone. Rome's residents come from all over Italy, especially from Tuscany, the south and Sardinia, to work in the ministries (it is the mecca of civil servants). But the true cooking of Lazio is the cooking of Rome, and it can be found in the taverns and trattorias of the city and in the restaurants in the hills around the city known as the Castelli Romani where Romans escape in the evenings and weekends to enjoy the cool fresh air of the lakes and forests.

Romans have always liked to eat out, a tradition which does not exist to the same extent in most of the rest of Italy. Years ago they went to *osterie fuori porta* (taverns outside the city gates), which sold wine. Groups of friends got together, whole families went, many of them taking their own food, cooked at home and still hot in the saucepan. In the taverns they were given bottles of wine and a sheet of paper to put on the table. They sang, laughed and fought, and the wine flowed until everyone was drunk – at least that is how they remember it. Trattorias were one step up from the taverns. They sold wine and *paniotelle* (bread with butter and anchovies) and one or two home pasta dishes.

I cannot think of a more pleasant and convivial eating place than a Roman one, especially when the weather and the traffic make it possible to sit outside. People go out to restaurants to enjoy themselves, to express themselves and to look at others. It is like going to the theatre. There is an atmosphere of noisy cordiality and joyfulness.

The capital and heart of Italy, once centre of the Roman Empire and capital of the Papal States, Rome is not the capital of Italian cooking. Roman cooking has few elements and all of them are cheap, simply prepared and without frills: a matter of making a virtue out of necessity. It is their very simplicity that is attractive, and something in the way the Romans mix garlic, rosemary and white wine, the way they roast, simmer and deep-fry in a mixture of lard and olive oil, that makes everything taste good.

In the past, pork fat was used in great quantities (every family in Lazio had a pig, which kept them supplied for a year). Now, in line with modern ideas about healthy eating, its place has gradually been taken by olive oil. Many rich vegetable soups, which once gained flavour from pork fat, now have a dribble of olive oil poured on at the end. Roman dishes are all homely and rooted in popular tradition, but the food is really sensual. A popular saying, '*Più se spenne, peggio se magna*' (The more you spend, the worse you eat), is strongly felt. Romans really love their simple food and don't like fancy dishes.

It seems strange that the only cooking anyone knows of in this city of triumphal arches, grandiose monuments, frescoed basilicas and extravagant Renaissance villas is the food of the poor. No dishes, it seems, have come out of the palaces of the aristocracy or from the kitchens of the cardinals other than *abbacchio arrosto*, roast baby lamb – so young that, it is said, 'it has not yet eaten grass' and 'it is more full of its mother's milk than of blood', flavoured with garlic and rosemary; *porchetta*, suckling pig boned and stuffed with garlic and fennel; and *saltimbocca*, thin slices of veal fried with prosciutto and a sage leaf so called because they are said to be so good they 'jump in the mouth'.

Roman cooking is based on pasta, dried beans and offal. This is characteristic of peasant cooking everywhere in Italy, but nowhere more than here. Great quantities of offal were always available in Rome because the nobles and churchmen, who ate so much meat, would eat only the best cuts. Popes were notoriously interested in food and they entertained and were entertained lavishly. How the priests liked their food remains a secret, but what the princes of the Church rejected is the basis of the dishes the Romans love. Many favourite dishes were born in the Testaccio district, in trattorias near slaughterhouses where the rejects (in slaughterhouse jargon *il quinto quarto*, 'the fifth quarter', of the animal) were used up.

Among these popular dishes is *coda alla vaccinara*, a rich oxtail stew (*vaccinari* is used in Rome for 'butchers'). *Zampetti all'agro* are calf's feet served with a green sauce made from anchovies, capers, sweet onions, pickled gherkins and garlic, all finely chopped, bound with potato and thinned with olive oil and vinegar. *Rigatoni alla pajata* (or *pagliata*) is pasta topped with the intestines of newborn veal still full of milk (don't squirm, they are delicious!) cooked with onions, white wine and tomatoes and flavoured with cloves and garlic. These dishes are now hard to get and have become expensive delicacies. *Coratella d'abbacchio* is newborn lamb's heart, liver, lungs and spleen fried with onion and white wine.

Offal is prepared in various other ways. Heart is marinated with oil and garlic and grilled or fried in slices. Liver is grilled and served with a squeeze of lemon, or is dipped in beaten egg and flour then fried in oil and served with lemon, or is sautéed with onions and finished with a wine sauce. Brains are breaded and fried. Kidneys are simply grilled or cooked with plenty of marsala and a squeeze of lemon, or they are cooked with mushrooms and served on toast. Sweetbreads are grilled, sautéed in butter and lemon or cooked in white wine. Calf's head is cooked with onion, garlic, tomatoes and parsley. Tongue is served cold in a salad. *Nervetti* is a boiled veal and calf's foot salad where the meat is cut into strips and dressed, still warm, with oil and vinegar, salt and pepper. Tripe is flavoured with mint and cloves and served with plenty of grated pecorino.

In Lazio the meat used is mostly lamb (the provinces are shepherds' territory and are second only to Sardinia in the number of sheep raised) and pork. Young milk-fed animals and *castrato* (castrated lamb), which has a fatty tender flesh, are especially prized. Baby lamb is cooked hunter's style, as *abbacchio alla cacciatora*, simmered with oil, vinegar, garlic, sage and rosemary; or stewed, as *abbacchio brodettato*, with an egg and lemon sauce.

Here, in the centre of Italy, where the fresh egg pasta of Emilia meets the dry hard pasta of the south, both kinds are eaten. Homemade varieties (if they are to be used in soups they are made without eggs) include sagne, frascarelli, maccheroni, pizzicotti, gnocchetti, falloni, ciufulitti (there are at least two thousand dialect names for pasta varieties in Italy). The most famous Roman pasta dish (they call it 'the immortal') is *bucatini* or *spaghetti all'amatriciana*. The dish originated in Amatrice, a small town that was once part of the Abruzzi,

whose men went to work as cooks in Rome. The sauce is made with *guanciale*, cured meat from the pig's cheek (purists claim that it must be from this part, but you could try bacon) fried in olive oil with a piece of chilli, a few tomatoes and grated pecorino romano, hard, sharp sheep's cheese. The common belief is that another famous dish, *spaghetti alla carbonara*, is Umbrian and was brought to Lazio by *carbonari* (coal men); actually, it is a relatively new dish, and some say it was inspired by the American GIs with their bacon and egg rations. Other favourite pasta dishes are fettuccine (egg noodles) with ricotta and pepper; *spaghetti cacio e pepe* with grated pecorino and plenty of coarsely grated black pepper; and *spaghetti ajo e ojo*, dressed simply with olive oil in which garlic has been fried then removed.

There are some good Roman soups. *Stracciatella* has eggs beaten into a delicate broth. *Minestra di fagioli* is made with beans, herbs and garlic. A soup said to date from Roman times is *zuppa di farro*, made with whole wheat. Many maintain that Caesar's troops conquered the world on *farro* (wheat made up the rations they carried), broad beans, lettuce and pecorino.

Other first courses are *calascioni*, huge ravioli filled with ricotta, spinach and egg and baked in the oven; *fregnacce*, a speciality of Viterbo, thin pancakes quickly poached (it makes them lovely and soft) and served with fresh cheese; and the famous *gnocchi alla romana*. The gnocchi are made from a thick dough of semolina, milk and egg which is poured on to a wet surface and cut into rounds. The gnocchi are baked with a dribble of butter and grated cheese and served with a light tomato and basil sauce or a meat sauce. These gnocchi are a Thursday dish: no one has been able to tell me why.

There is splendid fish and seafood in the restaurants along the coast and in Rome, but there are no authentic, local fish dishes. The people of Lazio started cooking seafood only 30 years ago. In the past, fish, like meat, was only for the tables of cardinals and princes. The people cooked eels (from the Tiber) with garlic, capers, anchovies and white wine, and peas in springtime, and the usual *baccalà* (salt cod) deep-fried or cooked in tomato sauce with raisins and pine nuts. And they always managed to get scampi.

The countryside above Rome is rich with volcanic soil and provides an abundance of vegetables. *Carciofi*, artichokes, are the most popular and most important, and there are several varieties. One, called *romagnolo*, *romanesco* or *mammolo*, is round, sweet and so tender you can eat it raw. There are many ways of serving artichokes: raw, dipped in olive oil or in a vinaigrette dressing; *sott'olio*, preserved in oil; *alla matticella*, brushed with oil flavoured with chopped mint and grilled over burning vine prunings; and, in the springtime, with onion, peas and ham. *Carciofi alla romana* are artichokes stuffed with garlic and mint and cooked in a mixture of oil and water. The famous *carciofi alla giudea* (Jewish style) were popularised by restaurants in the old ghetto, where there was once a large Jewish community. The choke is removed, the hard ends of the leaves are trimmed, and they are opened out like the petals of a flower. The artichokes are then deep-fried, head down, in not very hot oil. They are cooked slowly for half an hour, fried a minute or two in very hot oil in another pan until they are slightly brown and crisp, sprayed with salted water and served immediately with pepper. *Carciofi alla giudea* are heavenly, but they can be prepared only with the entirely edible *romaneschi*. Among other vegetables are a special lettuce with long tender leaves, turnips, beets, broccoli, peppers, sweet white onions, delicate peas, broad beans (so tender they are eaten raw with cheese) and different types of green beans, including a yellow variety called *quarantini*.

Central Italians have adopted the marvellous habit, which started in Rome, of bringing out a dish full of different raw vegetables to be dipped in *pinzimonio*, olive oil with only salt and pepper. Romans also prepare *misticanza*, a mixture of lettuce and wild salad leaves which might include rocket, *rughetta* and *puntarelle*, a type of wild, rather bitter chicory, dressed with olive oil, vinegar, garlic and anchovy.

Deep-frying is a typically Roman way of cooking. It used to be done outdoors to tempt passers-by and is said to have been started in the Jewish ghetto. Romans deep-fry everything: tiny lamb chops, brains, sweetbreads, liver, artichokes, courgettes, ricotta, apples, pears, pieces of bread, provatura cheese, salt cod. The vegetables are dipped in batter, the rest in egg and breadcrumbs. The classic Roman *fritto misto*, made with brains, sweetbreads, liver, artichokes, courgettes, apples, pears and bread dipped in milk, is a favourite antipasto. One of my favourite antipasti is *fiori di zucca farciti*, courgette flowers stuffed with mozzarella mixed with parsley and a bit of anchovy, dipped in egg and flour and then deep-fried.

Serving antipasti is not an old tradition. Restaurants started offering them only twenty years ago, but now they offer a huge selection to choose from. Some are old peasant snacks, such as *bruschetta*, hot toast rubbed with garlic and sprinkled with salt, pepper and olive oil;

panzanella, moistened bread soaked in olive oil and topped with chopped tomatoes; *crostini di midollo*, toast spread with bone marrow; a salad of tomatoes with oil, garlic and torn basil leaves; and roasted peppers, peeled and simply dressed with seasoned oil. You may also come across *crostini di provatura*, skewered cubes of soft cheese alternated with pieces of bread spread with melted butter and a touch of mashed anchovy, heated in the oven. *Supplì al telefono* are rice croquettes filled with meat sauce and mushrooms or simply with bits of mozzarella (which, melted and stringy, resembles telephone cords – hence the name). Frittatas with onions, herbs and vegetables, or with ricotta and ham, and local strong-tasting salty cured hams (some made with garlic, salt and pepper) also have a place on the antipasto table.

At the end of a meal come fresh or aged sheep's-milk cheeses made in the same provincial centres as salami and cured ham (the whey, mixed with cereals, is fed to the pigs), or local buffalo-milk mozzarella and other southern cheeses such as provolone, smoked provola and caciocavallo. Cheese is followed by sweet wine and liqueurs served with *tozzetti* (almond and hazelnut biscuits) and little round *ciambellini* to dunk in the wine. There are few desserts: *zuppa inglese*, a version of trifle, and cherry and plum tarts. People buy marvellous fresh ricotta in little baskets straight from shepherds and eat it mixed with sugar and fresh-roasted coffee, or with honey and cinnamon. Many meals conclude with anise-flavoured sambuca, a sweet liqueur that Romans drink after dinner with *mosche* (literally, flies) in the form of roasted coffee beans floating on top; they also pour sambuca into their morning coffee.

Inspired by the country's mood of returning to its roots, food writers in Rome are looking for their heritage in the Roman Empire. The Renaissance had revelled briefly through a period of fascination with the ancients before tiring of sensation and reverting to the sobriety associated with the Etruscans. Now Rome's gastronomes seek out references to food in the poetry and writings of imperial Rome, studying in particular the treatise on food by Apicius, one of the few food writers we know of from the period (his actual treatise, *De re coquinaria*, has never been found; only his pupils' notes on it remain), and they compare these references with modern Roman cooking. Apicius was an apostle of complication and extravagance. He describes interminable banquets with every conceivable victual from fish cooked alive at the table to peacocks and flamingos cooked and then re-covered in their plumage. Each dish required ten spices and several cooking processes; in the end it must have been difficult to recognise what the dishes and their ingredients were by either look or taste. The gastronomic reputation of ancient Rome rests on accounts of its spectacular feasting, but banquets were an exceptional feature of Roman life and only two hundred families could afford to give them. The feeling of those who cook in Rome today is that nothing much has been inherited from the times of Lucullus except the talent of being *mangioni*, good eaters.

The Wines of Lazio

On summer evenings Romans flock to the Castelli Romani, a range of hills of volcanic formation south-east of Rome with vine-covered slopes, olive groves and chestnut woods, lakes, clusters of little towns and princely villas, to enjoy the local food and wine. The Castelli wines – Frascati, Marino, Velletri, Coli Albani, Colli Lanuvini and Montecompatri-Colonna – are almost all white. Dry or semi-sweet, and derived from Malvasia and Trebbiano grapes, they are unassuming and easy to drink. At their best they are soft, scented and fruity with a bitter almond touch to the aftertaste.

Frascati is the reputed capital of the Castelli and its wine is the most renowned and plentiful, but modern production, especially of the dry variety, does not live up to the old name and true Frascati remains a mirage for most. For the production of Frascati *amabile* (semi-sweet) or *dolce*, or *cannelino*, as the sweet wine is also known, grapes affected by *marciume nobile* (a mould referred to as 'noble rot') may be used or a little concentrated must may be added.

Despite the dominance of white wines, two unclassified reds are among the most esteemed wines in Lazio. They are Fiorano Rosso, produced from a delicious blend of Cabernet Franc and Merlot, and the magnificent and rare Torre Ercolana, which marries these two grapes with Rome's native Cesanese.

SWEET AND SOUR ONIONS
Cipolline in agrodolce

SERVES 4

800g (1¾lb) small pickling onions
50g (2oz) butter
1 tablespoon olive oil

1–3 tablespoons sugar, or more to taste
150ml (5fl oz) white wine vinegar
Salt and pepper

Boil the onions for 1 minute and peel them while they are still warm. Melt the butter and oil in a frying pan and add 1 tablespoon sugar, then the vinegar. Put in the onions, sprinkle with salt and pepper and a little water to cover. Stir well, cover and cook very slowly for 1½–2 hours, checking every so often and adding more water if necessary and shaking the pan so that the onions do not stick. Taste. Add more sugar, if you like, after 1 hour. Serve hot or warm.

Variations

Some cooks in Lazio add a little potato flour and a little stock to the cooking juices and serve the onions with oven-toasted croûtons. Others add a tablespoon of tomato paste to the juices.

In Sicily they make sweet and sour onions with raisins and pine nuts; you can eat them cold. Butter is not used, and the dish is coloured with tomato paste.

BAKED COURGETTE BOATS
Zucchine ripiene

Most regions have their own way of stuffing courgettes. I particularly like this one.

SERVES 4

4 medium courgettes

125g (4oz) veal

1 slice ham

1 tablespoon tomato paste

2 tablespoons grated parmesan

1 small tomato, finely chopped

2 tablespoons breadcrumbs

1 egg

2 tablespoons chopped parsley

A few sprigs of marjoram or oregano, chopped

A good pinch of nutmeg

Salt and pepper

Olive oil

Trim the ends of the courgettes and boil in salted water until you can pierce them with a sharp, pointed knife. Drain and cut them lengthwise. Remove some of the pulp with an apple corer (save for use in soup or salad) and place the courgette shells in an oiled baking dish.

For the filling, chop the veal and ham or blend in the food processor. Mix and work to a paste with the rest of the ingredients except the oil. The mixture, like all fillings, should be strongly flavoured. Stuff the hollowed-out courgette shells with a heaped tablespoon each. Brush the tops with oil and bake in the oven at 200°C (400°F, gas mark 6) for about 35 minutes. Serve hot.

MASHED POTATO AND TOMATO CAKE
Frittata di patate alla romana

This recipe was given to me by Filippo Porcelli, who serves it as an antipasto at his restaurant, Checco er Carrettiere, in the Trastevere district of Rome. His mother made this popular Roman dish when the restaurant first opened. It is called *frittata*, although it is not made with eggs.

SERVES 4

1 large onion, chopped

2 tablespoons olive oil

350g (12oz) tomatoes, peeled and cut into pieces

120ml (4fl oz) dry white wine

Salt and pepper

500g (1lb) potatoes in their skins

Fry the onion in olive oil on very low heat until very soft but hardly coloured, stirring often. Add the tomatoes and wine, season with salt and pepper and simmer for 30 minutes, or until reduced to a thick sauce.

In the meantime, scrub the potatoes and boil them until soft, then peel and mash them. Add gradually to the tomato sauce, letting each spoonful become absorbed, until you have a firm, slightly moist texture. Serve hot or cold, shaped into a cake.

BROTH WITH EGG
Stracciatella alla romana

Stracciatella makes a very pleasant light soup if the broth is good.

SERVES 4

4 eggs
4 tablespoons freshly grated parmesan
Salt

A pinch of nutmeg
1 litre (1¾ pints) meat stock or consommé

Beat the eggs with a fork, add the cheese, a pinch of salt and a pinch of nutmeg.

Heat the stock and, when it comes to the boil, take it off the heat and pour in the eggs, beating all the time. Simmer for 5 minutes on moderate heat and serve at once.

CHESTNUT SOUP
Zuppa di castagne

SERVES 6

125g (4oz) pancetta or unsmoked bacon, finely
    chopped
1 onion, finely chopped
2 cloves garlic, finely chopped
2 tablespoons olive oil
250g (8oz) tomatoes, peeled and chopped, or
    1 can chopped tomatoes

3 tablespoons finely chopped parsley
350g (12oz) shelled fresh chestnuts, or dried
    chestnuts, soaked overnight and drained
200g (7oz) chickpeas, soaked overnight and drained
2 litres (3¼ pints) meat stock
Salt
1 small dried chilli, crushed

Fry the pancetta or bacon, onion and garlic in a large pan in the oil until lightly coloured. Add the tomatoes and parsley and stir for 1–2 minutes. Add the dried chestnuts, if using, and the chickpeas, cover with stock, add salt and the chilli, and simmer gently, covered, for about 2 hours. If using fresh chestnuts, slit the skin, roast under the grill, peel, and add them after 1 hour.

SPAGHETTI WITH EGGS AND BACON
Spaghetti alla carbonara

SERVES 4

250g (8oz) pancetta or unsmoked streaky bacon
1 clove garlic, lightly crushed
3 eggs
400g (14oz) spaghetti

Salt and black pepper
3 tablespoons grated parmesan
3 tablespoons grated pecorino

Fry the bacon in a wide pan in its own fat; add the garlic and remove it when well browned. Break the eggs into a bowl and beat well.

Cook the spaghetti in plenty of boiling salted water until al dente.

Put the spaghetti in the pan with the bacon, stir well and take the pan off the heat. Add the beaten eggs, a pinch of salt, plenty of pepper and a tablespoon each of parmesan and pecorino. Stir until the eggs form a fluid yellow cream, then add the remaining cheese, stir again and serve on hot plates.

SEMOLINA GNOCCHI
Gnocchi alla romana

SERVES 4

1 litre (1³/₄ pints) milk

Salt

125g (4oz) butter

275g (10oz) semolina

75g (3oz) freshly grated parmesan

2 egg yolks

A good pinch of nutmeg

Heat the milk with a pinch of salt and 15g (½oz) butter. When it boils, sprinkle on the semolina and keep stirring vigorously to avoid lumps forming. When it is smoothly blended in, simmer for 15–20 minutes, stirring from time to time.

Take the pan off the heat, add half the cheese and the egg yolks and nutmeg and stir well. Pour the mixture on to a smooth, wet surface and spread about 1cm (½in) thick. Level off the surface using a wet spatula. When cool and set, cut out circles about 5cm (2in) in diameter, using a small glass or a pastry cutter.

Butter a baking dish and arrange the gnocchi, slightly overlapping, in a single layer. Melt the remaining butter, sprinkle it on and cook in the oven at 200°C (400°F, gas mark 6) for about 25 minutes, or until the surface of the gnocchi forms a golden crust. Serve hot.

Variation

Serve the gnocchi with a tomato and basil sauce such as the one on page 19.

VEAL COOKED WITH HAM AND SAGE
Saltimbocca alla romana

This recipe is from Severino of Da Severino in Rome. He entertains his clients with Roman jokes and piano-playing when he feels in the mood. One morning he produced one Roman dish after another so that I could taste while he explained the culinary past and recited a little poem he had written celebrating *saltimbocca*.

SERVES 4

Salt and pepper

1 tablespoon flour

8 slices veal, about 75–125g (3–4oz) each

8 slices of ham, the same size as the veal

8 fresh sage leaves

4 tablespoons olive oil

250ml (8fl oz) white wine

50g (2oz) butter

Salt, pepper and flour the slices of veal. Place a slice of ham on top of each and then a sage leaf. Fasten together with a cocktail stick.

Heat the oil in a large frying pan and fry the *saltimbocca* on a high heat for about 2 minutes on each side. Drain off the oil and pour in the white wine. Allow it to evaporate quickly.

Serve the *saltimbocca* on heated plates. Melt the butter quickly in the pan with the cooking juices and pour this sauce over the meat.

OXTAIL STEW WITH CELERY
Coda alla vaccinara

We cannot buy oxtail in Britain today but I include the recipe in the expectation that it will be available again. This takes time but in the end you are more than rewarded.

SERVES 8

2kg (4lb) oxtail, cut into pieces
1 carrot
1 leek
1 stalk celery
A sprig of thyme
2 bay leaves
Salt and pepper
125g (4oz) streaky bacon, chopped
1 onion, finely chopped
2 cloves garlic, finely chopped

3–4 tablespoons olive oil
2 sprigs of marjoram, chopped
300ml ($\frac{1}{2}$ pint) dry white wine
1kg (2lb) tomatoes, peeled and chopped
A good pinch of nutmeg
1 teaspoon cinnamon
1kg (2lb) celery hearts, cut into pieces
2 tablespoons raisins
2 tablespoons pine nuts

Trim the fat and wash the oxtail. Cover with water in a large saucepan, bring to the boil, simmer for 10 minutes, then drain and throw the water away. Return the oxtail to the pan, cover with water, bring to the boil and remove all the scum. Add the carrot, leek and celery, thyme and bay leaves. Season and simmer for 3 hours. Lift out the oxtail with a slotted spoon and keep the stock for later.

In another saucepan, fry the bacon, onion and garlic in oil until the fat has melted and the onion is golden. Add the marjoram and put in the oxtail pieces. Turn them over, then pour in the wine. Add the tomatoes, salt, pepper, nutmeg and cinnamon, and simmer for 1 hour, or until the meat is so tender that it comes off the bone, adding a little of the stock when necessary.

In the meantime, cut the celery hearts into large pieces and cook in salted boiling water until tender but still crisp. Drain and put them in with the oxtail. Add the raisins and pine nuts and cook 10 minutes more. Serve hot.

CHICKEN WITH PEPPERS
Padellata di pollo e peperoni

A very old and very good Roman dish.

SERVES 4

1 onion, chopped
4 tablespoons olive oil
2 cloves garlic, finely chopped
1 chicken, skinned and cut into pieces

3 yellow and red peppers, cut into 1cm ($\frac{1}{2}$in) strips
    lengthwise
Salt and pepper
A few sprigs of basil or marjoram, chopped (optional)

In a large frying pan, fry the onion in oil until soft; add the garlic and, when the aroma rises, put in the chicken and turn to brown all over. Add the peppers, season with salt and pepper and cook gently, covered, stirring occasionally and moistening with a little water if it seems too dry, for about 25 minutes, or until the chicken is done and the peppers are soft. Sprinkle in the basil or marjoram, if using, towards the end.

BRAINS WITH BUTTER AND LEMON
Cervella al limone

I include this recipe in the expectation that we will be able to eat brains in Britain again.

SERVES 4

4 lamb's or 2 calf's brains, soaked in a few
    changes of cold water
1 tablespoon vinegar

125g (4oz) butter
Juice of 1–2 lemons
2 tablespoons chopped parsley

Remove as much of the covering membrane as possible without tearing the delicate flesh. Blanch the brains in water with a dash of vinegar for moments only until firm. Lift out with a slotted spoon and cut into bite-sized pieces.

Heat the butter until foaming and hazel-coloured, add the brains and the lemon juice and cook gently for 5 minutes until golden brown. Sprinkle with parsley and serve.

Variations
Add 2 tablespoons chopped black olives and 1 tablespoon chopped capers.

MUSHROOMS WITH GARLIC
Funghi trifolati

SERVES 4

350g (12oz) porcini, shiitake or other
    mushrooms
15g (1/2oz) butter
2–3 tablespoons olive oil

2 cloves garlic, finely chopped
Salt and pepper
2–3 tablespoons chopped parsley

Wash the mushrooms and thickly slice them or leave them whole if very small. Heat the butter and oil in a pan and add the garlic and mushrooms. Sprinkle with salt and pepper and cook very gently, stirring every now and then, until the mushrooms are done, adding a few tablespoons of water if too dry. Add the chopped parsley and serve hot as an antipasto or side dish.

Note
In northern Italy these mushrooms are often served on a slice of grilled polenta or as a sauce for tagliatelle.

MIXED SALAD
Insalata mista

With this salad you can improvise.

SERVES 6

1 head lettuce
12 radishes, sliced
1/2 cucumber, sliced
4 tomatoes, cut in wedges
1 fennel bulb, sliced

1 celery heart, sliced
1 green or yellow pepper, cut into strips
1 mild onion or a bunch of spring onions, thinly
    sliced

For the dressing

2 anchovy fillets, finely chopped
1 tablespoon capers, finely chopped
1 clove garlic, crushed

4 tablespoons olive oil
1 tablespoon wine vinegar
Salt and pepper

Wash and dry the lettuce and discard the outer wilted leaves. Tear the leaves into pieces and put them in a bowl with the rest of the ingredients.

Mix the dressing ingredients or blend them in a food processor and toss into the salad when you are ready to serve.

POACHED CHICORY
Indivia belga lessa

SERVES 4

4 large heads chicory
Salt

About 1 litre (1³/₄ pints) water or chicken stock
3–4 tablespoons olive oil

Trim the chicory and poach in salted water or stock until it is just tender. Drain and arrange in a small baking dish. Pour in the oil and turn the chicory to cover well. Serve as is, or bake in the oven at 200°C (400°F, gas mark 6) for 15 minutes, or until very slightly coloured.

STRAWBERRIES WITH LEMON AND SUGAR
Fragole al limone

When wild strawberries are in season you find them everywhere in Italy. In Lazio the best are at Nemi (a strawberry festival is held there in June). Lemon brings out and intensifies the flavour and perfume of even the most ordinary cultivated strawberries.

SERVES 4

700g (1¹/₂lb) strawberries
Juice of 1¹/₂ lemons

3 tablespoons sugar, or to taste

Leave small strawberries whole and cut the larger ones in halves or quarters. Steep for 20 minutes in the lemon juice and sugar.

Variations

You can also steep in orange juice or red wine, or serve the berries with whipped cream.

RICOTTA CAKE
Budino di ricotta

Ricotta is the great cooking cheese of Italy, and many regions have their own ricotta cakes for special occasions. For sweets, sheep's-milk ricotta is said to be the best. This Roman dessert is more a pudding than a cake; in Rome it is made with the marvellous local sheep's-milk ricotta.

SERVES 6

500g (1lb) ricotta
4 eggs, separated
3 tablespoons flour
250g (8oz) sugar

1 teaspoon ground cinnamon
Grated rind of 2 lemons
5 tablespoons rum
Icing sugar

Mash the ricotta and beat well with the egg yolks. Stir in the flour, sugar, cinnamon, grated lemon rind and the rum and mix well. Beat the egg whites until stiff, fold in and pour into a buttered and floured 25cm (10in) cake tin. Bake in the oven at 180°C (350°F, gas mark 4) for about 40 minutes, or until it is firm.

Serve hot or cold dusted with icing sugar.

Abruzzi & Molise

Abruzzi and Molise

These two mountain regions, which until recently were united as one, are very much alike: silent and empty, with high peaks, hills covered with forests, valleys dotted with sheep, and limpid rivers cutting into the mountainsides.

Their rural and pastoral cooking traditions are similar – simple and old. *Maccheroni alla chitarra*, a pasta made by rolling out strips of egg dough over a row of thin wire threads stretched on a wooden frame like strings on a guitar, dates from the fourteenth century. It is eaten with a hare sauce or lamb stew. Lamb and *castrato* (castrated mutton, very tender, with plenty of fat) and the wild foods of the hills and mountains – mushrooms, asparagus, endives, chard and *cipollacci* (bitter tubers that look like small onions) – are cooked here, as are potatoes, cardoons, celery, fennel, tomatoes and cabbage, which are cultivated. The regions grow cannellini beans, and the lentils of Capracotta in Molise vie with those of Castelluccio in Umbria for the title of best in Italy. Wheat is also grown (the excellence of the pasta, considered the best in Italy, is attributed to the quality of the water), as are maize, grapes, olives that produce oil of exceptional quality, and various types of fruit. At Piano di Navelli in Abruzzi saffron is grown (a priest is said to have brought the crocuses back from Persia). Most characteristic of the cooking are the little hot red chillies, lovingly called *diavolilli* (little devils), that go into everything, fresh or dried or in powdered form. *Olio santo*, olive oil in which a *diavolillo* has been steeping, is always at hand.

A meal starts with cheese or with ham and salami. *Mortadella di Campotosto* is an oval salami with a stick of lard running through the centre, and *soppressata* has many streaks of fat. *Ventricina* is a peppery salami flavoured with fennel and orange peel. The smoked hams of Rionero Sannitico are famous, as are the *mulette* of Macchiagodena. *Fegato dolce* (literally, sweet liver), liver and other offal mixed with honey, crystallised citrus peel and pistachio nuts, and *fegato pazzo* (crazy liver), very hot with *diavolilli*, are two unusual Abruzzi sausages. *Nirvi e musse* is pickled baby veal's head.

The seafood dishes of the coast – raw shellfish and raw baby squid with lemon, grills, mixed fry, *scapece* (fried fish marinated in vinegar) – are the usual ones of the south, with the difference that the fish soups and sauces that accompany pasta and risotto are always cooked *in bianco*, without tomatoes, and are peppered with a very generous amount of *diavolillo*.

Abruzzi has a special connection with cooking through Villa Santa Maria, a village squeezed between two great rocks on a hillside among the highest Apennine peaks on the banks of the river Sangro, where many of Italy's best chefs come from. Villa Santa Maria's tradition of dedication to cooking dates back to the sixteenth century when it was owned by the princes Caracciolo, who kept it as a hunting retreat for the summer months. The princes and their friends liked the way the local boys cooked game, and so they brought them back to cook for them at their palaces in Naples. Since then, virtually every young man of Villa Santa Maria has become a cook. First they cooked for families in Naples, and eventually they went to cook in restaurants and for kings and presidents all over the world. Already in 1607 a document in the kitchens of the Gonzagas in Mantua noted that a certain Vincenzo Pavia from Villa Santa Maria had the exclusive right to make pasta by hand in all the lands owned by the Gonzagas. In 1939 a cooking school was started in the village, and in 1962 it was transformed into a state hotel and culinary institute. Young boys from neighbouring villages and from all over Italy come to be taught by the famous dynasties of chefs – the Stanzianis, Marchitellis, Spaventas, Nardizzis, Sabatinis and di Lellos – and chefs from the world over sign up for week-long courses.

The Sagra dei Cuochi del Sangro (festival of the cooks of the river Sangro) is held once a year in Villa Santa Maria, which is called the 'land of international cooking' because the chefs teach classic French and international cooking. Recently, however, on popular demand, they have started to put local dishes – their wives' cooking – on the curriculum. It is the simple cooking of an isolated world which still lives in the past, but you can feel the influence of Apulia, where for centuries generations of Abruzzi and Molise shepherds spent winters with their sheep, and also of Naples, where the chefs of the past learned their trade. Among these are grand game dishes and elaborate ones such as *crespelle*.

The Wines of Abruzzi and Molise

Abruzzi has two great wines: Montepulciano d'Abruzzo (Montepulciano is the name of the region's grape, and the wine is not to be confused with the Tuscan Vino Nobile di Montepulciano) is rated as one of the best wines in Italy. It is plummily rich and mellow yet fresh and with an acid bite. Cerasuolo is the cherry pink rosé version of the same wine. Trebbiano d'Abruzzo is a sharp, dry white wine.

Molise's two wines, Biferno and Pentro, are similar to those of Abruzzi, and they, too, have a Tuscan feel.

GARLIC TOAST
Bruschetta

Bruschetta is found from Tuscany, where it is called *fettunta* (oiled slice), all the way down to Apulia, where very ripe tomato is rubbed into it.

Toast slices of rough country bread on the grill on both sides until golden brown. While still hot, rub one side all over with crushed whole cloves of garlic (you will need $1/2$ clove for each slice). Arrange the toast on a plate and sprinkle with salt, pepper and olive oil (about 1 tablespoon for each slice). Serve hot.

GRILLED CHEESE
Caciocavallo o scamorza alla brace

Grill thick slices of caciocavallo or scamorza (the latter is similar to mozzarella) on a barbecue or under the grill until they start to brown. Serve bubbling hot, sprinkled with pepper and accompanied by country bread.

CURLY ENDIVE SOUP
Zuppa di cicoria

This soup is usually made with wild endive, which is quite bitter.

SERVES 6

2 heads curly endive
Salt
1.5 litres (2$1/2$ pints) light chicken or meat stock
Pepper

3 tablespoons olive oil
50g (2oz) grated pecorino or parmesan
6 slices bread, toasted

Wash the endive and boil in salted water for a few minutes until soft, then drain (this gets rid of some of the bitterness). Chop it finely, in a food processor if you like, and add to the boiling stock. Add pepper and serve with a dribble of olive oil and plenty of pecorino or parmesan, accompanied by toasted bread.

Variation
You can also beat the cheese with eggs and then beat this mixture into the soup off the heat, just before serving, so that the soup becomes creamy.

CURLY ENDIVE AND CANNELLINI BEAN SOUP
Cicoria e fagioli

Although there is no liquid in it, this is served as a soup.

SERVES 6

1 head curly endive	1 small red chilli, fresh or dried
Salt	250g (8oz) can small white cannellini beans, drained
3 cloves garlic	and rinsed
4–5 tablespoons olive oil	6 slices bread, toasted

Wash and drain the endive and boil in salted water for 3–4 minutes, then drain and chop. Bruise the garlic and heat it in 3 tablespoons olive oil until slightly coloured. Add the endive and red chilli and stir well. Add the beans and cook for a few minutes. Remove the garlic and chilli and serve with a dribble of olive oil and toasted bread.

SPAGHETTI WITH CHEESE AND PEPPER
Spaghetti al cacio e pepe

This very simple spaghetti seems to be the favourite of professional cooks. After a day of preparing rich food, this is what they eat.

SERVES 4

400g (14oz) spaghetti	1 teaspoon black peppercorns, crushed with
Salt	mortar and pestle or coarsely ground
100g (3$\frac{1}{2}$oz) freshly grated pecorino or parmesan	

Boil the spaghetti in plenty of salted water until al dente, and drain, reserving a little of the cooking water. Moisten with a few tablespoons of this water, sprinkle with grated cheese and pepper, stir well and serve very hot.

PASTA WITH CHICKPEAS
Pasta coi ceci

This comforting, rustic winter dish can be served as a pasta dish or as a soup. What lifts it out of the ordinary is the addition of good olive oil and hot red chilli at the end, just before serving.

SERVES 4–6

250g (8oz) chickpeas, soaked for a few hours or overnight and drained	250g (8oz) pasta, either tagliatelle, broken into short lengths, or small shells

For the stock

500g (1lb) chicken wings	1 clove garlic
1 large onion	3 bay leaves
1 stalk celery	Salt
1 carrot (optional)	

For the sauce

3–4 tablespoons olive oil	Hot chilli powder to taste

Put the chicken wings in a large saucepan of cold water and bring to the boil. Skim the surface, add the vegetables, garlic, bay leaves and drained chickpeas.

Simmer gently, covered, for about 1$\frac{1}{4}$ hours. When the chickpeas are tender, take out the chicken and bay leaves and season with salt. Take the meat off the wings and return to the stock. There should be plenty of liquid. Add the pasta and cook for 10 minutes, stirring occasionally, until done.

To 3–4 tablespoons of the hot stock add the same amount of olive oil and some hot chilli powder. Mix and pour it over each serving.

LINGUINE WITH WALNUTS
Linguine con le noci

SERVES 4

400g (14oz) linguine or spaghetti

Salt

2–3 cloves garlic, crushed

250g (8oz) walnuts, finely chopped

4 tablespoons finely chopped parsley

A pinch of hot chilli powder (optional)

175ml (6fl oz) olive oil

Boil the linguine or spaghetti in salted water until al dente. Beat the rest of the ingredients into the olive oil, then mix well with the drained pasta, and serve.

ROAST LAMB WITH MINT
Agnello al forno

This lamb dish is from Antonio di Lello and Antonio Stanziani's *La cucina dei grandi cuochi di Villa Santa Maria*. I met Signor Stanziani, who teaches at the professional cooking institute, in the village square, where older men sit and talk of their days cooking in the far corners of the world.

SERVES 8

A leg of lamb, about 2kg (4lb), boned

Salt and pepper

3–4 cloves garlic, crushed

1 large bunch of mint, chopped

3 tablespoons olive oil

Juice of 1 lemon

1 stalk celery, finely chopped

1 carrot, finely chopped

1 onion, finely chopped

Open out the leg of lamb, season and cover with the garlic and half the mint. Roll it up and tie with string. Season outside and place in a roasting tin, fat side up. Pour over oil and lemon juice. Surround with the vegetables and place in a preheated oven at 230°C (450°F, gas mark 8).

Turn the heat down at once to 220°C (425°F, gas mark 7). Roast for 30 minutes. Turn the heat down to 180°C (350°F, gas mark 4), add 250ml (8fl oz) water and roast for a little over 1 hour. The meat should be crisp and brown, but very tender, pink and juicy inside. If you like it very rare, leave the meat at 220°C (425°F, gas mark 7) for just over 1 hour.

Strain the cooking juices. Skim off as much fat as you can. Mix in the rest of the mint and pour a little sauce over each serving.

Note

The vegetables, reduced to a purée to which you could add a glass of white wine to counteract the fat, make a good sauce in which to reheat any left-over lamb gently.

LAMB WITH EGG AND LEMON SAUCE
Agnello brodettato

An Easter dish, with echoes of Greece.

SERVES 6

1 onion, finely sliced

4 tablespoons sunflower oil

1kg (2lb) shoulder or leg of lamb, trimmed of fat
    and cut into 2.5cm (1in) cubes

1/2 bottle dry white wine

Salt and plenty of pepper

A good pinch of nutmeg

3 egg yolks

Juice of 1/2–1 lemon

3 tablespoons finely chopped parsley

Fry the onion in oil until soft. Add the meat and turn to brown the pieces all over. Add the wine, salt, pepper and nutmeg and simmer gently, covered, for up to 2 hours, or until the meat is extremely tender; adding water to keep it moist. There should be a good amount of sauce.

When you are ready to serve, beat the egg yolks with the lemon juice and parsley in a little bowl and stir this into the stew. Leave very briefly on the heat, stirring constantly until the sauce thickens, but do not let it boil or the eggs will curdle.

GRILLED LAMB CHOPS
Costolette di agnello alla brace

Grilling over embers is a popular way of cooking all over Italy, but it is more common in the south, where they are masters of the art.

SERVES 4

4 lamb chops
3 tablespoons olive oil
Juice of $\frac{1}{2}$ lemon, or more to taste
2 cloves garlic, crushed

A sprig of rosemary
Salt and pepper
4 tomatoes
1 lemon, quartered

Marinate the chops in a mixture of olive oil, lemon juice, garlic, rosemary and pepper for about 1 hour. Sprinkle with salt and cook for 10–15 minutes on a hot grill, turning over once, until well browned but still pink and juicy inside. While the chops are cooking, heat the tomatoes on the grill until they soften and the peel can be pulled off easily.

Serve with lemon quarters and tomatoes crushed on the plate with a fork.

RABBIT WITH WINE AND HERBS
Coniglio in tegame

SERVES 4

1 young, tender rabbit, about 1.1kg (2$\frac{1}{2}$lb), cut
   into pieces
2 tablespoons sunflower oil
Salt and pepper

A sprig of rosemary
A few sage leaves
150ml (5fl oz) dry white wine

Brown the rabbit pieces lightly all over in the oil in a large sauté pan. Add salt and pepper, rosemary and sage and pour in the wine. Simmer gently, turning the pieces over occasionally, for 15–25 minutes, until very tender.

PHEASANT CASSEROLE
Fagiano in casseruola

This, like Roast Lamb with Mint (page 169), is inspired by di Lello and Stanziani's collection of dishes.

SERVES 4

125g (4oz) streaky bacon, diced
2 pheasants, 1–1.1kg (2–2$\frac{1}{2}$lb) each
2–3 tablespoons olive oil
1 small onion, chopped
1 clove garlic, chopped
A few sage leaves

300g (10oz) black olives, pitted
250ml (8fl oz) red wine
Salt and pepper
50ml (2fl oz) brandy
2–3 tablespoons chopped parsley

Fry the bacon in a flameproof casserole, remove it and turn the pheasants slowly in the fat, adding olive oil if necessary, until golden. Add onion and garlic and cook for a few minutes. Mix these with the pheasant livers, sage, half the olives and the bacon and fill the cavity of each pheasant. Pour the wine over, season and cook, tightly covered, in an oven preheated to 170°C (325°F, gas mark 3) for about 1 hour, or until tender. To serve, cut the birds in half. Add the brandy and the rest of the olives to the casserole juices and heat through. Serve the meat with the stuffing, sprinkled with parsley and the sauce poured over.

CHICKEN, HUNTER STYLE
Pollo alla cacciatora

SERVES 4

125g (4oz) pancetta or unsmoked bacon chopped
3 tablespoons olive oil
1 chicken, about 1.5kg (3lb)
2 cloves garlic, chopped
500g (1lb) tomatoes, peeled and chopped
150ml (5fl oz) dry white wine

Salt and pepper
A sprig of sage
A sprig of rosemary
2 bay leaves
250g (8oz) mushrooms, sliced

In a large pot or flameproof casserole, fry the pancetta or bacon in the oil for 1 minute or so, then add the chicken and brown it all over. Add the garlic and, when the aroma rises, the tomatoes and the rest of the ingredients. Simmer for 50–60 minutes, or until the chicken is tender, turning over once.

WOOD PIGEON WITH WINE AND HERBS
Palomba in tegame

You can use squab and other small game birds in this way.

SERVES 4

4 wood pigeons
3 tablespoons olive oil
400ml (14fl oz) red or dry white wine
600ml (1 pint) chicken stock
4 tablespoons white wine vinegar
Grated rind of 1 lemon
2 sprigs of sage

2 sprigs of rosemary
2 bay leaves
2 cloves garlic, crushed
5 cloves
1 tablespoon juniper berries, crushed
Salt and pepper

In a flameproof casserole, brown the wood pigeons all over in oil. Add the rest of the ingredients and simmer, covered, for 15–20 minutes, or until done, turning the birds over once. Remove, reduce the sauce by half and return the birds to heat through before serving with the strained sauce.

BROCCOLI WITH BUTTER AND LEMON
Broccoli al limone

SERVES 4–6

1kg (2lb) broccoli
Salt
25g (1oz) butter

Juice of 1 lemon
Pepper

Rinse the broccoli, trim the stalks and divide into florets. Boil in salted water until the stalks are barely tender; drain. Put the broccoli back into the pan with the butter and lemon juice, heat through, and stir to coat. Sprinkle with pepper and serve hot.

Campania

Campania

Below Rome and the 'poverty line', where Italy becomes dry and almost entirely mountainous, is southern Italy, which Italians call the Mezzogiorno. Once backward and primitive, it is still a different world from the north: warm, passionate, generous, steeped in religion and superstition, centred on the family and tradition. They say that history conspired with geography to make it poor.

Because it was unified under the same rulers – colonised by the ancient Greeks, then part of the Roman and Byzantine empires and subsequently dominated by the Normans, Angevins and Aragonese – the regions of the south are fairly homogeneous compared with the rest of Italy, and they belong more to the Mediterranean. The Greeks planted olive trees, vines and durum wheat. Raisins and pine nuts, honey and almonds, orange blossom water and the method of stuffing vegetables came from the Arabs, who ruled Sicily, and from Byzantium; and there is a very strong influence from France and Spain.

The south was a separate kingdom for much of its past: there was the Norman Kingdom of the Two Sicilies, an Angevin monarchy, and the Spanish Kingdom of Naples. The land was owned by the king, the Church and a few baronial families while the peasantry were disenfranchised serfs, the poorest in Europe, tied to the soil, living in abject poverty and oppression in caves and hovels. If you wonder about their legendary joy of living, you are told that it was their way of living for the moment and of making the best of what they had. Making the best of the *piccole cose* (little things) they had is also the basis of southern cooking.

At the end of the nineteenth century, when their only hope was to emigrate, peasants left by the millions for the Americas and for countries around the Mediterranean such as Tunisia and Egypt. Of the five million Italians who went to America between 1880 and 1920, four million came from the south. No ethnic community has had as powerful an influence on American food as they have. Many went into the food business, bringing to it elements of their own home cooking. A new style, a blend from the different regions adapted to the tastes of the New World and bearing little resemblance to the native tradition, was born. And from there the pizzas and pastas and ice creams of southern Italy went on to conquer the world.

Southern Italian food was considered poor and unhealthy (social workers were sent to encourage Italian-Americans to change their eating habits) until American dieticians discovered the merits of a healthy, low-cholesterol Mediterranean diet. Now it is one of the most fashionable cuisines. Rich in grain, vegetables and dried beans, with plenty of fish, little meat and with oil as the cooking medium, it is full of flavours and aromas and what Italians call *fantasia*.

The cooking of Naples, the centre of power in the south since the fourteenth century, is a dominant influence, and many dishes are common to all the regions of the south. But there is great diversity in the form of local variations. It is a characteristic of the south that people did not spread out in the countryside but huddled together in towns and villages on hilltops to protect themselves from bandits, the traditional scourge of the area. The distances and lack of transportation meant that with little contact with others, each village continued to cook in its own special way.

The people of the coast adore fish and buy it fresh when the boats come in. Fishermen still go out to sea in their boats at night and come back in the morning, but there is not much variety left in this part of the Mediterranean. Few households can afford all the types of fish restaurants offer. However, there is plenty of small fish, especially anchovies and sardines, for everyone.

Although the south has the longest coastline in Italy, inland they hardly cook fish. In the past people feared the sea and were suspicious of its products. They lived high up on mountains, next to castles and monasteries far away from the coast, as a protection against piracy and invasion. For peasants the sea did not exist.

The cooking of the hills and mountains is based on

dried eggless hard-wheat pasta – spaghetti, macaroni, vermicelli (there are dozens more commercial types) – and the pasta is still often made by hand; tiny lumps of flour-and-water dough are squashed into little ears, hats, shells, snails and butterflies, or dough is rolled around wires or knitting needles. Pasta is cooked until it is less than tender and a little cooking water or a drop of oil (never butter) is added to keep the pasta moist and slithering. Pasta may be eaten twice a day, but it is always different. Everyone knows the famous southern tomato sauce with fried onions or garlic and herbs. But the variety of sauces and ingredients that are mixed with pasta is endless. Every pasta shape has its own special sauce – with turnip greens, rocket, cauliflower, courgettes, aubergine, peppers, peas and potatoes, lentils, chickpeas and beans, sausage, ricotta, olives, or anchovies – each alone or in combination.

Doughy foods such as pizza and focaccia (a bread brushed with olive oil and herbs) are another staple of southern cooking. *Sfogliata rustica* and *pizza rustica* are big puff pastry and shortcrust pies, respectively, filled with cheese and ham and salami, and sometimes spinach. Half-moon-shaped calzoni are filled with ricotta, mozzarella and raw ham. Panzerotti are like fried ravioli. Then there are *torte* made with a sweet shortcrust pastry and filled with pasta.

Vegetables are the triumph and glory of southern cooking. Campania's highly fertile black volcanic soil, which yields four crops a year in the plain above Naples, provides an unbelievably rich harvest, as does the Apulian plain. Vegetables – the familiar ones of the Mediterranean – are planted between olive and fruit trees, which also serve as a trellis for vines that climb over them. They are eaten as a first or a main course. *Sott'olio* (reserved in oil) or *sott'aceto* (pickled in vinegar), they are real delicacies and make ready antipasti. Young tender vegetables such as artichokes, broad beans and fennel are eaten raw as a side dish, with seasoned olive oil as a dip. Broad beans are used here as much as in Egypt, and in the same ways, mashed into a purée and dressed with oil. Turnip greens (rather than the roots) and a kind of wild endive are also widely used. Aubergines, courgettes and little onions are cooked in *agrodolce* (vinegar and sugar) and eaten cold.

Another common way of preparing vegetables is to slice them and cook them arranged in layers in clay pots. The handmade pots, which are called *tielle* and *pignatte*, and which are a legacy from Spain, are supposed to give a better flavour. Lentils, beans and chickpeas go into soups and pasta dishes. Aubergines, courgettes, peppers and tomatoes are often stuffed. Fillings, based on rice, pasta or breadcrumbs, are enlivened with bits of ham or salami, chopped olives and capers, onions and tomatoes, parsley and cheese.

Fritto misto is an assortment of different vegetables dipped in egg and breadcrumbs or in batter and then deep-fried. It may include courgette blossoms or slices, artichoke hearts, aubergine, potato croquettes, rice balls and cubes of cheese. It is an irresistible dish, done for special occasions: it is not easy to prepare, as you must proceed with the frying while eating – *friggendo mangiando*.

Monasteries and convents have always been associated with vegetables (as well as with liqueurs and sweets), and many vegetable dishes were developed by them. For centuries they had vast holdings and produced fruit and vegetables for the market. In the eighteenth century it was said that half the soil of Naples was held by the Church. With a population of fewer than five million, the kingdom supported twenty-one archbishops, one hundred and sixty-five bishops and abbots, fifty thousand priests and as many monks and nuns. During Lent, clergy and lay alike did not eat meat; some orders never ate meat at all.

Little meat is eaten in the south. In the past, most people ate it only once a year – at Carnival time. It is mainly lamb (the mountains are full of shepherds and their flocks) and pork in the hilltop villages. But it is good meat, full of flavour because the flocks and herds (there are some cattle too) graze in pastures rich in aromatic herbs and berries, and the small black pigs feed on acorns in the forests. Meat is mostly cooked directly over the fire with only herbs and a little olive oil. Lesser cuts are cooked slowly, for a long time, in stews. They are also made into *polpette* (meatballs) or *involtini* (meat rolls), which may be stuffed with ham, parsley and grated pecorino or with pine nuts and raisins. Rabbits and chicken are kept, and there is still wild boar and a few game birds.

Every winter at pig-sticking time, in the hills and mountains, pigs are turned into cured and smoked hams, bacon, black pudding, *zampetti* (stuffed pig's feet) and all kinds of salami. Among the sausages are *cervellata*, made with red wine and fennel seeds; *capocollo*, soaked in wine must with pepper and smoked over oakwood; and *soppressata, 'nduglie* and very hot *morsello* – all three full of red chilli. The pork fat is melted down and kept for cooking.

The classic fresh cheeses of the south are made with sheep, goat, cow or buffalo milk and are some of the best

Italy has to offer. They are eaten as a first or second course and make wonderful melting cheeses for cooking. The most famous, *mozzarella di bufala*, is a speciality of Naples, near which great herds of buffalo are raised. It is said they originated in India, but they have been in the once marshy areas of Campania since Roman times. Mild, porcelain-white stringy mozzarella is pulled and made into small balls and braids. Eaten fresh on the day it is made, it is something really fabulous – nothing like the vacuum-packed variety. When made with cow's milk it is called *fior di latte*.

Mozzarella is eaten as is, sometimes with a dribble of olive oil and a sprinkling of salt and pepper or as an antipasto with tomatoes and basil. It is called *impannata* when dipped in egg and breadcrumbs and deep-fried and *in carrozza* when fried between pieces of bread (the bread is sometimes dipped in milk). *Crostini* are prepared with mozzarella on toast, with chopped anchovy, tomatoes and a sprinkling of oregano, all put under the grill. Scamorza, made in the mountains and similar to mozzarella, is grilled over the fire until brown, and is eaten while still hot and creamy inside.

Caciocavallo, pear-shaped with a small ball at the top, is so called because the cheeses are tied up and hung in pairs astride a pole (*a cavallo* – literally, on horseback). It is semi-hard and strong-flavoured and can be eaten fresh, ripened or smoked. It can also be grilled or fried and used for cooking. Ricotta is eaten fresh and creamy or fermented and strong. Cacioricotta, hard salted ricotta, is used for grating. Goat's cheese is flavoured with herbs. Pecorino, made from sheep's milk, is mild or piquant and is sometimes preserved in oil or left to dry and then used for grating. Provola and provolone, both plain and smoked, also come from the south. Other specialities are tuma and burrino, or butirro, which has butter trapped in the middle.

All the people in Campania seem to be crowded into Naples while the land around the city is empty, abandoned by everyone except the elderly for northern Italy, Germany and Switzerland. The exuberant, chaotic, desperately lively Naples of the Camorra (the local Mafia) and the decaying slums was once the splendid, gay and powerful capital of the great kingdom of the south. The Spanish kings especially had a love of splendour and good living. From the time Alfonso, King of Aragon and Sicily, became King of Naples in 1442 and his court began to attract scholars and artists, Naples remained a centre of good food. Although *spagnolismo* (Spanish high living) was restricted to those near the court, the nobility owned vast areas of land and ruled as despotic lords from their country retreats. Their dishes became the carnival and festive foods of the south.

The cooking of Naples took its present shape in the eighteenth century when the crops brought back from the Americas by the Spaniards became widespread. Peppers and tomatoes especially had a dramatic effect in the kitchen: from green to yellow, everything became red. Today tomatoes are all-important – an ever-present ingredient, almost a religion. Tomatoes were married with pasta, which had come as early as the thirteenth century from Sicily, where the Arabs had introduced it. Soon the *mangiafoglie* (leaf eaters) became *mangiamaccheroni* (pasta eaters) and Naples became the queen of *maccheroni* (the general term for long pasta).

The glittering capital of the south was a magnet for the thousands who poured in from the countryside looking for work with the nobility. A tradition of street food sprang up to cater for these *disgraziati lazzaroni* (wretched good-for-nothings), as they were called, who lived on the street, waiting for work. Raw shellfish, snails bubbling in tomato sauce, tripe, innards of every kind, pizza, fruit and pasta were sold from colourful stalls. *Maccheroni* were first seen here by visitors from abroad, many of whom wrote of their amazement at finding Neapolitans eating the long strips with their hands.

Even today, people can remember *maccheroni* hanging on washing lines across the streets to dry. Sea towns had the ideal weather, with alternating hot and cold air, for drying pasta in the least possible time, so that it could keep, and they became centres of a thriving cottage industry. In 1840 the first large industrial pasta-making plant opened in Naples at Torre Annunziata. Hundreds more followed and exported their products all over the world.

Pizza was also born in Naples when tomatoes were teamed with bread. It is the ideal fast food for a city where everyone is always out in the street. Neapolitans still make the best – very thin, crisp and brown outside and soft inside, with a light topping. Although there are endless varieties now in the UK and elsewhere, the only ones local people eat are *pizza napoletana*, with tomato and garlic; *pizza alla marinara*, with tomato, olives and anchovies; and *pizza Margherita*, with tomato, mozzarella and a whiff of parsley, oregano or basil. The Pizzeria Piltro in Naples boasts that its original owner, Raffaele Esposito, invented the *pizza Margherita* with its green, red and white colours in honour of Queen Margherita of Savoy, wife of King Umberto I, who sent for a pizza when she came to the city to escape a cholera epidemic.

It is not all poor food in Naples. Something remains of the old Spanish Bourbon court cuisine. At the end of the eighteenth century King Ferdinand's queen, Maria Carolina, dazzled by her sister Marie Antoinette's court of Versailles, asked her to send the best cooks of France. So started an era of French influence with the Naples aristocracy. Those were the days when Sir William Hamilton was British ambassador and his wife, Emma, the mistress of Nelson, was the bosom friend of Maria Carolina.

According to legend, the king was a populist and insisted that *maccheroni* be served every day at the palace. His wife complained that palace etiquette did not permit eating with the hands, so the palace cook devised dishes that could be eaten easily with a fork and did not need to be sucked in while the sauce splattered. *Sformato Ferdinando*, with meatballs, chicken livers and black truffles, is still served, as are other refined and elaborate dishes such as *timballo di maccheroni, crespelle* (little pancakes), *sartù di riso* (a layered rice cake) and *gattò di patate*, filled with ham and cheese. These and some Neapolitan sweets – *babà* (baba); *sfogliatelle*, puff pastries filled with ricotta and candied fruit, often eaten hot; *pastiera*, an Easter cake now found all over Italy, all year round; *rococò*, orange-flavoured almond rings made at Christmastime; *zeppole di San Giuseppe*, fritters stuffed with a pastry cream; *croccante*, made with hard caramel and chopped nuts sculpted into extraordinary shapes; and the famous *zuppa inglese*, made with rum-soaked madeira cake and chocolate cream – came out of the old court kitchens. After the French Revolution, French cooks came to work for the Naples nobility in great numbers. *Monsù* (the dialect word for cook) is derived from the French *monsieur*. The first Neapolitan cookery book, *Il cuoco galante* (The Gallant Cook), written by Vincenzo Corrado in 1765, features mainly French dishes eaten at the tables of wealthy and noble families. *La cucina teorica pratica* (Practical Theoretical Cooking), written in 1837 by Don Ippolito Cavalcanti, Duca di Buonvicino, was also about French cooking, but it included some Neapolitan recipes in the local vernacular.

Now people prefer the simpler foods, but they all still make ragù, the prince of Neapolitan foods, which takes all day. Rolls of meat are stuffed with parsley, garlic, cheese, raisins and pine nuts and simmered slowly in wine with bacon and tomatoes. They call it *ragù del guardiaporta* because it needs someone like a doorman to watch over it lovingly and to keep adding water while it simmers away. The sauce is served by itself with pasta as a first course, and then the meat rolls are served as the second.

Desserts play an important role on religious festive days. Many were once the speciality of convents. Most are made with almonds or ricotta, and there are walnuts, wine must, honey, orange blossom water and dried and crystallised fruit. But the usual way to end a meal is with fresh fruit – citrus fruits, figs, apricots and peaches, cherries, grapes, melons, apples and pears – and ice cream and sorbet, which are magnificent.

Italian coffee is perhaps the most appreciated in the world, and Neapolitans claim to make the best with their coffee-pot, *la napoletana*, which is the oldest in Italy. To make coffee in it, water goes into the bottom half; filter-fine, double-roasted coffee grounds go into a metal filter placed on top; then a top half with a filter and a spout is screwed on with the spout pointing down. The pot is put over heat, and when the water boils it is turned over upside-down, so that the water slowly filters through the grounds into the part with the spout. *La napoletana* does not produce as strong and bitter a coffee as the famous *moka* pot or as espresso machines, which extract coffee by steam and pressure, but it is a method that, Neapolitans say, obtains the purest flavour and preserves the maximum aroma.

The Wines of Campania

Campania produces large quantities of wine but very few good ones. The best, which rate with Italy's most distinguished, are made in the hills around Avelino where three very ancient vines – Aglianico, Greco and Fiano – have, through careful selection, been brought to international repute. Taurasi is an austere, long-ageing red made from Aglianico grapes (the name derives from the word *Hellenic*). It is extraordinarily rich and complex with a magnificent bouquet.

Fiano de Avellino, an exceptionally dry white with the memory of pears, peaches and hazelnuts in the flavour, has such a strong character that it is very much an acquired taste. Greco di Tufo, a very dry white, has an almond flavour with lemon and liquorice.

Lacryma Christi del Vesuvio, the region's famous wine made from grapes grown on the slopes of Vesuvius and its environs, is red, white or rosé, and the white can be still or sparkling, dry or sweet. But the quality is usually found to be abysmal.

The islands of Capri and Ischia off the coast make pleasant wines.

CLASSIC NEAPOLITAN PIZZA
Pizza alla napoletana

While more than half the regions of Italy now claim their own special pizza, and an infinity of modern versions, many of them inspired by American preparations, can be found throughout the country, old Neapolitan classics remain the favourites. A homemade pizza (basically a flat round of bread with a topping) cannot compete with one made in a wood-fired baker's oven, but it can be very good if your oven gets really hot enough.

Basic dough for pizzas

500g (1lb) plain flour, sifted, plus extra for flouring
½–1 teaspoon salt
15g (½oz) dried yeast
About 250ml (8fl oz) warm water
Pinch of sugar
About 3 tablespoons olive oil for the bowl and the baking sheets

Put all but 25g (1oz) of the flour in a large bowl with the salt. Dissolve the yeast in 120ml (4fl oz) of the water with the sugar. When it begins to froth, pour the yeast mixture into the flour, then pour in the rest of the warm water gradually, first mixing with a wooden spoon, then working the flour into the liquid with your hands. Add only just enough water so that the dough holds together in a ball (it is difficult to be precise with quantities because flour varies from one country to another in its capacity to absorb water, and even flour made from wheat from the same field varies from year to year). Knead for 10–15 minutes, until the dough is smooth and elastic, adding a little more flour if it is too sticky. Pour a tablespoon of oil in the bowl and turn the ball of dough in it to cover it well with oil so that a dry crust does not form when it rises. Cover the bowl with a damp cloth and leave to rise in a warm place for 1–2 hours until doubled in size.

Punch the dough down and work it a little with your hands; then divide into four balls to make four individual pizzas. Roll out each ball of dough on a lightly floured surface with a lightly floured rolling pin into a 23cm (9in) circle about 0.5cm (¼in) thick. Pinch the edges, if you like, to make a slight rim and place on well-oiled baking sheets or in round pie dishes.

Cover with one of the following toppings (the quantities given are for an individual pizza) and bake in the hottest part of the oven at the highest possible setting for about 15–20 minutes, or until the crust is crisp and coloured.

Pizza aglio, olio e origano. Brush with 3 tablespoons olive oil and sprinkle with 3 finely chopped cloves of garlic, 1 tablespoon finely chopped oregano (or 1 teaspoon dried oregano), salt and pepper.

Pizza aglio, olio e pomodoro. Do the same as above but add a few tablespoons canned peeled tomatoes, well drained of juice and chopped.

Pizza Margherita. Spread with 2 well-drained and chopped canned peeled tomatoes and sprinkle with some diced very good quality mozzarella, 1 tablespoon grated pecorino or parmesan, a few torn basil leaves, salt and pepper, and drizzle with olive oil.

Pizza Margherita bianca. Use the same ingredients as above but without the tomatoes and with more mozzarella.

Pizza alla marinara. Spread with 2 well-drained and chopped canned tomatoes and sprinkle with ½ tablespoon capers, 1 tablespoon good-tasting pitted black olives, 4 chopped anchovies, salt and pepper.

COUNTRY PIZZA
Pizza rustica

This pizza is an unusual combination of sweet pastry and savoury filling. Rich pies, once festive country dishes, are now part of the restaurant and fast-food trade. I tasted a few different and very delicious ones at Ciro, in the centre of Naples, where people at neighbouring tables told me they had come almost every working day for twenty or thirty years and they always ordered the same things.

SERVES 8

For the pastry
125g (4oz) unsalted butter
50g (2oz) sugar

1 egg
250g (8oz) flour

For the filling
6 eggs, separated
500g (1lb) ricotta
50–125g (2–4oz) salami, cut very thick
50g (2oz) ham, cut thick
125g (4oz) mozzarella

125g (4oz) smoked mozzarella or other smoked
  cheese
2 tablespoons grated parmesan
Salt and pepper

To prepare the pastry dough, cream the butter and sugar and beat in the egg, then add enough of the flour gradually, mixing well, until you have a soft dough. Cover with clingfilm and leave in a cool place for 1 hour.

For the filling, beat the egg yolks one at a time into the ricotta. Chop the salami, ham, mozzarella and smoked cheese into small cubes and add them. Add the parmesan and seasoning. Beat the egg whites until stiff and gently fold in.

Butter and flour a 23cm (9in) tart tin. Divide the pastry into two pieces, one twice as big as the other. Roll out the larger piece and use to line the tin. Add the filling. Roll out the rest of the dough, cover and seal the edges. Prick the surface all over with a fork. Bake in a preheated oven at 190°C (375°F, gas mark 5) for about 50 minutes.

Note
The top may be brushed with beaten egg yolk or milk to brown nicely.

SPINACH AND HAM PIE
Torta rustica con spinaci

This thick vegetable pie, which you find all the way down to Calabria and Sicily, is not very different from the famous Ligurian *torta pasqualina*, made with artichokes and ricotta.

SERVES 6

For the pastry

250g (8oz) flour

50g (2oz) sugar

Pinch of salt

Grated zest of $\frac{1}{2}$ lemon

125g (4oz) unsalted butter

3 egg yolks

Beaten egg, for glazing

For the filling

500g (1lb) fresh spinach

Salt and pepper

250g (8oz) medium tomatoes, peeled and sliced

175g (6oz) cooked ham, diced

500g (1lb) mozzarella, sliced

Mix the flour, sugar, salt and lemon zest. Rub in the butter, then add the egg yolks and mix briefly until the pastry holds together in a soft ball, adding a little water if necessary. Cover with clingfilm and leave in a cool place.

Wash and trim the spinach and cook it, covered, until it crumples. Add salt and pepper.

Divide the dough into two parts, with one slightly larger. Roll out the larger part and line a greased and floured 23cm (9in) tart tin with it. Drain the spinach, squeeze dry and spread over the pastry shell. Lay the tomato slices on top. Sprinkle with ham and salt and pepper and cover with mozzarella.

Roll out the rest of the dough and cover the pan, tucking it into the sides. Prick with a fork, brush with beaten egg and bake in the oven at 230°C (450°F, gas mark 8) for 10 minutes, then lower the oven to 150°C (300°F, gas mark 2) and bake 30 minutes more, or until golden.

Variation

Substitute 6 frozen or canned artichoke hearts, well drained and sliced, for the spinach.

TOMATO AND MOZZARELLA SALAD
Insalata di pomodori e mozzarella

Use fresh or imported mozzarella, making sure that it does not taste stale.

SERVES 4

2 large ripe tomatoes, sliced

350g (12oz) mozzarella, sliced

Salt and pepper

5–6 tablespoons olive oil

A few sprigs of basil, coarsely chopped

Arrange the tomatoes and mozzarella on a flat serving dish. Dress with salt, pepper and olive oil and sprinkle with basil.

COURGETTE SALAD
Zucchine scapece

SERVES 4

500g (1lb) courgettes
Salt
Oil for frying

2 cloves garlic, sliced
A few sprigs of mint, chopped
1–2 tablespoons wine vinegar

Slice the courgettes, not too thinly. Sprinkle with salt and let stand for 1 hour, then rinse and dry thoroughly.

Fry quickly, a few slices at a time, in hot shallow oil, turning them over once, until lightly browned. Add the garlic towards the end.

Drain on absorbent paper towels, then place in a bowl, with mint, garlic and vinegar sprinkled between the layers. Leave to marinate for a few hours before serving cold.

Variations

For a sharper version, add some hot chilli powder to the frying oil.

A modern procedure is to marinate thinly sliced or chopped raw courgettes for a day in a mixture of oil, vinegar, salt, pepper, garlic and mint.

BROAD BEANS WITH SHEEP'S OR GOAT'S CHEESE
Fave stufate al cacio

When broad beans have just come into season and are very young and tender, they are eaten raw with their pods and skins removed. At Ristorante Cappuccini Convento the beans are served cooked, and with goat cheese. The restaurant is in what was once a convent, carved out high on a cliff overlooking the Amalfi road. The chefs there like to cook vegetable dishes from the old convents of the region.

SERVES 4

1kg (2lb) fresh broad beans in the shell
1 large onion, chopped
4 tablespoons olive oil

Salt and pepper
250g (8oz) soft, lightly salted sheep or goat cheese,
    thickly sliced

Shell the broad beans. Fry the onion in the oil until golden. Add the beans, stir for 1–2 minutes, then cover with water, season with salt and pepper, and simmer about 15 minutes, or until they are very tender and the liquid is absorbed. Serve hot with the cheese, warmed under the grill, on the same serving dish.

SARDINES IN SPICY SAUCE
Sardine alla scapece

Luca, who has a little restaurant called Alfonso a Mare in a fishing cove at Praiano on the Amalfi coast, gave me this recipe.

SERVES 8

1.5kg (3lb) fresh sardines	1kg (2lb) onions
Juice of 1 lemon	175–250ml (6–8fl oz) vinegar
Salt	1 whole head garlic
Flour	2 chillies, preferably fresh
Olive oil	8 tablespoons finely chopped mint leaves

Gut and clean the sardines; remove the heads and backbones if you wish. Soak them in water, lemon juice and 1 teaspoon salt for about 30 minutes to remove the strong flavour. Drain and pat dry. Dip the sardines in flour, fry in olive oil, drain on absorbent paper towels, and sprinkle with salt.

Cut the onions into biggish rings and fry in 2 tablespoons oil. When half cooked, pour in the vinegar and cook until it has nearly evaporated. Chop the garlic and chillies, and add them and the chopped mint to the onion and cook a little longer.

Place the sardines in a serving dish and cover with the sauce. Leave for several hours to marinate. Before serving, add a little more olive oil and some mint.

SEAFOOD SALAD
Insalata di frutti di mare

You can make a salad with only one or two kinds of seafood, dressed with oil and lemon.

SERVES 12 OR MORE

2kg (4lb) mussels or a mixture with clams	6 large scallops
1 small octopus or baby ones (if you can find them), about 500g (1lb)	175ml (6fl oz) olive oil
500g (1lb) small or medium squid	Juice of 2–3 lemons
500g (1lb) uncooked prawns	Salt and pepper
	8 tablespoons finely chopped parsley

Clean the mussels and clams, if using them, steam them open (see page 18) and remove them from their shells. Clean the octopus (see page 18) and simmer in the strained liquor of the mussels and clams with added water for 30 minutes, or until tender. Clean the squid (see page 18), cut the body into rings and add to the octopus. Five minutes later, add the prawns and scallops; cook only moments, until the prawns turn red and the squid and scallops become opaque. Drain quickly.

Cut the octopus into small pieces and peel the prawns. Cut the scallops in half. Arrange on a serving dish with the squid and mussels. Dress with a mixture of olive oil and lemon juice, salt and pepper. Leave to marinate in a cool place for at least 1 hour before serving. Sprinkle with chopped parsley.

BOILED OCTOPUS
Polpo affogato

This way of boiling octopus whole (*affogato* literally means drowned) is very popular all around the coast in the south. It is simple and attractive, especially when the double-tentacled *verace* are used. The tentacles curl up like the petals of a curious pink and white flower. It is usually served as an appetiser.

SERVES 8

2 small or 1 large octopus, about 1kg (2lb)
Salt
4 tablespoons olive oil
Juice of 1 lemon

Pepper
2 cloves garlic, crushed
4 tablespoons finely chopped parsley

Clean the octopus (see page 18). Blanch in boiling water for 1 minute, or until the scum rises; then throw away the water and boil in fresh salted water until tender. Octopuses weighing less than 500g (1lb) take from 25–45 minutes; larger ones can take up to 1½ hours.

Drain and dress with olive oil and lemon juice, salt and pepper and a sprinkling of garlic and parsley. The octopus is usually served hot or warm, cut into slices, but it is also very good cold.

COURGETTE SOUP
Minestra di zucchine

This easy soup is light, fresh and aromatic.

SERVES 6

350g (12oz) courgettes, finely chopped
1–2 tablespoons olive oil
1 litre (1¾ pints) light chicken stock
Salt and pepper

2 eggs
3 tablespoons finely chopped parsley
3 tablespoons finely chopped basil
3–4 tablespoons grated pecorino or parmesan

Fry the courgettes quickly in oil until lightly coloured. Add the stock, salt and pepper and simmer 15–20 minutes, or until tender. Beat the eggs with the herbs and the cheese and pour into the soup, beating well, just before serving. Do not let it boil.

PASTA WITH GARLIC AND OIL
Pasta aglio e olio

The poorest pasta dish of the south is one of the most popular.

SERVES 4

400g (14oz) spaghetti or bucatini
Salt
5 cloves garlic, crushed

1 small chilli, finely chopped or crushed (optional)
120ml (4fl oz) or more olive oil
8 tablespoons finely chopped parsley

Start cooking the pasta in plenty of salted boiling water, and make the sauce. Beat the garlic and, if you like, the chilli (if this is used the dish is called *aglio, olio e peperoncino*) and salt into the olive oil. When the pasta is cooked al dente, drain quickly and dress with the oil mixture and a generous sprinkling of parsley. Do not add grated cheese.

You may fry the garlic until slightly coloured in a little of the oil if you do not like it raw.

Variation

Other herbs, such as basil and mint, are sometimes added with the parsley. A restaurant in Trapani, in Sicily, uses thirteen, including marjoram, oregano, thyme, sage and rosemary, and calls it *spaghetti alle erbe*. You might like to try this.

SPAGHETTI WITH CHERRY TOMATOES
Spaghetti con pomodorini

Spaghetti dressed with fried onion or garlic and tomato pulp cooked down to a smooth sauce has travelled around the world, but this way, with barely cooked cherry tomatoes served on top of the pasta, is more popular in Naples and the Italian south today.

SERVES 4–6

500g (1lb) spaghetti or other pasta

Salt

3–4 cloves garlic, chopped

3 tablespoons or more olive oil

1kg (2lb) small or cherry tomatoes, halved

1 teaspoon sugar

1 small chilli, seeded and chopped (optional)

4 tablespoons coarsely chopped basil or parsley

Grated pecorino or parmesan

Cook the pasta in rapidly boiling salted water, stirring occasionally so that it does not stick, until only just tender. Drain.

Fry the garlic in the oil until golden. Add the tomatoes, sugar, chilli, if using, and herbs, and cook until soft.

Serve the tomatoes on top of the pasta, moistening with a little cooking water or oil if you like. The last to be served are supposed to be luckiest because they get the best of the sauce. Pass the cheese around.

Variations

For another, more usual tomato sauce, fry 1 chopped onion or 2 chopped cloves garlic in 2 tablespoons oil until golden, and add 1–1.5kg (2–3lb) peeled and chopped tomatoes. Stir in 2 tablespoons tomato paste if you like, season with salt, pepper and 1 teaspoon sugar, and simmer until quite thick, then add a few sprigs of parsley and basil, finely chopped.

For *maccheroni al pomodoro al forno* (baked macaroni with tomato sauce), mix 500g (1lb) pasta with a hole, such as penne or rigatoni, cooked a little less than al dente, with the above tomato sauce and 4 tablespoons grated parmesan in a baking dish. Stir in 250g (8oz) diced mozzarella and, if you like, also 350g (12oz) ricotta. Cover with a sprinkling of breadcrumbs and a few shavings of butter and bake in the oven at 180°C (350°F, gas mark 4) for 30 minutes, or until golden.

SPAGHETTI WITH OLIVES, CAPERS AND ANCHOVIES
Spaghetti alla puttanesca

No one knows the origin of this curious name, which literally means whore's style, but it appeared forty years ago. The sauce is very popular all over Italy and is served also with vermicelli or linguine. Large black *gaeta* olives are used.

SERVES 4

3 cloves garlic, chopped

4–5 tablespoons olive oil

500g (1lb) tomatoes, peeled and chopped

4 tablespoons capers, squeezed

125g (4oz) fleshy, tasty black olives, pitted

1 small hot chilli, chopped

A few sprigs of oregano

125g (4oz) anchovy fillets, finely chopped

4 tablespoons finely chopped parsley

Salt

500g (1lb) spaghetti, vermicelli or linguine

Fry the garlic in 2 tablespoons olive oil until golden. Add the tomatoes, capers, olives, chilli and oregano, and simmer for about 10 minutes, then add the rest of the oil. A minute before serving, add the anchovies and parsley, and salt if necessary (you may not need it).

Cook the pasta in boiling salted water until al dente, drain quickly and serve dressed with the sauce.

SPAGHETTI WITH MUSSELS
Spaghetti alle cozze in bianco

Spaghetti with shellfish – usually *vongole* (clams) – is the most popular dish on the southern coast. Other pasta, such as linguine and vermicelli, and other shellfish, such as *cozze* (mussels) or *datteri* (sea dates), are also used, and the sauce is made with or without tomatoes. There are those who like to remove the shellfish from the shells and those who prefer to leave them in – mainly for aesthetic reasons.

SERVES 4

1kg (2lb) mussels	2 cloves garlic, chopped
400g (14oz) spaghetti	4 tablespoons olive oil
Salt and pepper	3 tablespoons finely chopped parsley

Clean and open the mussels in a large pan (see page 18). Remove them from their shells or leave them in, as you wish. Strain the liquor from the pan.

Cook the spaghetti in plenty of vigorously boiling salted water until it is al dente.

In the meantime, fry the garlic in oil and add the strained mussel liquor. Boil vigorously to reduce the liquor, then add the mussels, sprinkle with salt and pepper and cook for a moment longer: the mussels need only be heated through.

Drain the spaghetti, cover with the mussels and sprinkle with parsley. Do not serve grated cheese.

Variations

For *spaghetti alle cozze coi pomodori* (with tomatoes), add 4 medium very ripe peeled and chopped tomatoes with the strained mussel liquor to the garlic when it begins to colour. Simmer until reduced to a thick sauce, then continue as in basic recipe.

CANNELLONI WITH MUSHROOMS
Cannelloni ai funghi

Cannelloni were born in Amalfi, which was once a great naval power and important centre of trade with the East. The town made itself a free republic in 839, and it boasts a style of cooking of its own.

For this recipe and the following, you can use homemade pasta or bought fresh lasagne.

SERVES 6–8

200g (7oz) flour	2 eggs
Salt	

For the filling

500g (1lb) mushrooms, coarsely chopped	2 tablespoons grated parmesan
1 clove garlic, crushed	A good pinch of nutmeg
3 tablespoons olive oil	50g (2oz) prosciutto, cut into squares
Salt and pepper	125g (4oz) gruyère, thinly sliced
400g (14oz) ricotta	

For the béchamel sauce

40g (1½oz) butter	A good pinch of nutmeg
3 tablespoons flour	Salt for boiling the pasta
600ml (1 pint) hot milk	1 tablespoon oil for boiling the pasta
Salt and pepper	
2 tablespoons grated parmesan	25g (1oz) butter, melted

Make the dough as described on pages 110–111, and roll it out thinly (but not quite as thinly as for tagliatelle). Cut into fourteen 10 × 15cm (4 × 6in) rectangles. Or use bought lasagne.

To make the filling, cook the mushrooms with the garlic in the oil for about 10 minutes, adding salt and pepper. Mash the ricotta and mix in the parmesan, salt, pepper, nutmeg and mushrooms.

To make the béchamel sauce, melt the butter, add the flour and stir well with a wooden spoon to blend them. Gradually add the milk and keep stirring until the sauce thickens. Add salt, pepper and nutmeg.

Now cook the pasta rectangles, a few at a time, in plenty of salted boiling water with oil to keep them from sticking. While still a little firm, lift out with a slotted spoon, drain and lay them out on a slightly damp cloth.

To assemble the cannelloni, place a small piece of prosciutto in the centre of each pasta rectangle, cover with a slice of gruyère and top with a heaped tablespoon of filling, in a thin line. Then roll up the pasta.

Spread 3 tablespoons of the béchamel on the bottom of a baking dish and arrange the rolled cannelloni in a single layer in it. Cover with the rest of the sauce, sprinkle with grated parmesan and melted butter, and bake in the oven at 200°C (400°F, gas mark 6) for 30 minutes. Serve very hot.

CANNELLONI STUFFED WITH CHEESE IN TOMATO SAUCE
Cannelloni alla sorrentina

SERVES 6

200g (7oz) flour	2 eggs
Salt	

For the sauce

2 cloves garlic, finely chopped	Salt
2 tablespoons olive oil	Black pepper or a good pinch of hot chilli powder
500g (1lb) ripe tomatoes, chopped	3 tablespoons chopped basil or parsley, or both
1 teaspoon sugar	

For the filling

300g (10oz) ricotta	4 tablespoons finely chopped parsley
2 eggs	250g (8oz) mozzarella, diced
50g (2oz) grated parmesan or pecorino	75g (3oz) cooked ham, finely chopped
Salt and pepper	
Salt for boiling the pasta	50g (2oz) grated parmesan or pecorino
1 tablespoon oil for boiling the pasta	

Make the dough as described on pages 110–111, and roll out thinly (but not quite as thinly as for tagliatelle). Cut into fourteen 10 × 15cm (4 × 6in) rectangles. Or use bought lasagne.

To make the sauce, fry the garlic in the oil until golden; add the tomatoes, sugar, salt and black pepper or chilli and simmer gently for about 10 minutes, or until reduced to a thick consistency. Add the basil and/or parsley.

To make the filling, mash the ricotta with the eggs. Add the parmesan, salt, pepper, parsley, mozzarella and ham, and mix well.

Boil the pasta rectangles, a few at a time, in plenty of salted boiling water with oil to keep them from sticking. Drain while still a little firm and lay on a damp cloth. Place 2 tablespoons of filling in a line in the centre of each and roll up. Spread a few tablespoons of sauce on the bottom of a baking dish and arrange the rolled cannelloni in a layer on top. Sprinkle with parmesan or pecorino and cover with the rest of the sauce. Bake in the oven at 200°C (400°F, gas mark 6) for 30 minutes, or until browned. Serve very hot.

Variations

Pour béchamel sauce (see preceding recipe) on top or use it instead of the tomato sauce.

AUBERGINE AND PASTA TIMBALE
Timballo alle melanzane

When Naples was ruled by a Spanish branch of the French Bourbons, the French cooks who came with them put pasta dishes into moulds for a more elegant presentation.

SERVES 6–8

700g (1½lb) aubergines
Salt and pepper
Olive oil for frying
2 cloves garlic, crushed
700g (1½lb) tomatoes, peeled and chopped
1 teaspoon sugar

4 tablespoons chopped basil leaves
400g (14oz) penne, ziti and other short macaroni
500g (1lb) mozzarella, diced
6 tablespoons grated parmesan
300g (10oz) ricotta

Slice the aubergines lengthwise into about 0.75cm (⅓in) slices; sprinkle with salt and leave for 1 hour; rinse and dry. Fry in hot oil, turning over once until browned.

Make a sauce: fry the garlic in 2 tablespoons oil, add the tomatoes, salt, pepper and sugar and simmer for 15 minutes. Add the basil.

Boil the macaroni in salted water until half cooked; drain. Line an ovenproof bowl about 15cm (6in) deep and 23cm (9in) in diameter with overlapping aubergine slices. Fill with alternate layers of pasta, tomato sauce, and the three cheeses.

Cover with foil, gently press down and bake in the oven at 200°C (400°F, gas mark 6) for 45 minutes. Unmould by turning the bowl upside-down on a serving platter. Serve very hot.

STUFFED PANCAKES
Crespelle ripiene

French cooks introduced *crêpes* (pancakes) to the Naples court. They are still very popular on the Amalfi and Campania coast.

SERVES 6–8

For the pancakes
400ml (14fl oz) milk
150g (5oz) flour

3 eggs, beaten
1 teaspoon salt

For a cheese filling
500g (1lb) ricotta
175g (6oz) mozzarella, diced
3 tablespoons grated parmesan

Salt and pepper
½ teaspoon grated nutmeg
4 tablespoons chopped parsley

For the sauce
700g (1½lb) tomatoes, peeled and chopped
2 tablespoons oil
Salt and pepper

1–2 teaspoons sugar
3 tablespoons chopped parsley

Oil to grease the frying pan and baking dish

To make the batter, gradually add the milk to the flour, beating vigorously; then add the eggs, salt and 4 tablespoons water (more if the batter seems too thick) and beat until smooth. Leave to rest for 30 minutes.

Into a greased heavy-bottomed or a non-stick frying pan on medium heat pour half a ladleful of batter and move the pan so that the batter runs all over the bottom. As soon as the pancake sets and is easily detached, turn it over and cook the other side. Repeat, stacking pancakes in a pile.

For the filling, mash the ricotta, add mozzarella, parmesan, salt, pepper, nutmeg and parsley and mix well. It should be strongly seasoned since the pancakes are bland.

Put a generous line of filling on each pancake, then roll up and arrange side by side in an oiled baking dish.

For the sauce, simmer the tomatoes in oil until soft, seasoning with salt, pepper and sugar. Crush them with a fork and let the sauce reduce and thicken a little. Add parsley, then pour over the *crespelle*. Bake in the oven at 220°C (425°F, gas mark 7) to heat through.

Variations

Spinach and cheese filling. Fry 1 large chopped onion in 2 tablespoons oil until soft, mix with 500g (1lb) fresh spinach or 300g (10oz) frozen whole-leaf spinach that has been boiled, squeezed dry and finely chopped, and 175g (6oz) ricotta. Season strongly with salt, pepper, nutmeg and 2–3 tablespoons grated parmesan.

Mushroom filling. Lightly cook 500g (1lb) mushrooms (the fleshy shiitake and oyster mushrooms are particularly good for this) – cut into pieces if they are too big – in 4 tablespoons oil. Add salt and pepper and 120ml (4fl oz) dry white wine, and cook for about 15 minutes, raising the heat towards the end to evaporate the wine. Drain the mushrooms and finely chop – but do not turn them into mush – in a food processor. Add 3 tablespoons double cream and about 2 tablespoons finely chopped parsley.

NEAPOLITAN RICE CAKE WITH A MEATBALL FILLING
Sartù di riso

Neapolitan cooking is a cooking of extremes – from stark simplicity to grandiose baroque. When I made this dish I thought it was too much trouble and that I would not include the recipe in this book, but then it fed so many people and it was so appreciated that it stayed in. Other versions of *sartù* have the filling showing not at the top as here but in layers in the middle.

This used to be a festive dish, but now you will find it in almost every self-service restaurant.

SERVES 16

For the meatballs

250g (8oz) chopped or minced lamb, beef or
   pork
2 slices bread, soaked in milk and squeezed dry
4–5 tablespoons grated parmesan
2 eggs

2 cloves garlic, crushed
Salt and pepper
4 tablespoons finely chopped parsley
Oil for frying

For the rest of the filling

1 onion, chopped
3 tablespoons olive oil
1 clove garlic, finely chopped
250g (8oz) mushrooms, cut into small pieces
2 small spicy sausages, skinned and cut into
   small pieces
125g (4oz) cooked small fresh peas or frozen
   petits pois

50g (2oz) prosciutto
500g (1lb) tomatoes, peeled and chopped
Salt and pepper
125g (4oz) chicken livers, cut into small pieces
250g (8oz) mozzarella, cut into small pieces
2 hard-boiled eggs, cut into small pieces

For the tomato sauce

2 cloves garlic, finely chopped
2 tablespoons olive oil
1kg (2lb) tomatoes, peeled and chopped

1 teaspoon sugar
Salt and pepper
3 tablespoons chopped basil leaves or parsley

For the rice

700g (1¹/₂lb) Arborio rice

Salt

125g (4oz) butter, cut into pieces

Butter to grease the tin

2 eggs plus 1 yolk, lightly beaten

75g (3oz) freshly grated parmesan

Breadcrumbs to dust the tin

To prepare the filling, mix the meatball ingredients in a blender or food processor and shape the paste into balls the size of large olives. Fry in hot oil, shaking the pan to brown them all over, then drain on absorbent paper towels.

For the rest of the filling, fry the onion in oil until soft, add the garlic and mushrooms and fry for about 5 minutes. Add the sausage, peas, prosciutto and tomatoes, season with salt and pepper and simmer gently until the liquid is reduced. Add the chicken livers and cook for 1–2 minutes. Stir in the meatballs, mozzarella and hard-boiled eggs, and set aside.

To make the sauce, fry the garlic in oil until golden, add the tomatoes, sugar, salt and pepper and simmer for about 25 minutes. Add the herbs.

Boil the rice in plenty of salted water for about 10 minutes until it is almost al dente, drain, place in a bowl, and stir in the butter, eggs, egg yolk and parmesan. Line a 30 × 7.5cm (12 × 3in) springform tin with foil. Grease with butter and sprinkle generously with breadcrumbs. When the rice mixture has cooled, make a ring in the pan with three-quarters of it, packing it around the sides and leaving a hollow in the middle. Pour the filling into the hollow and cover with the remaining rice. Sprinkle lightly with breadcrumbs and bake in the oven at 200°C (400°F, gas mark 6) for about 25 minutes, or until the top is lightly coloured. Unmould and serve with the tomato sauce.

AUBERGINES BAKED WITH TOMATOES AND CHEESE

Parmigiana di melanzane

You find versions of this dish all over Italy, usually with several layers of aubergine, but I particularly like this one.

SERVES 4

Salt

700g (1¹/₂lb) aubergines, thickly sliced

1 clove garlic, crushed

Olive oil

500g (1lb) ripe tomatoes, peeled and chopped

1 teaspoon sugar

Pepper

2 tablespoons chopped basil or mint leaves

250g (8oz) mozzarella, diced

5 tablespoons grated parmesan

Salt the aubergine slices and leave for 30 minutes to let the juices run out.

Fry the garlic in 2 tablespoons olive oil until the aroma rises. Add the tomatoes, sugar, a little salt and pepper and the basil or mint, and cook vigorously to reduce to a thick sauce.

Rinse and drain the aubergine slices. Dry them and deep-fry in hot oil, turning over once, and drain on absorbent paper towels.

Arrange the slices in a baking dish, cover with the tomato sauce, sprinkle with the cheeses and bake in the oven at 180°C (350°F, gas mark 4) for about 30 minutes.

NEAPOLITAN BAKED TOMATOES
Pomodori gratinati

This Neapolitan way of cooking tomatoes has been adopted all over Italy.

SERVES 4

4 large tomatoes, ripe but firm

4 tablespoons chopped parsley

1 clove garlic, crushed

4 tablespoons fresh breadcrumbs

4 tablespoons olive oil

Salt

A few sprigs of marjoram, chopped

1 tablespoon capers (optional)

Cut the tomatoes in half. Mix the parsley and garlic with the breadcrumbs, oil, salt, marjoram and capers, if using.

Place the tomatoes, cut side up, in a greased baking dish, cover them with the parsley and breadcrumb mixture and place in a preheated oven at 180°C (350°F, gas mark 4) for about 30 minutes. Turn up the oven to 190°C (375°F, gas mark 5) to make them crisp. Do not let them get too soft. Eat hot or warm.

POTATO CAKE
Gattò di patate

This delicious combination of creamy mashed potatoes baked with several kinds of cheese and salami is a good thing to make for a large number of people. Use Naples salami, which is soft and coarsely chopped, peppery and garlicky.

SERVES 10 OR MORE

1.5kg (3lb) floury potatoes

Salt and pepper

125g (4oz) mozzarella, cut into small pieces

125g (4oz) provolone, preferably sharp, cut into small pieces

75g (3oz) mortadella, chopped

75g (3oz) salami, preferably Neapolitan, chopped

75g (3oz) freshly grated parmesan

65g (2½oz) butter

4 egg yolks

Freshly grated nutmeg

Breadcrumbs

Peel the potatoes, cut them in large pieces and boil them in salted water until soft. Drain and mash them to a purée. Mix well with all the cheeses and salami, 50g (2oz) butter cut into bits, and the egg yolks, and season with salt, pepper and nutmeg.

Butter a deep baking dish or cake tin and dust with breadcrumbs. Pour in the mixture, sprinkle the top with butter shavings and breadcrumbs and bake in the oven at 180°C (350°F, gas mark 4) for about 30 minutes, or until golden. Unmould and serve hot.

NEAPOLITAN EASTER PIE

Pastiera napoletana

This Neapolitan Easter dish is now sold in pastry shops all over Italy throughout the year. There are many versions. This one is a little unusual and comes from Ristorante Cappuccini Convento.

SERVES 10

For the pastry

125g (4oz) unsalted butter
125g (4oz) granulated sugar

1 egg or 2 egg yolks
250g (8oz) flour

For the filling

500g (1lb) very fresh ricotta
125g (4oz) granulated sugar
Ground cinnamon
Grated rind and juice of 1 lemon
4 tablespoons orange flower water

125g (4oz) candied orange or mixed peel, chopped
6 eggs, separated
600ml (1 pint) milk
125g (4oz) vermicelli
Salt

Butter for greasing the tin
1 egg yolk (optional)

Icing sugar

To make the pastry, cream the butter and sugar, add the egg or egg yolks. Gradually add the flour; mixing well to a soft dough.

For the filling, add to the ricotta all but 2 tablespoons of the sugar, plus a good sprinkling of cinnamon, half the grated lemon rind and the juice, all the orange flower water and the candied peel. Add the egg yolks, one at a time, beating them in carefully. (Save about half a yolk, if you like, or use another yolk later; to brush the top of the pie.)

Boil the milk in a small pan and stir in the vermicelli. Gently simmer it in the milk with the remaining 2 tablespoons sugar, a pinch of salt, a pinch of cinnamon and the rest of the lemon rind, until the pasta has absorbed all the milk. A teaspoon of oil in the liquid will prevent the vermicelli from sticking. While it is still warm, blend the pasta carefully into the ricotta mixture. Gently fold in the beaten egg whites.

Roll out two-thirds of the pastry and lay it in a buttered 23 or 25cm (9 or 10in) springform or cake tin. Press the pastry into the base of the tin and around the sides. Pour in the filling.

Roll out the remaining pastry (you may have to add more flour to make a stiffer dough). Cut into long strips. Arrange these in a lattice on top of the filling. Brush the top with egg yolk, if you wish. Bake in the oven at 190°C (375°F, gas mark 5) for about 50 minutes, checking near the end of the time. Dust with icing sugar. Serve slightly warm or cold.

ORANGE GRANITA

Granita all'arancia

1 litre (1³⁄₄ pints) freshly squeezed orange juice
   (you may use the bottled kind)

Juice of 1 lemon, or 2 tablespoons orange flower
   water
4–6 tablespoons sugar

Beat all the ingredients together. Taste for sweetness. Pour into ice-cube trays and freeze, covered with clingfilm.

Take the frozen cubes out when you are ready to serve and blend in the food processor to a fine, smooth, soft texture. The granita can go back into the freezer and be eaten later.

Variations

You can do the same with the juice of mandarin oranges and other fruit.

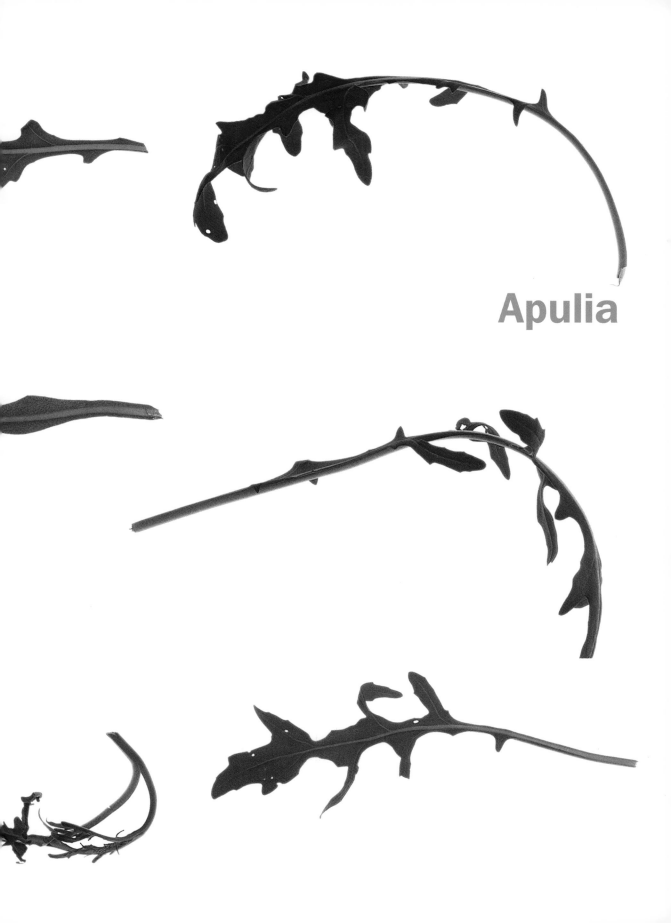

Apulia

Apulian food touches the heart, partly because Apulians are so incredibly warm and hospitable. Throughout Italy food is never just a matter of sustenance; it is part of the art of living, and there is always a sense of joy when you sit down to eat. In Apulia, in the 'heel' of the country, where emotions are heightened, the pleasures of the table are heightened too.

It may have something to do with the enchantment that this beautiful and ancient land produces with its endless coastline; the giant, contorted olive trees and white houses clinging together in clusters; the mysterious beehive-shaped *trulli*, dwellings with conical roofs (I saw one used as a wood oven for making bread and another full of pigeons); and the magnificent *foresta umbra* in the mountainous Gargano promontory, the spur of the Italian boot.

The cooking evokes an ancient past and distant lands. My first experience of Apulian food was *'ncapriata di fave*, mashed broad beans with olive oil, which is exactly like a dish made in Egypt. The second was *triya con i ceci* (pasta and chickpeas; *triya* is an old Arab word for pasta), also an Arab dish.

The coastal cities, because of their position in the middle of the Mediterranean, prospered through trade with the Near East and North Africa. Bari feels like a Levantine merchant city. The Arabs had a foothold in Apulia for a long time. Some came as traders, some as mercenaries called in by warring cities and governing families, some had their pirates' nests there. Sicilian Moslems failed to expand into the mainland, so they raided constantly. That is why there are fortified towers around the coast and why many dishes echo those of Arab lands.

The earliest, most powerful and longest-lasting influence in the area was Greek (the Greeks had colonies all along the coast), and it was renewed under the rule of Byzantium, which was the major force in the south until the tenth century. The fish soups found in every coastal town are Greek, as are many words in the fishermen's jargon.

The golden age of a place usually leaves its mark on the kitchen, and for this part of Italy it was during the reign of Frederick II of Hohenstaufen in the thirteenth century. The splendours of his court and his banquets are constantly evoked in gastronomic conventions. It was a time when Apulia was rich and powerful: Frederick was King of Sicily, Holy Roman Emperor and King of Jerusalem (he led a Crusade). His throne and capital were in Palermo but he loved Apulia and had a palace in Foggia and a hunting lodge in Andria. Frederick brought a cosmopolitan feel to the kitchen. He liked to surround himself with philosophers, scientists and poets, who were mostly French, German, Arab and Jewish scholars. His cook Bernardo, who was famous for his *scapece* (preserved fish), prepared many foreign, especially Arab, foods. Although Apulia fell into decline when Naples became the centre of power in the south in the fourteenth century, the cooking of Frederick's glittering period remained. Apulia was also ruled by the Normans, Angevins and Spaniards, but they had little impact in the kitchen. You do find, however, dishes such as *tiella*, layers of potatoes, rice and vegetables, and sometimes mussels, cooked in a clay pot called a *tiella*; this is said to be related to paella (and is very like the *tian* of southern France, which may also be of Spanish origin).

Until recently Apulian cooking was not considered worthy of interest because it was poor. In Milan a certain Peppino Strippoli had a successful chain of seventeen Apulian restaurants, but they offered modest fare. Today Apulian cooking is celebrated as the best example of what Americans call the healthy Mediterranean diet and attracts chefs from abroad on gastronomic pilgrimages. It is still humble food, based on bread and pasta and things that grow wild in the fields. There is offal and horse meat, and not very long ago donkey meat was used for sausages. *Maccheroni con pesce fsciuto* (dialect for *scappato*) means 'macaroni with fish that escaped'. It is pasta with a sauce made with tomatoes, onions and stones from the bottom of the sea encrusted with microscopic molluscs and algae, which give the sauce a taste of seafood. But the cooking has great qualities. Its beauty lies in its sheer simplicity.

Apulia is rich now – it is the richest part of the south. The past twenty years have seen a profound economic and social transformation. Industries have mushroomed. There are pasta manufacturing, olive-oil refining, canning, wine-making, industrial cheese-making, prosperous tobacco and clothing industries as well as steel and petroleum-processing plants. Thousands have left the land, traditional farming has declined, and modern agriculture with new technology has intensified. Young people have gone to northern Italy and settled there, and to Germany and Switzerland to work. Towns have grown. Food habits have changed with the way of life. Young women go to work and are no longer able or willing to spend hours making pasta by hand or watching the ragù as it simmers *da sole a sole*, from dawn to dusk.

But tradition has been kept up in the villages in the interior. Those who remain continue to kill pigs and make sausages, dry tomatoes in the sun and preserve vegetables in oil and in vinegar, cherries in alcohol, figs in honey, olives in brine, fish in salt or vinegar. And the new middle class and the rich of Lecce, Taranto and Bari, which is the new industrial and commercial capital of the south, take pride in keeping up the traditional foods.

Apulia's advantage over its poverty-stricken neighbours is that the region is nearly all plain and highly fertile, while theirs are entirely mountainous. The climate is hot and dry, but hard wheat, olives and grapes, typical of the Mediterranean and needing little moisture, grow profusely. The long roots of the vines and olive trees, seeking out water deep into the soil, help them resist the attacks of Mediterranean winds. Apulia is the greatest olive-oil and wine producer of Italy. The giant olive trees yield excellent oil with a strong flavour and perfume; much of the oil goes to make up the blends of Tuscany.

Almond trees, for which Apulia is also famous, and fruit trees are squeezed in among the olives, and vegetables grow among the grapevines. There are few rivers, and water comes from an aqueduct fed by the river Sele in Campania, enough to produce splendid tomatoes, artichokes, fennel, cauliflower, broad beans, asparagus, radicchio and much more. The brilliant sun brings a great intensity of flavour and fragrance to the fruit – there are plums, peaches, cherries, figs, apricots, citrus fruit and melons – and to the vegetables.

Tomatoes, especially, are exquisite. People buy them in huge quantities from growers and preserve them to last the winter. They cook them down and turn them into pulp (*pomodori in bottiglia*: literally, bottled) or put whole raw pieces, as they are, in jars which they then sterilise (*pomodori a pezzi*: in pieces) and use them to make sauces for pasta. *Conserva*, a salted, concentrated paste, is left on large terracotta plates in the sun. Rows of these plates are spread out on balconies and terraces. The paste becomes so strong that you need only a teaspoonful in a stew. For *pomodori sott'olio*, firm ripe tomatoes are halved, salted and left on boards to dry in the sun, cut side up. Then they are washed with vinegar and preserved in olive oil, sometimes with a chilli, garlic, capers or herbs. A variation is to put the tomato halves together with a little grated pecorino between them. *Pomodori a penduli* or *al filo* are tiny tomatoes, with hard but very edible skins, which are hung up in huge bunches with thread. They last the winter without spoiling and remain sweet and full of juice. Many vegetables, such as aubergine, mushrooms and artichokes, are preserved in oil.

A meal in Apulia usually starts with these preserves and an assortment of cured meats and salami. Capocollo is raw ham salted and covered in black pepper, smoked over oak wood, and cured for six or seven months; it is then washed in vinegar and wine, covered in red pepper and stuffed in a sausage skin for further curing. At Martina Franca, hams are immersed in *vino cotto* (boiled-down wine), covered in peppercorns, put into sausage casings, then smoked and seasoned. The cervellata of Martina Franca is a mixed veal and pork sausage flavoured with fennel seeds. *Soppressata* is a pork salami with lemon rind, cinnamon and cloves.

Cheese is eaten as an antipasto or as a meal. Apulia is a great cheese-making region with small artisan establishments and large industrial ones. They are spread out throughout the area, but Gioia del Colle, Andria, Alberobello, Acquaviva delle Fonti and Foggia are important centres. They all make mozzarella as *bocconcini* (bite-sized balls) and *trecce* (braids). Mozzarella is popular with the producers because it does not need ageing and does not require a large capital investment. But unless it is vacuum-packed, it must be delivered immediately and eaten fresh on the day it is made. Caciocavallo and provolone are seasoned for at least 180 days. Pecorino has a delicious peppery flavour when it is made with milk of sheep that have grazed around lentisk trees.

Everything is eaten with bread, which, with oil and wine, is a staple of the Apulian diet. Enormous amounts are consumed. One of the traditional breads is a giant, strong-tasting loaf which lasts several days and improves with time. *Ciambella* is a ring with a small hole. It is cut open and dried out in the oven, and becomes the kind of dry food that shepherds and peasants take to the fields. They dip it in water and sprinkle it with olive oil, salt and pepper and sometimes also chopped tomatoes and onion to make *bruschetta* or *frisedda*.

In the fields, peasants make a cold soup, *cialledda*, by putting water, salt and olive oil in a bowl, cutting up tomatoes, onions and cucumber, and breaking in the bread. *Taralli* are plain bread rings that are first boiled, then baked. They are quite hard and are meant to be dunked in wine.

People in Apulia still like to make pasta at home, with flour and water, and sometimes with flour and eggs. Their most famous pasta is their beloved orecchiette (little ears), which they eat every day. In dialect they are called *recchie* or *recchietelle*. Every village has its special way of making them. The dough is first rolled into a thin sausage shape and then cut into little discs with a knife. Some people indent the discs by pressing with their thumb, some squash them with the round end of a knife, some turn them inside out. Tiny ones are called *chianchiarelle*, larger ones *pociacche*. *Pestazzule* are little discs like orecchiette but not as deep. *Cavatelli* are like closed orecchiette. They also make *turcinelli* (little spirals), *stacchiotte* (like seashells) and *fusilli* with a hole in the centre (these are called the same but are different from the more familiar corkscrew fusilli). *Mignucchie* are shaped like little gnocchi. *Fenescecchie* are longish macaroni made by hand by rolling dough and wrapping it around a thin wire. *Strascenate* (called *stagghiotti* in Brindisi) are large rectangles pressed down on a piece of ridged wood. *Troccoli* are typical of Foggia. Women like to make all these sitting at a table in the street, when friends are around.

Pasta takes a long time to make, but the sauces are simple – barely cooked tomatoes; creamy, strong, fermented ricotta; toasted breadcrumbs and garlic; the liquor of a fish stew. The favourite sauce is made with *cime di rape* (turnip greens) with chopped anchovies. Others are made with broccoli and cauliflower, beans and chickpeas, fennel and rocket. The grand festive sauce for special occasions is ragù, a meat stew with veal or horse meat.

Wild things, picked in the fields or found between the vines, have an important place in everyday cooking. *Lampascioni* are curious tubers like hyacinth bulbs. They have an unusual bitter flavour and are generally boiled and served with oil and vinegar as an antipasto, roasted on the fire, cooked in *vino cotto* or put into omelettes and stews. Wild chicory and fennel, rocket, cardoons, thin wild asparagus and an incredible variety of wild leaves and plants – *caccialepre, crispigni, borraggine, ruchetta, marasciuli, acetosa, erimosa* and *ravastrello* – lend their strong, often bitter flavour to enhance some of the blander, plainer foods. Vegetables are eaten as a first or second course. Always simply cooked, they are little triumphs of gastronomy. There are herbs (no spices) and occasional embellishments such as olives, anchovies, almonds, toasted breadcrumbs, eggs and cheese.

With such a coastline and the sea always in the background, the importance of fish can be no surprise. One of the best appetisers of Apulia is raw seafood. It is a great thrill to buy it from the *bancarelle* (stands) on the waterfront around Bari and Taranto, where the enormous variety of shellfish includes oysters, scallops, mussels, clams, sea urchins, sea dates and razor clams. Vendors open them for you to eat raw, with only the perfume of the sea or, at most, a squeeze of lemon. Much of the seafood preparation, as everywhere in Italy, is as simple as possible, to preserve the natural flavours.

Lamb and mutton, pork and game are eaten, but not in large quantities. Every winter, shepherds from the high plateaux of the Gargano and Abruzzi and Molise bring down thousands of sheep to graze. They exchange cheese and lamb for olive oil, wine and vegetables. In many villages the butcher roasts the meat in his stone oven and sells it to his customers already cooked.

There is a great deal of diversity in the cooking of Apulia. Peasants lived far from their fields, huddled together in towns that remained isolated and separate (once upon a time they had fought incessantly). But the principal differences are among the coast, plain and mountains. At Monte Sant'Angelo, on the Gargano, people remember the time, before roads and television transformed their closed world, when you could tell who was a peasant, who a shepherd, who an artisan, by the way they dressed and spoke and ate. Peasants and shepherds did not know how to cook fish. A few artisan families would wait for mules laden with fish to arrive in the piazza after several hours' trek up from the sea; they would then make fish soup and sell it.

Many Apulian sweets – *mustazzueli* (hard almond biscuits); *bocconoti* (pastries filled with cherry or quince jam); *pettue* (fritters); *zeppole* (a sort of doughnut stuffed with custard and preserved cherries); *carteddate* (fried pastry dipped in *vin cotto* or in honey, or dusted with sugar and honey) – can be found in all the southern regions; as elsewhere in the south, they are associated with religious festivals and special occasions. The famous *zuppa inglese* is made here with sponge cake soaked with liqueur and rum, then covered with custard and cherries in syrup.

Apulia specialises in little pastries, many of which are connected with religious festivals. *Carteddate*, coiled ribbons of flour, oil and white wine pastry, are made at Christmastime; *raffiuoli*, little sponges topped with lemon icing, are Easter sweets; *pupurate*, yeasty rings flavoured with fig syrup, grated orange rind, cinnamon, cloves and huge quantities of pepper, are Carnival sweets in the Gargano and Foggia area. An All Saints' Day special is *'u grane cuotte*, a mixture of boiled wheat, chopped walnuts and almonds, grated chocolate, chopped crystallised lemon peel, pomegranate seeds and tiny sugar-coated almonds, all bathed in boiled-down wine and dusted with cinnamon.

Many pastries belong to a town or village. *Castagnede*, little balls made with flour and chopped almonds and perfumed with grated lemon rind, are a speciality of Bari; *cauciuni*, filled with a mixture of mashed chickpeas, melted chocolate and boiled-down wine, are a speciality of the Gargano. Every area makes *taralli*, rings of bread dough which are first boiled, then baked, but they are always different – plain or peppery, flavoured with fennel seeds and sometimes covered with sugar frosting. Andria is famous for the manufacture of *mucci*, the sugar-coated almonds present at every wedding and baptism all over Italy (they are named after Giovanni Mucci, who started making the almonds there a hundred years ago), and coloured marzipan confections.

The Wines of Apulia

Apulia produces a fantastic flood of wine – more than any other region of Italy. Once, most of it was sent off to other parts of Italy and France for blending, distilling and for making into industrial alcohol. Grapes mature quickly in the scorching sun and produce potent wine of high alcoholic content suitable for blending. But in recent years, faced with a declining market, Apulia reduced its production and turned to making lighter quality wines.

High-tech has been brought in with temperature-controlled environments and refrigerated storage vats; new methods of vine training have been tried; old vines have been moved from plains to hills; and foreign ones have been planted. Apulia now grows Cabernet Franc, Chardonnay, Pinot Blanc, Sauvignon Blanc and Riesling and produces entirely new wines, while new methods of wine-making have brought out unexpected refinements in some of the mighty old ones. But they all still have a distinct personality redolent of the south.

Castel del Monte, in the province of Bari, makes a rich, complex, long-ageing red, a rosé that is one of Italy's most popular, and a dry white. Torre Quarto is a rich and sophisticated wine made from French Malbec grapes. Salice Salentino and Copertino are the best of a few rich, warm, fruity reds produced in the Salento Peninsula with native Primitivo, Negroamaro and Malvasia Nera grapes. Primitivo di Manduria Amabile is a semi-sweet red.

Locorotondo and Martina Franca make lovely, crisp, fragrant and delicately almond-flavoured whites with ancient grapes and modern styles. Donna Marzia is a full and fruity aromatic white made from Malvasia. Rosa del Golfo is a very aromatic and highly esteemed rosé, and Aleatico di Puglia is Apulia's sweet red.

TOMATO TOAST
Bruschetta al pomodoro

This traditional shepherds' and peasants' lunch has become a fashionable appetiser.

SERVES 4

8 small, thick slices of coarse country bread
1 clove garlic, cut in half
Salt and pepper
Olive oil

2 large, very ripe tomatoes, roughly cut
1 small sweet onion, chopped (optional)
4 anchovy fillets (optional)

Toast the bread on both sides. Rub one side with garlic, sprinkle with salt and pepper and olive oil. Cover with tomatoes and, if you like, a sprinkling of onion or half an anchovy fillet.

STUFFED AUBERGINE ROLLS
Involtini di melanzane alla mozzarella

SERVES 4–6

1 large aubergine, about 500g (1lb)	250g (8oz) mozzarella
Salt	8 or more basil leaves
Oil for frying	Freshly ground pepper

Thinly slice the aubergine lengthwise, salt and leave to drain for 1 hour. Rinse and dry. Fry quickly in hot oil until tender and slightly browned. Drain on absorbent paper towels.

Cut the mozzarella into slices, place a basil leaf on each slice, sprinkle with pepper. Roll each aubergine slice around a piece of cheese with a basil leaf and place in a baking dish. Grill until the cheese softens. Serve at once.

AUBERGINES, COUNTRY STYLE
Melanzane alla campagnola

The merit of this Apulian way of preparing aubergine is that it is not fried but grilled and marinated in olive oil. I first tasted this dish at the Vecchia Bari restaurant in Bari, where Don Peppino and Anna de Grasta neither salt the aubergine nor brush it with oil before grilling. When I tried it in many different ways I found that with the aubergine I used it was better to salt it first and brush it with oil. What matters is that the aubergine is marinated long enough before serving.

SERVES 8

6 medium aubergines, peeled and thinly sliced	6–8 cloves garlic, or to taste, chopped
Salt	A few sprigs of oregano, chopped
120ml (4fl oz) or more olive oil	A few sprigs of mint, chopped
Pepper	A few drops of wine vinegar (optional)

Sprinkle the aubergine with salt and let it drain for 1 hour to extract the juices; rinse and dry.

Lightly brush with oil and grill the aubergine slices over embers, on a lightly oiled grid, or under the grill, until they are lightly browned, turning them over once.

Place the aubergine on a serving plate and sprinkle with pepper, garlic, herbs and, if you like, a few drops of vinegar. Finish with a generous dribble of olive oil and let the aubergine absorb the dressing for about 7 hours before serving.

Variations

In a Sicilian version the aubergine is sprinkled with a sweet and sour sauce made by boiling 2 tablespoons sugar in 4 tablespoons wine vinegar and then adding olive oil. The Sicilians also like to fry the garlic and to add a pinch of cayenne.

STUFFED PEPPER ROLLS

Involtini di peperoni alla barese

SERVES 12 OR MORE

6 large green, red or yellow peppers

4 heaped tablespoons breadcrumbs

4–5 anchovy fillets (washed if preserved in salt),
   finely chopped

1 tablespoon capers, chopped

2 tablespoons sultanas, chopped

2 tablespoons pine nuts, roasted

4 tablespoons chopped parsley

Salt and pepper

3 tablespoons or more olive oil

Wash and dry the peppers and put them whole on a baking sheet in an oven set at the hottest possible setting for about 25 minutes, or until they are soft and the skin is brown and blistered, turning them once to brown them evenly. Put them in a heavy-duty plastic bag, close it and leave for 10 minutes (this loosens the skins further and makes peeling easier). Peel the peppers while still hot but cool enough to handle; cut in half lengthwise and remove the stems and seeds, but try to keep some of the juice.

Mix the breadcrumbs with the rest of the ingredients, adding just enough oil and some of the pepper juice to bind the mixture. Put a tablespoon of filling on each half pepper and roll up. Arrange the rolls side by side in a serving dish and serve cold.

To serve hot, put the rolls in a lightly oiled baking dish and bake in the oven at 190°C (375°F, gas mark 5) for 15–20 minutes.

Variation

Make a filling with 4 tablespoons olive oil; 6–8 tablespoons freshly toasted breadcrumbs; the following, all chopped: 2 tablespoons toasted pine nuts, 2 tablespoons sultanas, 24 pitted black olives, 2 anchovy fillets, 2 tablespoons capers, 2 tablespoons parsley; and salt and pepper. You might like this one even better.

RAW MARINATED FISH

Il crudo

Absolutely fresh fish, particularly anchovies and sardines, but also other kinds such as red mullet, hake, smelts, pickerel, sea bream, whitebait, are eaten raw with a dressing of oil and lemon. They are also first marinated in lemon juice, which 'cooks' them in a way, and then dressed.

SERVES 4

500g (1lb) sardines, smelts or other very fresh fish

2 lemons

1 clove garlic, crushed

4 tablespoons olive oil

$\frac{1}{2}$ mild onion, finely chopped

Salt

Black pepper or ground hot chilli powder

4 tablespoons finely chopped parsley

Scale and gut the fish, remove heads, fins and tails and pull off backbones. Wash and dry the fillets and marinate in the juice of $1\frac{1}{2}$ lemons mixed with the garlic for 1 day, covered, in the refrigerator.

Drain and dress with a mixture of oil, the remaining lemon juice, the chopped onion, salt and black pepper or chilli. Serve sprinkled with parsley.

LITTLE FRIED CHEESE PASTIES
Panzerotti

MAKES ABOUT 60

For the dough

500g (1lb) plain flour

4 eggs

4 tablespoons oil

Salt

For the filling

250g (8oz) ricotta

2 eggs

125g (4oz) smoked provola or other strong
  cheese, diced

4 tablespoons chopped parsley

250g (8oz) mozzarella, diced

250g (8oz) soft fresh salami or ham, diced

125g (4oz) freshly grated parmesan

Salt and pepper

Oil for deep-frying

Make the dough (it is like pasta dough). Put the flour in a bowl; make a well in the centre and break in the eggs. Add the oil and the salt. Mix it all with a fork at first and then with your fingers. Knead well to form a smooth, elastic dough, dusting it with flour if it gets sticky. It should be smooth and silky. Wrap the dough in clingfilm and leave it to rest for at least 30 minutes in the refrigerator.

Meanwhile, make the filling. Put the ricotta into a bowl and break the eggs over the cheese. Mix in all the other ingredients. Season with salt and pepper.

Roll out the pasta as thinly as you can, then cut into 30 × 10cm (12 × 4in) rectangles. Place little spoonfuls of the filling along one side about 1cm (½in) from the edge. Wet the edge slightly, fold the other edge over and press firmly so that the dough sticks together around the filling. Using a glass or a round pastry cutter, cut along the folded seam to make half-moon shapes. This is a traditional way of making panzerotti. You may find it easier to cut out circles on a sheet of pasta, place spoonfuls of filling in the centre, fold over it to form a half-moon, then pinch the open edges and twist them so that they are firmly closed.

Leave to rest for 30 minutes, then lower them into very hot oil and turn down the heat slightly so that they do not burn. Cook for a very short time: they will quickly turn brown and crisp. Turn them once. Drain and serve hot.

Variations

Use pizza dough (see page 178). Another filling might be mozzarella and chopped tomato with salt and pepper, or a mixture of ricotta cheese, cooked spinach and mozzarella.

FISH SOUP
Zuppa di pesce

All kinds of fish and seafood are used, and every town and village has its favourites. The Adriatic and Ionian seas yield a great variety of fish. Any of these may be included: sole, flounder, turbot or brill, red mullet, bass, sea bream, monkfish, John Dory, hake, sardines, anchovy, eel, cuttlefish, squid, baby octopus, mussels, clams, prawns or lobster. *Scorfano*, a local rockfish, is often, but not always, included to give flavour to the liquor and then removed. You can substitute any firm white fish that you want and make the soup as cheap and as easy as you like. The secret is to give each fish the right amount of cooking it needs and no more.

SERVES 10

2kg (4lb) assorted fish
700g (1½lb) squid or cuttlefish
500g (1lb) mussels or clams
250g (8oz) unpeeled prawns
2 onions, finely chopped
2–3 cloves garlic, finely chopped (optional)
5–6 tablespoons olive oil
2 small chillies, seeded and finely chopped (optional)

4 medium tomatoes, peeled and chopped
250ml (8fl oz) or more dry white wine
Salt and pepper
2 tablespoons wine vinegar (optional)
1 teaspoon or more sugar (optional)
4 tablespoons finely chopped parsley
10 slices of bread, toasted

Clean and scale the fish whole or cut it into pieces if it is large. Clean the squid or cuttlefish (see page 18), and cut the bodies into rings (you can leave tiny ones whole) and divide the tentacles into small clusters. Clean and open the mussels or clams in a large saucepan (see page 18) and strain their liquor. Leave some in the shell and remove the rest.

In a very large flameproof casserole or clay dish, fry the onions and garlic, if using, in oil until golden. Add the chillies, if using, then the tomatoes and cook gently for 10 minutes; then add the wine, the shellfish liquor, salt, pepper and vinegar, if using, and cook 15 minutes more. Add sugar if the tomatoes are not sweet enough.

Start putting in the fish and shellfish, each according to the length of cooking time it requires: first the squid (tiny ones which take hardly any time should go in last) and the firmer-fleshed monkfish, then the delicate-fleshed fish such as the mullets and John Dory and prawns, which need only minutes. The cooked mussels and clams go in at the end.

Sprinkle with parsley and serve in bowls accompanied by toasted bread or *bruschetta* (page 197).

BAKED MUSSELS
Cozze arraganate

SERVES 6–8

2kg (4lb) mussels
6 tablespoons breadcrumbs
120ml (4fl oz) olive oil

6 tablespoons chopped parsley
Pepper
2 cloves garlic, crushed

Clean the mussels and steam them open (see page 18). Strain the liquid and reserve. Remove half of each shell and leave the mussels on the remaining halves.

Mix the breadcrumbs, half the oil, the parsley, pepper and garlic together, and moisten with a little mussel liquor.

Sprinkle each mussel with a little of the breadcrumb mixture and arrange in one or more roasting tins. Pour the rest of the oil over them and put them in a very hot oven at 220°C (425°F, gas mark 7) for about 10 minutes, or until the breadcrumbs are golden, or put them under the grill for moments only.

Variation
Dry white wine or tomato juice may be sprinkled on the mussels.

CALZONE
Calzone pugliese

Calzone means, literally, 'pants'.

FOR 6 CALZONI

Basic dough for 4 pizzas (page 178)	1–2 tablespoons capers
6 tablespoons olive oil	8 anchovy fillets, finely chopped
1 large onion, chopped	Salt and pepper
500g (1lb) tomatoes, peeled and chopped	4 tablespoons finely chopped parsley
50g (2oz) pitted black olives	

Prepare the dough as in the recipe on page 178, adding 4 tablespoons olive oil and working it in with the warm water.

For the filling, fry the onion in the remaining 2 tablespoons olive oil until soft, then add the tomatoes, olives, capers and anchovies. Season with salt and pepper and cook for 10 minutes. Add the parsley.

Divide the risen dough into six balls. Roll each out as thinly as you can on a lightly floured board with a lightly floured rolling pin into circles about 23cm (9in) in diameter. Place them on well-oiled baking sheets and spread the filling on half of each circle, leaving a 2cm (³⁄₄in) margin on the edge. Moisten this margin with water and fold the other half of the dough over the filling so that the edges meet, making a half-moon. Press the edges firmly together and pinch them to seal the pies.

Bake in the hottest part of your oven for about 25 minutes, or until crisp and brown. Serve immediately, hot and fresh.

Variations
For *calzoni con prosciutto* (with ham), fill with layers of sliced ripe tomatoes, sliced mozzarella and cooked ham cut in strips, sprinkling each layer with salt and pepper and grated pecorino or parmesan.

A *calzone di magro* – with onions only – is made on the first day of Lent. The onions are half cooked in oil, then simmered in milk. Sometimes pitted olives and slices of fresh cheese are added.

BROAD BEAN PUREE
'Ncapriata

Paola Pettini, who cooked this famous, ancient dish for me, runs a popular cooking school in Bari. She started by demonstrating in restaurants, and she now travels around the countryside recording recipes. She is passionately committed to preserving old regional traditions.

Dried broad bean purée was always poor food, the kind peasants took to the fields. Even in Roman times it was given to slaves and gladiators. Now it is very popular again, even chic, in Apulia, Sicily and Calabria.

In Calabria, where it is called *macco di fave*, and in Sicily, where it is *maccu*, the bean purée is combined with cooked pasta such as tagliolini or *paternostri* (which are like ditalini), or with rice, while in Sardinia it is called *favata* and is combined with tomatoes and cardoons. *'Ncapriata* partners the bland taste of the beans with bitter wild chicory or with spring onions and peppers. Although it is quite thick, it is served as a soup.

SERVES 4

350g (12oz) dried broad beans, skinned	2 medium onions, chopped
2 stalks celery, chopped	Salt
1 large potato, chopped	120ml (4fl oz) or more olive oil

Soak the beans in water overnight. Drain and rinse and put them in a saucepan with the celery, potato and onions. Cover with water and cook on low heat for about 2 hours. During the last stages of cooking add salt and a little oil, mixing well. Purée the mixture in a food processor, then beat in more olive oil.

Note

This purée is usually served with boiled wild chicory, for which you may use cultivated curly endive, dressed in oil. Or accompany with fried peppers, onions and tomatoes served on the same platter.

PASTA WITH TURNIP GREENS
Orecchiette e cime di rape

This is the most typical of Apulian country dishes. Many emigrants have bags of orecchiette sent to them regularly. If you can't find them, make the dish with pasta shells. Apulians grow turnips for the leaves. Turnip greens are available in some parts of the UK.

SERVES 4

700g (1½lb) turnip greens
Salt
350g (12oz) orecchiette

3 tablespoons olive oil
1 clove garlic, crushed
2 anchovy fillets, chopped

Wash the turnip greens and remove any hard stems. Boil in salted water. After about 10 minutes, add the pasta and cook until al dente.

Put the oil and garlic in a pan and brown. Add the anchovies and break them up. Drain the pasta and turnip greens, and toss with the garlic and anchovy sauce. Stir and serve.

MIXED FRIED FISH AND SEAFOOD
Fritto misto di mare

One of the most delicious ways of cooking fish and seafood in Italy is to give it a light coating of flour and deep-fry it in very hot olive oil. Every region and coastal town has its own particular assortment of mixed fry. In Naples and on the Campanian coast it is red mullet, baby cuttlefish, prawns and nothing else. In Liguria it can include sardines, anchovies, little soles, young hake, tiny octopus and squid. But the differences are blurred now as seaside restaurants put in whatever they think is expected by tourists.

SERVES 4

1kg (2lb) fish and seafood, such as sardines, sprats, whitebait, smelts, sole, hake, small cuttlefish, tiny squid, large raw prawns
Salt

Flour
Olive oil for frying
A few sprigs of parsley
2 lemons, cut in wedges

Scale, clean and gut small fish but leave the heads on. Wash, drain and dry on absorbent paper towels. Large fish can be filleted or cut into steaks. Leave tiny cuttlefish whole (they do not need cleaning); clean squid and larger cuttlefish (see page 18) and cut the bodies into rings. Take the heads off the prawns but do not remove the shells. Season with salt and roll everything except the prawns in flour. (You can also peel the prawns and dip them in flour, then in beaten egg, so as to give them a thick protective crust.)

Use a large frying pan with high sides so that the fish are not crowded and the oil does not boil over. Do medium-sized fish and steaks or fillets first, quickly, a few at a time, and of roughly the same size. Plunge in very hot oil (olive oil can reach higher temperatures than other oils without deteriorating, and gives the very best results), then lower the heat to allow them to cook through without burning. The temperature depends on their size. Lift out with a slotted spoon when cooked and crisp and golden. Drain on absorbent paper towels and keep hot in the oven while you fry the tiny fish, prawns, squid and cuttlefish, all of which need moments only.

Serve very hot, garnished with parsley, and accompanied by lemon wedges.

GRILLED FISH AND SEAFOOD
Grigliata di mare

Ai ferri or *in gratella* (on an oiled grill over the embers of a wood fire) and, more commonly, *sulla piastra* (on a hot griddle) are popular ways of cooking fish and seafood all over Italy. Both methods are referred to as *grigliate*.

Although every kind of fish can be done in this way, each type needs a particular treatment. Some fish are grilled whole, large firm ones are cut into steaks. Unless they are very oily, like sardines and eels, they need marinating (preferably for 30 minutes) and brushing frequently with olive oil, melted butter or a marinade to prevent them from drying out. The fish is sometimes rolled in flour (in Sicily they use breadcrumbs) and then smeared with oil or melted butter or the marinade, which forms a crust that keeps the flesh moist. It is cooked, turning over once, over gentle heat, until the flesh turns opaque and just begins to flake.

To prepare fish for cooking whole, clean, scale and rinse but do not take off the head. For large and medium fish, make a few cuts diagonally with the point of a knife so that the flesh cooks evenly and the skin does not burst. If the fish is very large (more than 1.5kg [3lb]), place it 15–20cm (6–8in) from the fire. If it is of medium size, place it 13cm (5in) away. Splitting the fish in half through the back cuts the cooking time and gives the smoky taste to a larger surface. The cooking time varies, depending on the size and type of fish, from about 15 minutes, for a 1kg (2lb) lean fish, to 45 minutes for a 5kg (10lb) oily one, and also according to the fire. Give the first side longer than the second and turn over more than once if the fish is large and firm enough. Place small fish 10cm (4in) from the fire and turn over once. (A hinged basket makes this easier.) They take from 5–12 minutes. Skewer eels rolled up in a coil.

Large fish with a firm flesh, such as tuna, swordfish, monkfish and turbot, are cut into steaks and grilled for 8–10 minutes. They are also sometimes cut into 1cm (½in) cubes, which are then threaded on skewers with a bay leaf between each piece.

Lobster is cut in half and grilled, shell side down, for 10–20 minutes, or until almost done (the flesh should be brushed with olive oil or a marinade); then it is turned and the flesh side is given 1–2 minutes more. Claws are left a few minutes longer on the fire.

Prawns are grilled in their shells, with only the heads removed. King-size prawns (*scampi* or *gamberoni*) are cut open from the underside and flattened, so that they open out like butterflies. They are marinated and grilled for only 4–5 minutes (mostly shell side down).

Shellfish such as oysters, mussels and clams are also put on the fire for about 5 minutes, until they open.

Small squid and cuttlefish are good on the griddle (see cleaning instructions on page 18). They are dipped in olive oil and cooked for 5–10 minutes.

With a good selection of fish and shellfish you can make a splendid *grigliata mista* (mixed grill). Serve sizzling hot with a sauce (it can also be the marinade), sprinkled with plenty of chopped parsley, accompanied by lemon wedges.

Marinades and sauces

The usual marinade and sauce, which is poured over at the end or served in a bowl, is a mixture of olive oil, lemon juice, salt and pepper. It is the simplest and, to most tastes, the best.

In the north they often use melted butter instead of oil or a mixture of the two.

To the above mixture, add a little crushed garlic and chopped herbs such as marjoram, oregano, fennel, basil, rosemary, sage or bay leaf. You could also add fresh tomato pulp, a little hot chilli powder, 2–3 finely chopped anchovies, or vinegar or white wine instead of lemon juice.

FISH IN FRESH TOMATO SAUCE

Pesce alla marinara

SERVES 4

2 cloves garlic, chopped

4 tablespoons olive oil

4 medium tomatoes, peeled, seeded and
    chopped

Salt and pepper

1kg (2lb) fish, such as small sea bass, monkfish,
    hake, halibut and cod, whole or cut into steaks

A few sprigs of parsley, finely chopped

Heat the garlic in the oil in a large pan. Add the tomatoes, salt and pepper and cook for 10 minutes, or until the sauce is reduced. Add 300ml ($\frac{1}{2}$ pint) water and cook 5 minutes longer. Put the fish in and simmer gently, covered, until it is done, from 4 minutes for thin fish steaks to about 15 minutes for monkfish tails. The flesh should just begin to flake from the bone. Add parsley and serve.

STEWED OCTOPUS

Polpi in umido

In Puglia they mostly use baby octopus, *polipetti*, for this dish. If you cannot find them, you can use larger ones.

SERVES 4

500g (1lb) octopus

2 tablespoons olive oil

2 cloves garlic, chopped

3 medium tomatoes, peeled and chopped

300ml ($\frac{1}{2}$ pint) dry white or red wine

Salt and pepper

2 teaspoons sugar

4 tablespoons chopped parsley

Clean the octopus (see page 18). Blanch for 1 minute in boiling water and throw out the water (this is to get rid of the scum that forms). The octopus firms and curls up. Cut into pieces and fry lightly in olive oil, turning them over once. Add garlic and, as it begins to colour, add the tomatoes, wine, salt and pepper and a little sugar. Cover with water and simmer until tender, 20 minutes for baby octopus, up to 50 minutes for a medium one. Sprinkle with parsley. Serve hot or cold.

Variation

For *polpi arrabbiati* (literally, mad octopus), add 2 chopped anchovies, 2 small chillies and 2 tablespoons capers at the start.

BAKED RICE AND MUSSELS
Tiella alla barese

SERVES 6

2 medium onions, peeled and sliced

500g (1lb) tomatoes, sliced

500g (1lb) potatoes, peeled and sliced

350g (12oz) courgettes, sliced

2 tablespoons finely chopped parsley

2 cloves garlic, crushed

350g (11oz) Arborio rice

3–4 tablespoons olive oil

250ml (8fl oz) stock or water

Salt

500g (1lb) mussels

In a clay pot put alternating layers of onion, tomato, potato and courgette, sprinkling parsley mixed with garlic in between each. Cover with rice. Pour in the oil and just enough stock or salted water to cover the rice.

Scrub and wash the mussels thoroughly and remove the beards. Open them by steaming in 1cm (½in) water in a covered pan. Strain the liquor and pour it over the rice.

Bake, covered, in the oven at 180°C (350°F, gas mark 4) for about 40 minutes, or until the rice is tender, adding water if necessary.

Discard any mussels that did not open, take the rest out of their shells and put them back on the half-shell. Lay them on top of the rice and put the pot back in the oven for a few more minutes.

BAKED SEA BASS
Spigola al forno

Sea bass is the grandest, favourite fish, so appreciated in Apulia that only the minimum treatment is tolerated.

SERVES 6

1 sea bass, 1.5–2kg (3–4lb)

Salt

Olive oil

Scale, wash and gut the fish but leave the liver and any roe. Sprinkle lightly with salt inside and out and rub with olive oil. Wrap loosely in a large sheet of foil, twisting the edges together so as to have a tightly closed but baggy package.

Bake in the oven at 220°C (425°F, gas mark 7) for 25–40 minutes. Eat it as it is, in its juices, with nothing to detract from the delicate flavour.

Note

If you must, serve it with a sauce of olive oil beaten with lemon juice and a little salt.

STUFFED MEAT ROLLS WITH MEAT SAUCE
Braciole al ragù

This dish is a Sunday special in all the south. The sauce is served first with fusilli or other pasta, and the meat rolls are served as the second course.

SERVES 6

1.1kg (2½lb) beef topside, thinly sliced (lamb, pork or veal can also be used)

Salt and pepper

125g (4oz) pecorino, grated, or sharp provolone, thinly sliced

4 cloves garlic, crushed

8 tablespoons chopped parsley, or a few basil leaves, chopped

Olive oil

125g (4oz) pancetta or unsmoked bacon (optional)

6 spring onions or 1 onion, chopped

1kg (2lb) tomatoes, peeled and chopped

2 tablespoons tomato paste

250ml (8fl oz) or more red or dry white wine

Flatten the beef slices by putting them between two pieces of greaseproof paper and pounding them with a meat mallet, and season.

Mix together the pecorino or provolone, three of the garlic cloves, and the parsley or basil. Spread the mixture on the beef slices and, folding in the sides, roll each up into a small package and tie with thread.

Fry the rolls in 2–3 tablespoons oil, turning them until they are nicely brown all over; then remove them. In the same oil, fry the bacon, if using, spring onions or onion and remaining garlic. Add the tomatoes, tomato paste and wine.

Put in the rolls and simmer, covered, on very low heat for 2 hours, watching to make sure they do not burn, and adding more wine or water to keep the meat covered. Or put in a low oven at 170°C (325°F, gas mark 3), tightly covered, for 2 hours.

Remove the thread before serving.

Variation
In Naples they put raisins and pine nuts in the meat rolls.

RICOTTA ICE CREAM
Gelato di ricotta

This is a modern way of using ricotta that I came across in Bari. It makes a very easy and very lovely dessert, which you may accompany with fruits in wine or in syrup.

SERVES 6–8

5 egg yolks

125g (4oz) caster sugar

5 tablespoons rum or cognac, or to taste

500g (1lb) very fresh ricotta

Put the egg yolks in a blender with the sugar and blend until fluffy and pale, then add the rum or cognac and the ricotta and blend to a light cream. Line a mould with clingfilm, pour in the mixture and cover with another piece of clingfilm. Leave in the freezer for at least 3 hours. To serve, remove the clingfilm and turn out the *gelato* on to a plate.

Variations
You may add a few drops of vanilla essence or the grated rind of a lemon or a teaspoon or two of cinnamon, but I prefer the *gelato* as is.

Basilicata

Basilicata

Basilicata has much in common with its neighbours, especially Apulia. But Basilicata is the poor relative, being almost entirely mountainous, beset by floods and land-slides, and having only a short coastline where the mountains rise abruptly from the sea. And Basilicata has always been far from the centre of power.

Here, too, pasta made at home is the queen of the table. The difference is that here the sauces are very hot with chilli. Cooks in Basilicata put *peperoncino* (red pepper) into everything. There are many varieties, ranging from very hot to mild and sweet. They are used fresh, chopped up or whole, or dried (they can be seen hanging everywhere in Basilicata), or in powdered form or preserved in oil – this gives the oil a very powerful kick. In the days when there was malaria in this region, *peperoncino* was thought to cure it.

Another characteristic of the cooking of Basilicata is the preponderance of pork. Sheep, goat and game are eaten, but every family has at least one pig. There is an old saying in dialect: *'Cu' si marita sta contentu 'nu giornu, cu' ammazza 'u porcu sta contentu n'annu'*, which means, 'He who gets married is happy for one day, he who kills a pig is happy for a year'. Pigs are reared for sausages, cured ham and salami. Older people in Basilicata say they want something to give their children when they visit and something for them to take away. (Most of the young people leave the region.)

The famous lucaneca (called luganega in the north), which can be fresh, smoked or dry and is said to have been made since Roman times, derives its name from Lucania, the other name for Basilicata. *Pezzente* is a poor man's salami, made with liver, lungs and other offal seasoned with garlic and pepper. *Soppressata*, a large flattened, oval sausage made with ginger and plenty of black and red pepper, is preserved in oil. It can be eaten raw, grilled or fried and is also dried and smoked. *Salsicce sott'olio* (sausages preserved in oil) are typical of Basilicata, where it is often too hot and sometimes not high and windy enough to cure them properly.

The usual cheeses of the south – manteca, provolone, caciocavallo, provola, mozzarella, buttiro and pecorino – are also made here; but strong, sharp flavours are preferred, and cheeses that are meant to be aged are aged for even longer here than elsewhere. A speciality of Matera is *ricotta forte*, a creamy fermented ricotta so strong it overpowers you when you open its container.

The sweets of Basilicata – *sciù* from Avigliano; *sospiri di Matera* (literally, sighs), tiny macaroons; *panzarotti*, filled with mashed chickpeas and chocolate; *scarcedda*, stuffed with ricotta and sugar – appear on festive occasions.

The Wines of Basilicata

Basilicata has only one great wine – the red Aglianico del Vulture. It is made from the Aglianico grapes of ancient Greek origin which grow two thousand feet up the side of the extinct volcano Monte Vulture. The cool air makes a superb dry wine with a rich almondy fruit and high acidity, and when it is aged, it attains exceptional depth and harmony. There are also slightly sweet and sparkling versions.

ROASTED PEPPER SALAD
Insalata di peperoni arrostiti

I have eaten pepper salad all over Italy, sometimes dressed with oil and vinegar and with trimmings such as capers, chopped anchovies and garlic. But this simple dish, with nothing to detract from the special flavour and texture of the peppers, makes an ideal antipasto and a good accompaniment to all kinds of cold meats.

SERVES 6

6 large peppers, preferably red and yellow

4–5 tablespoons olive oil

Salt and pepper

It is easier to roast peppers in the oven than to grill them, and they are just as good. Put them on a baking sheet on the top shelf of a very hot oven (240°C, 475°F, gas mark 9) and bake for 20–30 minutes, turning them once on their side, until they are soft and the skin is blistered and browned in parts. Put them into a heavy-duty plastic bag, close tightly and leave for at least 10–15 minutes. (This loosens the skins further and makes peeling easier.) When you remove the peppers, save the juice from the bag.

When the peppers are still hot but cool enough to handle, peel off the skin. Cut them in half, remove the stems and seeds, then cut the soft flesh into strips lengthwise (these can be wide or thin). Pour some of the juice that has collected in the bag over them and serve cold, dressed with olive oil, salt and pepper.

BROAD BEAN STEW
Ciaudedda

SERVES 4

1 large onion, sliced

3 tablespoons olive oil

125g (4oz) pancetta or unsmoked bacon,
    chopped

1kg (2lb) broad beans, weighed in the
    pods

4–8 artichoke hearts, quartered
    (canned or frozen can be substituted)

500g (1lb) potatoes, peeled and sliced

Salt and pepper

Fry the onion in the oil with the bacon until golden. Add the podded broad beans, artichoke hearts and potatoes, season with salt and pepper, barely cover with water and cook, stirring often, and moistening with a little water, for 20–30 minutes, or until the vegetables are done.

FRIED EGGS WITH MOZZARELLA
Uova al piatto con mozzarella

SERVES 2

1 clove garlic, chopped

2 tablespoons olive oil

250g (8oz) mozzarella, sliced

2 eggs

Salt and pepper

A few basil leaves, chopped

Fry the garlic in oil in a frying pan until it begins to colour. Put in the mozzarella, break the eggs on top, season with salt and pepper and sprinkle with basil. Gently fry until the mozzarella bubbles and the eggs are cooked.

POTATOES WITH CHILLI
Patate con diavolicchio

SERVES 4

2 large potatoes

Salt

2 cloves garlic, crushed

1 small hot chilli, finely chopped,
    or ¼ teaspoon hot chilli powder

4 tablespoons olive oil

2 tablespoons finely chopped parsley

Boil the potatoes in their skins in salted water. When cooked, peel and slice them. Fry the garlic with the chopped chilli or chilli powder in 1½ tablespoons olive oil until the garlic colours. Remove from the heat, stir in the rest of the oil and dress the potatoes. Sprinkle with salt and parsley and serve cold.

FRIED MEAT PATTIES
Polpettine fritte

These patties, which came to Basilicata from Sicily, make very good finger food for a party; just make them a little smaller.

SERVES 4

500g (1lb) pork, chopped or minced	Salt and pepper
4 tablespoons breadcrumbs	2 tablespoons raisins, coarsely chopped
1 tomato, peeled and chopped	2 tablespoons pine nuts, toasted
4 tablespoons grated parmesan	Oil for frying
$\frac{1}{2}$ mild onion, grated	

Blend the meat with the breadcrumbs, tomato, cheese, onion and seasoning in a food processor. Mix in the raisins and pine nuts. Take lumps the size of a large egg, shape into little cakes and fry in hot oil until done, turning over once to brown them all over. Drain on absorbent paper towels before serving. You can also dip the cakes in more breadcrumbs before frying.

LAMB STEW
Cutturiddi

SERVES 6

1kg (2lb) stewing lamb	Sprig of rosemary
2 tablespoons olive oil	2 bay leaves
4 little onions	Salt
2 cloves garlic, sliced	A good pinch of hot chilli powder
4 tomatoes, peeled	350ml (12fl oz) dry white wine

Cut the meat into 3cm (1¼in) pieces and remove as much fat as you can. Brown the pieces all over in hot oil in a large pan. Put in the rest of the ingredients. Cover with water and cook, covered, for 1½ hours or longer, until the meat is very tender, adding water if necessary.

BAKED ONIONS
Cipolle al forno

SERVES 6

3 large sweet (Spanish) onions, unpeeled	1 tablespoon vinegar (optional)
3 tablespoons olive oil	Salt and pepper

Bake the onions whole in the oven at 200°C (400°F, gas mark 6) for 50–60 minutes, or until they feel very soft. Peel them when they are cool enough to handle and cut into thick slices.

Dress with a mixture of oil, vinegar if you like, and salt and pepper. Serve warm or cold.

MIXED VEGETABLES, LUCANIA STYLE
Erbe alla lucana

This is made in quantities to last over a few days; it is served hot or cold with bread or toast. *Lucana* refers to Lucania, the old name for Basilicata.

SERVES 6–8

Salt

700g (1½lb) aubergine, cut in 2.5cm
    (1in) cubes

3 medium onions, sliced

2 large yellow peppers, seeded and cut
    into strips

Olive oil

2–3 cloves garlic, chopped

700g (1½lb) tomatoes, peeled and
    chopped

1 teaspoon sugar

1 teaspoon ground ginger

A good pinch of hot chilli powder

4 tablespoons chopped basil leaves

8 tablespoons chopped parsley

Salt the aubergine and leave for 1 hour to degorge the juice. Wash and dry the pieces.

Fry the onions, peppers and aubergine separately in hot but not deep oil, turning them over once, until tender and browned a little (the onions and peppers should be crisp). Drain on absorbent paper towels and sprinkle with a little salt.

Prepare a tomato sauce in a large pan. Fry the garlic in 2 tablespoons oil until the aroma rises, then add the tomatoes, salt, sugar, ginger and chilli powder, and simmer for 15 minutes, or until the sauce thickens.

Stir in the fried vegetables and the herbs and simmer gently for about 5 minutes.

Note

It is also good to serve the fried vegetables and the sauce separately to accompany them.

ALMOND MILK

Latte di mandorle

125g (4oz) blanched almonds

3 tablespoons sugar, or to taste

750ml (1¼ pints) water

Chop or grind the almonds as finely as you can in the food processor. Add the sugar and water (as much of it as the processor will hold) and blend for a good amount of time until the water turns milky white. Pour into a jug and keep in the refrigerator, covered, for a few hours to infuse further. Strain through a fine strainer and serve very cold.

Note

In Sardinia they add a tablespoon of orange flower water.

APRICOT GRANITA

Gremolata di albicocche

You will find orange flower water in Middle Eastern stores. Jasmine water is very rare (I found it in Sicily and in Thailand). But if the apricots have a good flavour of their own they will not need these perfumes.

SERVES 6

125g (4oz) or more sugar

250ml (8fl oz) water

Juice of 1 lemon

500g (1lb) very ripe apricots, pitted

1–2 tablespoons jasmine or orange flower
    water (optional)

Boil the sugar and water until the sugar melts (the amount needed depends on the sweetness of the fruit), add the lemon juice and let the syrup cool a little, then blend with the apricots to a cream. Pour into ice-cube trays, cover with clingfilm and freeze for a few hours until hard. Just before serving, put the frozen apricot cubes in the food processor, a few at a time, and process to a very soft cream. You can put it in a serving bowl and return it to the freezer, covered with clingfilm, until a few minutes before you are ready to serve.

Calabria

Calabria

Bordered by Campania and two seas, Calabria, the 'toe' of Italy, is largely mountainous, a quarter of it wooded, with great plateaux and plains and a few rivers. It is splendid in its great desolation, and stunningly beautiful, with mountains dropping into the sea, woodlands full of chestnut, lovely bays and medieval towns perched high above the sea. Like the Sicilian coast which is so near, the Calabrian coast is lined with olive groves, citrus orchards and fig trees, and tuna and swordfish are caught in large numbers in the waters here. Tuna is preserved in oil and the roe is salted and pressed to make *bottarga*. Swordfish is so common it is almost a symbol of the Calabrian coast. It is cooked in a double boiler with olive oil, herbs and lemon juice, and it is fried and grilled as steaks or as *involtini*, thin slices rolled around a stuffing of capers and olives with breadcrumbs. On the southern coast, whitebait, which is caught in large quantities, is dried on wooden tables in the sun, dusted with hot chilli powder, then preserved in oil to make an explosive delicacy variously called *mustica*, *rosamarina* and c*aviale di Crucoli* (Crucoli caviar), which is eaten with bread and also used to flavour sauces.

There is lamb. And the pig is celebrated. Every family has at least one, even in the towns, they say. The little black, svelte, hairy animals run free around the villages and are treated as though they were sacred. But in October their feasting ends and their owners' feasting begins, and it continues throughout the winter. The perishable parts are eaten first accompanied by a huge *soffritto*, a dish of aubergine, onions, peppers and tomatoes. Pork is roasted in pieces on skewers or whole on the spit, baked or fried, and is even boiled for breakfast, when it is eaten with marinated aubergine and *pitta*, a round soft bread. Calabrian sausage, ham and salami are famous for their strong peppery flavouring which comes from spices and fennel seeds.

Cheeses have the flavour of wild mountain herbs heated by the sun, and they taste different in every village. There are caciocavallo, impanata, rinusu, tuma, mozzarella, and scamorza; buttiro, with an outer crust and a soft butter centre; provola, smoked or not; and every shepherd makes his own pecorino. Cheese is served for breakfast, lunch and supper. Pasta is made at home from flour and water, and it comes in a variety of shapes; most often it is rolled *a firriettu* (around a wire) to make a hole. Among the various types are *fusilli*, *fischietti* (literally, little whistles), *bucatini*, *paternostri*, *filatieddi*, *ricci di donna* (women's curls), *canneroni*, *strangolapreti* (priest-stranglers), *lagane*, *sagne* and *pizzicotti* (pinches). *Pasta grattata* is grated pasta dough that goes into soups.

Aubergine is the most important vegetable. There are hundreds of ways of cooking it, and even the tiniest village has its own speciality. It is stuffed with minced meat or with anchovies and olives, then baked; slices are rolled around caciocavallo, then breaded and fried; *melanzane a scapece* is aubergine marinated in vinegar; *polpette di melanzane* are little croquettes of mashed boiled aubergine mixed with garlic, cheese and parsley, then breaded and fried. Other parts of Italy have a version of *parmigiana di melanzane* but Calabrians prepare the grandest, with layers of fried aubergines, chopped hard-boiled eggs, meatballs and slices of mozzarella, each sprinkled with tomato sauce and grated pecorino (I do not give the recipe as it is not my favourite).

Other Calabrian specialities are pasta with snails; *macco di fave*, a soup of mashed dried broad beans with olive oil, chilli and grated pecorino; and *patate alla tiana*, baked potatoes and tomatoes with a topping of grated pecorino which is like the Provençal *tian*. There are echoes from distant lands, such as *pitta*, which may have its origins in Greece, and sweets made with almonds and other nuts and honey, flavoured with orange flower water and aniseed, which are Arab and Sicilian (they have names like *anime beate*, blissful spirits). One speciality is dried figs stuffed with almonds or walnuts and soaked in honey. Another, *cubbaita*, is made of honey and sesame. Cannoli are filled with ricotta and candied fruit, and there are multi-coloured almond-paste confections.

The Wines of Calabria

Calabria has given a modern touch to some of the most ancient wines in the world. Its only famous wine, Cirò is a direct descendant of the Cremissa that was offered to victorious Olympic athletes when southern Italy was ruled by Greece. It is now high-tech and fashionable, and it is still traditionally offered to Italian athletes. The red Cirò, made from the native grape Gaglioppo, is rich and velvety and long-ageing; the white, made from Greco grapes, is young and fresh, and there is also a pleasant rosé Cirò. A new stylish wine is Magno Megonio, made from the recently rediscovered Magliocco grapes.

Calabria's high mountains produce attractive reds from blends where Gaglioppo dominates. Donnici, Pollino and Savuto are highly alcoholic but also fresh and fragrant wines with a taste of wild berries.

Two dessert wines, Greco di Bianco and Mantonico di Bianco, made in the town of Bianco on the 'toe' of Italy, are of very ancient origin and said to have aphrodisiac properties. The finest, Greco di Bianco, has an alcoholic bouquet with a delicate hint of orange blossom.

MUSHROOMS PRESERVED IN OIL
Funghi sott'olio

This most popular Italian preserve makes a ready antipasto to serve with ham and salami. In Calabria it has a strong, peppery flavour.

Wash the mushrooms (porcini, shiitake or button mushrooms) well. Simmer in a mixture of 2 parts water to 1 part vinegar with salt to taste for 10–15 minutes, or until tender. Drain well and let the mushrooms dry on a cloth for 1 hour.

Pack into glass jars with a few garlic cloves, a tiny hot chilli and herbs such as bay leaf, rosemary, thyme or oregano. Cover with olive oil.

The mushrooms should be ready to eat in a few days and will last for months.

CHICKPEAS WITH GARLIC
Ceci all'aglio

This is a ritual Christmas dish which also makes a good appetiser to serve with drinks. It is usually peppery and very garlicky.

SERVES 6

250g (8oz) chickpeas
Salt
4 or more cloves garlic, chopped

About 120ml (4fl oz) olive oil
Black pepper or a touch of hot chilli powder

Soak the chickpeas in water for a few hours and drain. Boil for at least 1 hour in water to cover until tender, adding salt when they begin to soften. Drain very well and return to the pan.

Fry the garlic in 2–3 tablespoons oil until golden and mix into the chickpeas. Stir in the rest of the oil, sprinkle with salt and pepper or chilli, heat through and serve very hot.

This is also good cold.

STUFFED ARTICHOKE HEARTS
Carciofi ripieni

These days I would not make this dish myself with fresh artichokes. It takes too long to remove the leaves. I use frozen hearts (they are much better than canned ones).

SERVES 4

8 frozen artichoke hearts, defrosted
2 tablespoons olive or sunflower oil
250g (8oz) chopped or minced lamb, pork or veal
250g (8oz) grated pecorino or parmesan
Bunch of parsley, finely chopped (about
    4 tablespoons)

Salt and pepper
Juice of 1 lemon
1 tablespoon breadcrumbs
1 egg

Arrange the defrosted artichoke hearts in a lightly oiled baking dish.

Mix the meat, cheese, parsley, salt, pepper, lemon juice, breadcrumbs and egg until very well blended. Fill each heart with a little mound of the mixture and brush the top with oil. Pour a little water in the dish to keep the artichoke hearts moist and bake in the oven at 180°C (350°F, gas mark 4) for 25 minutes, or until browned.

Variation

Make a little tomato sauce (see page 19) and place the artichoke hearts in it in the baking dish.

ORANGE SALAD
Insalata di arancia

SERVES 4

4 juicy oranges

Salt and pepper

4–5 tablespoons olive oil

4 spring onions or 1 sweet red onion, finely chopped

Peel the oranges and remove the white pith. Thinly slice and lay the slices out on a serving plate. Remove the pips and sprinkle with salt and pepper, olive oil and spring onions or onion.

COURGETTE FLAN
Flan di zucchine

This elegant version of a rustic dish is from Gaetano Alia of Ristorante Alia at Castrovillari, Calabria.

SERVES 6

6 medium courgettes, sliced

Salt

4 eggs, separated

175g (6oz) grated parmesan or pecorino

Freshly grated nutmeg

Oil to grease ramekins or baking dish

Blanch the courgettes in boiling salted water for no longer than 1½ minutes. Mix the egg yolks with the cheese and nutmeg and stir the courgettes into the mixture. Grease individual ramekins or a baking dish. Beat the egg whites until stiff and fold into the mixture. Fill the ramekins or dish and bake in a moderate oven (180°C, 350°F, gas mark 4) for 25 minutes, or until puffed and golden on top. Serve hot.

TOMATOES STUFFED WITH VERMICELLI AND HERBS
Pomodori ripieni di vermicelli

The more usual fillings for stuffed tomatoes are based on rice or breadcrumbs. This 'poor man's stuffing' is quite delightful if you flavour it well.

SERVES 4

4 large beef tomatoes, about 1.1kg (2½lb)
125g (4oz) vermicelli
Salt
3 tablespoons or more olive oil
Bunch of parsley, finely chopped (about
    3 tablespoons)

Bunch of mint, finely chopped (about 3 tablespoons)
Bunch of basil, finely chopped (about 3 tablespoons)
2 cloves garlic, crushed
Pepper

Cut a slice off the stem ends of the tomatoes and keep them to use as lids. Scoop out the inside with a spoon (this can be used for tomato sauce).

Crush the vermicelli into small pieces with your hands. (In Calabria they also use other pasta such as ditalini or rigati.) Cook in plenty of boiling salted water until it is not quite al dente, and drain. Dress quickly with a mixture of oil, herbs, garlic and plenty of salt and pepper. Mix well and fill the tomatoes with this.

Place the stuffed tomatoes in an oiled baking dish and cover them with their tops. Bake in the oven at 170°C (325°F, gas mark 3) for about 30 minutes, or until the tomatoes are soft – but not too soft or they will fall apart when you serve them.

Variation

For a stronger-tasting filling, add 4 anchovies, 12 black olives, 1 tablespoon capers, all chopped, and a good pinch of hot chilli powder to the cooked vermicelli.

SWORDFISH OR TUNA WITH TOMATOES AND OLIVES
Pesce spada o tonno alla marinara

Bagnara specialises in swordfish, and tuna is brought in at several ports around the Calabrian coast. My own favourite is the swordfish.

SERVES 4

3 tablespoons olive oil
4 swordfish or tuna steaks, about 150g (5oz)
    each
75g (3oz) black olives, pitted and chopped
1 tablespoon capers

350g (12oz) tomatoes, peeled and chopped
A few sprigs of basil, chopped
Salt and pepper or hot chilli powder
2 tablespoons breadcrumbs

Brush a baking dish with oil and place the swordfish or tuna steaks in it. Cover with the olives and capers, the tomatoes and basil. Sprinkle with olive oil, salt and pepper and breadcrumbs and bake in the oven at 240°C (475°F, gas mark 9) for 20–30 minutes.

GRILLED SWORDFISH OR TUNA STEAKS

Pesce spada o tonno ai ferri

SERVES 4

2 medium tomatoes, peeled and seeded

4 tablespoons olive oil

Juice of $\frac{1}{2}$ lemon

A few sprigs of marjoram, chopped

Salt and black pepper or hot chilli powder

4 swordfish or tuna steaks, about 150g (5oz) each

Purée the tomatoes with the olive oil, lemon juice, marjoram, salt and pepper in a blender or food processor. Sprinkle the fish steaks with some of this sauce and cook over embers, under the grill or in a hot sauté pan for 6–10 minutes, or until the flesh only just turns opaque (do not overcook), turning the fish over once and sprinkling with more sauce.

Serve at once with the remaining sauce.

BONED LEG OF LAMB ON THE GRILL

Cosciotto di agnello alla brace

SERVES 6

1 small leg of lamb, or $\frac{1}{2}$ leg, about 2kg (4lb)

Salt and black pepper or hot chilli powder

4 cloves garlic, cut into slivers

4 tablespoons olive oil

Juice of 1 lemon

3 sprigs of rosemary or mint

Have the butcher bone the leg of lamb or do it yourself. Remove the fat, open the leg out and flatten it. Pierce the meat with a sharp, pointed knife in several places and push a sliver of garlic and a few rosemary or mint leaves into each hole. Marinate the meat for 1 hour in a mixture of olive oil, lemon juice, salt and pepper.

Place the lamb on an oiled grill over embers or under the grill of your oven, at least 7.5cm (3in) from the fire. After about 20 minutes, turn the meat and cook another 15–20 minutes, brushing occasionally with the marinade. It should be brown on the outside but still pink inside. Cut into the meat to see if it is done to your taste. If you want it well done, cook for another 15 minutes.

If you prefer, leave the fat on and cook the fat side first.

Sicily

In Palermo I was constantly reminded of Egypt – the impromptu visits, the streams of relatives hugging and kissing and sitting in a circle, and piles of food. In the north they explained it as '*il culto della famiglia e del mangiare*' – the cult of family and eating. Getting together is part of what the north envies as the southern joy of living. Here, any event, from a homecoming or a birthday to saints' days and weddings, is an occasion for a feast. Banqueting rooms in every tiny village are always packed. Feasting is also a matter of keeping up appearances, *la figura*, and extravagance (Sicilians call it *spagnolismo*, saying they learned it from the Spaniards) can reach incredible heights.

The island is so poor that much of the male population has to leave in search of livelihood, and yet not only is food important but the cooking is one of the most varied and exotic in Italy. The secret lies in the two thousand years of occupation. Being in the middle of the Mediterranean, Sicily was always desirable when this sea was the centre of the world. She was colonised by Greeks and Romans, Arabs and Normans; governed from Spain, Austria and Constantinople, and occupied by the French, Germans and English. Sicily not only was conquered but became the seat of the conquering kings, which lent grandeur to the island's cooking.

Sicilians do not break with the past. They can tell you that Greeks introduced honey and wine, olives and ricotta, focaccia and fish soup; that they prepare *maccu*, a broad bean purée, as was done in Roman times; that the Byzantines brought sharp cheeses and spicy biscuits, the Normans salt cod and *involtini* (stuffed meat or fish rolls), the Spaniards tomato sauce and sweet and sour flavours, the English dessert wines, and the Arabs much of what is theirs.

In 827 an army of Arabs – Berbers from North Africa and Spanish Moslems (Sicilians called them all Saracens) – landed on the island. They brought their laws and their language, their literature, arts and sciences and their religion; they irrigated the land and planted exotic fruits and vegetables around the cities. Used to nomadism, they encouraged people to raise sheep and goats. Stuffed vegetables, rice dishes, *cuscusu*, almond pastries, sorbets and even pasta are the heritage of their civilisation.

The fusion of cultures produced a rich and aromatic style of cooking where melted anchovies, garlic, red chillies, chocolate, wine (including sweet marsala), herbs (especially basil and mint), spices (including saffron), lemon and orange zest, olives and capers, almonds and pistachios, pine nuts and raisins, honey, orange blossoms and jasmine all play their part.

Sicilian cooking is both very humble – there is a bread soup with only salt, garlic, a bay leaf and a sprinkling of olive oil – and sumptuous, as in *cassata*, a cheesecake decorated with a fantasy of candied fruit and brightly painted marzipan. These extremes reflect the world of feudal landlords and serfs in which Sicily was locked until after the Second World War. Most of the land was owned by a powerful aristocracy that possessed feudal lordship over whole villages. They were absentee landlords who lived in town (Syracuse and Palermo were once among the largest and richest cities in the world) and whose extravagant lifestyle and obsession with status are legendary. The *cucina nobile* (also referred to as baronial and baroque) was based mainly on Arab and Spanish cooking and acquired a French touch in the eighteenth century, when head cooks in noble households were French (to this day head cooks are called *monzù*, from the French *monsieur*). Galantines of goose and pheasant pâtés appeared on tables; pasta was pressed into moulds for *timballi*, or encased in puff pastry in *tortiere*; layers of rice were shaped into *gattò*; and meat was cut into *medaglioni*.

The mantle of noble cooking has been taken over today by a thriving catering trade with a never-ending round of parties and banquets for up to four hundred people. Many of these take place in the great old palaces known to us from the movie *The Leopard*, which are rented for the occasion. Some chefs are capable of extraordinarily elaborate centrepieces. Mafia weddings, especially, can be mind-boggling affairs with meats and vegetables arranged in ornate, multi-coloured peacock shapes, and with monumental cakes.

In feudal days the great bulk of the population were shepherds (living in the mountains, many of them in huts with their animals), labourers and sharecroppers who surrendered more than half their produce in lieu of rent and still owed personal services to the master. It is their cooking, *cucina povera*, or rather their festive dishes (for it was only on special occasions that they ate well), with a few borrowings from the aristocratic kitchen, that is the popular and fashionable food today. It is based on the produce of the land. Everything that grows in Sicily has a pure, intense flavour because of the brilliant sun and the rich volcanic soil. Cereals take up much of the agricultural land: hard wheat, which is easy to grow but difficult to mill, is the main crop. Olive trees grow wild in the hills, and there are so many huge orange and lemon orchards (the region around Palermo called La Conca d'Oro is full of them) that their fragrance pervades the whole island. There are pistachios, hazelnuts, pine nuts and eighteen qualities of almonds (at Agrigento a festival is held when the almond trees flower).

Agriculture used to be backward and depressed because the low-investment cultivation of wheat, oranges and lemons suited absentee landlords best, and because this arcane rural world, oppressed by vendettas and banditry, was beset by anarchy. Harvests were often destroyed by drought, and until recently, in modern Sicily, agriculture was subordinated to industry. But there is now a new dynamism and shift towards the intensive cultivation of vegetables.

There is sheep farming on the hills, and cattle and some goats are raised. Animals are left to wander everywhere, almost wild, to graze as they can. The frequent movement of the herds between the coast and the mountains to escape extremes of climate is bad for their meat and milk, but the wild herbs they eat give both a wonderful flavour, and the cows are of breeds that produce an enormous amount of milk. All the milk, including that of sheep and goats, is turned into cheese. Sicilians make caciocavallo (Ragusa is famous for it) and provola and a variety of fresh and seasoned sheep's-milk cheese. When sheep cheese is just made, and without salt, it is called tuma; when it is salted it is *primu sale;* while still in the basket (*canestro*) it is called *canestrato;* and when it is hard and seasoned it becomes picurino – the famous pecorino, which is sometimes peppered.

Piacentinu, which is made in Enna and Piazza Armerina, includes saffron as well as pepper.

Ricotta is made by boiling the whey left over from cheese-making; creamy granules float to the top and are skimmed off and put into plastic baskets to drain and become firm. Sicilians claim that only sheep's-milk ricotta has the perfect flavour and texture for making the desserts that are their forte. Hard pecorino and ricotta, dried in the sun, are used for grating.

A Sicilian way of making a meal of fresh pecorino or caciocavallo is to cut the cheese into slices, heat it very gently for a few minutes in a frying pan with a little garlic and a sprinkling of vinegar and oregano until it softens, and then dip bread into it. They also fry the cheese and break an egg on top of it.

Pigs are farmed in Aragona, Biancavilla, Cefalù, Chiaramente Gulfi and Enna. The acorns and prickly pears they feed on give them a special flavour. There is a tradition on the island of making sausage for cooking, rather than the more customary salami for eating. In Nicosia they make an unusual salami by mixing rabbit with pork. Sicilians are famous for preserving fruit. Their crystallised fruit actually tastes of the fresh fruit. At Macchia di Giarre, at the foot of Mount Etna, they preserve cherries in alcohol; Caltagirone and Piazza Armerina are known for their delicious perfumed quince paste.

The fishing industry is most important, and ports specialise: Messina in swordfish, Trapani in tuna. At the time of the *mattanza del tonno*, tuna is fished in great nets; about eighty men are employed for six months for this. This method of fishing is supposed to yield fish with a better flavour. There is also a preserving industry: swordfish is dried, anchovies and sardines are preserved in salt, tuna in oil. Tuna roe is dried and pressed to make the highly prized delicacy *bottarga*.

Fish is one of the glories of Sicilian cooking. It is prepared in every possible way: marinated, grilled and deep-fried; in cakes, in little rolls and in stews. Anchovies are fried, then cooked in white wine with fennel seeds. Octopus is eaten warm with a dressing of olive oil. *Nunnate*, the transparent newborn fish, are made into fritters with egg and parsley or cooked in a delicate soup with olive oil, garlic and chopped olives. Red mullet is cooked in a paper bag with fennel seeds, oil and lemon. There are Sicilian specialties for the famous *baccalà* and *stoccafisso*, beloved in the Mediterranean.

The cooking of Sicily is the most exuberant and colourful in Italy. For the most part, you will find the same dishes all around the island, but there are different versions in every town. The west coast is more Oriental and exotic, with perfumes and spices, orange juice, sweet and sour flavours, and raisins and pine nuts everywhere. The region of Trapani, the one closest to Africa, specialises in *cuscusu*, a variant of the famous North African couscous. Preparing it involves skill and art: the coarse-grained semolina is cooked in a large clay dish called a *mafaradda*; it is flavoured with spices, sprinkled with water and rolled with the fingertips until the grains stick together to form granules; then it is steamed over water for an hour. A soup, *ghiotta*, made with various types of fish and fiery with red chilli, accompanies the semolina. On the east coast the people are more restrained in their tastes and prefer to use mainly herbs.

Controversy has always raged in Italy about the origins of pasta, but culinary historians now seem to agree that it first came to Sicily with the Arabs (there is still a very thin type called by its old Arab name, *itriya*), acquired its best-known shapes here and marched north, eventually taking the place of rice and polenta to become the national staple. Sicilian pasta is the dry kind made of the local hard wheat and water. *Pasta lunga* (spaghetti and macaroni) is preferred, as are little rings called anelletti. Several kinds are made by hand; gnocculi are cannelloni and gnucchitti are little shells, margherite are wavy, cavateddi look like half-closed mussels, and ditalini look like date stones. *Maccaruna di casa* are rolled around wheat stems. Lately egg tagliatelle has become popular.

There is a saying, '*Cambian sempre, come la salsa*' (always changing, like sauce), because the variety of sauces is so great. Pasta is eaten with every kind of vegetable – aubergine, courgettes, courgette blossoms and leaves, artichoke hearts, cauliflower, broccoli, broad beans, peas, potatoes, lentils, beans, chickpeas and chestnuts – and also with chicken livers, meatballs, bits of pancetta and sausage. *Pasta 'ncasciata* (in a mould) consists of layers of macaroni, fried chicken livers, meatballs, sliced aubergine, tomato pulp, bits of salami, basil, with grated cheese and eggs to bind it all into shape – real baroque cooking! But most pasta dishes are incredibly simple examples of just how attractive *cucina povera* can be. Peasants fed themselves entirely on pasta, so it had to be good, and they put in what they could. Typical sauces are made not just with the many vegetables but also with seafood – cuttlefish and their ink; clams, mussels and prawns; and newborn fish so small they look like a lump of jelly. These can be sardines, red mullet and other fish. Fishing for them is forbidden most of the year (the fishermen use special nets) but they always seem to be around.

Although antipasti are not in the Sicilian tradition (Sicilians ignore them; they can't wait for the pasta), restaurants serve a huge array, starting with simple things – very fresh ricotta; anchovies marinated in oil and lemon, with garlic and chilli; marinated caciocavallo or canestrato; crushed green olives flavoured with mint, fennel and garlic; and sliced *bottarga*, to be eaten on bread with a squeeze of lemon. Other appetisers include *crispedi*, fried dough combined with cheese or anchovy and wild fennel, served hot with a sprinkling of red pepper, and *frittelle di milinciani*, aubergine croquettes made with grated cheese, raisins and egg yolks. The most popular antipasti, when they are eaten, are vegetable fritters, of aubergine and courgette, for instance; sliced raw artichoke hearts; boiled cauliflower, fennel and cardoons; and *caponata*, a sweet and sour ratatouille of sorts.

There were rice fields in Trapani during Arab times, but cultivation ended when the island became too dry (there were once several rivers running across it). There are still a few rice dishes, however. The most famous, *arancini di riso* (rice balls shaped like *arancini*, little oranges), belong to the street, to the realm of the *friggitori*, who fry all kinds of things: the beloved *panelle*, like fat chips, made with chickpea flour; *cazzilli* (potato croquettes with parsley, grated cheese and chopped ham); vegetable fritters; and aubergine fans called *quaglie* because they look like quails in flight.

There are not many meat dishes – mostly grilled meats, meatballs, meat rolls with stuffing and offal. *Farsumagru* is a great roll stuffed with chopped hard-boiled eggs, salami, cheese and herbs. Many restaurants have goat stew on the menu. A speciality of the eastern side of the island is *coniglio nero*, rabbit cooked in dry white wine with bitter chocolate, cloves, fennel seeds and vinegar.

Vegetables are more important in Sicily than anywhere else in Italy: for centuries they constituted the meal. Aubergine is a special favourite. Introduced by the Arabs, it went out of favour when they left and was considered poisonous until the Renaissance; Carmelite monks, who had eaten aubergine in their monasteries in the East, brought it back into favour. There are said to be a hundred ways of preparing it, and as many for peppers. The most common way of dealing with vegetables such as aubergine, peppers, artichokes and pumpkin is to roast them over a charcoal fire and serve them with a sprinkling of olive oil, chopped garlic and parsley. Another is to cook them in a sweet and sour sauce, made with vinegar, sugar and a touch of mint and serve them cold.

Artichokes are very popular; an unusual variety with thorny leaves has a most delicious flavour. They are cooked with fried onion, orange and lemon juice and a little sugar or baked with layers of sliced potatoes in milk; the hearts are stuffed with sausage meat, raisins, pine nuts and grated pecorino and topped with egg. Mushrooms are baked with a topping of breadcrumbs, garlic, anchovy and basil or cooked with tomatoes, white wine, garlic, lemon juice and parsley. Cauliflower and broccoli are stewed in wine with fried onion and bits of anchovy and olives. And the vegetable dish that everyone waxes lyrical about is *frittedda* – broad beans, peas and artichokes sautéed with onions.

Despite the changes since the boom years of the 1960s, despite the fascination after the war with grilled meat and salads and with frozen foods, and despite the attraction of fast foods for the young, traditional cooking has survived in the home. Food is tied to the rituals of life. In addition to Christmas, New Year's Day, Easter, All Souls' Day and Carnival, there is always a religious feast, a holy day, a saint's day or a celebration to commemorate a historical event or the arrival of the seasons or ancient superstitions and magic. And there is special food and always a special pastry associated with each one of those days.

In the early Middle Ages cake-making was an accomplishment of nuns, and they still make them today. Several convents in Sicily, particularly in Palermo, became famous for their sweetmeats. The Monastero of Monreale is known for its *viscotta*, the New Abbey of Trapani for *sanguinazzi*, the Abbey of Alcamo for *minni di virgine* (virgin's breasts) and *gattò di ricotta*. At Erice they make *mustazzoli*, almond biscuits. The sisters of Martorana are famous for their vividly coloured marzipan fruits, those of St Catherine of Palermo for their cannoli, crisp pastry cylinders deep-fried then filled with ricotta mixed with sugar, vanilla, lemon zest, bits of chocolate and candied fruit or pumpkin. The nuns of the Convent of Valverde are famous for their *cassata* (in 1575 the diocesan synods prohibited the nuns from making *cassata* because it was too famous and too popular and the nuns did not have time to pray). The sisters of Santo Spirito, a Cistercian convent in Agrigento, who make a sweet *cuscusu* garnished with almonds and pistachios, pumpkin preserve and grated chocolate, say they make it exactly as was done in 1270: the recipe is a secret.

Many cloistered nuns are old now and their eyes are not good enough for embroidery, another typical activity, but they can still make pastries and crystallised fruits and marzipan sweets with extraordinary shapes and riotous colours. The almond paste differs according to the proportions of sugar and bitter almonds used and according to the flavouring – lemon, cinnamon, orange or lemon zest, flower water – and the sisters occasionally add their 'secret recipe' jam. I was told that their pastries have names like *brutti ma buoni* (ugly but good), *ossa di morti* (bones of the dead) and *sospiri* (sighs) because nuns are not supposed to enjoy themselves too much.

Pastry shops offer a large selection of sweets and often their own ice cream. Sicily is famous for her *granite* and *sorbetti* (*sciarbat* in dialect is the Arab word for sorbet). There is still talk of the way the Arabs fetched snow from Mount Etna to make them, and the habit of mixing sugar and jasmine water in a glass full of snow goes back to those times. Sicilians became the great masters of the art of ice cream making before anyone else in Europe, and it was a Sicilian, Procopio Coltelli, who opened the Café Procope in Paris in 1686, where ice cream was served for the first time in France. Among the joys of the island are the magnificent sorbets, *semifreddi* and *cassate* made with pure ingredients. An ice cream competition is held in Agrigento during the springtime almond blossom festival: that may be a good time to visit this beautiful island.

The Wines of Sicily

Sicily is, with Apulia, the largest wine-producing region in Italy. Together they are largely responsible for the European 'wine lake'. There is a great profusion of different vines and well over six hundred different bottled and labelled wines on the island.

Sicilian wines have always been known for their strength of character, high alcoholic content and sweetness, and they have been used for blending and distilling. But over the last twenty-five years the wine industries have been entirely transformed by modern technology. Now, floods of new modern wines, aimed at the international market – fresh, pure, light, dry wines, whites especially, big in body and rich in flavour and scent, but, except for some outstanding exceptions, indistinguishable and without much character – are produced industrially. And the old sweet wines and fortified wines, which had been eclipsed by fashion for so long, have been refined and brought into line with modern tastes. The best known are the marsalas, which are made from completely matured grapes, fortified with alcohol and processed with concentrated must and cooked wine, and then aged in wood. The dry Marsala Vergine and the long-aged Superiore Riserva especially are much respected and have recovered the honour of marsala. At its best, the wine is warm and complex with a delicious deep caramel flavour and an acid edge that makes it surprisingly refreshing for a fortified dessert wine. Good examples may be sweet or dryish and have a richly nutty, smoky character. Marsala can be served as an aperitif and as a dessert wine.

Another famous old wine is the Moscato di Pantelleria, produced on the tiny island of Pantelleria off the coast of Sicily, closer to Tunisia, from a local type of Muscat called Zibibbo (the Arabic word for raisin). It is also the basis of the dessert wine Passito di Pantelleria made from dried, shrivelled grapes. The grape gives the wines an intense characteristic fragrance and flavour.

Malvasia delle Lipari from the volcanic islands of the Aeolian archipelago, north of Messina, is made from Malvasia and other local grapes and has an extraordinary bouquet with hints of citrus and apricots. The sweet passito type is made with the dried grape, and the liquoroso is both sweet and fortified.

Dry wines now predominate in Sicily, and although few have international standing, there can be gems like the powerful and long-ageing pale cherry-red Cerasuolo di Vittoria; the appealing and elegant Etna Rosso, Rosato and Bianco from around Catania; and the rich, aromatic red Faro near Messina.

The most esteemed dry wines which have won international acclaim are the rich and raisiny Regaleali Rosso del Conte *riserva*, the fragrant white Rapitalà di Alcamo from near Palermo, the jasmine-scented Faustus Bianco and velvety red Faustus Rosso, and the famous Corvo wines. Corvo exemplifies the new perfectionist, highly professional, constantly experimenting spirit of the best industrialised wine-making in Sicily. Their whites, made from Inzolia and other native grapes, are reliably fresh, clean, smooth and vivacious. Their white Colomba Platino has an especially delicate and sharp quality.

ARTICHOKE HEARTS WITH ALMOND SAUCE
Carciofi alle mandorle

I discovered several new artichoke dishes on my last Sicilian trip, including pasta with artichokes, and artichoke bottoms stuffed with sausage meat, raisins and pine nuts. The following is not the most common but it is very appealing. Sicily has many different kinds of artichokes, including a mauve one with thorny leaves, and wild ones. In some varieties the leaves are so tender they can be eaten, and only the points are cut off.

SERVES 6

6 artichokes or frozen artichoke hearts
Salt
1/2 onion, grated
1 clove garlic, crushed
3 anchovies, chopped
100g (3 1/2oz) ground almonds
250ml (8fl oz) light chicken stock

4 tablespoons olive oil
1 tablespoon vinegar
1 tablespoon sugar
Juice of 1 lemon
White pepper
2 tablespoons capers, chopped (optional)
2 small pickled gherkins, chopped (optional)

If the leaves of the artichokes are not edible, cut them off close to the base and throw them away, then cut off the stems and trim the base. Boil the artichoke hearts and stems in salted water for about 30 minutes, then drain. With a pointed spoon, remove the choke from the middle. If using frozen hearts, simmer 3 minutes only.

For the sauce, fry the onion until golden, then the garlic. Add the anchovies and let them melt; then add the almonds, pour in the stock, and simmer for about 15 minutes until thick and creamy. Beat in the oil, vinegar, sugar and lemon and a little salt and pepper, adjusting the quantities to taste.

Arrange the artichoke hearts on individual plates, pour the sauce over them and garnish with capers and gherkins, if desired. Serve cold.

SWEET AND SOUR AUBERGINE

Caponata

This is made in large quantities by most families and kept in clay pots as a ready antipasto or an accompaniment to cold meats and fish. Some people add a little bitter cocoa to the sauce.

SERVES 4

Salt
700g (1½lb) aubergines, cut into cubes
Olive oil
1 onion, sliced
500g (1lb) tomatoes, peeled and chopped
Pepper

1 tablespoon capers
50g (2oz) green olives, pitted
3 stalks celery, cut into 1cm (½in) pieces
4 tablespoons wine vinegar
1 tablespoon sugar

Salt the aubergine and let the juices degorge for 1 hour. Rinse, dry and fry in hot olive oil until brown and tender. Drain on absorbent paper towels. Fry the onion in a little oil until golden, then add the tomatoes, salt and pepper and simmer for 15 minutes. Blanch the capers, olives and celery, drain, then add to the tomato sauce with the vinegar and sugar. Simmer for about 15 minutes until reduced a little, stirring occasionally, then mix with the cold aubergine. Leave to stand for at least 30 minutes.

Note

Serve garnished, if you like, with chopped almonds and parsley.

PEPPERS STUFFED WITH RICE

Peperoni ripieni di riso

Stuffed vegetables are almost a symbol of the Mediterranean, Arab in origin and infinitely varied. In Sicily they stuff aubergines, tomatoes and peppers, and although fillings vary, the base is usually breadcrumbs or rice.

SERVES 4

6 small peppers, red, yellow or green
1 onion, chopped
3 tablespoons olive oil
250g (8oz) Arborio rice
500g (1lb) tomatoes, peeled and chopped

Salt and pepper
1 teaspoon sugar
2 tablespoons finely chopped parsley
2 tablespoons finely chopped mint

Cut a slice off the stem end of the peppers. Keep these as lids and remove the seeds.

For the filling, fry the onion in 2 tablespoons oil until golden, add the rice and stir until it becomes transparent. Add the tomatoes, season with salt, pepper and sugar, and cook, moistening with 4–5 tablespoons water, for about 20 minutes, or until the rice is slightly underdone, adding a little more water if it becomes too dry. Stir in the herbs and fill the peppers with the rice mixture. Cover with their lids and pack into a baking dish.

Pour the rest of the oil and about a finger of water in the bottom of the dish, cover with foil and bake in the oven at 200°C (400°F, gas mark 6) for 30 minutes, or until the peppers are tender. They are best served cold.

Variation

If you like a stronger-tasting filling, add finely chopped olives (black or green), capers (with their vinegar squeezed out), a good pinch of hot chilli powder and the juice of 1 lemon.

RICE BALLS WITH CHEESE
Arancini di riso e ricotta

You find these rice balls the size of small oranges (*arancini* means 'little oranges') at old-fashioned *friggitori* and at *tavole calde* or other modern fast-food establishments. Tiny ones are prepared at home as party food to pass around. Some are mixed or stuffed with meat sauce and green peas, and sometimes the rice is cooked with saffron. This simple version with cheese (sometimes peas and ham go in) is often featured as part of a vegetable *fritto misto* throughout southern Italy.

SERVES 6 AS A STARTER

150g (5oz) Arborio rice

Salt

125g (4oz) ricotta, mashed

25g (1oz) freshly grated pecorino or parmesan

3 eggs, beaten

4 tablespoons finely chopped parsley

Pepper

Freshly grated nutmeg

125g (4oz) mozzarella, chopped

Flour

Fine breadcrumbs

Oil for frying

Boil the rice in 750ml (1¼ pints) salted water for about 17 minutes, or until tender. Let it cool and dry out for a few minutes on a large plate, then turn into a bowl and mix in the ricotta, grated pecorino or parmesan, two of the eggs and the parsley, and season generously with salt, pepper and nutmeg. Work well until the mixture sticks together like a paste, then work in the mozzarella.

Wash your hands and wet them to shape the rice into small walnut-sized balls. Roll first in flour, then in the remaining beaten egg and lastly in the breadcrumbs. Deep-fry in medium hot oil until golden. The oil should not be too hot, as the *arancini* must cook for 5 minutes to allow the cheese to melt, and they could brown too quickly. Drain on absorbent paper towels. You can reheat them in the oven when you are ready to serve.

Variations

A little powdered saffron can go into the water with the rice. Chopped fresh mint gives *arancini* a lovely fresh taste, and gorgonzola (though not a southern cheese) makes a good alternative to mozzarella.

TUNA AND POTATO SALAD
Insalata di tonno e patate

SERVES 6

4 medium new potatoes, boiled, peeled and
    thickly sliced

250g (8oz) canned tuna, broken into pieces

2 hard-boiled eggs, quartered

1–2 tablespoons capers, chopped

50g (2oz) anchovy fillets, chopped

4 pickled gherkins, chopped

Handful of black olives, pitted and chopped

Juice of 1 lemon

Salt and pepper

4–5 tablespoons olive oil

Put all the ingredients in a serving bowl and mix well. Let it stand for 1 hour before serving.

BREAD WITH OLIVES AND SAUSAGE
Pane con olive e salsiccia

Large braided loaves covered with sesame seeds are typically Sicilian. In small towns and villages, little bakeries bake the same breads that people make at home; some containing bits of olives, cheese, salami, herbs and even vegetables constitute a snack. This bread is a speciality of Agrigento.

700g (1½lb) strong flour
1 rounded teaspoon salt
5 tablespoons olive oil
1 packet active (easy-blend) dried yeast
Pinch of sugar

400ml (14fl oz) warm water
200g (7oz) black olives, pitted and chopped
250g (8oz) fresh soft salami, diced
A sprig of rosemary, chopped

Mix all but 40g (1½oz) of the flour, salt and 4 tablespoons of oil together in a bowl. Dissolve the yeast with the sugar in a little of the warm water and leave to froth for about 5 minutes. Mix it into the flour mixture and add enough of the remaining water to make a stiff sticky dough. Knead the dough for about 10 minutes, adding more flour if necessary, until it is smooth and elastic.

Put the remaining oil in a bowl, turn the dough in it to keep a crust from forming, and leave to rise in a warm place, covered with a damp cloth, for 1–2 hours, or until the dough doubles in bulk. Punch it down and knead again, and divide it into four balls. Divide the olives, salami and rosemary and work them well into each ball. Form 4 loaves, place them on oiled baking sheets and allow them to rise again to almost double their bulk. Bake in a preheated oven at 200°C (400°F, gas mark 6) for about 45 minutes, or until the loaves sound hollow when tapped.

VERMICELLI WITH PEPPERS, TOMATOES AND AUBERGINE
Vermicelli alla siracusana

SERVES 4

1 largish aubergine, cubed
Salt
1–2 yellow peppers
Olive oil for frying
1 clove garlic
2 anchovies, finely chopped
4–5 tomatoes, peeled and chopped

Pepper
8 black olives, pitted and cut into pieces
1 tablespoon capers, vinegar squeezed out, chopped
Small bunch of basil, chopped
400g (14oz) vermicelli
Grated caciocavallo or pecorino (optional)

Sprinkle the aubergine with salt, and let the juices run out for 1 hour, then rinse and dry them. Roast the pepper by turning it under the grill until the skin is brown and blistered. Seal it in a heavy-duty plastic bag and after about 10 minutes peel it (putting it in the bag makes it easier). Remove the seeds and cut the pepper into strips.

In a large pan, fry the aubergine in oil (start with 3–4 tablespoons but you may need more), turning to brown it all over. Add the garlic and, when the aroma rises, the anchovies and then the tomatoes. Season with salt and pepper and simmer about 15 minutes, or until the aubergine is tender. Add the olives, capers, basil and pepper strips, and cook a minute longer.

Cook the vermicelli in plenty of boiling salted water until al dente. Drain and serve topped with the sauce. Pass the grated cheese around, if desired.

PASTA WITH RAW TOMATO SAUCE
Pasta a picchi pacchi

I first had this splendid dish – a relatively new one – at a restaurant called PG in Trapani, where a whole soccer team ordered what sounded like 'pik pak'. No one can explain where the name comes from. It is sometimes called *pasta al pesto*, because some of the ingredients are pounded with a pestle and mortar.

All the sauce ingredients are raw. Everyone describes them differently: sometimes there is very little tomato; sometimes there are no almonds and sometimes they are toasted; various other herbs can join basil; and opinions are divided as to whether you should add grated cheese.

SERVES 4

6 medium tomatoes, peeled, chopped and well
   drained
4 tablespoons olive oil
50g (2oz) blanched almonds, very finely chopped
   or pounded (not ground)
2–3 cloves garlic, crushed
Good bunch of basil, chopped or pounded

Salt and pepper
1 teaspoon sugar (optional)
$\frac{1}{2}$ small chilli, finely chopped, or a pinch of hot chilli
   powder (optional)
400g (14oz) spaghetti or bucatini
Grated pecorino or caciocavallo (optional)

To prepare the sauce, put all the ingredients except the pasta and cheese in a bowl to steep, covered, for at least 1 hour so that the flavours have time to infuse (pounding extracts more of the basil's fragrance).

Cook the pasta until al dente in boiling salted water. Drain and dress with the raw sauce (which should be at room temperature). Many prefer to eat this without cheese, as I do, but pass it around if you like.

PASTA WITH COURGETTES AND AUBERGINES
Pasta con zucchine e melanzane

There are many pasta dishes with courgettes and aubergines. In Palermo I was offered a plate with two small, whole deep-fried aubergines on top. They were sliced, but not all the way through, so they remained attached at one end and opened out like fans (these aubergine fans are called *quaglie*, quails, because they look like the birds). I also had spaghetti topped with courgettes cut into little sticks and fried. A famous speciality of Catania, *pasta alla Norma*, has pieces of aubergine in a tomato sauce. The following way of serving both vegetables is a popular one.

SERVES 4

2 large aubergines, cut in half lengthwise and
   sliced thinly into half-moon shapes
6 medium courgettes, sliced thinly lengthwise
Salt
1 onion, chopped
Olive oil
700g (1$\frac{1}{2}$lb) tomatoes, peeled and chopped

2 cloves garlic, finely chopped
$\frac{1}{2}$ small chilli, finely chopped, or a pinch of hot chilli
   powder (optional)
Black pepper
1 teaspoon sugar
3 tablespoons chopped basil leaves
400g (14oz) spaghetti

Sprinkle the aubergines and courgettes with salt and leave them for 1 hour to drain.

To make the tomato sauce, fry the onion in 2 tablespoons oil until soft, then add the tomatoes and garlic; season with salt, chilli, if using, black pepper and sugar, and cook for about 25 minutes, or until the sauce has reduced to a thick consistency, adding the basil towards the end.

Press the aubergine slices between two plates to squeeze out as much juice as possible. Rinse and dry the aubergines and courgettes, then deep-fry quickly in hot oil until lightly browned and tender. Drain on absorbent paper towels. Arrange in a flat ovenproof dish and heat through in the oven before serving.

Boil the pasta in plenty of boiling salted water until al dente, then drain quickly and dress with the tomato sauce. Present the vegetable slices separately.

Note

You can sprinkle the courgette and aubergine with flour and shake them in a colander before frying.

PASTA WITH BROCCOLI
Ditali coi broccoli

SERVES 4

700g (1½lb) broccoli, or 1 small cauliflower
Salt
350g (12oz) ditali or penne
4 tablespoons olive oil
1 clove garlic, finely chopped

8–10 anchovy fillets, chopped
125g (4oz) green olives
1 red chilli, finely chopped (optional)
6 tablespoons freshly toasted breadcrumbs

Trim and cut the broccoli or cauliflower into florets. Boil in plenty of salted water until tender and drain, reserving the cooking water. Use the water to cook the pasta, for 10–12 minutes.

Heat the oil with the garlic in a small pan until the aroma rises, then add the anchovies and mash them well. When the pasta is al dente, drain and mix quickly with the anchovy sauce, adding a little more olive oil if you like. Add the olives, pitted if you prefer, broccoli or cauliflower and chilli, if using, and serve sprinkled with breadcrumbs.

PASTA WITH SARDINES
Pasta con le sarde

This is the most typical of Sicilian pasta dishes. The wild fennel leaves, which lend a distinctive flavour, can be replaced with cultivated fennel tops.

SERVES 6

12–14 fresh sardines
Salt
1 medium onion, chopped
Olive oil
8 tablespoons chopped green fennel leaves

25g (1oz) raisins, soaked in water
50g (2oz) pine nuts
Flour
500g (1lb) spaghetti
6 tablespoons fine breadcrumbs, toasted

Scale, clean and bone the sardines and remove the heads. Open them out flat. Wash and salt them.

Fry the onion in 2 tablespoons of oil until golden, then add the fennel and cook gently. Add the drained raisins and the pine nuts and cook through.

Flour the sardines lightly and deep-fry in oil. Boil the spaghetti until al dente and drain. Mix the spaghetti with the fennel mixture and add a spoonful or two of raw olive oil, if you like, and one or two of pasta water. Arrange the sardines on top.

Pass the breadcrumbs around for everyone to sprinkle on top. (Breadcrumbs, known as 'poor man's parmesan', were sprinkled over pasta by the poor, who could not afford the real thing.)

RICE AND AUBERGINE MOULD
Risu e milinciani 'a palermitana

Rice is not an everyday dish in Sicily as it is in the Veneto, Lombardy and Piedmont. Apart from the little *arancini*, rice dishes are reserved for special occasions. It is often said that although the unification of Italy meant a conquering of the south by the north, in gastronomic matters the conquests went the other way – pasta and pizza went north but polenta and risottos were never adopted in the south. In the *Guida all'Italia gastronomica*, Massimo Alberini and Giorgio Mistretta trace the southern aversion for rice to the First World War, when southern soldiers fighting in the trenches received disgusting rations of gluey rice and swore never to eat risotto.

But Sicily does have her own much-liked rice dishes. This one is a speciality of Palermo.

SERVES 6

2 large aubergines, sliced about 0.75cm ($\frac{1}{3}$in) thick
Salt
Olive oil
2 medium onions, chopped
500g (1lb) tomatoes, peeled and chopped
Pepper

1 teaspoon sugar
3 tablespoons chopped parsley
3 tablespoons chopped basil
250g (8oz) Arborio rice
About 1.75 litres (3 pints) light chicken stock
Grated caciocavallo or ricotta salata

Sprinkle the aubergine slices with salt and leave for about 1 hour. Press between two plates to squeeze out as much juice as possible. Rinse and dry, then fry in hot olive oil, turning them over once, until tender and lightly browned. Lay them on several layers of absorbent paper towels with more paper towels on top, and press gently to get rid of excess oil.

Make a tomato sauce. Fry the onions in 2 tablespoons oil until very soft and golden. Add the tomatoes, salt, pepper and sugar and simmer for 15 minutes until reduced, then remove from the heat and add the parsley and basil.

Now boil the rice in plenty of chicken stock for about 15 minutes, or until tender but still firm. Drain, throwing away the excess stock.

Line a round mould or ovenproof bowl with the overlapping aubergine slices and fill with alternating layers of rice and tomato sauce with sprinklings of grated caciocavallo or ricotta salata. Bake, covered with foil, in the oven at 200°C (400°F, gas mark 6) for about 25 minutes. Turn out of the mould and serve hot.

SWORDFISH STEAKS IN WHITE WINE WITH TOMATOES
Pesce spada alla siciliana

SERVES 4

1 small onion, chopped
1 stalk celery, chopped
1 clove garlic, finely chopped
2 bay leaves
2 tablespoons olive oil
3 tomatoes, peeled and chopped

1 teaspoon sugar
300ml ($\frac{1}{2}$ pint) or more dry white wine
Salt and pepper
2 slices swordfish, about 250g (8oz) each, skin removed

Fry the onion, celery, garlic and bay leaves in the olive oil until softened. Add the tomatoes and sugar and cook, stirring, for 1 minute. Pour in the wine, season with salt and pepper, simmer for 5 minutes and put in the swordfish. Poach for less than 10 minutes, or until the flesh becomes opaque, turning the slices over once. Serve hot or cold.

STUFFED SQUID OR CUTTLEFISH
Calamari o seppie imbottite

SERVES 4

8 medium or 16 tiny squid or cuttlefish
50g (2oz) fresh breadcrumbs
2 anchovies, finely chopped
Bunch of parsley, chopped (about 4 tablespoons)
2 cloves garlic, crushed

Salt and pepper
4 tablespoons olive oil
5 medium tomatoes, peeled and chopped
250ml (8fl oz) dry white wine
1 teaspoon sugar (optional)

Clean the squid or cuttlefish (see page 18).

For the filling, mix the breadcrumbs with the chopped tentacles, anchovies, all but about 2 tablespoons of the parsley, and garlic, add salt and pepper and 2 tablespoons of oil, and moisten with a few drops of water to bind the mixture. Fill the squid or cuttlefish three-quarters full (they shrink and the filling expands when they are cooked, so it will spill out if they are too full). It is usually advised to sew up the openings but I don't bother. Fry gently on all sides in the remaining oil and remove.

Make the sauce in the same pan. Put in the tomatoes and white wine, a little salt and sugar, if using, and cook 10 minutes. Add the fish and simmer gently until tender, from 5 minutes if they are very small to 15–20 minutes if medium. Serve hot or cold, sprinkled with the remaining parsley.

STUFFED SARDINES
Sarde a beccaficu

SERVES 6

1kg (2lb) fresh sardines
1 medium onion, chopped
Olive oil
250g (8oz) fresh breadcrumbs
Good bunch of parsley, chopped (about
    4 tablespoons)

75–125g (3–4oz) pitted green olives, chopped
2 tablespoons capers
Juice and grated rind of 1 orange and 1 lemon
Salt and pepper
12 bay leaves
Juice of 1 lemon

Scale, gut and clean the sardines, split them open and remove the head and backbone. Fry the onion gently in 3 tablespoons oil. When golden, add breadcrumbs, parsley, olives and capers, moisten with orange and lemon juice, add the rinds and season well. Place a spoonful on each sardine and roll up, starting from the neck.

Arrange in an oiled baking dish, with a bay leaf between each. Sprinkle with a little more oil and the lemon juice and bake, uncovered, in the oven at 180°C (350°F, gas mark 4) for 10–15 minutes. Serve hot or cold.

Variations

You might want to try this stuffing from the eastern part of Sicily. Omit the olives, capers and orange juice and add instead 2 tablespoons pine nuts, 2 tablespoons raisins and 6 finely chopped anchovies.

Or do as they do in Messina: stuff thin slices of swordfish instead of sardines and grill them.

MUSSELS WITH LEMON
Cozze al limone

SERVES 6

1kg (2lb) mussels
Juice of 1 lemon
120ml (4fl oz) or more olive oil

Salt and pepper
3 tablespoons finely chopped parsley

Prepare the mussels as described on page 18. Remove the top part of the shell. Mix the rest of the ingredients. Pour a little into each half-shell.

BRAISED VEGETABLES
Frittedda o frittella

This is served alone as a first course or side dish, as a soup with stock added or as a sauce with pasta.

SERVES 4

500g (1lb) fresh broad beans, in the pod
500g (1lb) fresh peas, in the pod
12 spring onions, coarsely chopped

4 artichoke hearts, quartered
About 4 tablespoons olive oil
Salt and pepper

Shell the broad beans and the peas. Put all the vegetables in a pan with the oil and cook very gently for a few minutes. Season and add a ladleful of water and cook, stirring occasionally and adding a little more water now and then, for about 45 minutes, or until the vegetables are tender. In Sicily they like them very soft.

Variation

This can be eaten cold, in which case a little lemon juice, sugar and a few leaves of mint are added during the cooking.

VEAL SCALOPPINE WITH MARSALA
Scaloppini cu Marsala

SERVES 4

700g (1½lb) veal scaloppine
Flour
50g (2oz) butter

1 tablespoon sunflower oil
120ml (4fl oz) dry marsala
Salt and pepper

Coat the veal with flour and quickly fry in half the butter and the oil until brown. Add the marsala, evaporate a little, then remove the meat from the pan, season and keep warm. Reduce the sauce, whisk in the remaining cold butter, cut into pieces, and pour over the veal.

Variations

You may omit the flour and use only oil without butter.

Pork tenderloin can be cut into medallions and cooked in the same way.

LIVER IN SWEET AND SOUR SAUCE
Ficatu all'agru e duci

This is from Paolo Cascino's book *Cucina di Sicilia*. Considered the greatest cook in Sicily, he now teaches at a hotel and catering school in Palermo, where students learn how to plan feasts of thirty and even forty dishes.

SERVES 4

700g (1½lb) calf's liver, thinly sliced

Salt and pepper

Breadcrumbs

Sunflower oil

3 cloves garlic, crushed

1 tablespoon sugar

3 tablespoons wine vinegar

1 teaspoon chopped fresh mint

Season the liver and dip in breadcrumbs. Fry very quickly for 2–3 minutes on each side in oil, put on a plate and keep warm.

Fry the garlic and sugar in 2 tablespoons oil until golden, being careful they do not burn. When the sugar is caramelised, add the vinegar, let it evaporate and add the mint.

Pour over the liver and eat hot or cold.

SWEET AND SOUR RABBIT
Coniglio all'agrodolce

SERVES 4

1 onion, sliced

2–3 tablespoons olive or sunflower oil

1 rabbit, about 1.1kg (2½lb), cut into pieces

Flour

300ml (½ pint) red wine

1 bay leaf

A sprig of rosemary

Salt and pepper

1 tablespoon sugar

2 tablespoons white wine vinegar

2 tablespoons pine nuts, toasted

1 tablespoon raisins

2 tablespoons pitted and chopped green or black olives

Fry the onion in oil (I prefer using sunflower oil here) until soft and golden. Roll the rabbit pieces in flour and fry lightly, turning to brown them all over. Cover with red wine, add the bay leaf and rosemary, salt and pepper and simmer for 20 minutes. Add sugar and vinegar, the pine nuts, raisins and olives and raise the heat to evaporate the vinegar for 1–2 minutes (its taste should not be too powerful).

'ALMOND BLOSSOM' PASTRY
Fior di mandorla

Most of the pastries in Sicily are Arab in origin and based on almonds. Angelo Lauria, pastry-maker of Licata near Agrigento, offers a huge and delicious range. This was my favourite.

MAKES ABOUT 30

400g (14oz) ground almonds
250g (8oz) sugar
100g (3½oz) honey
1 teaspoon cinnamon

Grated rind of 1 lemon
2 egg whites
Icing sugar

Mix the ground almonds, sugar, honey, cinnamon and lemon rind, and add only just enough egg white to make a soft firm dough (it is important not to add more than you need).

Start kneading the mixture when it is still dry, like damp sand, and the oil in the almonds will help hold it together.

Shape into little cakes about 5cm (2in) in diameter and place on greased foil on a baking sheet. Bake in a preheated oven at 150°C (300°F, gas mark 2) for 20 minutes.

Let them cool, place on a serving plate and dust with icing sugar.

MELON GRANITA
Granita al melone

Sicily's ice creams have conquered the world, and they still have an enormous place in Sicilian life. They are made by pastry-makers, who also make candies, almond pastries and savoury tarts. Curiously, many of these pastry-makers are of Swiss origin and they have added their own ways of making ice cream with eggs and cream to the Sicilian classics such as cassata and granita. There are always new flavours, new *bombe* and new styles – now ice cream is stuffed into brioches for eating in the hand. But old favourites, such as melon granita, remain, and people still make them at home.

Choose a sweet, perfumed and very ripe melon. This is the kind of confection you should make to taste; the amount of sugar you add depends on the sweetness of the melon.

SERVES 8

2 ripe melons, preferably cantaloupe, to make
    750ml (1¼ pints) pulp
125g (4oz) sugar, or to taste (optional)

Juice of 1 lemon
1–3 teaspoons jasmine or orange flower water
    (optional)

Cut up the melon, peel it and remove the seeds. Blend to a liquid, adding sugar, if necessary (if the melon is very sweet you do not need to add any sugar), and lemon juice, and flower water if you like. Jasmine water is hard to get (I have found it only in Sicily and Thailand), but orange flower water is available in Middle Eastern and Oriental stores (you can use the larger quantity as it is usually rather weak).

Pour into an ice-cube tray, cover with clingfilm and let it freeze hard. Just before serving, put the cubes in a food processor and process a few at a time until light and frothy, or process in advance and put the granita back in the freezer, covered, for serving later.

COFFEE GRANITA
Granita al caffè con panna

SERVES 6

4 tablespoons sugar, or to taste
1 litre (1¾ pints) good strong black coffee

300ml (½ pint) whipped cream (optional)

Dissolve the sugar in the coffee while it is still hot (it is best made not too sweet). Let it cool, then pour into ice-cube trays. Cover with plastic wrap and put in the freezer for several hours.

Just before serving take out the required amount of ice cubes and process in a food processor to a soft or crunchy consistency. Serve in glasses, topped, if you like, with the whipped cream.

ALMOND OR HAZELNUT ICE CREAM
Semifreddo alle mandorle o alle nocciole

Antonio Tantillo, chef at the Charleston in Palermo, gave me this recipe.

SERVES 6

125g (4oz) blanched almonds or hazelnuts
75g (3oz) granulated sugar
600ml (1 pint) double cream

2 eggs, separated
100g (3$\frac{1}{2}$oz) sifted icing sugar
2 tablespoons maraschino

To make the praline, toast the nuts lightly in a dry frying pan, shaking the pan. Add the sugar and stir until melted and golden brown. Pour on to a lightly oiled baking sheet and, when cool, break into pieces and blend for a few seconds to pulverise.

To make the mousse, beat the cream until thick. Beat the egg yolks with 25g (1oz) icing sugar until pale. Beat the whites until stiff, then add the rest of the icing sugar and beat until the mixture stands in stiff peaks. Fold the yolks into the cream, then fold in the egg whites and the praline and stir in the maraschino.

Use a mould with foil, spoon in the cream mixture, level and cover with foil. Freeze for 24 hours. Leave to stand for a few minutes before unmoulding.

CASSATA, PALERMO STYLE
Cassata palermitana

Confectioners cover this Sicilian classic with marzipan, fondant icing and baroque decorations. The icing given here is simpler.

350g (12oz) sponge cake, thinly sliced
3–4 tablespoons rum or marsala (optional)
350g (12oz) ricotta
125g (4oz) caster sugar
A few drops vanilla essence
50g (2oz) candied fruit, chopped

50g (2oz) candied orange peel, chopped
50g (2oz) bitter chocolate, chopped or grated
350g (12oz) icing sugar
A few drops green food colouring
About 200g (7oz) whole mixed glacé fruits or candied
    peel

Line the sides and bottom of a 20cm (8in) mould with foil, then line with sponge cake, keeping some to cover the top. Sprinkle with half the rum or marsala, if using.

Mix the ricotta, caster sugar and vanilla in the blender. Stir in the chopped candied fruit and the peel and chocolate. Spoon the mixture into the mould, cover with the remaining slices of sponge cake and sprinkle with the rest of the alcohol, if using. Cover with foil and press down well, then refrigerate for a few hours.

Melt the icing sugar in a double boiler with 1–2 drops green food colouring and a few tablespoons water. Stir continuously with a wooden spoon and be careful it does not brown. Unmould the cassata and cover with the icing.

Decorate with mixed candied peel or glacé fruits and serve in very thin slices.

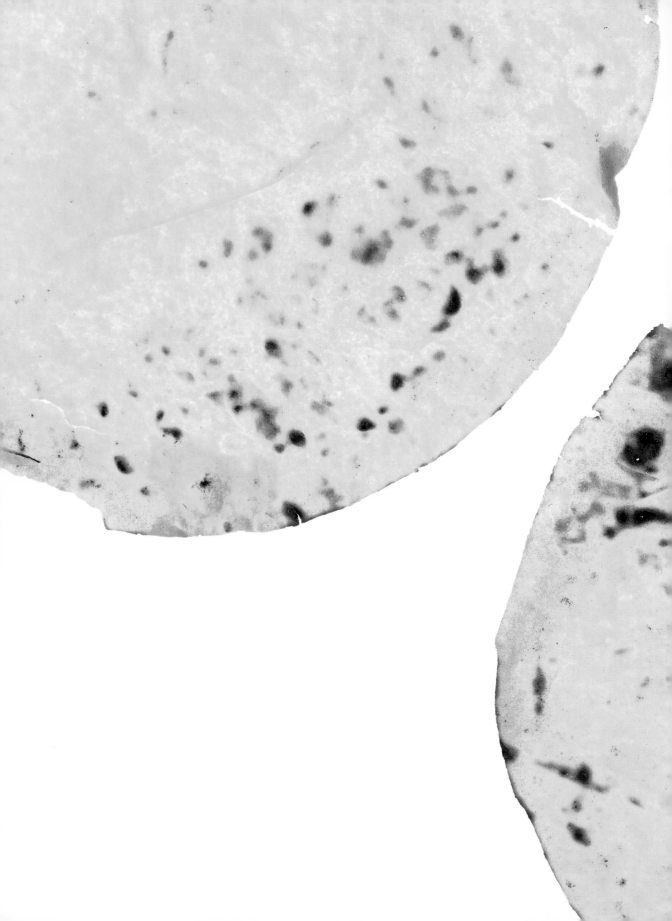

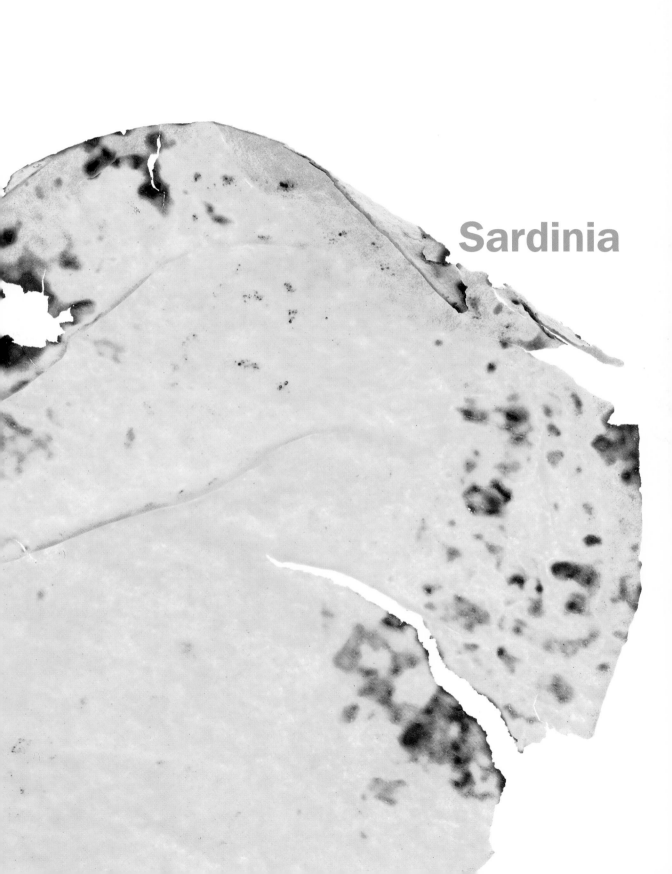

Sardinia

'It's a prehistoric dish,' explained the owner of a small restaurant at Cabras near Oristano, referring to a grey mullet preserved with a herb from the *laguna*. I had arrived through a landscape dotted with the remains of cone-shaped towers (*nuraghi*) dating from 1200 BC, and the menu in Sardinian, which sounds like Latin to me, reinforced the sensation of the remote past. But the development of luxury hotels, villas and marinas on the Sardinian coast has brought a mushrooming of restaurants that offer what they think tourists want. The first seafood restaurant opened in Cagliari twenty years ago; now there are two hundred there. They claim that the inspiration for the new cooking of the sea came from local fishermen.

Sardinians are people of the interior. They hate the sea and they don't like fish. Those who live on the coast are from outside or of mixed ethnic ancestry. Fishermen are Genoese, Neapolitan, Sicilian (they have taken over tuna fishing), Arab and Catalan (they still speak thirteenth-century Catalan). Their influence can be detected in the dishes and cooking terms: *burrida* and *ciuppin* are Genoese for fish stew, *scabeccio* is Spanish, and a Neapolitan fish soup has a Spanish name, *cassola*, derived from the pot. The result is a very varied list of fish and seafood, simply cooked and delicious. *Buttariga*, the salted and pressed roe of grey mullet or tuna, sliced very thinly and served as an appetiser with olive oil and lemon juice or dried and grated over pasta or rice, is a speciality. Lobster, grilled, boiled or cooked in white wine, is another. Oysters and sea urchins are served raw with lemon juice. Octopus is boiled and seasoned with oil and vinegar, garlic and parsley. There are baby crabs and jumbo prawns. Mussels, clams, sea dates and other shellfish are cooked in white wine with saffron (it grows here), with or without tomatoes. Squid is served stuffed. Cuttlefish is cooked in its ink. Newborn fish (*gianchetti*) are made into fritters. Sea anemones are battered and fried, as are little fish. You will find most of the Mediterranean fish grilled over charcoal or fried (they are first dipped in semolina, which gives them a good crust).

Anchovies, eels, tuna, red and grey mullet, swordfish, sea bass and sea bream are most popular. Coastal Sardinians have their own versions of Italian fish soups, seafood pastas and risottos (rice grows here too) made with prawns, shellfish, squid, cuttlefish and sea urchins.

Sardinia had many foreign invaders and conquerors, starting with the Phoenicians, Carthaginians and Romans. They stayed on the coast while the Sardinians retreated into the interior, and they left few traces in the kitchen. *Fregula*, semolina granules made by moistening the grain and rolling it gently with the fingertips, which go into fish soups, are supposed to have been introduced by the Romans. The Byzantines introduced ways of making cheese. The Arabs brought rice, milk puddings and almond pastries. Spanish domination lasted for four centuries and peopled Alghero with Catalans. Saffron, meat pies (*empanadas*), and the mixed meat stew *lepudrida* (in Spanish *olla podrida*) are part of the Spanish heritage.

Italian civilisation (and dishes) came, for the first time since the Romans, with the Pisans and Genoese in the eleventh century. The two struggled for control of the island until the arrival of the Spaniards in the fourteenth century. Cagliari became the centre of Pisan power in the south-west (where you can still hear medieval Tuscan) and Sassari became the bastion of Genoese influence in the north-west. Prominent Pisan and Genoese families married into the native aristocracy. The merchant classes flourished. Monks settled from Italy and developed agriculture.

In the eighteenth century Sardinia was acquired by the Piedmontese House of Savoy and the Duke of Savoy became King of Sardinia. The bonds between Sardinia and Piedmont became close when the court of Savoy, driven from Turin by Napoleon, found refuge in Cagliari in 1799. The Piedmontese promoted rural improvement and initiated a movement back to the coast. They introduced stuffed pasta, their agnolotti, which were transformed into *culingiones* and *angiolottus*. The

Piedmontese King of Sardinia, Victor Emmanuel II, became the first king of Italy in 1861. But Sardinia remained isolated from the mainland and her regional cooking is the most distinctive in Italy. Outside influences made little impression on the cooking of Sardinia. The interior of the island was never penetrated; it was always poor, primitive, sparsely populated, independent and lawless.

The true Sardinia is the mountains and the forests and the silent lonely life of the shepherd. It has not changed much despite television and industrialisation, road-building and marinas. Hidden in remote villages where life seems to have stopped a hundred years ago, people have clung to their old traditions, many of which are of extreme antiquity, and their cooking reflects their simple and archaic way of life.

There are shepherd villages and peasant villages (agriculture and pig rearing are practised in the western part of the island and on the coastal plains), but every family produces its own olive oil (trees grow wild), wine (mostly sweet wine for festive occasions) and *acquavite*, and grows its own vegetables: artichokes, fennel, celery, broad beans, tomatoes and others. The main industrial crop of the island is durum wheat, and there is fruit. The climate is very hot and dry, and winds tear at the land, making it difficult to cultivate. Every family kills a pig or two in the winter and makes cured ham and sausages. The Sardinian diet is based on meat (mainly lamb and pork), including game (wild boar, hare, partridge), cheese and bread. The flesh of the animals has a delicate flavour derived from the wild herbs and berries tangled in the scrub which covers the mountains. The most typical food is suckling pig (*porceddu*) roasted in the open until the crust is brown and crackling. Baby lamb or kid and wild boar are done in the same way. Salt is the only seasoning; the flavour comes from the burning wood (juniper, holm oak, myrtle and vine cuttings) and from the branch that serves as a spit, which is traditionally stuck upright into the ground. At the end, the roast may be wrapped in myrtle leaves and wild herbs, so that their perfume permeates the meat. Another way, laying the meat over heated stones in a pit lined with myrtle, rosemary, thyme and other herbs, with a fire burning on top, is still used by hunters to cook wild boar to melting tenderness, and was originally how animal thieves and poachers hid their booty while it cooked.

Myrtle leaves are a favourite flavouring. According to legend, the plant was brought by the Jews (who used it for ritual purposes) when they were deported to the island by the Roman emperor Tiberius. A delicacy is boiled chicken or birds left in a bag with myrtle leaves for at least a day until the perfume is absorbed.

Even cheese acquires a characteristic flavour from herbs. Sheep's-milk cheese is produced industrially but it is still also made by shepherds in the old way in their own sheepfolds (*ovili*) in the hills. Pecorino, a mature hard cheese that can be used for grating over pasta, is one of Italy's most popular cheeses and is exported all over the world. Fiore sardo, toscanello, calcagno, foggiano, romano, pepato (with peppercorns), crotonese and semicotto can be eaten soft and fresh or hard and piquant, after six months' maturing. Caprino and bonassai are slightly sour and soft. There are several types of ricotta apart from the fresh and creamy one, which must be eaten quickly; ricotta salata is salted and should be used within fifteen to twenty days; ricotta infornata, baked until it is dark outside but still soft inside, keeps longer; and ricotta forte is fermented and strong-tasting.

Dolce sardo is a soft cheese made with goat's milk, and fresa is from cow's milk. *Peddas* and *taedas* are varieties of caciocavallo. One of the best cheeses I have ever eaten is *casumarzu*, which means 'rotten cheese', or *casu beciu*, which means 'old cheese'. Fresh cheese is used for cooking. It is grilled until it is golden, or is fried with onions and a sprinkling of vinegar. Fresh cheese is the basis of many soups and the filling for both savoury and sweet pies, fritters and cheesecakes.

The most typical Sardinian bread is the crisp, paper-thin *pani carasau* made in large round sheets and called *carta di musica* by mainland Italians because of the noise it makes when you eat it. It keeps well and shepherds have always taken it with them when they spend months away from the village, wandering with their flocks from highland to lowland pastures. (Now most are motorised and can go home for the night.) Brushed with oil, baked again and eaten hot, it becomes delicious *mazzamuru*. Softened in water, it is layered or rolled up like lasagne or cannelloni to make *pani fratau*, filled with tomato or meat sauce and topped with grated cheese and a poached egg.

Every village has its own special breads (there are supposed to be five hundred types), biscuits and cakes. On festive occasions villagers work their breads into fine lacy, sculptured designs featuring leaves and flowers and little birds or animals. Some motifs have ancient religious and magical significance. In this religious and superstitious land, every saint's day, holy day and pagan event is a festive occasion and sweets are part of the celebrations. There are hundreds of pastries, most of them made with almonds (sometimes with cheese) and flavoured with orange, lemon, vanilla, saffron, orange flower or jasmine water, aniseed or honey. An unusual, bitter honey is made by bees that feed on the bitter red fruit of *corbezzolo*, or arbutus.

Crowded in little towns and villages (once for protection from brigands), in tightly knit clans of relatives (same last names are common), with a powerful communal spirit, isolated from their neighbours, with little outside contact and perpetual feuding, Sardinians have preserved their individual cultures (including banditry and vendetta), their local dialects and their dishes. That is why, although it is simple, the cooking is extraordinarily rich in regional specialities. 'If a village grows potatoes,' I was told, 'there are a hundred ways of preparing them. The neighbouring village may do a hundred things with aubergine.' (I wonder if counting in hundreds is a thing picked up from the Arabs!) Villages also have their own ways of using entrails, tripe, heart, brains, feet, testicles and stomachs. Sardinian food is poor food because many people live at subsistence level. But can roast meat served with raw tender artichokes and fennel dipped in vinaigrette, stews with wine and herbs, pasta dough mixed with saffron, plates of wild mushrooms and asparagus be called poor food?

I don't know if it is because Sardinians are unbelievably generous and hospitable and their land so beautiful, or because their food evokes the simple life or the remote past, or because it is simply so good, but it provokes strong emotion of the kind you never forget.

The Wines of Sardinia

The vines in Sardinia are extremely ancient and some originated in Spain in the fourteenth century, so the wines have a character of their own, quite different from those of the rest of Italy. Most of the grapes are grown by seventy thousand smallholders who furnish the thirty-nine cooperatives which process the wine for local consumption (the surplus goes to France and Germany). With the exception of wine from the Sella & Mosca company in Alghero, which is one of Europe's biggest wine estates, the dozen or so labels come from very small producers.

Vernaccia di Oristano is the most Sardinian of wines, made from the native Vernaccia grape. It is aged in chestnut barrels into a sherry-like, amber-coloured, gloriously rich mellow wine with an intense perfume of flowers and pleasantly bitter flavour. The dry *superiore* version is one of Italy's most appreciated aperitif wines.

White wines to note are Malvasia di Cagliari, Vermentino di Gallura, Nuragus di Cagliari and Nasco di Cagliari, Torbato di Alghero, Dorato di Sorso, and the fragrant Moscato di Cagliari. Notable reds are Campidano di Terralba, Carignano del Sulcis, Girò di Cagliari, Mandrolisai and Monica di Cagliari. Cannonau di Sardegna is the big, strong, powerful voluptuous red wine that accompanies game and meat when they are cooked out in the open on the mountains in winter.

Sardinia has a traditionally long range of dessert wines, both the liquid gold and velvety red varieties, which come in a range from sweet to dry and fortified. Everyone makes their own at home.

CHEESE RAVIOLI
Culingiones

Natalina Laconi and her sister make these beautifully crafted little ravioli at their restaurant Su Meriagu at Quartu Sant Andrea, Cagliari, with a variety of different fillings (including mashed potatoes and spinach).

SERVES 4

Fresh Egg Pasta (see pages 110–111)
600g (1lb 6oz) fresh Pecorino or other bland soft
    soft cheese or well-drained mashed cottage
    cheese
2 eggs
Bunch of mint, finely chopped (about 2
    tablespoons)

Salt and pepper
Grated rind of $\frac{1}{2}$ orange (optional)
Freshly grated nutmeg (optional)
$\frac{1}{4}$ teaspoon powdered saffron, dissolved in a drop of
    hot water (optional)
2 tablespoons or more melted butter
Grated pecorino

Prepare the pasta according to the directions on pages 110–111. For the filling, mix the cheese, eggs, mint, salt and pepper, orange rind, nutmeg and saffron, if using, in a bowl. Roll out the pasta dough to a thin sheet on a lightly floured surface. Cut into 6cm (2½in) circles with a pastry cutter. Put a heaped teaspoonful of filling in the centre (a little to one side) of each. Fold over to make a half-moon shape, then pinch the edges together and twist to make a tight, festooned edge. Boil the ravioli in plenty of salted water for 5 minutes and drain as soon as they are done. Coat with butter and serve with grated pecorino.

Variation
You may also serve the ravioli with fresh tomato sauce and grated cheese.

SEAFOOD PASTA
Pasta con frutti di mare

SERVES 6

1kg (2lb) mussels or clams
4 sea scallops (optional)
250g (8oz) small squid
250g (8oz) large or jumbo prawns
3 cloves garlic, finely chopped
3 tablespoons olive oil
1 hot red chilli, fresh or dried, finely chopped or
    crumbled, or a pinch of hot chilli powder (optional)

4 medium tomatoes, peeled and chopped (optional)
250ml (8fl oz) dry white wine
Salt and pepper
Bunch of parsley, finely chopped (about
    3 tablespoons)
550g (1¼lb) spaghettini, tagliolini or tagliatelle

Clean the mussels or clams and steam them open (see page 18). When they are cool, take them out of their shells and filter the liquid (keep it for the sauce). Cut the scallops, if using, into 2–4 pieces. Clean the squid (see page 18) and cut the bodies into rings. Peel the prawns.

Fry the garlic in oil just until it begins to colour. Add chilli and tomatoes if you like, the liquid from the shells, and the wine. Season with salt and pepper and simmer for 10 minutes to reduce a little. Add the squid and prawns and cook for a few minutes only until the prawns turn pink and the squid opaque. Add the mussels or clams and scallops and the parsley and reheat when the pasta is ready to serve.

Cook the pasta in plenty of boiling salted water until al dente and serve with the sauce.

Variation
A pinch of saffron occasionally goes into the sauce.

At Cipriani in Venice they make a seafood sauce with champagne and add cream.

PASTA WITH HARE SAUCE
Pasta con sugo di lepre

A similar sauce for pasta is made in several regions; in Sardinia hare is still plentiful. You could use rabbit instead.

SERVES 4–6

50g (2oz) pancetta or unsmoked bacon, chopped
4 tablespoons olive oil
1 small hare, about 1.5kg (3lb), cut into pieces
2 medium onions, sliced
2 cloves garlic, crushed
1–2 tablespoons flour
1 bottle (750 ml) red wine

Salt and pepper
3 cloves
1 teaspoon cinnamon
A few sprigs of rosemary or thyme
500g (1lb) spaghetti
Grated pecorino

Fry the bacon in oil, add the pieces of hare and turn to brown them all over. Remove from the pan and gently fry the onion and garlic until soft. Stir in the flour and add the wine. Put the pieces of hare back in the pan, add salt and pepper, the cloves, cinnamon and rosemary or thyme, and simmer for 1 hour, stirring occasionally. Finish the cooking on a high heat if necessary to reduce the sauce. Cook the spaghetti in plenty of boiling salted water until al dente, strain and dress with the hare stew and pecorino.

Note

The hare can also be removed from the sauce, which is served with the pasta as a first course. The hare is then served separately.

FRIED JUMBO PRAWNS
Gamberoni in tegame

SERVES 4

500g (1lb) jumbo prawns
2 cloves garlic, crushed
½ small chilli, chopped (optional)
4 tablespoons olive oil

Salt
2 tablespoons finely chopped parsley
About 4 tablespoons *acquavite* or grappa

Wash the prawns and remove the heads and little legs. Fry them quickly with the garlic and chilli, if using, in the oil for a few minutes until they turn pink. Sprinkle with salt and parsley. Just before serving, pour in the *acquavite* or grappa and set it alight.

LAMB WITH OLIVES
Agnello con olive

Lamb with olives is a very Mediterranean combination. The wine, garlic and chilli give it a Sardinian touch.

SERVES 6

1.1kg (2½lb) lamb, leg or shoulder, cut into
   2.5cm (1in) cubes
4–5 tablespoons olive oil
2 medium onions
½–1 fresh red chilli, seeds removed, or a good
   pinch of hot chilli powder

1 clove garlic
120ml (4fl oz) or more red or dry white wine
175–225g (6–8oz) richly flavoured black olives
Salt

Cook the lamb in a pan in 2–3 tablespoons oil on a medium heat until brown. Remove from the pan. Chop the onions, chilli and garlic to a very fine pulp in a food processor and add it to the pan with a little more oil.

Cook, stirring, until golden brown, add the wine, stir and increase the heat to let it evaporate. Reduce the heat as low as possible and add the olives and lamb.

Season, cover and cook, adding water or more wine if it becomes too dry, for about 45 minutes, or until the meat is very tender.

FRIED CHEESE PASTRIES WITH HONEY
Sebadas

This is the most popular sweet in Sardinia. The combination of pastry, hot melting cheese and honey is most appealing. They use a very particular semi-soft, bland ewe's-milk cheese, but a mixture of mozzarella and ricotta makes a good substitute.

For the pastry
500g (1lb) strong flour

4 eggs

Pinch of salt

50g (2oz) butter, softened

For the filling
500g (1lb) mozzarella, cut into small cubes

500g (1lb) ricotta

1 egg white or yolk (optional)

Vegetable oil for frying

Grated rind of 2 large oranges

250g (8oz) clear honey, to serve

Mix the flour with the eggs and salt and knead well. Add the butter, a little at a time, so that it is absorbed thoroughly. Knead well to a soft elastic dough, adding a little water if necessary: it should be firm but not sticky. When the required consistency is achieved, pull or roll out the pastry thinly and cut out 10cm (4in) circles.

For the filling, blend the cheeses and orange rind. Put 2 teaspoons in the centre of half the pastry circles and put the remaining circles on top as lids. Seal the edges well: it is much easier to do this if you moisten around the borders of the pastry bottoms with water or egg white or yolk, using your finger.

Fill a large pan with oil and deep-fry the pastries over medium heat, two at a time, making sure they do not brown. They take only a few minutes. Serve immediately and pass around clear honey (warmed if you like) for everyone to help themselves. In Sardinia, they sometimes use melted bitter honey.

RICOTTA DESSERT WITH HONEY AND ORANGE JUICE
Dolce di ricotta

This is a little different from the Roman dessert made with ricotta. You will need a good fragrant honey.

SERVES 6

350g (12oz) ricotta

125g (4oz) almonds, finely chopped

2 bitter almonds, or a few drops almond essence

250g (8oz) clear honey

3 eggs

Butter to grease the dish

2 tablespoons breadcrumbs

Juice of 1 orange

Blend the ricotta in a blender, then add the almonds, almond essence, nearly 125g (4oz) honey, and the eggs.

Grease a flan dish with butter and dust with breadcrumbs, then pour in the ricotta mixture. Bake in the oven at 200°C (400°F, gas mark 6) for about 45 minutes, or until firm and the top is golden. Unmould. Beat the orange juice into the remaining honey and pour over.

Serve cold. It is even better the next day.

Index